THE WPA HISTORY OF THE NEGRO IN PITTSBURGH

A John D. S. and Aida C. Truxall Book

The WPA History of the Negro in Pittsburgh

edited by
Laurence A. Glasco

University of Pittsburgh Press

Published by the University of Pittsburgh Press
Pittsburgh, Pa., 15260

Copyright © 2004, University of Pittsburgh Press

Manufactured in the United States of America

Printed on acid-free paper

10 9 8 7 6 5 4 3 2 1

Library of Congress Cataloging-in-Publication Data

The WPA history of the Negro in Pittsburgh / edited by Laurence A. Glasco.
   p.   cm.
   First publication of the unfinished manuscript "The Negro in Pittsburgh"
produced by the Federal Writers' Project in Pennsylvania.
   Includes bibliographical references and index.
   ISBN 0-8229-4232-1 (cloth: alk. paper)
   1. African Americans—Pennsylvania—Pittsburgh—History. 2. African
Americans—Pennsylvania—Pittsburgh—Social conditions. 3. African
Americans—Pennsylvania— Pittsburgh—Interviews. 4. Pittsburgh (Pa.)—History.
5. Pittsburgh (Pa.)—Race relations. 6. Pittsburgh (Pa.)—Biography. 7. African
Americans—Pennsylvania—History. I. Title: History of the Negro in Pittsburgh.
II. Title: Negro in Pittsburgh. III. Glasco, Laurence Admiral. IV. Federal Writers'
Project (Pa.)
  F159.P69N495 2004
  974.8'8600496073—dc22   2004003404

CONTENTS

Note: Chapter numbers are not consecutive due to missing chapters in the original manuscript.

ACKNOWLEDGMENTS

I want to thank the Pennsylvania Historical and Museum Commission, which gave a grant to help with typing the manuscript, and the Western Pennsylvania Research and Historical Society and its executive director, Bernard Morris. I also want to acknowledge the assistance of Jialu Wu, as well as students in History of Black Pittsburgh, Fall 1996: Paul Bender, Mike Bercik, Jeffrey Brick, Ursula Brown, Neil Burton, Emily Cantor, Laquetta Carter, Jason Chavis, Jan d'Arcangela, Joe Devine, Valerie Drayton, Talia Duck, Fred Dukes, Beryl Everett, Fran Fernald, Carla Fisher, Felicia Gardner, Yvette Glover, Arlener Hicks, Rose Nuhfer, Greg Obsincs, Paul Quigley, Jane Wallis, and Bob Zebrasky. I especially want to thank Deborah Meade, senior editor at the University of Pittsburgh Press, for her skill in catching errors and suggesting improvements. And finally, I want to thank my wife Ingrid for her patience and support.

THE WPA HISTORY OF THE NEGRO IN PITTSBURGH

Introduction to the Published Volume

Dedicated to the memory of Professor Clarence Rollo Turner,
1943–1993

"The Negro in Pittsburgh" has had a long and curious career. The Federal
Writers' Project, which produced the manuscript, was terminated in 1939 before
work was completed. The manuscript languished in the Pennsylvania State Library in Harrisburg, largely forgotten and neglected, until it was rediscovered
and microfilmed in 1970. Even then, the manuscript failed to attract the attention
it deserved. One scholar, Clarence Rollo Turner, a professor in the Black Studies
department at the University of Pittsburgh, realized its value and very much
wanted to have the manuscript published. Like the original project, however,
Turner's plans never came to fruition; his work was abruptly ended by his sudden, premature death. This published version of "The Negro in Pittsburgh" is
dedicated to Turner's memory.[1]

"The Negro in Pittsburgh" provides both the scholar and the general public
with a unique source for learning the history of the city's black population. Although never completed, at more than seven hundred typewritten pages, it is the

---

1. For this published edition, errors of grammar, spelling, and fact have been remedied as much
as possible without altering the apparent intent of the author. To enhance the narrative flow and
logical organization of the manuscript, some duplicate text has been eliminated and a modest
amount of other text has been rearranged. Substantive editorial emendations in the text have been
noted in brackets or footnotes; all numbered footnotes are editorial comments added for this published edition.

most ambitious attempt to write the history of Pittsburgh's black population.[2] Chapter titles give an idea of its broad coverage: "The Shadow of the Plantation," "The Negro on the Frontier," The Early Community, 1804–1860," "Abolition Years," "Civil Rights," "The Negro Wage Worker," "Church, School and Press," "The Later Community," "Folkways," "Arts and Culture," and "The People Speak," with interviews of twenty-four black Pittsburghers. The manuscript contains some primary sources, perhaps most notably the 1837 "Memorial of Pittsburgh's Free Citizens of Color" protesting the disfranchisement of African Americans by the Commonwealth of Pennsylvania,[3] and two poems by George B. Vashon, lawyer and son of Pittsburgh's leading black businessman and abolitionist. A bibliography, plus excerpts from books, documents, government reports, and local newspapers round out the original manuscript. Twenty to thirty photographs by Rosalie Gwathmey and nationally recognized documentary photographer Luke Swank were planned but never appeared in the document.[4]

The original manuscript contains three tables of contents, all of which differ slightly from each other. One of these is reproduced for this edition to give some idea of the original intentions of the editor. No single table of contents from the original corresponds exactly to the manuscript materials actually microfilmed.

2. To date, the only overall survey of the history of blacks in Pittsburgh is Laurence Glasco, "Double Burden: The Black Experience in Pittsburgh," in *City at the Point: Essays on the Social History of Pittsburgh*, ed. Samuel P. Hays, 69–109 (Pittsburgh: University of Pittsburgh Press, 1989). Studies which focus on the years between the two world wars include: Andrew Buni, *Robert L. Vann of the Pittsburgh Courier: Politics and Black Journalism*, (Pittsburgh: University of Pittsburgh Press, 1974); Arthur J. Edmunds (with research by Margaret Albert), *Daybreakers: The Story of the Urban League of Pittsburgh, The First Sixty-Five Years* (Pittsburgh: Urban League of Pittsburgh, 1999); Peter Gottlieb, *Making Their Own Way: Southern Blacks' Migration to Pittsburgh, 1916–1930* (Urbana: University of Illinois Press, 1987); John Bodnar, Roger Simon, and Michael P. Weber, *Lives of Their Own: Blacks, Italians, and Poles in Pittsburgh, 1900–1960* (Urbana: University of Illinois Press, 1982); and Rob Ruck, *Sandlot Seasons: Sport in Black Pittsburgh* (Urbana: University of Illinois Press, 1987). Ann Wilmoth's "Pittsburgh and the Blacks: A Short History," (Ph.D. diss., Penn State University, 1975), focuses on the pre–Civil War era.

3. The original table of contents reproduced for the published edition lists this document as "Memorial of the Free Citizens of Color in *Political Destiny of the Colored Race on the American Continent*." This may refer to a document by Martin Delany: "Political Destiny of the Colored Race on the American Continent," located in the Index of the Report of the Select Committee on House Resolution No. 576, printed July 1862, by the House of Representatives. See http://www.libraries.wvu.edu/delany/mrdwrit.htm.

For more information on the disfranchisement of Pennsylvania's blacks, which is what occasioned "Memorial of the Free Citizens of Color," see Eric L. Smith, "The End of Black Voting Rights in Pennsylvania: African Americans and the Pennsylvania Constitutional Convention of 1837–1838," *Pennsylvania History* 65, no. 3 (1998): 279–99; and Eric L. Smith, "The Pittsburgh Memorial: A Forgotten Document of Pittsburgh History," *Pittsburgh History*, 80, no. 3 (1997): 106–11.

4. Mention of the photographs appears in a note toward the end of the original appendix. We do not know what became of those photographs, or if in fact any were submitted to the project. In

Some chapters were never written, some had their titles changed, and some appear more than once. For this edition, chapters that appeared twice (sometimes in slightly different forms) have been blended. These include "The Early Community," "Abolition Years," and "Folkways." The original tables of contents call for separate chapters on church, schools, and the press, but the microfilmed material shows one combined chapter on these topics. The microfilmed appendix material amounts to some 119 pages, and contains more (and different) items than are indicated in any of the tables of contents.[5] The appendices included in the present edition represent only the most interesting and significant of the original appendix materials. The original did not contain maps; these have been added for the present edition.

"The Negro in Pittsburgh" was one of many projects sponsored by the Federal Writers' Project (FWP), a branch of the Depression-era Works Progress Administration (WPA). The FWP was created in 1935 to provide jobs for unemployed writers, editors, and research workers, in the same way that the WPA provided work for unemployed manual laborers. Although conceived as something of a white-collar version of leaf-raking jobs, the FWP quickly became more than that when its director, Henry Alsberg, hit on the idea of producing a series of state and city guide books for the nation. Published under the rubric of the American Guide Series, these guides soon became classics of Americana. A second set of FWP publications dealt with folklore, sayings, superstitions, music, legends, and oral histories of the American people.

A third initiative of the Federal Writers' Project involved studies of ethnic and racial minorities. Alsberg's conviction that the experience of minority groups formed an important part of the story of America was a radical departure at a time when immigrants and blacks were regarded with suspicion, if not outright hostility, and the image of the "melting pot" was one in which their values and beliefs were to be melted down and recast in the dominant Anglo-Saxon, Protestant

---

an e-mail communication with the author on November 24, 2003, Howard Bossen, author of a forthcoming book on Luke Swank, mentioned a series of photographs Swank took of Logan Street, a predominantly Jewish commercial street that was frequented by all the races and ethnic groups of the Hill District: "The Logan Street series is composed of a group of mounted, signed, and labeled photographs. On the front of these images, in Swank's handwriting, is the notation, 'Logan St. Jan. 1939.' Enough images with this notation were found in the Luke Swank collection in the Carnegie Library [of Pittsburgh] that they clearly constitute a series. It is not possible to determine if only these photographs were included in the series or if others at one time were included. The Logan Street series presents the diversity of cultures and street activities that existed along Logan Street in the late 1930s. The time frame and subject matter make it plausible that these photographs might be the ones referred to in the Federal Writers' Project papers, although there is no way to prove this."

5. For a full list of the microfilmed materials, please see appendix 6.

mold. FWP ethnic studies included *The Italians of New York, The Jewish Lands-manschaften of New York* (in Yiddish), *The Armenians of Massachusetts,* and *The Swedes and Finns of New Jersey.*

Alsberg did not neglect the role of African Americans in making up the American mosaic. To ensure blacks' involvement in the projects, Alsberg set up a Negro section of the FWP and, to head up that division, he recruited a distin-guished black academic and professor of English at Howard University, Sterling Brown. Brown not only recruited black writers, but made certain that the tone of the writings in the state and city guides portrayed blacks in an integral, balanced, and accurate manner. The most notable FWP study of blacks was *The Negro of Virginia.* Produced by an all-black unit at Hampton Institute, *The Negro of Vir-ginia* appeared in 1940 to rave reviews, and is still in print. The FWP sponsored several other studies of blacks, only a few of which were ever published. The Chicago FWP produced a ninety-five-page pamphlet, *Cavalcade of the American Negro,* and in 1967, New York published an informal social history, *The Negro in New York,* a quarter of a century after its project had ended. In 1993, the Univer-sity of Mississippi Press published *The Florida Negro,* which includes contribu-tions by Zora Neale Hurston.[6]

"The Negro in Pittsburgh" was part of this broader involvement by the Penn-sylvania Historical Commission in the FWP's American Guide Series. The Com-monwealth was quite active in that program, and teams of researchers and writers published such works as *Pennsylvania: A Guide to the Keystone State* (1940) and *Philadelphia: A Guide to the Nation's Birthplace* (1937) in addition to separate studies of Jews, Poles, Irish, Hungarians, and blacks in Philadelphia, plus Men-nonites, Schwenkfelders, Swedes, and Pennsylvania Germans.[7]

In 1939, conservative Congressmen abruptly terminated the Federal Writers' Project because of its liberal politics and sympathetic treatment of racial and eth-nic groups. In its brief existence, between 1936 and 1939, the FWP left a lasting legacy. It provided work for some 6,600 unemployed men and women, including

6. Jerre Mangione's *The Dream and the Deal: The Federal Writers' Project, 1935–1943* (Boston: Little, Brown & Company, 1972) is the best study of the agency. The introduction in Gary McDonogh, *The Florida Negro: A Federal Writers' Project Legacy* (Jackson: University Press of Mississippi, 1993), contains good background material on the Federal Writers' Project studies of the history and culture of black Americans.

7. The full records of the "Works Progress Administration's Pennsylvania Historical Survey" have been microfilmed in seventy-nine rolls of film, including eight rolls called "WPA Ethnic Sur-vey, 1938–1941." Ruth Hodge, *Guide to African American Resources at the Pennsylvania State Ar-chives* (Harrisburg: Pennsylvania Historical and Museum Commission, 2000), is an excellent guide to the Harrisburg holdings. "The Negro in Philadelphia" was Job 63, Roll 2; "The Negro in Pitts-burgh" was Job 64, Roll 1 of the "WPA Ethnic Survey." Originals are still housed in the Pennsylva-nia State Archives. The microfilm copy used for this publication of "The Negro in Pittsburgh" is housed in Hillman Library, University of Pittsburgh, microfilm F35#2.

such leading authors as Claude McKay, Richard Wright, Ralph Ellison, Nelson Algren, and Saul Bellow, and it published more than one thousand books and pamphlets.

At the time it was terminated, the FWP had a substantial, but unknown, number of studies in the pipeline. Like "The Negro in Pittsburgh," these have remained largely ignored and hidden away. Jerre Mangione's outstanding study, *The Dream and the Deal: The Federal Writers' Project, 1935–1943*, helped keep the memory alive. The book inspired John Cole, director of the Center for the Book at the Library of Congress, who since 1978 has been working to make the FWP materials accessible. The results have been encouraging. A number of biographies have appeared of the FWP's more celebrated alumni, and the Library of Congress has recently put some three thousand oral history interviews on its Web site. But, as a recent *New York Times* article pointed out, "no one has yet tackled a broad-based study of the thousands of untested but talented young writers" who worked for the FWP.[8] J. Ernest Wright and his coworkers would undoubtedly figure among that group.

Microfilming "The Negro in Pittsburgh" did little to raise the manuscript's visibility. Scholarly studies of black Pittsburgh that have appeared since the manuscript's discovery and filming make only passing references to it or do not mention it at all.[9] The public has virtually no memory of the project. Frank Bolden, the former city editor for the *Pittsburgh Courier* and the most knowledgeable individual about black Pittsburgh during that era, only vaguely recalled the project and the manuscript. Walter Worthington, the other leading historian of black Pittsburgh, had only a vague memory of Wright and of the project. Perhaps one reason for the public's lack of awareness of the project was a feeling among its workers that the manuscript was the exclusive property of the government and was not to be discussed without permission. This was the impression, for example, of Marian Holmes, one of the workers on the Pittsburgh project, who, when I interviewed her, was at first reluctant to talk. Mrs. Holmes responded warily to my queries and asked whether I represented the federal government before agreeing to discuss the project.[10]

It is not easy piecing together the origin of "The Negro in Pittsburgh." No

8. Douglas Brinkley, "Unmasking the Writers of the W.P.A.," *New York Times*, August 2, 2003. The Library of Congress maintains "American Life Histories, Manuscripts from the Federal Writers' Project, 1936–1940" at http://memory.loc.gov/ammem/wpaintro/wpahome.html; FWP interviews with 2,300 ex-slaves is at . . . ammem/snhtml.

9. Andrew Buni, in *Robert L. Vann of the Pittsburgh Courier*, for example, notes that the manuscript had recently been discovered and that Professor Turner was preparing it for publication. Buni, however, made no use of the manuscript.

10. Based on personal communications between the author and Bolden, Worthington, and Holmes.

one has yet located archival materials authorizing its inception, and the project's editor is no longer living. We do know that the editor, J. Ernest Wright, earned his M.A. and Ph.D. in English from the University of Pittsburgh. He taught there as an adjunct instructor in the English Department from 1924 to 1934, when he was released along with some one hundred other faculty members in a Depression-era retrenchment. Following his dismissal, Wright worked on several historical projects with the Western Pennsylvania Historical Survey. The Survey was sponsored by the Buhl Foundation, the Historical Society of Western Pennsylvania, and the University of Pittsburgh. Between 1938 and 1940 it published a number of monographs on the history of western Pennsylvania, two of which, dealing with the colonial era, were authored by Wright.

While still engaged by the Survey, Wright began work on "The Negro in Pittsburgh." It is not known how Wright, who was white, became interested in African American history. He was not trained in Black Studies, and the field was not in academic favor at the time. One possibility is that Wright had a rebellious streak. His doctoral dissertation investigated the English Victorian novelist William Hale White, the pseudonym of Mark Rutherford, who had been expelled from college for holding heretical religious views, and whose writings, according to one critic, are intense and "deal with religious problems or with ordeals of the heart, the intellect, or the conscience."[11] Wright's graduate studies also helped prepare him for writing about historical topics. His master's thesis examined the life and work of George Gissing, a late Victorian English novelist who depicted the lives of those in the lower middle class, and who wrote in a naturalistic style that sought to capture the reality of the world around him. Wright, moreover, was comfortable around blacks, and socialized with them, something seldom done in those days. Marian Holmes recalls that the racial atmosphere on the project was harmonious, and Vivian Hewitt, an African American graduate student at Carnegie Tech at the time, recalls being at a party given by Wright that was attended by a number of black social workers.[12]

Wright's commitment to racial justice created difficulties for him during the war years. Hired as a substitute teacher by Har-Brack Union High School in Natrona Heights, a suburb of Pittsburgh, he was summarily fired in 1944 after being accused of using profanity and failing to "follow textbooks." Wright admitted that he had used some profanity, but only when condemning intolerance. He

11. *Encyclopedia Britannica*, DVD-ROM 2000, s.v. "Rutherford, Mark."
12. Vivian Hewitt, telephone conversation with author, May 23, 1998. Wright lived on Andover Terrace in the Schenley Farms Terrace neighborhood, part of the Upper Hill near Oakland. At the time, it was an almost all-white neighborhood with a considerable number of residents who were faculty at the University of Pittsburgh.

claimed his dismissal stemmed from his criticism of anti-Semitic remarks made by some of his students, including the daughter of the principal. The principal did complain that Wright had used his classroom to discuss race relations. The case made local headlines when 250 students went out in a three-day strike to protest his firing and the school board's refusal to allow him to present his side of the story.

For reasons that are not clear, John Bowman, chancellor of the University of Pittsburgh, waded into the fray with a statement to the press that, despite "traces of brilliance," Wright had been dismissed from the University in 1934 because, on the whole, "he was not a capable man" and "was not competent enough to conduct an English course."[13] Others clearly did not feel that way, for Wright went on to teach at Rutgers University in New Jersey and at the New School for Social Research in New York.[14]

For the project "The Negro in Pittsburgh," Wright appears to have assembled a predominantly African American group of authors: one version of the table of contents cites eleven blacks as chapter authors and coauthors. The employment of so many on a single project was unusual; despite the efforts of Henry Alsberg and Sterling Brown, blacks made up only 2 percent of the FWP's workforce nationally.[15] The most involved Pittsburgh author was Abram T. Hall, a Chicago native and son of a prominent Methodist minister who had established that city's first African American church. Born in 1851, Hall worked as a land agent in Kansas and as a columnist for the *Cincinnati Enquirer* and the *Chicago Tribune*. In 1883 or 1889[16] Hall moved to Pittsburgh, where he helped establish the city's first Negro fire company, and in 1896 began a forty-two-year career as a counter clerk in the City Treasurer's Office.

Hall had good credentials. From 1897 to 1931 he edited "Afro-American Notes," a weekly column that appeared in Pittsburgh's leading Republican newspaper, the *Press*. "Afro-American Notes" was unusual for its time in that it appeared in a predominantly white newspaper and was edited by a black man. The column was a type of community bulletin board, primarily used for posting no-

---

13. *Pittsburgh Sun Telegraph,* January 27 and February 11, 1944; *Pittsburgh Post-Gazette,* January 28, 1944; *Pittsburgh Press,* January 27, 1944. Several investigations of Wright's dismissal were undertaken by the Western Pennsylvania Council of B'nai B'rith in cooperation with Dr. William Young, director of the Pittsburgh Round-Table of the National Conference of Christians and Jews, and committees of the American Legion and the Veterans of Foreign Wars.

14. Wright died in 1958 at the age of sixty-four. Obituary, *New York Times,* May 11, 1958.

15. Monty Penkower, *The Federal Writers Project: A Study in Government Patronage of the Arts* (Urbana: University of Illinois Press, 1977).

16. Hall's obituary in the *Pittsburgh Press,* January 9, 1951, says he came to Pittsburgh in 1883, whereas the *Pittsburgh Courier's* obituary, January 13, 1951, states the year as 1889.

tices of upcoming events, out-of-town visitors, and local marriages, births, and deaths.[17]

In 1938 Hall retired from the City Treasurer's office, and this may have been the year in which he began working on "The Negro in Pittsburgh." He is listed as author of "Folkways," and as coauthor of "The Shadow of the Plantation," "The Early Community, 1804–1860," and of the "Press" section of the chapter "Church, School and Press."

Hall's long residence in Pittsburgh and his newspaper work helped prime him for writing chapters on both the history and the lifestyles of black Pittsburghers. He also had a gift for words, having published a book of poems. On the occasion of his seventy-fifth birthday, Hall wrote:

> I've passed another milestone along life's devious way,
> The trail's becoming shorter with each succeeding day.
> My flesh is growing weaker, my spirit unabashed
> Peers forth to glimpse the future with courage still undashed.
> The shore-line of the past looms up with vistas fond and sweet;
> What lies beyond horizon's bound, is mine to guess and meet.[18]

Hall was one of two exceptionally well-prepared members of Wright's team. The other was Homer Brown, listed as the author of the manuscript's chapter on civil rights. The table of contents indicates Brown was to also write a chapter on politics, but that chapter presumably was not written, for it is missing from the manuscript. Brown was the city's leading black politician and later judge. A graduate of the University of Pittsburgh School of Law, Brown was a practicing lawyer, the head of the local NAACP, a member of the Pennsylvania State Assembly, and, toward the end of a very long and distinguished career, a judge of the Court of Common Pleas in Pittsburgh.[19]

The project's other black participants were well educated but did not have backgrounds that particularly qualified them to write historical accounts. Most were teachers, preachers, and social workers—three of the white-collar fields open to blacks at the time. Fred Holmes, listed with Abram Hall as coauthor of the first chapter, "The Shadow of the Plantation," was a caseworker for the Department of Public Assistance and a member of the Association of Negro Social Workers. Mrs. Sydney Taylor-Brown, listed as author of "The Negro on the

17. Dr. John W. Browning, a pharmacist who had come to Pittsburgh from Montgomery, Alabama, began the "Afro-American Notes" column in 1896 (see chapter 7, "Church, School and Press"). After only eight months as editor, Browning died, and the column was taken over by Hall.

18. Hall died January 7, 1951, just a few months before his one-hundredth birthday.

19. Constance Cunningham, "Homer S. Brown: First Black Political Leader in Pittsburgh," *Journal of Negro History* 66 (Winter 1981–82): 304–17

Frontier" and coauthor of "The Early Community," was a social worker affiliated with the Federation of Social Agencies (and, incidentally, the daughter of the world-famous black bicyclist Marshall "Major" Taylor). William E. Hill, credited with "The Negro Wage Worker," was the former industrial secretary of the Urban League and quite knowledgeable about labor matters, and James Dorsey, listed as author of a chapter called "The Later Community," was the director of the Ammon Recreation Center. Mrs. Don Dammond (Ellen Craft), descendant of the famous runaway slaves William and Ellen Craft and daughter of the director of the Centre Avenue branch of the YMCA, is listed as author of the chapter, "The People Speak." Mrs. Dammond was an employee of the Pittsburgh Housing Authority, and her husband was the head of the YMCA. Reverend H. R. Tolliver, pastor of Grace Memorial Presbyterian Church, Mrs. Paul Jones of Herron Hill Jr. High School and James M. Albriton, a probation officer, and P. L. Prattis, editor of the *Pittsburgh Courier,* are listed as the project's authors on church, school, and the press, respectively.

Two of the authors were white, and each brought excellent qualifications to the project. Dr. F. F. Holbrook was the director of the Western Pennsylvania Historical Survey, the director of the Historical Society of Western Pennsylvania, and the editor of the Historical Society's journal. He came to Pittsburgh from Minnesota, where he had coauthored a two-volume history of Minnesota in the First World War. The other white author was Frances Weller, a prominent figure in Pittsburgh music circles and associate editor of *Musical Forecast*, a monthly journal published in Pittsburgh. Weller came to Pittsburgh in 1916 from upstate New York. She worked in radio and, for the last eighteen years of her life, wrote a column called "Siftings," which covered local musical activities. From her vantage point at *Musical Forecast*, Weller was a close observer of Pittsburgh's music scene and a knowledgeable supporter of black musical activities. Her column of August 1941, for example, highlighted the National Association of Negro Musicians in Pittsburgh and recommended the group's performance of the opera *Aida,* enthusiastically urging "the best attention to the event from the lovers of good opera hereabouts!"[20]

The true, as opposed to the attributed, authorship of the chapters of "The Negro in Pittsburgh" presents a considerable mystery. It may be interesting to note that the original table of contents heads the columns of names with the word "consultants" rather than "authors." Unfortunately, there is no way at present to confirm that the thirteen individuals listed in the table of contents were the actual authors, or were even involved with the manuscript. Only two individuals listed in the table of contents could be interviewed in preparation for the published

20. Frances Weller, "Siftings," *Musical Forecast* (August 1941): 4.

edition, and neither recalled working on the project. Mrs. Sydney Taylor-Brown was quite surprised to learn that she was listed as author of two chapters, for she had no recollection of the project. She speculated that perhaps at her advanced age she had simply forgotten having worked on the project. Mrs. Don Dammond, who now lives in California, has a good recollection of her years in Pittsburgh, and emphatically states that she never worked on such a project. Mrs. Marian Holmes, listed as the typist for three of the manuscript's chapters in the original table of contents, has vivid recollections of both Wright and of working as a researcher on the project. Her memories of the experience help to confirm Brown's and Dammond's lack of awareness of the project, for she reports that apart from herself, the project had only one other black worker—E. Marie Coleman, who worked as a secretary.[21]

If Mrs. Holmes is correct and there were only two black workers on the project, the mystery deepens as to why so many blacks are listed as authors. Were they put on the sheets to satisfy some mandate from Washington that required black participation? Did the authors—both black and white—work at home or at another office, perhaps making use of the materials gathered by Holmes, Coleman, and the others at Carnegie Public Library? Such an arrangement prevailed at some other Federal Writers' Projects.

Whatever the origins of the project, whatever the composition of the research and writing team, the value of the manuscript ultimately must stand or fall on its own merits—its thoroughness, accuracy, coverage, objectivity, documentation, analysis, and readability. On these counts, "The Negro in Pittsburgh" presents a mixed story, with both strengths and weaknesses.

Part of the problem in evaluating the manuscript stems from the fact that its preparation was terminated prematurely, before final editing of most chapters. Congress cut funding for the Federal Writers' Project in 1939, and formally terminated it in 1943. The 1939 cut required states to put up 25 percent of the funds. Miraculously, many of the financially strapped states did so for a time, and in the

21. Marian Holmes, interview with author, May 23, 1998. Mrs. Holmes is the widow of Dr. Carroll Holmes, a leading researcher on tuberculosis who had an appointment to the University of Pittsburgh medical school. Mrs. Holmes recalls reporting to work each morning at the Historical Society and then going over to the nearby Carnegie Public Library where, along with five or six young, college-educated white workers, she probed primary sources for information. Mrs. Holmes adds: "A lot of writers in the FWP were communists. I don't know about Wright. I steered clear of politics. I didn't apply for the position [on the project], I was recommended." After the project ended, Mrs. Holmes wanted to use the knowledge she had gained to help write the history of blacks in Pittsburgh. Toward that end she helped to establish the Western Pennsylvania Historical and Research Association (WPHRA), founded in 1957 to record and maintain the historical record of African Americans in the Pittsburgh region. Its original membership included Walter Worthington and Mrs. Holmes's project coworker, Marie Coleman. The WPHRA is still in operation, although with an increasingly smaller membership.

process asserted greater control over what projects would and would not be continued. The exact dynamics of the process in Pennsylvania are unclear, but it appears that "The Negro in Pittsburgh" limped along until the spring of 1941. That inference is based on the dates typed into the headings of various chapters. For example, the chapter "Arts and Culture" was typed in February 1941, and the bibliography was typed on May 28, 1941. As a result of this drawn-out termination of the project, chapters are in various stages of completion, and much of the manuscript bears the characteristics one would expect from a rough draft—editorial markings, repeated material, some grammatical, spelling, and typing errors, and some unfinished thoughts.[22] Overall, however, the manuscript is quite readable, reflecting the goal of clarity for all of the Federal Writers' Project documents. Undoubtedly "The Negro in Pittsburgh" benefited from the pen of Wright, who is listed at the head of each chapter (except "The Shadow of the Plantation") as "rewriteman." In general, the quality of writing is high—the anecdotes are telling, and the prose is crisp and even lyrical on occasion.

The downside of readability, however, is an absence of the usual scholarly apparatus, especially footnotes. In the interest of general accessibility, most Writers' Project publications lack footnotes, and this is true of "The Negro in Pittsburgh." In a number of cases, however, authors have embedded newspaper or manuscript citations in the text itself (sometimes with only an approximate date). For example, some of the passages that appear in the manuscript for "The Negro in Pittsburgh" were taken, sometimes verbatim, and sometimes with minimal paraphrasing, from other sources. The most notable example of this occurs in chapter 3, where biographies of prominent blacks of Pittsburgh rely heavily— sometimes entirely—on Martin Delany's *The Condition, Elevation, Emigration, and Destiny of the Colored People of the United States*. While Delany is sometimes cited and quoted (and even profiled), at other times his passages appear without reference. It is possible that those who prepared the manuscript used other source materials in the same way. How can this practice be explained? Perhaps this manuscript was in such an early stage that it was still just a collection of data, and the writers meant to rewrite and refashion the "borrowed" portions at a later date. Perhaps typists left out indentations in the formatting that would have been meant to show reproduced extracts. Perhaps some of the people preparing the manuscript did not fully appreciate the nature of proper citation. The lack of footnotes and proper citations reduces the manuscript's value to scholars.

---

22. Some chapters are present only in what is called "pre-final" form: "The Shadow of the Plantation," "The Negro Wage Worker," "Church, School and Press," and "The Later Community." Others are available only in "final" form: "The Negro on the Frontier," "Civil Rights," "Arts and Culture," "The People Speak," the bibliography, and the appendices. "The Early Community," "Abolition Years," and "Folkways" are present in both "pre-final" and "final" form.

The manuscript's coverage is uneven. Part of that asymmetry is temporal, as the frontier and antebellum periods are more thoroughly researched and documented than the post–Civil War era. The unevenness is also topical. Because the chapter on politics is missing from the manuscript, we lack anything approaching a good understanding of the political evolution of black Pittsburghers. This omission is only partly remedied by Brown's chapter on civil rights, which is more historical than contemporary and which focuses more on discrimination than on blacks' efforts to counter that discrimination. Moreover, there is no discussion of black businesses, of women, of youth and/or the family, or of economic conditions and standard of living. These gaps are remarkable especially because during the 1920s, the students in the sociology and economics departments at the University of Pittsburgh produced quite a few masters' theses on the social conditions of black migrants and the black community.

Despite its flaws, "The Negro in Pittsburgh" is still our most comprehensive single source of information for reconstructing the history of black Pittsburgh. It maintains a nice balance between objectivity and empathy; it is not filled with special pleadings or invective. It clearly points out the discrimination faced by blacks and, where appropriate, includes the participation of whites in blacks' struggles to overcome the barriers they faced. Perhaps the most important value of the manuscript is that it brings together a wealth of useful information not available elsewhere. For example, the appendix contains a number of useful newspaper accounts, particularly from the nineteenth century, along with documents such as an 1837 petition of Pittsburgh blacks to the state assembly that is not otherwise easily obtainable.

Of course, the best way to evaluate "The Negro in Pittsburgh" is to look at individual chapters, each of which has distinctive qualities and characteristics. The manuscript's introduction, "The Shadow of the Plantation," offers an almost lyrical reflection on the history and meaning of being black in Pittsburgh. It provides thumbnail sketches of the various neighborhoods in which blacks resided, and describes the strivings of the black population in an often inhospitable environment. The chapter closes on a note of sadness and pathos by describing the mood of black Pittsburghers during the Great Depression.

Equally strong are three chapters covering the pre–Civil War era. "The Negro on the Frontier" provides the most detailed treatment we have of blacks at the time of Pittsburgh's settlement. It documents and describes the lives of black laborers, servants, and slaves in the earliest history of the region. As the founding families of Pittsburgh, such as the Nevilles and Craigs, arrived from Virginia, they brought slaves with them. The chapter explores the contradiction of a region and people concerned with freedom from British tyranny yet tolerant of slave ownership within their society. "The Early Community, 1804–1860" describes the role of blacks in developing and settling the Hill District and the favorable image held by whites and by parts of the local press of these early black residents. The chapter describes the era's leading black business and community leaders and highlights how in the 1830s Pittsburgh's black population was transformed into a community through an outburst of institutional development. New institutions that developed at this time included the A.M.E. Church, the Temperance Society, the Moral Reform Society, Martin Delany's *Mystery* newspaper, and antislavery and Underground Railroad organizations. It also describes the leading businesspeople of the period—John Vashon, who ran a bath house, Henry Collins, a real estate developer, John and Lady Julius, owners of a prominent cafe and concert hall, Owen Barrett, developer of patent medicines, and Lewis Woodson, barber and civic leader. "Abolition Years" is probably the strongest of the three early historical chapters. Based on primary research, it includes good accounts of local black leaders and provides an overview of Pittsburgh's antislavery movement and underground railroad, as well as a hilarious poem by Jane Grey Swisshelm, Pittsburgh's famous antislavery feminist, which skewered her proslavery detractors.

Three post–Civil War chapters are also strong. "Folkways" is beautifully written, often witty, and always informative. It opens with the assertion, "There exists in Pittsburgh a Negro way of life as individual as the Italian, the Jewish, the Polish, or native-white way of living." The chapter describes the social life of the middle and upper classes of Pittsburgh's black community, paying particular attention to the pre–Civil War genteel society and its class consciousness. The chapter also sympathetically describes the "folk," including their bars, night spots, lodges, churches and street slang, in addition to such folkloric aspects as the songs of street vendors, the operation of the "numbers," the rent parties, the drugs, folk medicines and superstitions, conjuring, and voodoo. "Arts and Culture" discusses literary and social clubs, such as the Loendi and Aurora Reading clubs, as well as the Negro Drama League of the 1930s. Highlighting blacks' musical activity, the chapter documents an aspect of black Pittsburgh history that has been largely forgotten—the strong interest in what today would be called European or "high" culture. In the early twentieth century, black Pittsburghers took a keen interest in classical music, and supported a number of concert orchestras. Black Pittsburgh is especially noted for the large number of jazz greats either born or raised here, and "Arts and Culture" provides wonderful sketches of Pittsburgh jazz greats and jazz spots. The manuscript's final chapter, "The People Speak," offers fascinating and original material based on interviews with a number of black, mostly middle-class Pittsburghers, in which they relate their feelings about Pittsburgh and race relations. Their ruminations show the diversity of opinion among Pittsburgh's black population, and help to humanize the study.

The manuscript contains four relatively weak chapters, victims, perhaps, of the project's early termination. "Civil Rights," which provides a historical overview of racial discrimination experienced by black Pittsburghers, is quite brief. It focuses on the pre–Civil War era, with discussions of slavery on the frontier, efforts of slaveholders to evade the gradual emancipation laws of the 1780s, segregation of blacks in local theaters and other places of public access in the nineteenth century, creation of a segregated school system in the 1830s, and disfranchisement of Pennsylvania's blacks in 1838. Treatment of the period following the Civil War provides some useful information, but is short and schematic. "The Later Community" also deals with its material in a cursory fashion. This is especially unfortunate considering that the chapter's time period includes the years following the First World War, when industrial jobs finally opened for blacks and thousands responded to the opportunities by migrating here from the Deep South. The result of that migration was an unprecedented vitalization of community life in the 1920s: the establishment of nationally prominent baseball teams (the Pittsburgh Crawfords and Homestead Grays), the founding of a nationally influential newspaper (the *Pittsburgh Courier*), the expansion of organizations such as the Urban League and NAACP, and the development of a vibrant jazz scene. "The Negro Wage Worker" also suffers from brevity, which is unfortunate given the fact that the opening of industrial jobs to black workers created black Pittsburgh's first blue-collar labor force—one with enormous problems of adjustment that deserve to be explored. "Church, School and Press" contains useful information, but each section provides just a tantalizing introduction to its subject. Martin Delany's abolitionist paper the *Mystery* is well known, and the *Pittsburgh Courier*, founded in 1910, is still in existence. Especially intriguing, however, is the chapter's listing of a substantial number of now-forgotten and unavailable black newspapers. These include the *Meteor* (1890–1894), the *Western Enterprise* (c. 1897), the *Pioneer* (1907), the *Progressive Afro-American* (1919), the *Competitor* (edited by Robert Vann of the *Pittsburgh Courier* in 1920), the *Crusader*, the *Citizen*, the *Vanguard*, and the *Triangle Advocate*. Curiously lacking from this impressive list is the *Colored Home Journal*, at least one issue of which (October 1903) is in the possession of a local family. One can only wonder where these papers were at the time of the writing of "The Negro in Pittsburgh," and where they might be today.

In sum, the historical chapters are both the strongest and weakest of the manuscript. The weak chapters, it must be stressed, are weak primarily because they are too brief to provide enough factual information about these topics, which had not really been explored until that time. Yet this is really the first effort to write a historical survey of blacks in Pittsburgh, and for that reason everything (or virtually everything) that is included is important and useful. "The Negro in Pittsburgh," then, is a valuable manuscript and a pioneering effort, one that can be read with confidence and profit by the contemporary reader. It is by no means the last effort to produce a general history of blacks in Pittsburgh, but it is certainly a worthy first.

The Negro in Pittsburgh

J. Ernest Wright

compiler

ORIGINAL TABLE OF CONTENTS*

*The original manuscript contains three versions of the table of contents. One has been reproduced here in its entirety. None of the tables of contents correspond exactly to the materials microfilmed from the collection. Within the text and in the table of contents for the published edition, chapter titles have been reproduced as they appeared in the microfilmed chapters, rather than in any one version of the table of contents. The microfilmed appendix contains more (and different) items than are indicated in any version of the table of contents. For notes on the selection process for the published edition, please see the introduction. For the content and order of material in the microfilm for "The Negro in Pittsburgh," please see appendix 6.

CHAPTER 1

The Shadow of the Plantation

———•◦•———

Typist: Brooks / July 13, 1939 / Pre-final

Pittsburgh lies fifty miles north of the Mason Dixon line, the accepted dividing line between those two great districts of the nation known as the North and the South. Below this line lies Dixie, the Old South, the Deep South, the once Solid South, dominated by the plantation with its one-crop system of agriculture. Here lies the Kingdom of Jim Crow, with its Black Belt, sharecroppers, backdoor movies, Jim Crow streetcars and trains, disenfranchised citizens, and lynch law.

North of this line are the chief industrial centers of the country, a dozen cities in which the Negro people have developed communities such as Harlem, the South Side of Chicago, South Philadelphia, and the Hill in Pittsburgh. To these settlements have migrated hundreds of thousands of southern Negroes. Here they vote and serve on juries, send representatives to Congress and state legislatures, participate in county and city government, publish newspapers, attend school and college with their white neighbors, ride unrestricted on train and streetcar, attend the same theaters and movies.

The Negro people are one of the many national groups that make Pittsburgh dynamic. In streets, shops and foundries, in parks, churches and concert halls one sees almost every race and nation, hears almost every tongue spoken—white, yellow, black, red. Turk, West Indian, Japanese, Mexican, Chinese American, French, Finn, Magyar, Slav, Welsh and Irish inhabit their little sections and preserve their customs, traditions and languages while they become active citizens. Of every five people making their home in Pittsburgh, three are either foreign born or Negro. Of all Americans, the Negro people in 1930 made up almost one tenth, of all Pennsylvanians about one seventh. And of Pittsburghers the Negro people make up roughly one twelfth. Among northern cities, Pittsburgh ranks ninth in its number of Negro people.

In Pennsylvania the Negro population is concentrated in eight counties. Four of these—Beaver, Westmoreland, Allegheny and Washington—are in the Western Pennsylvania steel district. This fact is basic in determining the manner and condition of living for the 54,983 Negro people who make their homes in this northern industrial city.

Steel is the barometer of the standard of living in Pittsburgh. When the mills roar and shake the earth, men in Pittsburgh have jobs. The worker feels secure. Unquestionably, the greater number of Negroes are wage workers. In 1930, of the city's employed people 26,121 were Negroes. One third were steelworkers, glassworkers, laborers, carpenters, and workers in manufacturing and industry. Almost half of these were in domestic and personal service—servants, chauffeurs, barbers, and the like. One sixth worked in trade and transportation, or were small shop owners, bus and car repairmen. All others—white collar and professional workers—were but seven percent or one fifteenth of the whole.

The welfare of the Negro worker, then, is a gauge of the welfare of the Negro community. And in turn the welfare of the Negro and other national groups who predominate in the mills, factories, and offices helps gauge the social and cultural temperament of Pittsburgh.

In other respects the Negro people of Pittsburgh help determine the character of the city. Pittsburgh has had from its beginning a strong liberal tradition, never completely lost sight of in the growth of industrial paternalism, and stoutly defended by national minorities who make up the majority of its citizens. The extent to which these national groups enjoyed prosperity, civil and social security, natural and cultural rights is, therefore, a standard of the enlightenment and progressive character of Pittsburgh.

The impact of the Negro people on the general mood of the city has been deep. The folkways of the dense population of the Hill and the Strip have been adopted by thousands of people. The food, drinks, dances, "jive," songs, proverbs, anecdotes, and the consciousness of peoples or nationalities living together within a community, for better and for worse, have been enhanced by the presence of thousands of Negro people.

Negroes participate broadly in the working of the complex organism of this modern industrial center. In paving the streets and digging tunnels through the rocky hills, in constructing the railroads that follow the three rivers, in erecting the skyscrapers of the downtown triangle, in repairing the cars and buses that provide transportation, in working behind the scenes in the department stores, in distributing mail, on river boats and along city wharves, or catering in restaurants and hotels, the Negro worker has contributed to the welfare of one of the first industrial regions of the world. The Negro professional—architect, lawyer, doctor, surveyor, social worker, accountant and clerk, City Assessor and Building Inspector, Workmen's Compensation Referee and Assistant in Labor and Industry—has recently added his training and skill. And on the culture of the region he has also left his mark. His music has exerted an influence from the time of Stephen Foster to Earl "Fatha" Hines, Bennie Carter, Leroy Eldridge, and "Honey Boy" Jones. Martin R. Delany did much for the national progress of the Negro through the publication of his *Condition, Elevation, Emigration, and Destiny of the Colored People of the United States*. The poetry of George B. Vashon— "Vincent Ogé," and "A Life Day"—marked a peak of achievement. Henry Ossawa Tanner, the painter, was born here. Johnny Woodruff, Olympic champion, enrolled at the University of Pittsburgh, and John Henry Lewis, the pugilist, makes Pittsburgh his home.

The Negro began his service in the Pittsburgh region with the establishment of the earliest frontier. As freeman, slave, and indentured servant, he aided in opening the Pittsburgh frontier to settlement. Legend says "Black Jack," a frontier scout and guide, was a Negro. But the deeds of this Herculean, swarthy frontiersman known as "Black Jack, the Hunter" or "Captain Jack, the Wild Hunter," supposed to have accompanied General Braddock as guide, were frontier myths which had their origin in a very real person, Captain Patrick Jack of the Cumberland Valley. The names of Charles Richards, however, a Negro tavern keeper in the frontier village, and of Benjamin Richards, a land merchant and cattle dealer, are inscribed on the petition drawn up in 1787 by residents of Pittsburgh and the neighborhood to set up Allegheny County.

Of the forties, the heyday of river traffic, when Charles Dickens visited Pittsburgh, when abolition and temperance societies were strong, Thomas A. Brown, employed on a river steamer, a man of character and intellect and the father of Hallie Q. Brown, said:

> The City of Pittsburgh boasted of stalwart characters in these days. Lewis Woodson, Augustus Green and William Wells, powerful pulpit orators; John Peck, the first Negro to own and control a fine Hair Goods Establishment; Joseph Miller, leader of the famous choir of Old Wylie Street Church; George B. Vashon, Samuel Neale, and Martin H. Freeman, noted professors of Avery College, and other city schools; Martin R. Delany, distinguished physician and scholar; George Knox, Jesse Wells, William Austin, Barney Mahoney, Matthew and Charles Jones and a host of others I could mention. Ah! These were giants in their day! Given a fair chance in the race of life they

would have measured arms with the greatest of earth's noblemen. They served their day and generation; noblemen they were in point of splendid service.

Harlem, South Chicago, South Philadelphia are cities in themselves. In these cities within cities have grown great and small industries, businesses, and social organizations, which give life within them a unity. Pittsburgh is different. Here the Negro people are concentrated not in one community only, but in half a dozen island-like groups into which and around which wash other nationalities— Poles, Italians, Jews (foreign-born and native), Germans, Irish, Russians, Mexicans, and Hungarians.

These islands of population are the Hill District, East Liberty, Homewood, the South Side, the Strip, Manchester, Woods Run, and Beltzhoover. In this city of heavy industry the Negro worker works not in his own community, but travels to the mills and factories, or to the downtown business section. Neither has Negro business grown up in the separate communities. Usually the Jew and the Italian have remained there to run groceries, drugstores, gas stations, variety stores, and movies. At times group tensions have formed and have been played upon by politicians and opportunists.

The history of the Hill is the usual sorry tale of deterioration from a once attractive living place. When the second part of the historic Woods plan of Pittsburgh was laid out in 1784, it contained four farms and 40 outlets lying along the Monongahela River from the present Grant Street to Frasier Street in Oakland, and along the Allegheny River from 11th Street at the edge of the Golden Triangle to 33rd Street in Lawrenceville. Farm number three on this plot consisted of 274 acres, owned by A. C. Reed, which, after the Revolutionary War was subdivided for a home for General Tannehill. This is now the heart of the Hill District. What is known as "The Hill" was populated slowly. In 1815 only thirteen of the town's 5,000 persons lived on Grant's Hill, but a business directory in 1837 listed 413 people on all that land now referred to as the Hill. These were chiefly merchants and professionals who had built in the growing suburb. As late as 1887 the Hill was still country land, set at wide intervals with good houses, some of them well-known for traditional hospitality. Several of the old homes survive, dilapidated reminders of former delightful prosperity. At the far end of the old Seventh Street Road was the Jacob Ewart farm and the house which later was for some years the Montefiore Hospital. The now dismal house adjoining the Irene Kaufmann Settlement was the home of General Moorhead, famous during the Civil War and for years afterwards for its feasts and festivities, and for such visitors as James Garfield, William McKinley, Horace Greeley and General Grant. The Rosalia Home for Foundlings on Cliff Street was the home of James P. Tanner. But wealth and social position gave way before the advance of the usual succession of new groups of people. As the city grew, the lower parts of the Hill, nearer the noise and dust of business and the smoke and grime of iron mills and foundries became peopled with Irish workers. These, as Jews settled among them, moved up the Hill. And then as the Negro people grew in population and took up the long-used houses on the lower slopes, the Jews also pushed further out.

So the successive tides of people have worked up the long slope and out towards Oakland, leaving finally the Negro people, largely, in the dwellings discarded by their predecessors; and leaving them for many years in alley-houses behind the dwellings of the Jewish, Italian and other foreign populations.

As early as the 1860's the lower section of the Hill was known as Hayti. By 1900, the Fifth Ward, where the Negro people of Pittsburgh are most concentrated, recorded 211. Within the next ten years the Negro population of this ward grew to 6,146 and by 1920 it had reached 10,383.

On the Hill, 25,000 or almost half of the Negro people of Pittsburgh now try to live, fighting poverty, squalor, disease, crime, vice—every human handicap. Here thrive saloons and speakeasies, gambling houses and pawn shops, pool rooms, dope dens, houses of prostitution and assignation.

The Hill is the symbol of the worst that a fiercely industrial city like Pittsburgh can do to human beings. Its dominant note is squalor. Narrow streets are lined with tawdry houses, dingy red, their scarred doorways and tottering porches often reached by crumbling wooden steps. Roofs sag. Walls lean. Window frames are rotted and patched. Chimneys are cracked and gaping with holes.

It rises, an abrupt, tremendous mound from the flat land between the three rivers. No street on the Hill runs level for more than a quarter of a mile. Dozens of them, many of which are dirt and ash, gullied by open sewers, climb almost perpendicular. Many break at a ravine or a cliff edge, convert themselves into long flights of wooden steps, hundred in a flight, and continue on the other side.

Along the Hill streetcars side-swipe parked automobiles and trucks, and wait for the driver to push or pry loose his vehicle. Curbs are broken, cobbles dislodged, macadam split and bulging. Doorways and curbs are littered with paper; discarded boxes and crates inconvenience the pedestrian. A dead cat may be crushed against a curb. A man may lie bleeding in the angle of a house wall.

The Hill is a district of small businesses trying to prosper—dingy pool rooms; the yellow fronted Big 4 Barber Shop or the garish green Cold Turkey Barber Shop; red front variety stores; smudgy, ill-smelling restaurants—Tom's Lunch, Mother's Lunch, Southern Bar-B-Que, Lucky Chop Suey, Rosa's Beauty Saloon or the Paradise Shoe Shine. An occasional broad plate glass window displays gold letter inscriptions—Hod Carriers Local 11 or Refuse Drivers and Collectors Local.

In the midst of squalor and dullness the New Granada Theater displays its glazed orange, green and purple front, pseudo-modern, pseudo-Spanish.

On hot summer days the Hill reaches its saturation point. Old wigged women sit on steps or in doorways clacking their Yiddish tongues. Drunks lurch past or stand reeling and singing on corners. Old men sleep in alleys or on church steps. On the pavements—their chief playground—children stretch out to draw or read. They dash between cruising trucks after wildly thrown balls. Prostitutes lean from windows or stand half-concealed in doorways—motioning trade with cigarettes held in white or black fingers.

From garbage wagons driven uncovered through the streets, the sun draws sickening odors. From open bars and cafes mechanical victrolas screech; the stale odor of beer and sweat drift out. Passing the ends of sun-seared alleys, one breathes the stink of urine.

And most of the people on the Hill fit appropriately into the background— impoverished Jews, Italians, Negroes; slump-shouldered men with hungry eyes; Negro women, spindle-legged from childhood rickets; spine-sagging, down-at-heel, listless men and women, or drink-blurred white and black faces screeching filth and strident jokes.

Here and there survives an old garden wall, a bit of iron grill work wrought in leaf and tendril. And occasionally a clean, modern storefront, or freshly painted, clean-curtained house front gives relief.

In summer every yellow clay hillside, ravine or discarded quarry—and there are dozens of these on the Hill—is overrun with sunflowers, from whose dense leaves glow hundreds of brown and yellow heads.

Schenley Heights, East Liberty and Homewood, to the Pittsburgh Negro, connote life lived in other ways than the social disorganization and disintegration of the Hill. In these sections professional and middle class people own their homes—some in the usual city row, some isolated from their neighbors by as much narrow ground as city crowding permits. Here lawyers, doctors, teachers, clerks, may take the air on a summer evening on front porches screened by vines. Hedges, though they bear as much grime as leaves, set off houses from street or neighbor. Front lawns with forsythia or hydrangea, gardens of pansies, hyacinths or geraniums or patches of lawn and a garden bench allow breathing space. Gardens and lawns with crocus, tulip, roses, iris, snapdragon, and aster give charming backgrounds for parties, fetes, weddings or social loitering. In these sections, radios, automobiles, vacations with pay, pianos and bathrooms, high school and university study, theater and concert attendance are more plentiful than in the Hill and the Strip, on the South Side or Woods Run.

In these communities living is organized on a level different from that of the Hill. Bridge clubs and literary clubs meet in comfortable, well-furnished living rooms. Invitational luncheons and dinners are served at well-laid tables. Musicals, formal parties, formal calls and entertaining maintain a "genteel tradition."

On the North Side, for more than a century pleasantly known as Allegheny, lies Manchester, once a green and open village, with lawns reaching to the river, and elm trees sheltering porticoed houses. This was Margaret Deland's *Old Chester*. In Manchester, Negro life is almost as old as the city itself. In Allegheny, too, was the Avery Mission settlement where one of the first Negro schools in the country was established. Here also Avery College taught the sciences and the humanities. In old Allegheny several of the earliest churches were founded. Part of the Avery Church settlement had grown up in streets easily reached by the spring flood of the Allegheny River. Year after year streets and houses were submerged and, when the waters subsided, left under layers of slime and mud. There came also to this settlement an influx of that human wreckage that found quarters most easily accessible near rivers and railroads. Old residents moved out, discouraged, and crowded into the Carrington Street and Manchester districts. Housing became an acute problem here, and with it grew problems of health, infant mortality, delinquency and other evils.

Carrington Street, Boyle Street and the Brighton Road district are not so decrepit as the lower Hill District and the South Side, not so substantial as Homewood and Schenley Heights. They are, nevertheless, among the less desirable parts of the city for living. Manchester and Woods Runs, with the South Side, are scarred by social decay. These are the steel-mill settlements—black, congested, sorry with mill grime, industrial disease, and misery. Ramshackle houses of frame or brick, when the mills are running, tremble with the beat of trip hammers and vibrating rollers. To these settlements in the early days of the iron industry came German and Irish mill workers, their numbers growing as the iron industry grew. Woods Run was largely English and Welsh laborers. Then came other workers in the usual succession—Italians, Poles and the various Slavs. In Manchester and Woods Run now the six thousand odd Negroes are chiefly families whose fathers do hard labor in the nearby mills. Today many of them live on relief. A few run small businesses for their own people—barber shops and restaurants, chiefly. Here, too, came many people from the South during and after the migration of the First World War. And here some special effects of this migration appeared sharply, for many of the newcomers brought their native community organizations with them—their preachers and congregations in particular. These groups, furthermore, kept to themselves and the older families held aloof in a belief in their social superiority because of longer residence in a northern city with its advantages for literacy, development of culture, "refinement" and achievement of somewhat greater economic security and a higher standard of living.

These North Side communities have developed their own social unity expressed in the North Side and Suburban Civic League of about 400 members, in women's clubs, in the Olympian Dramatic Club and in young people's social clubs. The pastors of sixteen churches form the Ministerial Association. Four or five doctors and three dentists practice.

"The Strip," once notorious as the "Stormy Ninth" Ward, is a narrow stretch of industrial slums between the Allegheny River and the Pennsylvania Railroad running from the Union Station almost to the old United States Arsenal. Very early it was the site of an Indian Village, Shannopin's Town. At its eastern end young Major Washington landed after his winter crossing of the Allegheny River on a raft, from which he had fallen into the frozen water. It was later laid out as Bayardstown, an early American residential suburb along the Braddock's Field Road. Not long afterwards, it became one of the level sections of city land, conveniently lying along the river banks, preempted by the early iron industry, and for years was inhabited by German, then Irish foundry and mill workers. As the Black Diamond Steel Mill was the first in the city to employ Negro workers, numbers of Negroes moved in with Poles and Slovaks, and the German and Irish drifted eastward.[1]

It is now a grimy backyard of the city, a kind of ghost city, a deserted mill area, discarded by industry, partly demolished; churches and schools for the most part have moved to neighboring sections. Once notorious for violent political battles, highjackers and gangsters, crime and delinquency, it became the site of one of the city's Hoovervilles, and is now a degenerated region of forlorn Negro, Polish, and Slovenian homes.

On the industrial South Side lives another island community of Negroes, five percent of the Germans, Poles, Hungarians, and Russians squeezed into the smoke and dust-corroded flats along the Monongahela River, or climbing the bleak hills just beyond the flats. Here again are the tawdry and barren homes of unskilled millworkers, washed and scorched to uniform dreary gray by rain and sun and falling cinders from mill stacks in whose hot shadow they stand. Dilapidated, dark from crowding together and from the smoke-filled air that settles around them, roofs leaking, steps broken, porches hanging—kitchens frequently used for sleeping, these houses are human habitations. Rooms of semi-darkness, where the plaster has fallen and rain seeps in, two beds, a table, a stove, and soap boxes or orange crates for chairs, sometimes house a family.

Here a number of southern Negroes have migrated in the last two decades, and formed two rival communities centering about a Methodist and a Baptist Church, finding amusement in two neighborhood theaters, several pool rooms and beer gardens. Negro youth of this section go to the Hill or to East Liberty for

1. Black Diamond was located in the Lawrenceville section of Pittsburgh.

dances. For the older residents, house to house visiting largely suffices for recreation.

Beltzhoover, a conservative community lying on the outer hills of the city, has a Negro population of approximately 2,000. This settlement grew rapidly when the Liberty Tubes were begun in 1924. Italian and southern black laborers employed on the construction of the tubes lived in shanties overhanging the tube area and, after completion of the tubes, many of them did not leave but moved into better houses. Residents from the degenerating parts of the Hill moved into the greener, more open district of Beltzhoover. Here they built or rented more modern types of homes than had been theirs on the Hill, sometimes graced with amenities like flower gardens. Beltzhoover has a less mobile population of millworkers, postal service employees, two physicians, a dentist, social workers, nurses, clerks and people in other occupations, about one third of whom are homeowners. The families of several school teachers, who because of the prejudice in our Pittsburgh school system must seek employment elsewhere, live there. The relief situation is less acute here than in the Hill, Manchester, or the Strip. It is a neighborly community. Frequently Negroes and whites visit back and forth. Occasionally in time of illness a white family takes home a Negro family's wash and vice versa. At Christmas, pudding and pastries are exchanged.

Community life is organized around two Baptist Churches, a Methodist Church, a Church of the Saints of God in Christ, a branch Sunday School of Bidwell Presbyterian Church, and, outside of the church, two Negro Democratic Clubs, a Negro Republican Club active only when primaries are held, a woman's Dorcas Circle. A club of young women, the Gay Hill-Toppers, raise funds to reduce the mortgage and interest on the Methodist Church building, and have programs of book reviews, lectures and discussions. For larger social activities the people indulge in much intra-city activity among other neighborhoods.

The economic basis upon which rests the social, political, and cultural life in Pittsburgh is weaker and more shifting than that of any other group. Because of such variability, as well as the existence of several communities rather than one concentrated settlement such as Harlem or South Chicago, the group mood and outlook has not established or coalesced; group unity has remained weak. In addition to economic instability and geographic separation there exists within the population itself the ancient order of three—rich man, poor man, and he who lives between, eager to lift himself into the class that enjoys luxuries, fearful of falling into that much larger group which suffers privation. Three fourths of Pittsburgh Negroes live in poverty, one sixth of them have the necessities of decent living, about one tenth maintain comfortable middle-class circumstances. Several have accumulated small fortunes; a few have incomes above $10,000 a year. Fifteen percent of the community own their own homes, as compared with about one third of the native whites and one half of the foreign born.[2]

Occupations, though limited, are various. In addition to those employed at common labor there are chauffeurs, janitors, commercial clerks, domestics. Besides these, Pittsburgh has a large professional group—attorneys, physicians and surgeons, pharmacists, actors and showmen, musicians and teachers of music, trained nurses, undertakers, dentists, school teachers, real estate dealers, engineers, an architect and other professionals. There are 143 clergymen and three artists and teachers of art.

A considerable number of small businesses thrive in the various neighborhoods—fruit and vegetable markets, groceries, or combination groceries and butcher shops; confectioneries, bakeries and fish markets, filling stations and garages; fuel and ice dealers, secondhand shops, drug stores with or without soda fountains; a millinery shop, a costume tailor, and greater than all, 133 eating and drinking places.

Among cities with a large Negro population, Pittsburgh ranks last in the number of Negro operated retail stores. In 1938, 81 such stores were run by Negro proprietors and firm members. Between 1929 and 1935 almost half [of Pittsburgh's Negro-owned retail stores, numbering 150 in 1929] closed.

In spite of economic, political and social achievement, the Negro in Pittsburgh, as anywhere else, is made to feel that he is a member of a minority group, and he lives not only under the disadvantages of all such groups but also under the added one of having a black skin. Programs and movements exist for encouraging the Slavs, the Italians and other nationalities to assimilate, and for hastening their adjustment to American society. Little has been done, however, to promote interracial relations, to explain Negro to white or white to Negro; to inform white students in schools of Negro history and culture. The quicker the adjustment of other nationalities the more desirable citizens they are thought to be. Such capability is taken as a mark of versatility and adaptability on the part of the Greek, the Italian, the Hungarian—of any group except the Negro. Instead of such help he meets obstacles.

He is kept conscious of the difficulty he faces to become a free, reliant, fully productive member of society. He is restricted in professional practice. Interns cannot practice in Pittsburgh hospitals; no Negro doctor is employed on a permanent hospital staff. At only one hospital are Negro nurses in service. No Negro students have been admitted to the School of Medicine at the University of Pitts-

2. The true figure for black property ownership was lower. See chapter 6, "Homeownership," in John Bodnar, Roger Simon, and Michael P. Weber, *Lives of Their Own: Blacks, Italians, and Poles in Pittsburgh, 1900–1960* (Champaign: University of Illinois Press, 1981).

burgh since 1914. Although civil service examinations are open to Negroes, practice teaching in the schools is not open; therefore, but two full-time teachers and a home visitor are employed by the Board of Education. He is barred, in spite of the Equal Rights Bills, from many restaurants and middle-class hotels. He is denied the free use of public swimming pools.

The dominant psychology of the Negro Pittsburgher has been that of the middle-class Negro who has achieved some reasonable economic security, is satisfied to maintain it and is, therefore, unwilling to risk rebuff, to excite animosity, to invite discomfort by participation in aspects of civic and social life other than those allotted him by a prejudiced community. He has kept largely to himself, in nationalist isolation or racial pride. He has felt that he belonged to a strategic group among his people. Lucretius-like, he has achieved a sense of well-being, rather from commiseration of those less fortunate than himself, than through complete economic and social participation.

For years the Negro community in Pittsburgh has, admittedly on the part of many of its members, lacked strong leadership. Under the handicaps of an environment dominated by heavy industry and divided into communities not strong enough or wealthy enough to support their own schools and colleges, there had developed no sizable intelligentsia, no strong group of intellectuals to bring conditions and problems to attention and discussion. Consequently, the Negro in Pittsburgh has been less articulate than elsewhere, slower in coming to social and cultural maturity. With such backwardness has gone passivity in political action. Divided into a half dozen communities, Negro voters have not been able until recently to place representatives in state or municipal bodies through which they might work for the welfare of their group.

New moods and attitudes, however, are forming. A little weary of being tolerated, philanthropized, patronized, kept in the shadow, the Negro people are becoming articulate. The depression has had its effect. It has jarred open doors; it has focused issues; it has coalesced groups; it has given voice to many needs and joined many hands. Many of the white population, white workers and middle class groups are waking to consciousness that most of their problems and the problems of their Negro neighbors are not separable. Jobs, relief, security, leisure and culture, education cannot be easily maintained in an economic crisis where division into many groups weakens the maintenance of these things by scattering social energy. What have in the past been looked on as psychological, social, national or racial differences, under the pressure of general social insecurity are coming to be understood as common economic interests. Social, national, racial and psychological levels have become more uniform and are more clearly divined as, at bottom, job levels or levels of economic opportunity. The Negro in Pittsburgh has two major desires—equal chance with all other groups to make a living; and the breaking down of prejudice against complete social, political, and cultural fruition. No longer does he accept his former primary role as a source of cheap labor nor his cultural role as perpetuator of stereotypes growing out of the white man's romantic conceptions—the Rastuses, the mammies. He has grown conscious of his value as builder; as millworker who supplies steel for American bridges, railroads and buildings; as road maker. He realizes his training for teaching, for producing music or painting. He believes in his capacity to administer justice in courts or magistrates' offices, to perform social service to his community. There is a growth of group unity—broader, more progressive, more liberal. Until the jolt of depression, neither Negro nor white had realized generally that the need of one is the problem of all, and that poverty, political and cultural restrictions of any one group are a drag on general progress. The lowest economic group naturally first felt the pressure, and responded first. Unemployed and W.P.A. workers, evicted tenants, relief clients organized into the Workers' Alliance, Tenants' Leagues, Housewives' Leagues, and similar groups were created to alleviate distress and maintain some degree of social security.

A bitter period of unemployment and relief subsistence more than anything else has awakened this, the largest and weightiest group. In waking, it has stirred the whole Negro community into thought and action. To bring forward the condition and elevation or integration of the Negro into the Pittsburgh scene the large community has begun to work through the National Negro Congress, the NAACP, a coordinating committee for jobs for Negroes, the Workers Council of the Urban League, and discussion groups formed by the Negro Branches of the YMCA and YWCA.

A tendency away from such movements as the Garveyites is manifest. At one time Herron Hill and Lower Wylie Avenue Branches of this movement enrolled several thousand members. But the "Back to Africa" idea did not take a strong hold in Pittsburgh. It was thought too narrow and unbecoming to the pride-of-race characteristic of many Negro people. Although in changing its name to the Universal Negro Improvement Association, the society claimed interest in improvement of the status of the Negro everywhere, it lost ground. Attempts to carry out its plan of Negro businesses by and for Negroes by establishing a few restaurants, laundries and similar enterprises proved unsuccessful. The Association held meetings and carried on propaganda campaigns. As late as 1938 they sent a delegate to their International Convention held in Toronto, Canada. They still maintain a small hall on the Hill. But the movement amounts to little now in the city.

Slowly but with acceleration the community is learning that the solution of its problems does not lie within the race itself, that education, economic independence, culture and employment skills alone will not dissipate the shadow of the plantation. More than that, they will not guard them against further discrimination, segregation, or national oppression in a crisis that has brought many new words into books and papers, one of the most frequently used of them—fascism.

Little wonder then, that diverse moods and attitudes have developed. Under the dominance of the southern tradition, under the northward reaching shadow of the plantation, the Negro in Pittsburgh has sought many adjustments. Whereas he wants chiefly to feel himself part of an industrial and social community he is constantly reminded that in many phases of the city's life he cannot yet join without uncomfortable consciousness of nationality. He may not live in the street of his choice. It is not long since a fiery cross was burned in front of the home of a physician who was not wanted in the district; the home of an attorney was stoned repeatedly until he withdrew to a Negro residential section. The old device of the more expensive restaurants and hotels ignoring Negroes at tables, or serving salt in their coffee is still practiced to circumvent the Equal Rights Bill. Settlement houses in the most congested Negro areas discourage or openly refuse their advantages to Negroes most in need of them.

Dominated by a feeling of race, the Negro nevertheless does not want to be thought of as an African or Ethiopian but as a Pittsburgher. Yet many Negroes have not yet assumed their share of responsibility in the development of a homogeneous community. Many have developed a retaliatory mood; they do not want, they say, to mingle with white citizens. They have come to feel "you don't want us; so we don't want you."

Such a mood may become resentful and suspicious of the outstretched hand of the white man. It results in isolation from the main currents of life; it rejects the stimulus of other ways of living and becomes inbred. Its worst aspect is "racism" or the false aspect of "race pride." This way of life, they say, is ours—this music, these churches, this form of sociability. Take it or leave it. Then, too, there are other attitudes, survivals from the more conciliatory elements in the history of the Negro in America. Jupiter Hammon, for instance, while thousands of slaves were revolting and making their escape, felt it his duty to bear slavery with patience, but opposed it as a system and urged manumission of Negro youth. Peter Williams, one of the early national figures, after the beginnings of the convention movement in the 1830's wished not to offend the powers of the Episcopal Church by an aggressive attitude in defense of Negro rights. This weak stand on the question of Negro liberation lost him prestige among his people. Men like Hammon and Williams lacked the aggression of Bishop Richard Allen, of Prince Hall or Martin Delany. The Hammonses and Williamses of today retard the integration of communities where Negroes live in large numbers, set off, but side by side with native born white and European, many of whom are eager to develop a unified community of friendly nationalities. Negro and white, native and European are coming however, to understand that the maintenance of national cultures within any social unit, city, county or country, if allowed to interact freely will produce a many colored harmonious whole, without losing them individuality of any single factor.

These attitudes of conciliation and retaliation endanger the flowering of people in such "melting pots" as Pittsburgh. Any national group which exists in too self-contained a manner becomes easy prey to dangerous social forces. Withdrawal and isolation or too great passivity make possible movements such as the White Crusaders who circularized the district in 1936 with a demand to "Put the Mason-Dixon line north of Pennsylvania." They encourage the burning of fiery crosses and impede the opening of many doors closed simply because the doors have not been pushed open.

A Negro woman wrote recently: "We Negroes teach our youth that the salvation of the Negro lies within the race itself; that, as soon as we become economically independent, educated, cultural, and skillful, we shall arrive. But wealth, education, culture and technological advancement did not save the Jew in Germany."

Martin R. Delany saw clearly, almost a century ago, the dangers of racism. He wrote: ". . . a fact worthy of observation, that wherever objects of oppression are the most easily distinguished by any peculiar or general characteristics, these people are the more easily oppressed. This is the case with modern Jews and many other people who have strongly marked, peculiar, or distinguishing characteristics. The policy of all those who proscribe any people, induce them to select as the objects of proscription, those who differed as much as possible, in some particulars, from themselves." These various attitudes taken by the Negro to his problem, whether individually, in groups, or in organizations such as the Garveyites, are attempts to explain his position and respond to it, to change his world, to develop and satisfy him more completely.

It behooves the Pittsburgh Negro in particular to educate himself, to clarify his attitudes to himself, and to educate white nationalities on the role of the Negro in American life, past and present. This he must do by intelligent use of the ballot, by energetic participation in programs such as that of the NAACP youth organizations, by promotion of sound legislation in behalf of all minorities, by introduction of Negro history into the schools, and by correction of the distortion of Negro history in texts now in use. More than all these he must participate in energetic attempts to integrate himself with progressive white groups, and especially he must participate more extensively in the progressive trade union movement. The Pittsburgh Negro has an important job to do in removing from northern cities the shadow of the plantation, and by extending his own democratic rights, extending democracy in the community at large.

CHAPTER 2

THE NEGRO ON THE FRONTIER

Typist: M. B. Holmes / Rewriteman: J. Ernest Wright /
February 5, 1940 / Final

Almost as early as the English and the Scotch-Irish, the Negro arrived on the western Pennsylvania frontier to claim it for the English and to settle it. With the first military expeditions, Negroes came as officers' men, as workers about the forts, and as soldiers. Legend says that at General Braddock's defeat in 1755, his Negro servant Will helped carry the General from the field and that Will later became the property of General Washington. This story lacks verification. Of the early frontiersmen—the buckskinned fellers-of-trees, the moccasined fur-capped trappers and hunters, the scouts and the rangers between the log forts and stations in the Monongahela country, records will probably never divulge how many were Negroes or how many were of mixed Negro, Indian, and white blood. Neither perhaps will they yield the names of the drovers and the cattle herders or the rifle men, drummers and fifers of the early military expeditions to the frontier. It is known that in the French and Indian Wars, Negroes from the Carolinas, Georgia, Virginia, and Maryland enlisted, but the rolls do not identify all of them.

In 1755 General Braddock set out from Georgetown, Maryland through the wilderness to wrest Fort Duquesne from the French. So narrow and rutted were the roads, so encumbered with boulders and fallen trees that the army could travel in columns only three and four deep, and consequently stretched four miles long. Braddock's great coach lumbered along as best it could. With the baggage train of two hundred wagons and twenty-five hundred horses were a number of Negro wagoners and drivers. One of these was Sandy or Samuel Jenkins, who was the property of Captain Broadwater of Fairfax County. Jenkins drove a provision train. He is said to have lived until 1849, when he died at the age of 115 at Lancaster, Ohio. At Fort Fredericktown, Maryland, when the army halted in May, 1755, the Negro recruits helped clear ground for camp, and paraded at two o'clock in the afternoon of that day. Further along his line of march, Braddock picked up other Negro recruits. Among them was Billy Brown of Frankfort, born in Africa and brought to America as a slave. In Capt. Walker's company was Jack Miner, a Negro from Bucks County, also Abraham Lawrence and Archibald Kelso. Two southern Negro recruits under Washington on this march were Gilbert and John Alton. There was also on Braddock's expedition a boy named Ishmael Titus, serving a master employed by the commissary to transport army stores with his two-horse wagon. A third horse was added to the team and on this horse Ishmael Titus rode.

Several years after Braddock's expedition, in 1758, other Negroes came to the frontier with General John Forbes' expedition. "Over a prodigious train of mountains and through deep and rocky woods," as Forbes wrote in his letters, the columns moved "over 400 miles of land carriage through an immense wilderness and the worst roads in the world." Their ship cannon were mounted on trucks. "The Howitzers had each nine horses, the twelve pounders seven and the wagons six." There were roads to cut, swamps to make passable. At times gun carriages had to be let down a hill with tackle. Wagons were demolished. Frequently when the columns halted to cut a passage over a mountain slope, a day's march did not exceed two miles. Forbes reports that "the horses (were) growing every day fainter, many of them dying." Finally the various regiments met at the Baystown Camp (now Bedford, Pennsylvania.) Here in the frozen muck and sleet, and in the log palisade at Fort Ligonier where General Forbes passed the last autumn days sending out scouts to reconnoiter the land about the forks of the Ohio were thirteen Negroes, eight of whom were with the Royal American Regiment. These men must have been wagoners, drovers, and servants. But at times they also took part in the military action. Three Negroes were reported attached to the Sixty-Seventh Regiment of the First Highlanders. In the Virginia regiments under Colonel Washington were listed thirty-six Negroes. Perhaps Negro troopers were among the scouts dispatched by Forbes to determine the number of French Canadians at Fort Duquesne, or what entrenchments had been thrown up between the fort and the rivers, or what guns were mounted and what parties were leaving the fort by day and by night to reconnoiter. If so, they were among those who returned to the outpost at Loyalhanna and made themselves known by yellow fillets worn about their heads and arms and by waving their match coats upon long poles. For these were the activities of soldiers encamped with Forbes on Laurel Hill before the final march upon the fort.

At the end of November, Forbes and his army moved from Loyalhanna to attack the Fort. They encamped for a night at Turtle Creek. The French had been warned of their coming. As the black and white troops prepared for their final move, the dull echoes of explosions shook the air. The French had blown up the fort and fled. And when the army reached the fork of the rivers next day they found only charred ruins—blackened shells of huts and other buildings above which stood a score of smoking chimneys. About the ground lay quantities of old carriages and wagon iron, guns, barrels, and a cartload of scalping knives. And, most eloquent of all, there stood a row of stakes to which were chained the charred bodies of five soldiers taken among General Grant's men.

In the gray half light of November 27, 1758, amid the smoking ruins of the abandoned French fort at the Point, General John Forbes, pallid and suffering, stood with Colonel Bouquet and Colonel George Washington while the drums rolled and the fifes played, and Colonel Armstrong fastened the flag of Britain to the flag rope. With the white troops forty-two Negro frontiersmen stood to watch the crosses of St. George and St. Andrew run up the flag staff, flutter in the cold river wind, and proclaim that Britain's empire had been ensured of its westernmost outpost. These forty-two Negro frontiersmen were encamped on the spot when for the first time in history a letter, from General John Forbes to Sir William Pitt bore the heading; "Pittsburgh, 27th November 1758." In his letter the general wrote to the Prime Minister,

> I have used the freedom of giving your name to Fort Duquesne, as I hope it was in some measure the being actuated by your spirits that now makes us Masters of the place. Nor could I help using the same freedom in the naming of two other Forts that I built (plans of which I send you) the one Fort Ligonier and the other Bedford. I hope the Name Fathers will take them under their protection. In which case these dreary deserts will soon be the richest and most fertile of any possessed by the British in North America.

Less than two weeks later Forbes and Bouquet left Fort Pitt. Colonel Hugh Mercer remained as commandant. In the spring of 1759 he wrote to Mr. Richard Peters, provincial secretary and superintendent of Indian affairs, for "two Negro girls and a boy about fourteen years old, to be paid for in fur."

With Mercer at the fort was left a garrison of several hundred green-coated Pennsylvania soldiers, Marylanders and Virginians, kilted Highlanders and scarlet-coated Royal Americans. The first weeks were occupied in building a stockade against winter and Indians, then in erecting a new fort, a square structure of earth work and logs with four bastions. A row of log cabins and bark huts was hastily built along the Monongahela river bank. Some of the log structures were of two stories, to be used as storehouses by traders. That spring of 1759 an Indian trading post was officially established at Fort Pitt. Among the Indian traders who established headquarters here were William Trent, Joseph Simon, David Franks, and Levi Andrew Levy. These formed a partnership in 1760 which lasted nine years. In their employ were Negroes who drove pack horses or wagon loads of paltry to the east.

George Morgan of the firm of Baynton, Wharton and Morgan, who also had stores in Pittsburgh, believed the company could establish a flour monopoly, bartering Negro slaves for wheat and flour on long-term credits. On a farm farther west he placed a number of unsold slaves at work erecting a log house and planting tobacco and corn.

To the trading post at Fort Pitt came also the Quaker James Kenny, in April 1759, with a pack-horse train of goods as a present for the Indians. Kenny made another visit in 1761. In his journal Kenny records many incidents in the life of this log trading post—that 100 horses arrived loaded with oats; that Geo. Croghan got a black eye in a fight with the Delaware chief Tedyuscung; that General John Stanwix arrived "with his train and set of music," that he was very plainly dressed and that "many bullocks and other provisions arrived." Kenny also says "ye South Branch of Potomac people are in droves along the road, going to Pittsburgh, some with flour and some with corn, oats, butter, cheese, etc." He met Colonel Curd and a party of wagons and pack horses going to the mouth of Redstone Creek to build some storehouses. He tells of the repairs on the fort banks, the quarrying and squaring of stone for a governor's house at the fort, the making of brick, the mowing and hay making along the riverbanks. He tells of deals in skins with the Indians, how they brought across the river in a flat about forty bushels of coal, and how he killed a turkey. He speaks of the other Indian traders—William Trent, and Levi Andrew Levy, and he records on August 4: "Levy's Negro ran away with the Indians last night."

That year, Kenny wrote in his diary (Nov. 20th):

> I have been informed by a Young Man that was order'd by ye Commanding Officer, Colonel Bouquet (this Sumer), to Number all ye Dwelling Houses without ye Fort marking the number on each Door that there was above one Hundred Houses but ye Highest number I have seen by beter acct there is 150 Houses, to take notice of I think was Seventy Eight, these being ye Inhabitants of Pittsburgh, where two years ago I have seen all ye Houses that were without ye Little Fort they had then, thrown Down, only One, which stands yet, also two that was within that little fort is now standing being ye Hospital now, all ye rest being Built since, which if ye Place continues to Increase near this manner it must soon be very large, which seems likely to me.

A few days later he wrote:

Many of ye inhabitants here have hired a school Master & Subscrib'd above Sixty Pounds for this Year to him, he has about Twenty-Scholars, likewise ye Soberer sort of People seems to Long for some public way of Worship, so ye School Master Reads ye Littany & Common Prayer on ye first Days to a Congregation of different Principals (he being a Prisbiterant) where they behave very Grave (as I hear), on ye occasion ye children also are brought to Church as they call it . . .

During its trading post days, Fort Pitt, or Pittsburgh, was the busiest point on the frontier. A score or more traders, their clerks, packers, wives and families, the garrison of the Fort, the Indians coming in with bundles of paltry, families of refugees fleeing Indian attack on the frontier settlements gave the place a rude, thriving air. The drums at daybreak set all within the fort at work until the gun fired late after sundown, the Indian robberies at night, the brawls between Indian and white men, the disastrous rise of the rivers that swept away the houses on the river bank with most of the stores of furs and supplies, the traffic with the Indian villages in the nearby country—Chartiers, Old Town, Logstown, Aliquippa's Town—colored life in the village.

In 1761, John Malcolm of Philadelphia wrote to Colonel Henry Bouquet, then stationed at Fort Pitt, that "a Negro man named Joe, a sawyer by trade" five feet four inches high had been left by Major Rogers on his return from Detroit to Fort Pitt in the custody of Colonel Bouquet. The sawyer Joe belonged to Mr. Thomas Cuthbert of Philadelphia. He was "of the mulatto cast," and the owner was afraid he might change his name, no doubt to evade return. The sawyer Joe was apparently one of a number of Negroes taken by the French and Indians. Lord Jeffrey Amherst wrote to Bouquet at Pittsburgh saying there were sundry claims for Negroes taken by the enemy and, "as a Considerable saving will arise to the public by restoring those Negroes; these are therefore to direct and require you, to deliver or Cause to be delivered to Mr. Cuthbert of Philadelphia, his Negro named Joe. . . ." Robert Morris also wrote to Bouquet at Mr. Cuthbert's request asking him to use his interest "in procuring the Negro man . . . to be sent down here (Philadelphia) as expeditiously as possible his detention from his masters service being a great hindrance to him in carrying on his business."

Bouquet wrote to Amherst on April 21, 1761 saying: "I send with Lieutenant Boutick the Negro Joe, to his Master Mr. Cuthbert of Philadelphia who is to give a receipt for him." Another Negro man, Tom Hyde, was held at the fort. In 1761 an act of Parliament provided for enlistment of servants as soldiers, the masters to be paid by recruiting officers from public funds. Hyde, however, was a free Negro. He had been a soldier in Colonel Fray's regiment, had been taken prisoner at Lake George and he too had been brought to Pittsburgh by Major Rogers.

Hyde had lived in Boston, and he claimed that his former master, Andrew Morgan, had given him his freedom in Europe. He was kept at Fort Pitt until September, when General Hancock wrote to Colonel Bouquet saying that Hyde was a free man with a wife and considerable effects in this country.

While Joe the sawyer, and Tom Hyde, the free soldier, were awaiting instructions they must have spent the summer months of their frontier life like all the other inhabitants of the fort and trading post—mending moccasins, cleaning arms, caulking the rips in canoes and bateaux, working in the smithy, the saw mill, or the storehouses, and reconnoitering the nearby woods and river banks.

During this period a tide of settlement had set in. Land was rapidly taken up within many miles of the fort. Land speculators like George Washington sent out gangs of indentured servants and Negro slaves under overseers to make the first log houses on their holdings. The holdings were then sold or leased to settlers.

By the time the western country joined the Revolution, Pittsburgh was no longer merely a trading post, nor was the Monongahela country around it an uncultivated wilderness dotted with a few frontier settlements of miserable log huts. By 1775 roads had been laid out to neighboring towns and villages of log and of stone houses. Taverns and inns accommodated express riders, military agents and many travelers. Grist mills and distilleries were meeting places where farmers discussed and argued frontier affairs—the Indian policy of the colony, whether the county around about was in reality under the jurisdiction of Virginia as the District of West Augusta, or whether it was Westmoreland County and rightfully part of Pennsylvania.

Fort Pitt, according to Rev. David McClure, was still a handsome and strong fortification, with barracks and comfortable houses, and one large brick house called the Governor's House. The village was a quarter-mile distant and consisted now of houses of hewn log. Although the first object of Rev. McClure's attention on his arrival was the number of poor drunken Indians, staggering and yelling through the village, and although the village was still the "headquarters of Indian traders and the resort of Indians of different and distant tribes who come to exchange their paltry and furs for rum, blankets and ammunition," there were other types of people now, and life had other aspects.

In the town itself men in satin knee breeches and cocked hats, ladies in panniered skirts and ribboned bonnets mingled with buckskin-clad traders and the uniformed garrison. Masonic meetings were held by the soldiers of the garrison. Concerts and plays were given. Courts sat for the Virginia district of West Augusta. At least half a dozen inns and taverns operated. Two ferries plied the Monongahela, and a ducking stool had been erected at the Point.

Englishmen from Maryland and Virginia settled in the town and in the surrounding country. The Nevilles, the Bells, the McNairs, Capt. Heath, and others had come up the Monongahela River valley, bringing their slaves with them, and settling on plantations near Fort Pitt.

No battles of the Revolutionary War were fought near Fort Pitt, but troops were raised to guard the frontier, and many men left for the east. Negroes served in the eastern engagements. But certainly in Pittsburgh there was no Lemuel Haynes, no Peter Salem, Salem Poore, or Austin Dabney. The sentiment of the Massachusetts Committee of Safety, that the use of Negro troops against the British would "reflect dishonor on the American colonies," was held at first throughout the thirteen colonies. Washington, when he took command of the colonial troops at Cambridge, protested the presence of Negro militia men. The Continental Congress instructed him to discharge all Negroes, free and slave. But when Lord Dunmore, the Tory Governor of Virginia, offered in 1775 to free all slaves who would fight in the British ranks, 25,000 Negroes in South Carolina enlisted, and Georgia lost about three fourths of her Negroes to the British. Then Washington revoked the order which prohibited enlistment of Negroes, and the records of everyone of the thirteen colonies record Negro troops, some in special regiments, such as that from Rhode Island which fought at Valley Forge, but most of them side by side with white soldiers. A Hessian officer observed in 1777: "no regiment is to be seen [among the Americans] in which there are not Negroes in abundance, and among them there are able-bodied, strong, and brave fellows." How many of the 4,000 Negroes in the Continental army were from Pittsburgh or Western Pennsylvania we do not know.

In the archives one military incident is recorded in which two Negro slaves were involved in a very minor and passive way. A band of Tory traitors to the Revolution had become active about Fort Pitt. General Hand, in charge of Fort Pitt at the time, had ordered a guard of soldiers to arrest the suspected Tories and bring them to the fort. The traitors were working from Alexander McKee's home on the Ohio River, at what is now McKees Rocks. They had got word of Hand's intention and fled. The band consisted of Capt. McKee, his cousin Robert Surplitt, Simon Girty, Matthew Elliot, a man named Higgins, and two Negro slaves belonging to McKee. It was the winter of 1777 and 1778. Washington and his army of Negro and white soldiers were enduring the winter at Valley Forge when Colonel John Proctor wrote a letter which mentions the incident. The crudity of its spelling and its pithy contents connote vividly the revolutionary frontier.

Westmoreland County, Apr ye 26th, 1778

Honored Sir,

I am in great need of a larg sum of Cash. I hope you will send me by the Bailor, Mr George Hendry, foure thousand Pounds if Posable; he is a safe

Hand, and what Ever sum you send me by him I will be answerable for. I would a ben Down myself, but though it unsave to lave Hom at this time.

Sir, I am able to inform you that Capt. Alexander McKee with sevin other Vilons is gon to the Indians, and since there is a serj't and twenty od men gon from Pittsburgh of the Soldiers. What may be the fate of this County God only knows, but at the Prisent it wears a most Dismal aspect.

I am Sir,
your Most sincere
and Very Humble Servt.,
JOHN PROCTOR.

During the Revolution Virginia claimed the Monongahela country as the district of West Augusta, although Westmoreland county had been set up by Pennsylvania. With a county seat and a log courthouse in Hannastown near Greensburg, the court exercised jurisdiction only over the eastern end of the county. In October 1776 Virginia divided the District of West Augusta, in which Pittsburgh was located, into three counties, Yohogania, Monongalia, and Ohio. Pittsburgh was in the Yohogania County. The courthouse, however was on Andrew Heath's plantation on the Monongahela River near Elizabeth. The dispute lasted until 1779, when delegates from the two states met in Baltimore and agreed to extend the Mason and Dixon line five degrees due West of the Delaware and from that point to run the boundary due north. The agreement was approved the following year, 1780, and in 1781 Pennsylvania erected Washington County west of the Monongahela and north of Ohio. Pittsburgh remained for the next six years in Westmoreland County.

On March 1, 1780 about a year and a half before the Revolution was ended by Cornwallis' surrender at Yorktown, and before the Virginia controversy had been settled, the Pennsylvania Assembly passed "An Act For the Gradual Abolition of Slavery," which provided that from that time on no child born in Pennsylvania could be a slave; that Negro and mulatto children born of slave mothers should be servants until they were twenty-eight years of age, and that all persons held in slavery at the time the bill was enacted should be registered before November 1, 1780 or be declared free. The registry was to give the number, names, sex, and age of all slaves held. Since the boundary between Pennsylvania and Virginia was not yet settled, many of those who recognized the Virginia authority refused to register their slaves. All of the representatives of Westmoreland County in the Pennsylvania assembly had opposed the passage of the bill. Violation of the act was common. Some owners openly kept up the slave trade outside of Pennsylvania. Masters sold their slaves into neighboring states or sent them into other states to work, where they remained slaves. Pregnant female slaves were sent beyond the state border so that their children would not be born on free Pennsylvania soil.

In 1782 a second act was passed and in 1788 a third act to enforce the act of 1780. The act of 1788 provided that the births of children of slaves should be registered; that husband and wife could not be separated more than ten miles without their consent; that pregnant females should not be send out of state, and it forbade slave-trade under a penalty of 1,000 pounds. Violations to even this act however, are to be found.

Between the passage of the two acts, that is immediately after the end of the Revolution and after the settlement of the Pennsylvania-Virginia Controversy in favor of Pennsylvania, many slave-holding settlers moved with their slaves from the district and took up land farther west, particularly in Kentucky, the new frontier where settlement had begun in 1774, and where they could maintain legal possession of their slaves.

Under these acts, however, most of the slaves in the district were registered. Robert Galbreath, the attorney, registered five; William Morrow, the inn-keeper registered eight; James Wall, a distiller and farmer who lived where Pitcairn now stands, registered five; Capt. Henry Heath, registered six; Conrad Winebiddle, one of the early German settlers and an ancestor of the Negleys and the Mellons, registered five; Jacob Castleman, another German farmer, registered eight; John Bell, registered eight; Thos. Parker, one of the physicians of the town, registered four. Dunning McNair, who built "Dumplin Hall" on his estate which is now Wilkinsburg, registered ten. Others who registered one or two slaves were John Woods, Pittsburgh's first surveyor; Devereaux Smith, one of the first justices of the peace for Westmoreland County; Samuel Ewalt, first Sheriff of Allegheny County and owner of the field in which stood the first log structure of the University of Pittsburgh; John Gibson, the Indian trader and frontiersman; Aenese Mackay, Revolutionary soldier and land owner; Edward Cook, judge, colonel, friend of George Washington and signer of the Declaration of Independence; Dorsey Pentecost, another justice of the peace when Allegheny County was formed, and others. Gen. John Neville lived on his estate "Bower Hill" in the style of a true Virginia planter with eighteen slaves. His son, Presley Neville, held nine slaves on his estate on the other side of the valley. Isaac Craig, landholder, Revolutionary officer, and early manufacturer, held eight.

It might have been expected that the church would have discredited slave holding, especially as the Pittsburgh frontier developed during and after the Revolutionary years, when theories of liberty and equality were in the air. Also, the Calvinist churches early secured dominance in the region. The Scots and Scotch-Irish colonists had their own stern principles of political and religious freedom. Yet not less than six of the most prominent of the early ministers themselves held Negroes in slavery. The Rev. James Finley recorded twelve male slaves, the Rev James Bright fourteen females, Rev Samuel Irwin, five. The Historian Boucher says that nearly all the elders and officers in the Presbyterian church held slaves.

The register for 1780–82 listed in the Pittsburgh district in what was then Westmoreland County—342 male slaves, 349 females and four whose sex was not given. The 1790 census listed 880 slaves in southwestern Pennsylvania. In 1790, when Allegheny County had been in existence two years, 159 slaves were recorded within its bounds. By 1800 the number had decreased to 79 and by 1810 to 24. One was recorded in 1820, but newspaper correspondents called attention to this as an error and in 1830 there were 27 recorded. None were recorded after that year. The percentage of the farms on which slave labor was employed was small, less than three percent for southwestern Pennsylvania. Most of the slaves held were farm servants. But by the nature of the frontier economy, even on the farms and particularly in a town like Pittsburgh, many of them followed other occupations. Some made shoes and boots at the last for shoemakers; others worked the bellows at forges for blacksmiths; some were valets, barbers, and messengers for ministers and doctors; still others cooked for and waited on wives and spinsters, heckled flax,[1] carded and spun wool and wove it into linen or linsey-woolsey, dyed it butternut yellow or blue and made it into dresses for frontier women. They served in the tap rooms and stable yards of inns. They worked at grindstones for millers. But chiefly they plowed the frontier farms with oxen and sowed them for farmers, reaped harvests with sickle and scythe and threshed the grain with flails.

That slavery did not take strong hold on the Western Pennsylvania frontier is due to several causes. The settlers' forts and military stations were democratic, largely without class rule or division. In almost every frontier situation one buckskin-clad man was as good as another, every linsey-clad frontier woman as valuable as another. Frontier people lived largely in isolation, where the individual counted for his full worth and they held vigorously to the idea of individual freedom, for which they had come to the frontier. Revolutionary feeling was strong in the district, although with all the talk of liberty, freedom and human rights, these concepts were not held to apply to the hundreds of slaves in the region. They were not granted the revolutionary rights of liberty and personal freedom. The principles expressed by the Northwest Ordinance of 1787 forbidding slavery in the territory immediately beyond the western boundary of Pennsylvania perhaps

1. To heckle flax is to separate the fibers with a comb called a hatchel.

had some influence in the Pittsburgh region. But the failure of slavery to take as firm hold here during the later frontier period as it took in the slave holding states immediately south of the Pennsylvania border was not so much due to these democratic ideas as to economic disadvantage.

Whereas the average southern plantation consisted of about six hundred acres, the average frontier farm had not more than thirty acres. Even those were not usual. The smaller northern farms furthermore, were sown in part with rye, in part with corn or wheat, and part of them was always a truck patch of potatoes, turnips, pumpkins and other vegetables requiring various skills in cultivation. Neither the large nor the small farms were restricted to a single, staple crop, like cotton, tobacco, or rice as were the plantations of the South. Moreover the nature of the pioneer precluded slave holding; the average pioneer was a poor but hardy man, who depended on help at busy times from neighbors who gathered for communal cabin raisings, flax-pullings, husking bees, and other farm labors. The cost of a slave was more than most struggling settlers could afford. Slaves sold in the community for any price between sixty and a hundred pounds, or three hundred to five hundred dollars.[2] In 1790 the average cost was about two hundred dollars. By 1815 it was two hundred and fifty dollars. And by 1850 it was one thousand dollars. But one thousand dollars even as early as 1790 was not an unusual price. A Presbyterian minister in the district, nevertheless, advertised "a mulatto worth fifty dollars." The cost of maintaining slaves presented further obstacles. On small southern plantations food, clothing and shelter averaged between thirty and forty dollars a year for the scantiest supplies. Large plantations in the cotton belt allowed twenty dollars per slave for maintenance. On the Pittsburgh frontier, however, costs were higher because quarters and food were generally of better quality and more plentiful. Another reason why slavery did not take deep root on the frontier was that from the days of early settlement commerce was as much developed here as was farming. Industry too, developed early. These occupations required semi-skilled workers and most slaves were not trained for either of them, although some belonged to blacksmiths and distillers and some worked at the early iron forges and iron foundries. The other industries—fur trading, cattle raising, ship-building—were less adapted to slave work than to that of indentured servants. Nevertheless, for a time slavery did take root on the western Pennsylvania frontier in the proportion of one slave to eighty-seven of the white population.

2. One dollar in 1800 would be worth about thirteen dollars today, while one dollar in 1850 would be worth about twenty-two dollars today. See Robert C. Sahr, "Consumer Price Index (CPI) Conversion Factors 1800 to Estimated 2013 to Convert to Dollars of 2002," Political Science Department, Oregon State University, http://oregonstate.edu/Dept/pol_sci/fac/sahr/cv2002.pdf (accessed January 7, 2004).

In eastern Pennsylvania, which had long passed the pioneer stage, the proportion was one to four hundred. Also slavery lasted longer in the southwestern counties than anywhere else in the State.

The condition of the slaves about Pittsburgh from the time Hugh Mercer sent for the two girls and a boy was mild. It was much like that of the indentured white servants except that the slave, until 1780, was held in perpetual servitude and passed on his state of servitude to his descendants. There was no opposition, as there was in the South, to education and care for moral and intellectual well-being. True, marriage and all such vital affairs were closely regulated, and punishment for offenses was heavier than it was for indentured servants, white or black. Woodson[3] says that the good treatment slaves received among the French, especially at Pittsburgh, which was the gateway to the northwest territory, tended to make Pittsburgh an asylum for such slaves as had sufficient courage to leave the wilderness for freedom. Pittsburgh was never accustomed to the more spectacular features of slavery—no cargoes of slaves were brought in, no shackled slave droves came or went, no auction block was present.

The status of free Negroes in the frontier community is indicated by the citation of Brissot de Warville, who traveled through the country about 1788 while studying the condition of Negroes in America for the French government. De Warville noted two cases of intermarriage between Negroes and whites in Pittsburgh. One was a Negro who had married an indentured French serving woman. From their marriage was born an attractive mulatto girl who married a surgeon of Nantes then stationed at Pittsburgh. Colonial Pennsylvania had forbidden by strict law the mingling of races, but this law was one of a number affecting the Negro which had been repealed in 1780.

During the decade after the Revolution, the decade in which these conditions matured, Pittsburgh had further changed its character. Though still a frontier town, it was acquiring some of the sophistication of the eastern cities. At this time Colonel John May passed through Pittsburgh on a business trip into Ohio. He had with him a considerable stock of goods and a number of employees. He described the town in 1788 as "an irregular, poorly built place. The number of houses, mostly built of logs, about one hundred and fifty. The inhabitants perhaps because they lead too easy a life incline to be extravagant and lazy. They are subject, however, to frequent alarms from the savages of the wilderness. . . ." The Colonel noted in his journal that "There are a number of Indians on the other side of the river. Many of them are often over in Pittsburgh. I cannot say that I am

3. Carter G. Woodson (1875–1950) founded the Association for the Study of Negro Life and History and the *Journal of Negro History*. See bibliography for some of his important historical studies.

fond of them, for they are frightfully ugly, and a pack of thieves and beggars. . . ."
One Sunday he wrote that

> Four Kentucky boats have gone down [the river] today. Surprising the number of these boats which have passed the place this spring. Two hundred are taken account of, and many go down in the night. We allow, at the least computation, twenty souls to a boat, and a great number of bodies without souls.

He crossed the river one afternoon with Generals Harmer, Parsons, and several other gentlemen, "in the 'Congress' barge, rowed by twelve men, in white uniforms and caps." The town was still as Arthur Lee had described it four years earlier in his often quoted description:

> Pittsburgh is inhabited almost entirely by Scots and Irish, who live in peltry log-houses, and are as dirty as in the north of Ireland, or even Scotland. There is a great deal of small trade carried on; the goods are bought at the vast expense of forty-five shillings per hundred weight, from Philadelphia and Baltimore. They take in the shops, money, wheat, flour, and skins. There are in the town four attorneys, two doctors, and not a priest of any persuasion, nor church, nor chapel; so that they are likely to be damned, *without benefit of clergy*. The rivers encroach fast on the town; and to such a degree, that, as a gentleman told me, the Allegheny had within thirty years of his memory, carried away one hundred yards. The place, I believe, will never be very considerable. Batteaux, pass daily, with whole families, stock and furniture, for Kentucky. . . .

Another traveler, however, Mrs. Mary Dewees, saw in the town, "a very handsome parlor, elegantly papered and well furnished, it appeared more like Philadelphia than any I have seen since I left the place." Mrs. Dewees "Drank tea at the French lady's [home] with several ladies and gentlemen of this place." This was the town in which lived four Negro families who have left their names in public records: Benjamin Richards, Charles Richards, David Saven and David Betty. This was the town in which Charles Richards kept one of the best taverns and in which Benjamin Richards carried on his cattle dealing and butcher business.

By 1788, Westmoreland County was so populous, and Hannastown, its county seat, so far away from Pittsburgh for ordinary court business that the citizens of Pittsburgh and the nearby country asked to have a new county organized.

"A Petition addressed to the General Assembly of Pennsylvania asking for the Creation of Allegheny County" was signed by 742 freemen of the Commonwealth of Pennsylvania who lived in the western part of the county. The list was headed by the names of John Crasby, Samuel Barr, Isaac Craig, Richard Butler, Hugh Ross, John Soull, Stephen Bayard, Nathaniel Bedford, Dunning McNair, Devereaux Smith. And among the signers of this petition to organize Allegheny County are those of four men easily identifiable as Negroes—Charles Richards, Benjamin Richards, David Saven, and David Betty.

Of Benjamin Richards, Martin R. Delany, a Negro who later published a paper here and practiced medicine, says

> Benjamin Richards, sen., of Pittsburgh, Pennsylvania, forty years ago, was one of the leading business men of the place. Being a butcher by trade, he carried on the business extensively, employing a white clerk, and held a heavy contract with the United States, supplying the various military posts with provisions. Mr. Richards possessed a large property in real estate, and was at one time reputed very wealthy, he and the later general O'H. [O'Hara] being considered the most wealthy individuals of the place. Mr. Richards taking the precedence; the estate of the general O'H. now being estimated at seven millions of dollars. Mr. Richards has been known to buy up a drove of cattle at one time. By mismanagement, he lost his estate, upon which many gentlemen are now living at ease in the city.

On a list of subscribers petitioning "For the Relief of the Citizens of Philadelphia in the cholera epidemic of 1793" are found the names of Benjamin Richards and Lucy Richards.

It was rare, in these days, for Negroes to possess a family name. Like men and women of Biblical times or the age of Homer, they were known simply as Joshua Luke, Esther or Sara. Through the deep woods and along the frontier roads near Pittsburgh, Rev. Robert Ayres had traveled on horseback in his black knee breeches, rain cape and cocked hat—his Bible under his arm, his rifle over his saddle. For farmers and river men of the frontier he held church service in cabins and log school houses. He married young couples and baptized their children, and he kept his "Church Register of Births and Baptisms" in a homemade paper notebook that is still preserved, yellow with a century and a half of existence, filled with the parson's sharp handwriting. In the back of the notebook a separate half dozen pages are headed "Blacks," where the parson recorded the baptisms of Negro and mulatto children born to the first dwellers in the region. Here are the names of children born in the first years of the life of the nation, when Allegheny County was first formed on the frontier of civilization. These unremembered black children would be men and women when the question of slavery began really to vex and agitate the country. As men and women they would see their fellow men steal into town at night by the Underground Railroad, or be kidnaped in the streets by day. But now they were children whose baptism Rev. Ayres noted in his register by their simple Christian names: "Cassey, belonging to Basil Brown;" Or Sammy son of Cloe, property of W. Wallace." Other entries are interesting— "Kether: Daughter of Will, the property of widow Huttern by his wife a free black woman, Name Princy," "Roberts, a mulatto property of James Carmichael." But already there occur a few family names—"Jemina, Daugher of Robert and Betsy Robinson, Property of Wm. Wallace."

Of slaves held in the town and the nearby countryside the records of the Court of Quarter Sessions of Allegheny County from 1789 to 1813 give simply Christian names. Many are Biblical names, the result of familiarity with almost the only book they knew: "Caleb a male"; Isaac, Solomon, Hannah, Noah, Delilah, "a black male child Abraham," and "Dorcas a Mulatto Girl." Here are other names traditional among Negroes, names by which a submerged people expressed their sense of poetic: Daphne, Sylph, Chloe, Nero, Pompey, Caesar. Occasionally a family name occurs, as when we read "Tom Moore, Born 30th July 1783 belonging to your humble servant Andrew McFarlane." McFarlane also entered "a mulatto Female Child named Libby Wheelan." Since parents are infrequently named it is difficult to know whether the name Negro or Mulatto is accurate or not.

When the *Pittsburgh Gazette* was established in 1786 this four-page weekly, issued from little Ramage band press that John Soull had transported across the Alleghenies, became a repository for many items, which, pieced together, help tell the story of the Negro in Pittsburgh. For years the *Gazette* carried advertisements of slave sales, of runaways and as the town grew and slavery or abolition became an issue it printed news stories of kidnapings and of antislavery meetings and other incidents. On May 23, 1787, for instance the *Gazette* advertised:

> To be sold to Any Person Residing with Country
> A Negro Wench.—She is an excellent cook and can
> do any kind of work in or out of doors. She had
> been registered in Westmoreland County. Produce
> will be taken, or cattle of any kind. Enquire of Col.
>
> John Gibson, Ft., Pitt

Slaves were bartered for cattle or farm produce. They were exposed to public sale: "Horses, cows, sheep, stills, Negroes, and household furniture." A farm of 360 acres was advertised for sale in the *Gazette* on February 2, 1790, the terms of payment to be half in cash and the balance in Negroes. Slaves were often sold at public outcry in the streets of Greensburg.

Of the advertisements for the return of runaway slaves, men and women mak-

ing the first individual, desperate attempts in the history of the region to gain
their freedom, the notice, which appeared on June 14, 1787, is typical:

> Ran away from the subscriber a Negro Fellow named
> Jack: five feet six or seven inches high, about forty
> years old, speaks bad English, he is of a swarthy
> complexion his hair more like a white man than a
> Negro's, it is supposed he will endeavor to pass for
> a freeman. Whoever takes up said Negro and delivers
> him to Thomas Girty in Pittsburgh, shall be generously
> rewarded by me.
>
> Signed.........David Steel

Since the *Gazette* circulated far beyond the limits of Pittsburgh itself, slave-
owners in outlying districts used its columns for such notices as the following,
which appeared on Dec. 2, 1793:

> Runaway from the subscriber, from Redstone Old
> Fort, on the 30th of November last, a Negro man
> named Jerry, by trade a blacksmith, of a yellowish
> complexion, about 34 or 35 years old, about 5 feet
> nine inches high; he had on when he went away a
> suit of white plains but very probably may change
> them, as he has a suit of green ditto with him, he is
> fond of spirits, and when a little intoxicated is apt
> to stammer. Also, a Negro Woman named NANNY,
> about 45 years old, very black; she had on when she
> went away a suit of green plains, I expect they will
> go the road to Winchester in Virginia, or they may
> attempt to pass for free Negroes—but I am under the
> apprehension that they will be concealed or
> harbored by some white person in that neighborhood.
> Any person that will apprehend said Negroes, and
> deliver them to Mr. John Forker, of Brownsville, who
> is fully authorized to receive them, shall be rewarded
> Twenty-Pounds, Virginia money, or one Hundred
> Dollars, if delivered to the subscriber in Scott County
> Kentucky.
>
> Metcalfe de Grassenriedt
>
> Pittsburgh, December 2, 1793

The *Tree of Liberty*, the second newspaper to be published in Pittsburgh, also advertised runaways. On April 9, 1803, it published the following notice:

Stop the Runaway:

On Sunday the 3d inst. absconded from the subscriber
his Mulatto man, named ISAAC, about 18 years old,
very tall and slender, remarkable from his lazy
slothful appearance, and from his having been lately
inoculated for the small pox and the marks of which
are still discernible on his face. He had on and took
with him a dark round about jacket a blue ditto with
a Buff Cape—one pair of blue pantaloons, a blue Surtout
Coat, 2 shirts and 2 striped Rugs, etc. Whoever returns
said servant to me confines him to any jail so that I may
get him again, shall receive TEN DOLLARS reward and
reasonable charges paid

O. Ormsby

Pittsburgh 6th April, 1803
N B I will dispose of the above described Mulatto on
very reasonable terms if apprehended.

On July 28 of the same year another notice appeared:

40 Dollars Reward
Stop the Runaway

Run away from the Subscriber's service, about the
3d of May last, a Mulatto man named MINOR about
19 or 20 years of age, about 6 feet high, straight
and well made, and might pass for white except his
hair, which is not very dark. He has two remarkable
scars on his face, one on his nose occasioned by a cut,
the other on this chin occasioned by a fall. By these
marks he can be immediately identified. Has on and
took with him a half worn blue linsey hunting shirt,
a swansdown jacket, and deep blue cloth overalls with
him. It is supposed he crossed the river at McKeesport.
He has probably steered over mountains or towards the lakes.
Whoever takes up the said Runaway or secures so that the
owner may get him again shall receive 40 dollars Reward and
reasonable expenses if brought more than 50 miles,

paid by the subscriber, living in Brooke Co., Va., 4
miles from West Liberty, on the side towards Washington

David Chambers

June 29, 1803
N B Persons at a distance, many directions will
please notice this advertisement, as it will be worthy
of their attention and make every inquiry possible in
this case.

The other is characteristically pictorial:

8 Dollars Reward

Run away from the subscriber on the 11th of Sept. last
a Likely Negro Wench named PRISS, aged 15,
about 5 feet 6 inches high,
slim-made, with a handsome face, a proud walk and
haughty appearance. Had on when she went away
a dark calico short gown, with a white and dye coloured
petticoat; a black wool hat and a bonnet with a yellow
handkerchief thereon. Whoever takes her up and
delivers her to the subscriber, shall receive the above
reward and reasonable charges.

Henry Westbay

Cannonsburg, Wash. Co.
Oct. 5, 1803
N. B. It is supposed she has gone towards Raccoon Cross
Creek, where her sister lives.

In 1789, the year in which President Washington made his triumphal march
from Mt. Vernon to New York to be inaugurated first President of the United
States of America, antislavery sentiment was strong enough in the Pittsburgh region to find organized expression. The *Pittsburgh Gazette*, on Feb. 14, 1789 [...]⁴

---

4. Text in the original manuscript terminates in mid-sentence. The *Gazette* of February 14,
1789 relates the following: (missing text is due to illegibility): "In a company of gentlemen at Washington, on [...] of February, an association, similar to that in Philadelphia, for the relief [?] of free
negroes, unlawfully held in bondage, and [?] agreed that two of the company should make a [...]
of the principles of their association, and that they would all meet again the next day."

CHAPTER 3

The Early Community, 1804–1860

———•◆•———

Typist: Marian Holmes / Rewriteman: J. Ernest Wright /
May 1, 1939 / Prefinal
Typist: M. B. Holmes / Rewriteman: J. Ernest Wright /
February 19, 1940 / Final

[Part I]

In 1800, twenty years after the Abolition Act of 1780 had set free the slaves in Pennsylvania, Pittsburgh was a town of 400 houses, many of which were still built from log, though some were of frame, and a few of brick. It was still a frontier town in spite of its two printing offices, the log university in Ewalt's field near the site of the present court house, its two glass factories, tin plate factory, rail splitting establishment, smith's shops and several shipbuilding enterprises. The town had but recently—1794—been incorporated as a borough. The first fire company had been organized, and owned a hand engine which had been brought from Philadelphia. The population was about 2,400, and of these 64 were Negro slaves. There were also a few "free men of color," but except for one or two names, their identity is lost.

One of the earliest records of Negro participation in town life is the petition addressed to the General Assembly of Pennsylvania asking for the Creation of Allegheny County, February 14, 1787. Among the signers were Charles and Benjamin Richards. A list of subscribers to "the relief of distressed citizens of Philadelphia" during the yellow fever epidemic of 1793, named Benjamin Richards as contributing fifty cents, Lucy Richards as contributing the same amount. Mrs. Hannah Brady is known to have been employed during these years by the

---

The original version of chapter 3 had uncollated sections; for this edition, part numbers have been added in brackets to distinguish each section.

Croghan Family. On her death, at the age of one hundred and two years, she was buried in the old Trinity Church Graveyard. "The Common Place Book" of Reverend Charles Taylor, first Rector of Trinity Episcopal Church, contains an entry of the marriage on January 7, 1813 of Charles Richards to "Miss ——." This is the only instance in the book of the name of one of the marriage parties being left blank. Charles Richards, son of Benjamin Richards of Pittsburgh, married Miss Felicia Fitzgerald, a native of Cork Ireland. Benjamin Richards was known in the early town as "Daddy Ben."

By 1815 Pittsburgh was a grimy town of a dozen streets, its shops and factories beginning to use steam engines driven by coal as fuel. Coal came from the 40 or 50 pits on Coal Hill, now Mt. Washington. Factories were multiplying in new suburbs like Sidneyville and Birmingham on the South Side. Birmingham was known for its glass manufacturers. It was already as black as Pittsburgh from the smoke of iron foundries. A century later, the steel mills of Birmingham (today the South Side) employed hundreds of Negroes. The Pittsburgh *Directory* for 1815, the first year the *Directory* was issued, listed the "Taxable inhabitants within the Borough of Pittsburgh and the several townships of Allegheny County." The total was thirty-five.

Steamboat building, too, was becoming a major industry. On many boats launched near the Point, Negroes found jobs as stewards, deck hands, and stewardesses; on the wharves, they found work as stevedores and "mudsills," or roustabouts. Cotton and woolen mills were increasing in number. Into these went many white women and girls. The jobs of servant and cook, which these women left vacant, were available to Negro women and girls. Jobs left vacant by white barbers, wig makers, river men, draymen and stewards on riverboats, who found jobs in iron and glass factories or went into the skilled work of boat building, were open to Negro men.

Northward migration began in the 1820s. Not only escaped slaves but free Negroes who thought a northern city gave comfort of living arrived in Pittsburgh in ever greater numbers. By the 1830s the Negro community had begun to take shape. In spite of poverty, prejudice, and lack of educational and cultural facilities, Negroes began to own homes, pay taxes, organize schools and beneficial societies, and build and organize churches—in other words to constitute not only a Negro population, but a Negro community.

Harris' Pittsburgh *Directory* for 1837 gives the various national groups in the city—native-born American 20,000; Irish 8,000; German 7,000; African 2,400; Scots 2,000; English 2,000; Welsh 1,500; French 600. One generation removed from those freed by the Act of 1780, Negroes now ranked third among the national minorities, being outnumbered only by the Irish and Germans. They had taken up residence in certain definite areas of the city. The section now known as the Lower Hill was already known as Hayti. Oliver Avenue, then known as Virgin Alley, was a street predominantly Negro. Here lived John Devaul, Lewis Davis, John Butler, Violet Jones, John Lewis, Solomon Norris (a dealer in new and second hand clothing), Amelia Sanders, Peter Sheppard (a boot and shoe black), John Templeton (a teacher) and Benjamin Wilkins (another dealer in second hand clothing).

In the 1830s, new thoroughfares were laid out from the heart of the city between the rivers to the growing suburbs of Arthursville, the district between the present Fullerton Street and Soho, where a number of Negroes had settled and founded a church, and to Minersville, then a professional, predominantly white, residential section. Pittsburgh was thriving, noisy with the coming and going of stage coaches, its hotel and inn yards packed with Conestoga wagons, the Monongahela wharves lined with packets and strident with river traffic. Streets were cobbled and noisy with the low, two-wheeled one-horse drays which made traffic heavy. City newspapers commented in 1835 on the recent erection of five new school houses, a prison, the Bank of Pittsburgh, and many improvements in Arthursville and Hayti. A night watch had just been instituted and a Board of Trade organized. The founding families of the city were still in control of municipal affairs—the Craigs, the Nevilles, the O'Haras, and the Dennys.

But now, too, there was a different quality to Negro life in the city. More than one family was known wherever Negro interests were being promoted. Nationally known now among antislavery, temperance, education, women's rights, and other reform movements were the Vashons, the Woodsons, the Richards, the Tanners, the Browns, the Pecks, Miss Ware, Mr. Templeton, A. D. Lewis and the Mahoneys.

These families by the 1840s had acquired homes marked by comfort, plenty, and a genuine culture. American middle class houses were as a rule anything but tasteful in the 1840s and the 1850s: horse hair furniture, shell and feather floral wreaths under glass on walls or parlor tables, curtains heavy and dark, carpets tacked unsanitarily into corners. The square piano was becoming a household object. Women played the guitar and sang sentimental ballads. Men wore side whiskers and tall beaver hats; women wore crinoline skirts, fissus[1] around their throats, and poke bonnets on their braided hair.

The Negro community in Pittsburgh had in 1835 organized its own Temperance Society, one of the first in Pittsburgh, with Richard Bryans, President; Martin R. Delany, Recording Secretary; William T. Greenly, Corresponding Secretary; Samuel Bruce, Vice President; William T. Greenly, Auditor. Listed as Male Managers were John B. Vashon, Samuel Reynolds, A. D. Lewis, Zelicher

---

1. "Fissus" is probably a misspelling of "fichus," triangular pieces of fabric worn by women in the Victorian era to cover the neck, throat, and shoulders, often crossed or tied in front to fill in low necklines.

Newman, Samuel Berry, C. T. Williamson. Female Managers were Nancy Jones, Hannah M'Grady, Grace Wiggins, Phoebe Collins, Mary Harrison, and Maria Jones. The society published 500 copies of its Constitution and by-laws.

Active also was the Moral Reform Society with 100 members. Its officers were Richard Bryans, President; A. D. Lewis, First Vice President; P. Jackson, Second Vice President; John N. Templeton, Recording Secretary; and John B. Vashon, Treasurer.

By the decade of the 1840s there were three black churches in Pittsburgh—two downtown and one in Arthursville. An African Public School enrolled 90 pupils with an average attendance of 70. This school was taught by Mr. Templeton, "a reputable man of color." The directors, however, were white.

In the town of Allegheny, across the river from downtown, Mrs. Lawrence, the wife of Reverend Lawrence, conducted a "select school for colored children, both male and female, in which the common branches are taught."

By the third decade of the century, Negro life in Pittsburgh had reached a high level. In any American city where abolition and antislavery movements were active, where education, women's rights, temperance and other reforms were advocated, the Vashons, the Woodsons, the Richards, the Tanners, the Browns, the Pecks, A. D. Lewis, and Martin Delany were in high repute.

Martin Robison Delany, for example, had come to Pittsburgh in 1831, and stayed to make his living as a leecher and cupper.[2] Delany was born in 1812, the son of free Negroes, Samuel and Pati Delany. His paternal grandfather was a member of the African Gullah tribe. His grandfather on his mother's side was a prince of the Mandingo tribe, who had been captured in the valley of the Niger, sold and brought to America along with the woman to whom he was betrothed. Mr. Delany came to Pittsburgh from Chambersburg, Pennsylvania, where the family had been compelled through persecution to move from Charles Town, in what is now West Virginia.[3] In Pittsburgh, young Mr. Delany, then nineteen, studied with Reverend Lewis Woodson, employed by the African Education Society. Two years later he was active in welfare organizations. He studied medicine with Dr. Andrew N. McDowell (who tended Charles Dickens on his Pittsburgh visit), with Dr. Francis, and with Dr. Joseph P. Gazzam. Delany was leader of the Theban Literary Society, which he had organized with the help of a student at Jefferson College. In their debates and discussions, Delany trained himself for writing and public speaking. These gifts he devoted to the abolition movement and to the general progress of his people. In 1843, Delany founded an abolitionist paper, *The Mystery*, which he edited for 5 years. On March 15, he married

2. A common medical practice in the early nineteenth century was to apply leeches and/or hot cups to draw out "bad" blood.

3. Charles Town is located near Harpers Ferry.

Katherine Richards, the daughter of the inn keeper, Charles Richards, and his wife Felicia Fitzgerald. Delany assisted Frederick Douglass in the publication of *The North Star* at Rochester, N.Y. In 1849, at the age of 37, he entered Harvard Medical School. He traveled and lectured, wrote a famous treatise *The Condition, Elevation, Emigration, and Destiny of the Colored People of the United States, Politically Considered*, and a novel, *Blake, or The Huts of America*. Delany played a conspicuous part in the calling of conventions to reconsider the whole question of the colonization of Africa by Negroes. He was chief commissioner of an exploration party to the Valley of the Niger for the purpose of science and general information. He wrote the expedition's official report. In 1879, he published *Principles of Ethnology: The Origin of Races and Color*. Delany opposed the mainline colonization schemes, considering the American Colonization Society as an agency of the slave holders. He laid down a clear basis for Booker T. Washington's advocacy of education along industrial lines.[4]

Equally significant in the history of the Negro, not only in Pittsburgh, but in the nation, was John Bathan Vashon.[5] Vashon came to Pittsburgh with his wife and son in 1829, from Carlisle, Pennsylvania, where he had kept a large livery stable and a "public saloon," popular with Dickinson College students. Born in 1792 at Norfolk, Virginia, Vashon's mother was a mulatto, his father a white man of French ancestry, who was an Indian Agent under President Van Buren. Vashon, at twenty, served in the War of 1812 as a common seaman aboard the "Revenge," cruising among the West Indies and along the coast of South America. He was made prisoner, exchanged, returned to Virginia and served with the land forces when Negroes of the neighborhood were called to prevent the British fleet from ascending the Potomac. In Carlisle, with his friend John Peck, he initiated the formation of a mutual improvement association known as the Lay Benevolent Society. A man of thirty seven when he arrived in Pittsburgh, he engaged in every progressive movement of the times. For livelihood he opened a barber shop and public baths, the first public baths for ladies west of the mountains.

In the Pittsburgh *Gazette*, on the fifth of May 1833, there appeared this item:

> On Saturday evening, at the invitation of Mr. Vashon, we visited, and examined his new Baths, and were highly gratified with the arrangement and furnishing of the establishment. In the lower story of the building, he has thirteen bathing rooms, for the use of gentlemen who may visit them, each

4. Much of the following text on Vashon, Richards, Hill, Collins, Julius, Barrett, and Freeman is taken from Martin R. Delany, *The Condition, Elevation, Emigration, and Destiny of the Colored People of the United States* (New York: Arno Press, 1968), 83–85, 101, 104–5, 107, 119, 122.

5. Vashon's middle name is sometimes recorded as Bethune or Bethume. Some of the biographical material about John and George Vashon related here is repeated later in this chapter.

supplied with an abundance of hot and cold water of the purest quality taken from La Belle Riviere and furnished with everything necessary to the complete enjoyment of that most delightful and refreshing luxury. The upper story is intended for the use of ladies, residing in or visiting this city, and is so richly furnished and well supplied with all things necessary and proper, that the maids themselves might be tempted to forsake their native fountains and resort to Mr. Vashon's City Baths. The location of these baths is well made. They are in a central situation, and yet in a very retired street. Every precaution has been taken to secure to the ladies' apartment the utmost privacy and security. The entrance is by a way entirely distinct and separate from that to the lower story, and from the moment a lady leaves the street she is invisible, expect to the female attendants.

John B. Vashon won respect in the community by a policy he initiated in another of his businesses—his barber shop. The *Pittsburgh Conference Journal* reprinted from the *Advocate* a notice strongly in the spirit of those days under the caption "Respect for the Sabbath":

> We are highly delighted to see the subjoined notice posted up in the elegant and well conducted establishment, on the corner of Third and Wood Streets. We hope the independent and justly commendable example of Messrs. Vashon and Colder will be followed by others in this city, and that its influence will extend out of it. When we hear of other instances we shall give them honorable mention. The following is addressed to their patrons: "Having had, for some time, under serious and anxious consideration the practice of transacting our calling, on the Sabbath as on the other days of the week, we have become firmly convinced that the habit is utterly irreconcilable to the conscientious—to those who profess to regard the command of their Creator, as their supreme guide, and consequently come to the conclusion of entirely discontinuing the practice of keeping open shop on the Sabbath Day. We hope to be complying with what we deem our duty to God, ourselves, and the highly moral and religious community in which we live.

John Vashon was among the first to promote National Negro conventions not only for the freeing of slaves but also for the struggle for equal rights in an expanding democratic republic. He claimed, before anything else, to be an American, a name he loved as dearly as he loved the word liberty. And he devoted his life to making them synonymous. He was the Pittsburgh agent for the distribution of William Lloyd Garrison's "Thoughts on Colonization" and for *The Liberator*. He persuaded leading Pittsburghers, such as Robert Bruce, the President of the University of Western Pennsylvania, to become active in the antislavery movement. In 1833, in the parlor of his house on Third Street, he organized the first antislavery society west of the Allegheny Mountains. He was one of the founders of the African Education Society, president of a Temperance Society, and of a Moral Reform Society.[6] On a visit to Boston, he saw William Lloyd Garrison being led by a mob who opposed his abolitionist activities. Vashon, an ex-solider, and a fiery lover of freedom, stood stricken and helpless, weeping at the sight. The next day he appeared at the prison with a new hat for Garrison to replace the one which had been cut by the knives of the men of "property and standing" from all parts of the city. In July 1853, Vashon was elected one the vice presidents of the National Convention of Colored Men at Rochester, N.Y. and was also a member of the Pennsylvania State Council. At the National Convention in Philadelphia in 1855, Vashon, who had never received a soldier's pension or government lands for his military service, insisted on taking his seat as a soldier delegate among the defenders of his country. At the station, on the way to the State Council and Military Convention, while he sat resting on his trunk, he died of a heart attack, the Citizen Soldier, lover of liberty and democratic equality.

John Vashon's son, George Boyar Vashon grew to manhood in the Pittsburgh of abolitionism, antislavery, and the underground railway. His father sent him to Oberlin College in 1840, from which he graduated with honors in 1844. In 1849, he took his M.A. at the theological seminary. For three years he taught at New York Central College, McGrawville, N.Y., a college established by the abolitionists. He returned to Pittsburgh to study law with Walter Forward, then Judge, and later Secretary of the Treasury of the United States. Vashon's application to be admitted to the bar in Pittsburgh was denied on account of his color. In 1847 he was admitted to the bar in New York City. For three years Vashon taught at College Faustin, in Port-au-Prince, Haiti. He returned to Pittsburgh and became head of the one school for Negro children in the city. George Boyer Vashon was "a ripe scholar, an accomplished essayist, a chaste classic poet." He was devoted to Byron, especially *Childe Harold* and he probably took Byron as his model, to whom he always referred by his full name, George Gordon Noel Byron. Vashon's poem "Vincent Ogé" attempted a more ambitious theme than any poem hitherto written by a Negro. It appeared in *Autographs for Freedom* and has a genuine sense of poetic values. "A Life Day" appeared in *The Semi-Centenary and the Retrospection of the African Methodist Episcopal Church*, by Daniel A. Payne, published in 1860. In the school in which he taught in Pittsburgh, Susan P. Smith also taught. The two were married in 1857. They had seven children.

Other Negroes participated in the business of the city. Benjamin Richards

6. Previously in the chapter, Vashon is said to have been one of the Male Managers of the Temperance Society in Pittsburgh and the Treasurer of the Moral Reform Society. Here it says that he was president of both organizations.

was one of the leading business men of the place. He carried on an extensive butcher establishment, employed a white clerk, and held a heavy contract with the United States government through which he supplied military posts with provisions. Mr. Richards bought cattle a drove at a time. He also owned much real estate. He and General James O'Hara were considered the most wealthy men in the city. Mr. Richards was even said to take precedence over the General.

A Mr. Hill, who came to Pittsburgh from Chillicothe, Ohio, was a leading tanner and currier, buying up hides and giving employment to many men. He, too, kept a white clerk who once a year took down the Ohio one or more flat boats loaded with leather and other domestic produce. Hill accumulated a fortune, but like Benjamin Richards, through endorsements, mis-transactions and failures, lost his wealth and died in Pittsburgh in poor circumstances. He gave his children a liberal education.

Henry M. Collins stood among men of national note because, "born a poor boy, and thrown upon the uncertainties of chance, Alger-like, he rose in the world through employment as river man to speculate in real estate." Martin Delany said of him:

> Though only rising forty, he had done more to improve the Sixth Ward of Pittsburgh than any other individual, save one, Captain W., who built on Company capital. Mr. Collins was the first person who commenced erecting an improved style of building; indeed, there was little else than old trees in that quarter of the city when Mr. Collins began. He continued to build, and dispose of handsome dwellings until a different class of citizen entirely was attracted to that part of town, among them, one of the oldest and most respectable and wealthy citizens, an ex-Alderman. After this, the wealthy citizens turned their attention to the District; and now, it is one of the most fashionable quarters of the city.

Then, too, in the pre-Civil War community there were "John Julius, and Lady." John Julius' real name was Julien Benoit. He was a "tall, good-looking Creole" from Louisiana, who bore the terrible gashes of the bayonet conspicuously on his neck from the War of 1812. He was one of the few Americans to meet Sir Edward Packenham's troops in single handed charges on the breastworks at New Orleans. He lamented more the injustice done him in the neglect of the government to grant his claim of money and lands in fulfillment of its promise for military service than he did any reverse of fortune with which he ever met. "John Julius and Lady" were for several years the proprietors of Concert Hall a Caffe, then the most fashionable resort for ladies and gentlemen in Pittsburgh. Mr. and Mrs. Julius held assemblies and balls attended by the first people of the city. Being himself a fine violinist and dancing master, he superintended the music and dancing. When General William Henry Harrison in 1840, then President elect of the United States, visited the city, his levee to the reception of the Ladies was held at Concert Hall, under the superintendence of "Monsieur John and Madame Edna Julius, the colored host and hostess."

Owen A. Barrett of Pittsburgh was the original proprietor of B. A. Fahnestock's Celebrated Vermifuge. Mr. Fahnestock raised Mr. Barrett from childhood, instructing him in all the science of practical pharmacy, continuing him in his employment after manhood, when Mr. Barrett discovered the "sovereign remedy" for lumbricalii, and as an act of gratitude to his benefactor, he communicated it to him, but not until he had fully tested its efficacy. The proprietor of the house, finding the remedy good, secured his patent, and never in the history of remedies in the United States has any equaled, at least in sale, this of B.A. Fahnestock's Vermifuge. Mr. Fahnestock, like a gentleman and Christian, has kept Mr. Barrett in his extensive house compounding this and other medicines, for sixteen or eighteen years.

These were the fortunate men in the city, men who had risen to independence, comfort, and even prosperity. There were some thousand others who made up the bulk of the community. Within three generations of freedom many of those who had come to Pittsburgh to advance themselves and their people had little to go on except the good wishes of the community. Even this they were not guaranteed. Many who became efficient and industrious were disliked because of successful competition with white laborers.

The Negro community had come a long way since the first appearance of Negro soldiers and body servants with the military expeditions into the frontier. From scattered slaves, indentured servants and one or two freemen, it had grown through manumission and through the more rapid and riskier ways of escape and by migrants and births of children to be a free community of people. From penniless, untaught, untrained men and women, it had developed to include journalists, musicians, writers, lecturers, and national leaders of a people. It had advanced by the brilliant struggle of Negroes and whites through years of national turbulence.

As in any group, numbers of them fell into poverty, or were forced by unemployment into idleness and crime. Yet, it is remarkable, collectively, how much they had achieved against unbelievable [prejudice and discrimination].[7] The examples of such prejudice are legion.

In 1826 the *City Directory* said:

> Another cause of regret is, that our Mayor's Court is so constantly infested with that race of persons politely termed 'people of color.' It shows

7. Bracketed material added for this published edition.

how liberally the law is meted out in this region. Far be it from us to say, that they should be deprived either of law or justice in the smallest degree; but it might be considered whether by countenancing the suits of the more worthless part of them, the interest of morality were promoted, or the good order of society increased.

Prejudice resulted in attacks on the community similar to those in Philadelphia and New England. *The Daily Advocate*, one morning in 1839, carried the following story:

> On Saturday evening the city was disturbed by a riot on the hill. It arose from a quarrel between some white and colored men, and ended in pulling down two or three tenements occupied by colored people. During the last part of the disgraceful business, a colored child was killed. The mayor and police at length arrived, and put a stop to the riotous proceedings. Several of the ringleaders were arrested and committed.

"The Spirit of the South," *The Daily Advocate* continues, instituted the fiendish spirit of mobbism, selecting either the dwellings or the business places of the prominent colored men of the city. And, of course, on another occasion, while this spirit was rife, they made an attack on the house of Mr. John B. Vashon.

In her paper, *The Saturday Evening Visitor*, Jane Grey Swisshelm, a staunch champion of all human rights and liberties, wrote in 1847[8]:

> Mr. Delany in his paper of yesterday complains of having been refused, or rather we should say conditionally refused, in an insulting manner, a passage in a stage coach from Buffalo. The reason for this treatment was, that the Doctor was a colored man. We really think it is time that sensible people should cease to manifest upon such occasions, prejudices so narrow. What harm could it be to anyone to ride in a coach with a well-dressed, well behaved, and intelligent colored man—for all this Dr. Delany undoubtedly is. The most cruel and cowardly thing in this world is a wanton insult to those who are powerless to defend themselves; and whose humility prevents them from giving offense. We have known a man possessing the education or manners of a gentleman to wantonly insult the feelings of these unfortunate people.

In a letter to his wife, written from Pittsburgh on August 12, 1847, William Lloyd Garrison pictures life here at mid-century. Frederick Douglass was to have come with Garrison from Harrisburg, but through trouble with tickets was com-

8. The following passage from the *Visitor* is repeated in chapter 5.

pelled to travel ahead of Garrison by several hours. Garrison recounts the trip over the mountains by stage coach to Pittsburgh:

> The route over the Allegheny Mountains, although a very beautiful and sublime one, is a very slow and difficult one, and with a crowded stage on a melting hot day, quite overpowering. It seemed to me almost interminable— almost equal to a trip across the Atlantic. Douglass was not allowed to sit at the eating table, on the way, and for two days and nights scarcely tasted a morsel of food. Oh, what brutality! Only think of it, and of the splendid reception given to him in all parts of Great Britain! On arriving at Pittsburgh, however, a different reception awaited him, which was also intended for me. A committee of twenty white and colored friends, with a colored band of music, who had sat up all night until three o'clock in the morning, met him to welcome him to the place, and to make eloquent music to him. Of course they were greatly disappointed at my not coming at that time.

Garrison continues with his account of the Pittsburgh doings:

> I arrived towards evening, entirely exhausted, but soon recovered myself by the good warm bath. A meeting had been held in the afternoon in the Temperance Hall which was ably addressed by Douglas. In the evening, we held one together in the same place, crowded to overflowing. Yesterday, we held three large meetings, two of them in the open air, and concluded last night with the greatest enthusiasm. This morning Saturday, we are off for New Brighton, where we are to have a meeting this afternoon and others tomorrow.

In another letter to his wife on August 16th, Garrison says:

> I scribbled a few hasty lines for you at Pittsburgh, just before leaving that busy, though dingy and homely city—a city which so closely resembles the manufacturing towns in England that I almost fancied that I was once more on the other side of the Atlantic. So, too, the enthusiasm manifested at our meetings was altogether in the English style. For example, at the close of our last meeting, three cheers were given to Douglass, three for Foster, and three for myself. Everything passed off in the most spirited and agreeable manner.

On Friday, Garrison took a steamer for Beaver, thence rode in an omnibus accompanied by several Negro friends from Pittsburgh: J. B. Vashon, son George, Dr. Delany, editor of *The Mystery*, "black as jet and fine fellow of great energy and spirit," and others including a Dr. Peck, "a fine promising colored young man, son of my old friend John Peck now of Pittsburgh, formerly of Carlisle, and a graduate of Rush Medical College in Chicago." Douglass, Garrison, and Dr. Peck spoke at New Brighton. Continuing the account of their journey, Garrison says of the boats that "colored persons are not allowed to sit at the regular table at meals." The Captain, upon being asked by Garrison, said that he had no objection but that some of the passengers might do so. Garrison made the rounds of the passengers and found that there was none.[9]

As the years drew dramatically nearer the crisis of 1861, the Negro community expanded, and knit itself into closer unity. It kept contact with the larger world, with conventions in Philadelphia and Rochester to organize Negroes for extension of liberties, with church conferences in Baltimore and Washington where churches in the western part of the country were promoted. Men like John Vashon and Martin Delany made speaking tours in the interest of abolition. They opened schools, public and private. They printed pamphlets and papers. The community vibrated with discussion and argument, for colonization in Africa and South or Central America or against colonization as slave holders' device to make slavery safe by ridding the country of free Negroes who stirred ambitions for freedom in the hearts and minds of their brothers in bondage. In parlors and churches, in barber shops and on street corners men opened their papers and read aloud the news of slave revolts in the South, of fugitives fleeing into Canada, of attacks on Negro communities in older cities. They read of the entrance of new territories into the Union, of the Dred Scott Decision, of the Compromise of 1850, and the Fugitive Law. They read of Kansas and John Brown.

Life, however, was not all struggle and politics in these mid-century years. There was the gaiety of parties and cotillions in homes and public halls. City newspapers gave space to social events in the Negro community. The *Commercial Journal* noted in March 1848 that "The Soiree of the Colored Baptist Church came off at Temperance Hall on Tuesday, Wednesday, and Thursday evenings" this week. In mid-June it announced that "the colored Masons celebrated St. John's Day this forenoon by a procession and address. Dinner was served at Stricklands where an address will be delivered in the evening." After 1837 when the Wilberforce Emancipation Act liberated 300,000 slaves in the British West Indies, American Negroes annually celebrated August 1st as Emancipation Day. Until that time Christmas and New Years had seemed to many the only days they wished to celebrate. The *Gazette* in 1852 said:

> The colored inhabitants of Allegheny County are preparing to celebrate the First of August, the anniversary of the Emancipation of the slaves in the British West India islands, in fine style. That day occurring on Sunday, as did the Fourth of July, the celebration will take place on Monday, in the fine grove

9. Chapter 5 includes Douglass's account of this boat trip.

in Manchester, on the estate of the late James Adams. A number of addresses will be delivered by eminent speakers, proceedings will prove very interesting, and friends are invited to attend.

On August 3, 1852, the paper said:

Our colored fellow citizens assembled yesterday in the grove on the property of the late Mr. Adams, below Manchester in large numbers, to celebrate the emancipation of the slaves in the British West India Islands. The day was a very fine one, and nothing occurred from the hour the exercises commenced, until their close to mar the harmony of the proceedings.

A fine band of music was in attendance, and booths had been erected, and refreshments of all kinds were supplied. All enjoyed themselves, and we were pleased to see the decorum which prevailed. Mr. T. Norris was called to the chair and Messrs. S. Green, H. Tanner, Simon Turfley, J. Jackson, T. Brown and H. B. Williamson were appointed vice presidents.

Messrs. Alfred M. Green and Ephraim Luckett acted as secretaries. After a prayer by the Reverend Levin Gross, the Chairman, in the absence of the orator of the day, delivered an address commemorative of the glories of the day which they had assembled to celebrate. After some fine music, the company adjourned to the tents for dinner.

The following delivered addresses: Professor Freeman of Allegheny Institute, S. Fleming, James Callan, Benton Kerr, and the Reverend Mr. Avery. Matthew T. Jones offered a series of appropriate resolutions which were unanimously adopted. Dr. M. R. Delany and Reverend Mr. Howell addressed the meeting, and after music, the assembly dispersed, and shortly afterwards returned to their several homes.[10]

There was also in these days the theater to attend, and it was attended, though the Negro audience was set off to themselves in one of the boxes. Yet, here, they could see the older Booth in *King Lear* and *Richard II*, or James Murdock in *Claude Melnotta* or Fennie Wallack, Edwin Forrest, Mathilda Herron, or Charlotte Cushman.[11] There was a band that played at large social affairs or at rallies and protest meetings. Concerts were held, too, at which young men of the Theban Literary Society orated between instrumental performances by young women in hoop skirts and corkscrew curls. Fairs and bazaars were organized by churches and philanthropic societies.

In a number of homes and families hospitality was traditional. There were dinners for out-of-town guests lecturing or visiting, for men who came to orga-

10. An account of the Emancipation Day celebration of 1845 is included in chapter 4.
11. This passage about the theater is repeated later in the chapter.

nize a convention, a church conference or an antislavery society, eminent men and women like William Lloyd Garrison or Wendell Phillips, Theodore Weld, Lucretia Mott, Bishop William Paul Quinn or Bishop John M. Brown, Fanny Wright or Frederick Douglass. These might be entertained at the home of the Reverend A. D. Lewis on Wood and Third Street (Market and Ferry) or Lewis Woodson on Liberty Street, the Browns on Hazel Street on the Hill, or at Hugh Tanner's on Knox Street in Arthursville, or the Vashons at Wood and Third, or John Templetons in Virgin Alley, or the Pecks at Penn and St. Clair Streets.[12]

The home of Mr. and Mrs. Thomas Arthur Brown on Hazel Street was known nation-wide for such hospitality and culture. It was a rest for travelers, and a refuge for fugitives. Mr. Brown had been a slave, held by relatives.[13] Mrs. Brown's grandfather had been an officer in the Revolutionary War. Her mother had been a slave. When the father died, the grandfather liberated mother and children, but cast them adrift on the world. The widow mother re-married. The family came north in a covered wagon drawn by four black horses. The children rode on a layer of feather beds and were comfortably covered with patchwork quilts. Their route was over the mountain, and at night they stopped, built a fire and ate from a well filled hamper the mother had packed. Often they were held by the patrol for hours while their papers were examined and certified. The Browns made their home in Pittsburgh on Hazel Street in Arthursville.[14]

[Part II]

The continuity of Negro life from the frontier into the era of industrial development, though attested by few documented facts in the first decades of the new period, is very real. The frontier had completed one historic task. In this task a number of Negroes were concerned. Military expeditions had won the wilderness from the French and Indians and established it as a colonial possession of the British crown. White settlers had built a vast fur trade, cultivated farms and turned the wilderness into profitable colonies under the mercantile system. At this stage also Negro slavery, and the labor of the region's few free Negroes, had assisted development. But the mercantile system made the colonies mere feeders of the mother country and prevented their free native development. To achieve

12. Some of the material relating the addresses of various family homes is repeated elsewhere in this chapter.

13. We don't know the details of Brown's upbringing. In general, mixed-race offspring caused tensions within the master's family, and for that reason might be sold off or sent away to live with friends or relatives. A lucky few were manumitted.

14. The tiny village of Arthursville was soon absorbed by an expanding city, and became part of the Hill.

such development, economic and political freedom was needed. The central issue of the time, therefore, became colonial independence, a break with the mother county, the destruction of the feudalistic subservience of the colonies under the mercantile system, and freedom for native capital to expand and native commerce and industry to develop. Only in this way could the country follow its rightful destiny. In this revolutionary task the particular service of the frontier—its farmers, their Negro slaves and servants, the traders and soldiers, both Negro and white—was to hold the west against British regiments, against Tory traders and Indian allies. In this they succeeded; but the democratic republic established by the Declaration of Independence, by Cornwallis's surrender, and by the Constitution with its Bill of Rights, did not give economic and political freedom to all groups who had fought to establish it. It did not grant universal suffrage; it did not abolish property qualifications for office holding; and it did not free from chattel slavery almost 700,000 Negroes held at that time. With the establishment of independence, the effects of the Industrial Revolution became at once apparent. But the industries which sprang up throughout the northern states demanded an open domestic market for their expansion. The growth of factories was to result in the construction of the greatest industrial system the world has known. But until the disputed lands of the west were guaranteed free from competitive slave labor and were freely open to expansion of northern industrial capital, industry could never reach its maximum development. National policy must be free from the dominance of the slave-holding South. Rivalry between the two sections became so intense that the preservation of the Union, of the Republic established in 1776, called for the destruction of southern slave economy and the breaking of the hold of the slaveocracy on national policies. The central issue of the nineteenth century, therefore, the issue complementary to that of the frontier, was the destruction of slavery, freedom of the Negro people. The rise of Pittsburgh to supremacy in the industrial world typified these historic movements, for with the opening of the new century its industrialization was dramatically rapid, and the growth of its Negro community and of the issues revolving around that growth almost as much so.

The 19th century opens with a roll of "Black Thunder" that presaged the rising storm of the next fifty years. In the autumn of 1800 the *Gazette* carried a letter from Richmond, Virginia, which spoke of "an alarming plot of the blacks having been discovered which was to have been put into effect last night, had it not been detected, in which an undistinguished massacre of the whites was to have taken place without regard to age or sex." The *Gazette* was "happy to report that the leaders are taken," and it had no doubt that they would "be brought to condign punishment." The incident referred to was Gabriel's revolt, a slave of Thomas Prosser. Gabriel was a Negro giant of six feet two inches. With his brothers

Solomon and Martin, and Jack Bowler, four years older than Gabriel and three inches taller, he had armed the slaves with clubs and swords which they had "been making since last harvest." Gabriel had intended to buy a piece of silk for a flag on which he would inscribe the motto "Death or Liberty." His brother Solomon had said, "Before he would any longer bear what he had borne, he would turn out and fight with his stick." Jack Bowler declared, "We have as much right to fight for our liberty as any men." But the thousand slaves who had gathered that night six miles out of Richmond were frustrated by a storm which flooded the rivers, tore down bridges, and made their well-laid military operation impossible. The conspiracy had reached not only throughout the Richmond neighborhood, but into adjacent counties, perhaps involving the whole state. Gabriel's army had expected that the poor whites would join the revolt. And orders had been issued to spare Quakers, Methodists, and Frenchmen. The Quakers they knew from long opposition of those people to slavery to be their friends. The Methodists, members of a frontier church, were democratic, and in general opposed the slaveocracy. As for the Frenchmen had they not recently carried through their own revolution under the slogan of "Liberty, Fraternity, Equality"? But Gabriel's revolt failed, and on October 7 he was hanged. Thirty-five other Negroes were executed. Two condemned slaves escaped. Ten were reprieved and banished. Nevertheless the warning thunder rolled.

On the first day of October in the year 1804 a newcomer to Pittsburgh, a young man who was to become deeply involved in the business and finance of the growing city, Mr. John Thaw, picked up the quill pen from his accounting desk and wrote to his father in Philadelphia:

> Pittsburgh is a fine Country Town . . . posses tolerable good and cheap markets, dear stores and bad society the Inhabitants being so much engrossed with political discussions that those of opposite sentiments can hardly think or speak well of each other—its a place by no means so enticing as Phila. and a person coming from thence should do it under the conviction of making money and bettering his circumstances, but not of Enjoying the pleasure either of a country or city life.

A visitor to Pittsburgh "found the town, which was called the Western Exchange a reflect of New York, the same earnest bustle, and the same national variety in its thickly thronging strangers.

The "Letters from a Swiss Farmer" said:

> The city of Pittsburgh is the largest place on the west side of the Allegheny Mountains . . . The pleasant region around here is full of high but fertile hills, well cultivated and thickly populated. The place itself consists of wide

straight streets ... and is built according to the plan of Philadelphia. The houses, which number over 300, without the warehouse, are in part of brick, but many of them are still of wood. Among the public buildings to be mentioned are the courthouse, the jail, the school, the Presbyterian church, and the German Lutheran Church.

Although Mr. Thaw found the town "by no means as enticing as Philadelphia," and "engrossed with political discussion," he also spoke of the family pride and of the distinction between classes. Mr. Thaw's letters give some further description of the town. The houses were generally two stories high. The old ones were principally of log and the new ones of brick construction. The streets were straight and narrow, but not paved, and were of course extremely muddy. A few planks had been laid in the mud by careful home owners. And the degree to which the frontier character of the town had been displaced is shown by Mr. Thaw's remark that, "As for Speculation [in real estate][15] there is no chance, landed property being already monopolized by monied men and held at very high prices."

"The national variety of its thronging strangers"—its Germans, French, Scots, Negroes, and Welsh, was enhanced by the river boatmen, Irish traders, honest mechanics, loafers and sharpers, young dandies in ruffles who gathered in tap-rooms and inn-yards for bull-baitings, cockfights, card games, or boxing matches "fought to the death." Each autumn these characters gathered with throngs from all the country round about at the annual races of the Jockey Club. The race track stood at the extreme north-eastern end of the town where the Fort Pitt Hotel now stands.

Cotillions and country dances were held in the assembly room of the Green Tree Tavern or the ball room of the "General Butler." Dancing classes met for ladies at three o'clock and for gentlemen at six. Concerts of vocal and instrumental music—the spinet, violin, cello, flute—were also given, and an amateur dramatic society performed in the "Great Room" of the court house.

The changes in town life were typical of the changes in American life at the beginning of the nineteenth century. They were due chiefly to the earnest building of a new society, to the intense development of industry and business and the making of money; to the development of one class of men, the employers, who owned and promoted the shops and factories, and another, the employees who worked in them. More and more mechanics became familiar sights in the streets and along the river wharves, no longer in leather breeches and aprons of their craft, but in long loose trousers and short tight-fitting sailors jackets or rounda-

15. Bracketed material appears in the original manuscript.

bouts, made in winter of linsey woolsey and in summer of nankeen, dimity, or linen.

In 1804, the year in which Mr. Thaw used his quill pen so graphically, the first regular stage coach service had been instituted between Pittsburgh and Philadelphia. The first factory for carding, spinning and weaving cotton yarns and material was established by Peter Kitonbend who came from Manchester, England. A tin factory employed 28 persons, a nail factory 30, the cotton factory 12. Shipbuilding gave employment to 30 workmen, boat-building to another 50. The ropewalks employed 30 workers.

How far this new society had developed is dramatically embodied in an incident that occurred in this year. The journeymen shoemakers, then called cordwainers, found their wages insufficient in proportion to the cost of living. When the price of their board was raised and their wages remained stationary, these journeymen shoemakers issued the following statement:

> Pittsburgh, December 19, 1804. This notice is intended to inform the traveling journeymen shoemakers of Pennsylvania, or of any other state, that the journeymen of this town made a turnout for higher wages. Two or three of their employers had a meeting, and having a number of apprentices thought proper to advise the other master shoemakers to raise the boarding from $1.50 to $2.50 per week. We think it our duty to give this notice to all journeymen shoemakers that they may be guarded against imposition. The following are the prices which we turned out for, Viz.: Fine shoes, 80 cents; coarse shoes, 75 cents; women's slippers, 75 cents; bootees, $2.00; long boots, $2.50; coffees, $2.50; N. B. We would not advise any journeymen to come here unless they want a seat of cobbling.

This was the first strike in Pittsburgh. Between this year 1804 and the year 1816 the shoemakers conducted five or six strikes. That of 1815 set a historical precedent. In the case of the "Commonwealth vs. Morrow," James Middle, proprietor of one of the shops, brought his striking employees into court charged with conspiracy and won the verdict. In this case Edward M. Stanton, later Lincoln's Secretary of War, won himself a reputation through the prosecution. These incidents meant that the old slave-holding, self-sufficient agricultural community was forever gone and that the foundations of the future industrial empire was laid. With that empire would be bound the destinies of millions of men and women of all creeds, faiths, nationalities, and races. The next century would tell the story of how this new society and its peoples tried to organize their pursuit of life, liberty and happiness and for many years one of its most dramatic themes would be the story of the Negro people.

Five years after this first strike occurred, that is in 1809, Oliver Evans built for his brother's stone grist mill on the Monongahela River front, a steam engine— the first steam engine west of the Allegheny Mountains. This was like the stroke of a genie, a magical thing that unleashed the tremendous energies of the industrial world. It was a world of steam and smoke, signifying the beginning of the industrial city of the future.

Already the black smoke of Pittsburgh was famous. It came from the round cannon-stoves and open grates of the homes and from the fires of the shops and factories, all supplied from the 40 or 50 pits on Coal Hill, now Mt. Washington. Every traveler commented on it. David Thomas said aptly that looking down on the city from the hilltops he was reminded "of the smoking logs of a new field"; and John Pearson's notes say of the place:

> We arrived at Pittsburgh, the Birmingham, the Manchester, and the Sheffield of America, according to some, but in my words a poor, gloomy, sickly receptacle, hardly fit for convicts of the worst description; no greater punishment could be inflicted, I am sure, upon our Bank note forgers than to send them to Pgh., yet this was the place where the hammers stunned your ears, and the manufactories struck you dumb with astonishment, so indeed they do when you can find them. There is one paper mill that employs 20 hands, one grist mill 8, and one nail shop that employs one poor old man, but no piano forte manufactory, as has been represented; there were 1,188 persons destitute of employment and the cry of distress was universal: this is the Birmingham of America, and let them deny it if they can.

John Meliah, a Scottish geographer and merchant, having visited Pittsburgh in 1810, recorded his impressions of the industrious town, including the boat building which for years afterwards was to have such an influence on the industry and commerce of the city:

> In the course of my walks through the streets I heard every where the sound of the hammer and anvil; all was alive; everything indicated the greatest industry, and attention to business. The markets were well stocked with provisions and fruit, and the vegetables were larger than any I had seen before. I ascended an eminence, called Grant's Hill, from whence I had a fine view of the town and country. I went accompanied by a friend to visit the glass-works, which we found in excellent order, and one of the workmen prepared for us some glassware of curious workmanship. In the neighborhood we saw a pottery, at which a great deal of very handsome earthen utensils are manufactured. I carried a letter of introduction to Mr. Roosevelt, the gentle-

man who had the management of the steam-boat which was on the Ohio. He was not at home, but I went to see the boat. It had lately been launched on the Monongahela River, and was the largest vessel I had ever seen which bore the name of a boat. Her dimensions were as follows: length 146 feet 6 inches; breadth 32 feet 6 inches; depth 12 feet; and she will draw four feet of water. She was originally intended to run between Pittsburgh and the falls of the Ohio, but she was found to be too large, and is now destined to run between New Orleans and Natchez. The ultimate design of the proprietors is to have six boats to ply between the falls and New Orleans, and five between the falls and Pittsburgh. Should this plan be practicable, and carried into full execution, it will be of incalculable advantage to the whole western country. . .

Pittsburgh's rivers and roads were making of the city a great trade mart. The nearby coal veins supplied plentiful fuel for its manufacturers. The sand from its river beds made the glass industry an easy development. When Napoleon Bonaparte had closed the Mississippi River to American traffic in 1800, three-eighths of the commerce of the United States was passing through the mouth of the Mississippi to the Gulf of Mexico. The wheat and livestock of the trans-Allegheny country were already important articles of commerce. From Pittsburgh went Conestoga wagons, flat boats, and keel boats laden with bar-iron, coarse linen, and glass bottles from the earliest manufactories; up the river came corn, beans, dried pork and sugar from New Orleans; cotton from Mississippi and Tennessee, tobacco from Kentucky. Galleys and ships brought Missouri lead, Mexican copper, Spanish wool and molasses from the West Indies. The launching of the *New Orleans* in March 1811, the first steamboat constructed in Pittsburgh and the first to ply the western rivers, revolutionized river traffic. The war of 1812 cut off the sea route to great volumes of American trade, which sent greater volumes of southern commerce into and through the town. The first hard surfaced turnpikes laid down in 1816 and 1817 strengthened industrial and commercial ties with the East and the West. Improved roads and river transport not only increased traffic in freight and built manufactures, it increased human traffic. In one year, 1817, some 22,000 Irish and Germans came into the country. A number of these moved west. An Englishman who migrated to Illinois that year said: "the old America seems to be breaking up and moving westward." One gatekeeper on the Pennsylvania turnpike counted over 500 wagons and 3000 immigrants passing his toll gate in a single month.

With this great traffic came ever greater numbers of the Negro people, all looking for work in the diverse, thriving industries, many seeking refuge from southern slavery. John F. Watson in 1809 had written the Philadelphia Quaker Anthony Benezet, "Blacks now call themselves colored people (a modern name) meaning thereby to disdain the appellation of Blacks or Negroes—they never had surnames until lately." Watson's statement is borne out both by newspaper accounts of the day and by the first Pittsburgh directories,[16] where the listings read:

Vashon, H.   (col)   barber and hairdresser
                             Third n Market

J. B.   (colored)   hair dressing saloon
                             Corner Wood and Third

By 1813 the flight of escaped southern slaves into Pennsylvania had assumed such proportions that a petition to the Legislature said there were 4,000 runaway slaves in Philadelphia alone. How many had reached Pittsburgh is not known. It is recorded, however, that between 1780 and 1813, 189 children had been born, 33 to slave parents. Besides this circumstance most of the slaves still living had been manumitted. Many were still house servants, but others had taken up occupations as mechanics in the young industries, as carpenters, boatmen, draymen, and masons or as seamstresses, cooks and other workers.

One of the few documents of the time which records incidents in the community is the "Commonplace Book" of Rev. John Taylor, Rector of Trinity Episcopal Church, which in 1813 records the marriage on "Jany 7" of "Charles Richard(s) to ——." Charles Richards was the son of Benjamin Richards, the cattle dealer. It was Charles Richards who, years later, described to Martin R. Delany the passage through the city streets in 1812 of 360 Negro marines in military pomp and naval array on their way to the Frigate *Constitution* then on Lake Erie under the command of Commodore Perry.

Pittsburgh had been incorporated as a city. Two years after the school opened the first bridge was built across the Allegheny River at St. Clair Street, now Sixth, and another was built over the Monongahela. The school was opened at the beginning of the first of the city's financial panics, when hundreds of workers were thrown idle upon the streets and upon charity. By 1819 one or two organizations had been formed to meet such emergencies and that year the *Mercury* said, "it was better for charitable organizations and corporate bodies to give WORK to the poor, rather than to support them in idleness."

The Missouri Compromise of 1820 opened another and more stirring decade in the formation of the Negro community. The question of the extension of slavery was now inseparably tied up with the opening of the West, free lands for the farmers, an expanding domestic market for industry, internal improvements, the

16. These listings actually appeared in *Harris' Pittsburgh Business Directory* of 1839, which was neither the first city directory (1815) nor the first to come out under the Harris name (1837). See the bibliography for further detail.

tariff, popular elections, manhood suffrage, and all the issues of the increasing social democracy known as Jacksonian Democracy.

The decade was susceptible to great democratic movements outside the nation but within the western hemisphere. Brazil won her independence in the first year of the decade, Bolivia in 1825, Peru in 1826, Chile in 1828. The founding of the Haitian Negro republic in 1798, whatever its subsequent course, had been a constant source of inspiration to the slaves of the southern states.[17] And in 1822 occurred another nation-shaking slave revolt under the leadership of Denmark Vesey, in Charleston, South Carolina.

Vesey had written to St. Domingo telling his plans and asking for aid. One witness said 6,600 Negroes were involved, another said 9,000. Simultaneous attacks were planned by boat from five points and from a sixth on horseback. The uprising was to take place in July. By the middle of June the Negroes had made 250 pikeheads and bayonets and over 300 daggers. Every store containing arms had been made note of, and instructions were given to all slaves who tended horses or could easily get them as to where they should be brought. Barbers had helped by making wigs for disguises. The date for the uprising was betrayed. Vesey tried to set the date ahead, but some of his confederates were eighty miles out of the city and could not be reached in time.

In Charleston 131 Negroes were arrested and 47 condemned. Twelve were pardoned and 26 acquitted. Thirty-eight were discharged by the court. Four white men—an American, a Scotsman, a Spaniard, and a German—were imprisoned and fined for aiding the slaves. Most of those executed followed the admonition of Peter Poyas, one of the leaders, "Die silent, as you shall see me do."

At the time there were 285 Negroes in Pittsburgh and another 409 in the surrounding county. Vesey's revolt was reported in the papers, and news came into the city by word of mouth. It was this year that the first Negro church was organized in the city.[18] Certainly at the church gatherings, in the little parlors of homes, and on the streets of this early American city, the incident must have been argued and discussed, with the meager information given by the *Gazette*, the *Mercury*, and the *Statesman* or with the more complete details brought in by underground telegraph.

From this time on a heavy northward migration set in, bringing into Pitts-

17. Some of the dates presented in this paragraph of the original manuscript are erroneous: Brazil was declared independent in 1822, Peru won independence in 1821, Chile in 1818, and Haiti in 1804.

18. The city's first African American congregation gathered in 1808 in the basement of a downtown apartment, but the city's first official congregation, called Bethel African Methodist Episcopal Church, was established in 1822. See [Patricia Mitchell,] *Beyond Adversity: Teaching About African Americans' Struggle for Equality in Western Pennsylvania, 1750–1990* (Pittsburgh: Historical Society of Western Pennsylvania, 1994), 4.

burgh ever larger numbers and an ever stronger sentiment towards the problems that came to center around the abolition of slavery. Pittsburgh was an incorporated city of over 10,000 people. Suburbs had sprung up or been laid out beyond the original wards—the Northern Liberties to the northeast with a population about 700; Kensington and Pipetown in the neighborhood of the present Dinwiddie and Colwell Streets; Birmingham, with several steam mills and an extensive lock manufactory, on the South Side; Arthursville, in the present Fullerton and Arthur Streets neighborhood; Minersville, a mile or two farther out the road; and across the Allegheny River the "very handsome, flourishing town called Allegheny." Population showed an increase in the numbers of Catholic Irish, characteristic of industrial towns of the times, and of other foreign-born residents, particularly Germans. Thirty-two attorneys and sixteen physicians practiced in the city; the Western University had grown from the Pittsburgh Academy and a paying high school met in the Unitarian Church, but the city had "no library, no athenaeum, no garden, no theater."

The once scattered group of a hundred or so slaves and indentured servants in the city and its environs at the end of the decade was now a population of more than a thousand free men and women. Of these almost 500 lived within the city, more than 500 in the suburbs and nearby country. There were free men and women. There were also still a small number of slaves. But, free, slave or indentured, they were not part of the city life as were the Germans, the Irish and the Welsh. However capable, they held no city offices, did not attend city schools, were segregated in the theater, and were not members of the scientific and literary societies. There were various economic levels within the group and consequently various social levels. But more important than such differences was the growing common need for the satisfaction of broader, common interests, religious and cultural aspirations, professional ambitions, and with the progress of time the overshadowing question of what status the Negro should hold in a community of whites. By formation of social groups into church congregations, literary societies, temperance and moral reform societies, charitable and beneficial organizations, and, perhaps more significant than all these, abolition and antislavery societies, were sought to counter the deepening perplexities of the community.

The strongest impetus to organization of Negro community life in the 1830s came from antislavery sentiment and those ideas growing out of it. The decade was one of struggle, struggle for the elevation of the people. To this struggle every aspect of life contributed. Leaders came forward within the community. Others came in and made it their home. Its affairs became more and more a part of national Negro history, part of the history of the nation. The years previous to this decade had been a kind of pre-history of the Negro in Pittsburgh, with scant and unclear records. With the 1830s events and sentiments with the Negro community could no longer be ignored in the press of the day. They were chronicled in books, pamphlets, and in legislative archives. Historical records began to accumulate. A distinctively Negro way of life took form. Its activities and moods, its social, political and cultural institutions assumed a particular character. The Negro church, the Negro temperance movement, the Negro schools, the Negro literary society and philanthropic society, while inevitably marked by general characteristics of such institutions, because of the stress and agitation of the times just as inevitably assumed specific Negro characteristics. They became the seed from which sprang the Negro culture of the pre-Civil War years.

This decade, like the preceding one, opened under the impact of an event that stirred the country. The ten years just ended had been marked by a severe economic depression. The price of cotton and of slaves had reached the lowest point touched until the Civil War. British antislavery agitation had grown strong. Mexico had abolished slavery in 1829 and, with Colombia, attempted to acquire Puerto Rico and Cuba and wipe out slavery in those territories. Slave revolts were reported from Venezuela, Brazil, Cuba, Martinique, the British West Indies, and in almost all of the southern states—North and South Carolina, Georgia, Alabama, Tennessee, Louisiana—and in the states immediately neighboring Pennsylvania—Delaware, Maryland and Virginia. These movements for national independence, with their resulting freedom of the slaves in these countries, with the memory of Denmark Vesey's revolt, and the persisting memory of Haiti, stirred southern Negroes once more to rally about a revolutionary leader. For many weeks after the beginning of September 1831 Pittsburgh newspapers, by column after column of letters and dispatches, brought to Negro and white readers the outbreak, progress, and suppression of Nat Turner's revolt in Northampton County, Virginia. The *Gazette* said in part on September 2:

> An express reached the Governor this morning informing him that an insurrection had broken out in Southampton, and that, by last accounts, there were 70 whites massacred, and the militia retreating. Another express to Petersburg says that the blacks are continuing their destruction; that 300 militia were retreating in a body, before six or eight hundred blacks. A shower of rain coming up as the militia were making an attack, wet the powder so much that they were compelled to retreat, being only armed with shotguns. The Negroes were armed with muskets, scythes, axes, etc., etc. Our volunteers are marching to the scene of action. A troop of cavalry left at four o'clock P. M. The artillery with four field pieces start in the steamboat Norfolk at six o'clock to land at Smithfield.

Turner had chosen July 4th, the anniversary of American Independence, for the day on which he would strike for freedom. Turner, however, was ill on the fourth. When the revolt broke, U. S. troops recently stationed in Virginia in anticipation of such uprising—cavalry, seamen, and marines—swarmed over the country and with the help of many inhabitants killed over a hundred slaves. Turner escaped into hiding. And it was not until November 4 that a letter appeared in the *Petersburg Intelligencer* giving an account of his capture. The letter was quoted in the Pittsburgh *Gazette* for November 11, the day on which Turner was hanged. The letter said:

> It appears that on Sunday morning last Mr. Phipps having his gun, and going over the land of Mr. Francis, (one of the first victims of the hellish crew) came to a place where a number of pines had been cut down, and perceiving a slight motion among them, cautiously approached, and when within a few yards discovered the villain who had so long eluded pursuit, endeavoring to ensconce himself in a kind of cave, the mouth of which was concealed with brush. Mr. P. raised his gun to fire, but Nat hailed him and offered surrender. Mr. P. ordered him to give up his arms. Nat then threw away an old sword which it seems was the only weapon which he had. The prisoner, as his captor came up, submissively laid himself on the ground, was then securely tied—without making the least resistance.

Turner's revolt was one of the first overt events leading to the final break between North and South. It had instant effect in every city, North and South. Severe repressive laws were enacted in all southern and border states. Southern antislavery societies disappeared; northern societies multiplied. The movement for colonization of Negroes in other countries was temporarily strengthened and northward migration of free Negroes intensified.

Concerning Nat Turner's revolt Frank R. Rollin's biography of Martin Delany says:

> It was also about the winter of 1831-32 that the little ripple, destined to be the great antislavery wave, against which the ship of state would madly contend, was noticed; for, almost simultaneously with the outbreak for freedom as Southampton, Va., known as Nat Turner's insurrection, appeared "Garrison's Thoughts on American Colonization."
>
> Then to the casual observer, the action of one was a ridiculous folly; that of the other, the wild fancies of a fanatic's brain. Now, there is a dark significance in that solitary figure, looming up in the dark background of slavery as an offering on the altar of freedom, in the home of Washington, preceded by that attempted at Charleston with Denmark Vesey at its head, followed by the closing scene at Harper's Ferry. In each of these there was a warning and a lesson as direct as those which the Hebrew lawgiver received amidst the

thunders of Sinai, but by which a slavery-blinded nation failed to profit, until the last great martyr of Osawatomie was offered up.

> When that great heart broke, 'twas a world that shook;
> From their slavish sleep a million awoke.

The revolt shocked the stubborn orthodoxy which had begun to settle over Pittsburgh's middle-class population. Church membership in this decade increased 400% in the city. Church buildings grew in number from 10 to 55, congregations from 15 to 76. Tract, bible, and temperance societies sprang up. When the first playhouse opened in 1833 a public controversy was waged in the papers over the immorality of the theater. The Sunday School Association attempted to prohibit steamboats from running on Sundays. Complaints were made against drinking and gambling on river boats. A temperance line of steamers plying between Pittsburgh and Louisville was supported by 99 leading commercial patrons. So strong did feeling become against dancing and card playing that the ladies who directed the Pittsburgh Orphan Asylum refused the receipts of the Washington Birthday Charity Ball because they were won from dancing.

This narrow piety was shot through with many cross currents. Fourierist and Swedenborgian societies flourished. The followers of Frances (Fanny) Wright published a newspaper, *The Manufacturer*, which attacked the hypocritical religiosity of the city, advocated the ideas of Voltaire, Rousseau, Fourier, and Robert Owen, and agitated for the formation of free-thinking agnostic groups. Crowds gathered in the public halls to hear these ideas discussed. Frances Wright lectured on "Knowledge," Emerson on "Worship," Lucy Stone on "Social and Industrial Disabilities of Women," Wendell Phillips on "The Philosophy of the Reformation of Slavery." Susan B. Anthony and Lucretia Mott addressed crowded halls. When Abby Kelly Foster spoke on antislavery, anti-religious and anti-state subjects, Temperance Hall was so packed with its listeners that women fainted, windows were broken, and the demagogic street preacher Joseph Barker, later elected mayor while in jail, rushed to the platform and denounced Mrs. Foster's remarks.

This decade put Andrew Jackson into the White House with an overwhelming majority—to which even Pennsylvania added its 30 electoral votes, although only one of her congressmen had voted against the re-chartering of the National Bank. Jacksonian Democracy became a great progressive movement, a complex of popular movements. The 1830s was the first decade in which all classes of people took part in governing their country. This decade saw the beginnings of a strong labor movement, important to an industrial city like Pittsburgh. In 1833 a Labor Party held its first national convention in Philadelphia and demanded higher wages, shorter hours—the working day was often as long as fifteen hours—

and more sanitary shops and factories. Working men protested the competition of convict labor, demanded free schools for their children and the abolition of imprisonment for debt. They won the abolition of property and religious qualifications for voting. They initiated movements for the improvement of the poor laws, prison laws, and for healthier, cleaner cities.

Public opinion on these questions was formed in Pittsburgh by four daily newspapers, eleven weeklies and ten other periodicals. Eighteen printing and nine binding establishments issued pamphlets, bulletins, broadsides, and tracts. And in this industry was reflected another movement of the decade: the journeyman printers of the city formed their first protective union. Besides the printers, thirteen other crafts formed unions. Then the trade union movement took on broader scope. They sent a delegate, James Murray, to the third Convention of Trades Unions in Military Hall in Philadelphia. At a Fourth of July picnic held by the Pittsburgh Trades Union in 1836, a speaker called attention to the growth of classes in the country, and to the accumulation of great wealth as the cause of this. Such growth, he said, corrupted legislatures, gave security to monopolists, and perverted the judiciary. The remedy, he declared, was the ballot box.

The rise of the Negro community was part of this democratic sweep forward. Through its own leaders, through mass movement within the community, through white philanthropy and through Negro and white co-operation in reforms, it worked out its passionate, progressive history in the forefront of the movements of the times.

At the end of the decade, Harris' Pittsburgh *Directory* listed the various nationalities that made up the polyglot city and its environs. Of native-born Americans there were 28,000. The Irish population had reached 10,000 and these were almost entirely Catholic. The Germans numbered 12,000, though a note appended said "Some of the most intelligent German gentlemen think the population 13,000." The Welsh population had reached 2,800. In a generation and a half succeeding the Abolition Act of 1780, free Negroes in the city now ranked fourth among the national groups, surpassing the 2,000 Englishmen, the 2,000 Scots and the 700 French, and were surpassed only by the Irish, Germans and the Welsh. Although they were scattered in various streets of the city, they were concentrated in the Lower Hill, already known as Hayti, in Arthursville around Roberts Street and the side streets off Fullerton, and in Allegheny. The more well-to-do families lived at various points in the present Golden Triangle—Charles Richards lived on Front Street, the present First Avenue; J. B. Vashon kept his baths at Wood and Third. Vashon's neighbor was A. D. Lewis, dealer in second hand clothing, preacher and prominent abolitionist. John Peck had his hair dressing and wig making establishment on St. Clair Street (now Sixth and Penn); Lewis Woodson, the preacher, was proprietor of a hair dressing saloon at 214 Lib-

erty; Martin R. Delany, leecher and bleeder, resided on "Fifth east of Wood."
Oliver Avenue, then known as Virgin Alley, was a street predominantly Negro.
Here lived John Devaul, laborer; Hannah Hopkins, laundress; Jacob Hopkins,
fireman; Frederick Livers, boatman; Solomon Morris, dealer in new and second
hand clothing; Peter Sheppard, a boot and shoe black; John Templeton, the
teacher; Benjamin Wilkins, another dealer in second hand clothing; and John
Butler, Violet Jones, John Lewis, Emily Snowden, and Amelia Sanders,
unidentified except as dwellers in the street. In Minersville lived Joseph Anderson, Tobias Balder and George Gardner, all boatmen; the Reverend Mr.
Lawrence, and a few years later the Tanners and the Browns. Most of the arrivals
in the city found dwellings in Hayti around Coal Lane, and similar small side
streets.

On the evening of 16 January, 1832 "the colored people of the city and vicinity of Pittsburgh convened in the African Church," a one story brick building in
Miltenberger's Alley on the present site of the Chamber of Commerce Building.
Realizing that "ignorance is the sole cause of the present degradation and bondage of the people of color," and "for the purpose of dispelling the moral gloom
that has long hung around us," they formed the African Education Society.

On New Years Day, 1835, the *Commercial Journal* recorded the formation of
what Martin R. Delany said was the first total abstinence society to be organized
in America by Negroes:

> At a meeting of the people of color of Pittsburgh and vicinity, in Bethel
> Church, Tuesday evening, 30th of December, for the purpose of forming a
> Temperance Society, the Rev. John Boggs was called to the chair, and Mr.
> Thomas Norris appointed Secretary.

It was "Resolved, unanimously, that the meeting proceed to form a Temperance Society." The Preamble to the Constitution said:

> Believing that moderate drinking leads the way to all the drunkenness in
> our land and the world—that total abstinence from intoxicating liquors is the
> only safe guard for the temperate—and that the future prospects of the two
> and a half million of our brethren who are now groaning, in our own country,
> beneath the iron hand of the oppressor, will depend materially upon the state
> of morals among the *free* people of color, we the undersigned colored inhab-
> itants of the city of Pittsburgh and vicinity pledge ourselves neither to *drink*,
> nor *buy*, nor *sell*, nor *give away* any intoxicating liquor, except when rendered
> necessary as a medicine, and prescribed by a physician, when one is to be
> obtained.

Article 2 of the Constitution declared:

> The object of this society shall be to collect and disseminate facts on the subject of Temperance—to guard the temperate, to reform the intemperate, to refine the morals of the colored people as far as our influence may extend; and that by virtue they may rise to the possession of those intellectual, civil and religious privileges which were designed by the beneficent Creator for the mutual enjoyment of all mankind.

The officers elected were: Pres., Rev. John Boggs; V. Pres., Richard Bryans; Thomas Norris, Secretary; Lewis Woodson, Auditor.

A Board of Managers consisted of: Wm. J. Greenly, Samuel Bruce, Martin R. Delany, Geo. Bell, Joseph Neel, Daniel Toner, J. B. Vashon, Phebe S. Collins, Nancy Jones, Mary J. Dockins, Nancy Morgan, Isabella Collins.[19]

Negro opinion of such movements is voiced in an article that appeared a few years later while the society was still flourishing. Contributions to the papers from the community were rare, and this is one of the first of its kind:

TEMPERANCE REFORM

> Mr. Editor—it is gratifying to see the colored portion of our community engaged in promoting the great Temperance Reform among themselves by the organization of distinct associations, and adopting the Washingtonian pledge. No one, untrammeled with the popular prejudices that operate so strongly against the unfortunate man of color, can for a moment withhold his approval for such an enterprise, being embraced and propagated by them; when we consider intemperance has accomplished its deadly effects among the black population in the same proportion as it has among the whites; therefore showing the propriety of measures, being brought into requisition of their own creation, to prevent its further progress. The black man receives an unrighteous stigma upon his nature, and is degraded on account of his color, in the erroneous judgment of a mortal like himself; but stands in these respects, perfect before his Creator; his moral worth is not depreciated, because he is of a different tinge.

> But the black man who indulges in intoxicating drinks, is considered wonderfully debased, and is frowned to earth by those who have had in their hearts the unrighteous prepossession spoken of above; Therefore, the more powerful the inducement is, for forming themselves in array against the use of alcoholic liquors.

---

19. Previously in this chapter, the text lists a different roster of officers and managers for the temperance society.

I visited the Society on last Tuesday evening, that convenes in the school room belonging to the people of color in our city, and to my great satisfaction the house was full by the time the exercises commenced, which progressed smoothly, without the slightest difficulty or interruption, during their continuation. Several addresses were delivered of the right cast, embracing a concise explanation of the important principle of Total Abstinence, as connected with the property of individuals, as well as the general welfare of mankind.

I found on inquiry, that the association numbered already 200 members, and was daily augmenting, so that an entire reformation of the blacks is not a hopeless project if continued on the present prosperity, a few months more. Though the black man's privileges are circumscribed, and consequently his enjoyments measurably curtailed; yet, the consciousness of a guiltless course of sobriety and industry in the walks of human life, will afford him some pleasure, in solitary seclusion from his oppressors, and upon a dying bed, when tottering mortality shall drop into the repository of all dead—the grave.

A FRIEND, AND WASHINGTONIAN,

Pittsburgh November 5, 1842.

In most American cities where abolition and antislavery movements were active, where free public education, women's rights, temperance and other reforms were advocated the names of leading Pittsburgh Negroes were known—J. B. Vashon, Lewis Woodson, John Peck, and above all, Martin R. Delany.

Martin Robison Delany was undoubtedly the outstanding leader of the community. He had come to Pittsburgh in 1831 as a youth of nineteen. He was born the son of Samuel and Pati Delany, at Charles Town, Virginia, (now West Virginia), May 6, 1812. Delany felt intense pride of birth and pride of race. By these he was motivated to turn his genius into the activities he did. Delany is symbolic of much of the history of the Negro in America. His biographer, Frank A. Rollin says of him:

> With the name Delany, a peculiarity illustrative of the man himself is manifested. Regarding it as not legally belonging to his family by consanguinity, and suspicious of its having been borrowed from the whites, as was the custom of those days, he expresses himself always as though it was distasteful to him, recalling associations of the servitude of his family. With these associations clinging to it, his pride revolts at retaining that which he believes originated with the oppressors of his ancestors; and though he has made it honorable in other lands besides our own, encircled it with the glory of a steadfast adherence to freedom's cause in the nation's darkest hours, and un-

compromising fidelity to his race, thus constituting him one of the brightest beacons for the rising generation, he eagerly awaits the opportunity for its erasure.

His pride of birth is traceable to his maternal as well as to his paternal grandfather, native Africans—on the father's side, pure Gullah; on the mother's, Mandingo. His father's father was a chieftain, captured with his family in war, sold to the slavers, and brought to America. He fled at one time from Virginia, where he was enslaved, taking with him his wife, and two sons, born to him on this continent and, after various wanderings, reached Little York—as Toronto, Canada, was then called—unmolested. But even there he was pursued and "by some fiction of law, international policy, old musty treaty, cozenly understood," says Major Delany, he was brought back to the United States.

The fallen old chief afterwards is said to have lost his life in an encounter with some slaveholder, who attempted to chastise him into submission.

On his mother's side the claim receives additional strength. The story runs that her father was an African prince, from the Niger valley regions of Central Africa; was captured when young, during hostilities between the Mandingoes, Fellahtas, and Houssa, sold, and brought to America at the same time with his betrothed Graci.

His name was Shango, surnamed Peace, from that of a great African deity of protection, which is represented in their worships as a ram's head with the attribute of fire.

The form and attributes of this deity are so described as to render it probable that the idol Shango, of modern Africa, is the same to which ancient Egypt paid divine homage under the name of Jupiter Ammon. This still remaining popular deity of all the region of Central Africa, is an evidence sufficient in itself to prove not only nativity, but descent. For in accordance with the laws of the people of that region, none took, save by inheritance, so sacred a name as Shango, and the one thus named was entitled to the chief power. From this source this American family claim their ancestry.

Shango, at an early period of his servitude in America, regained his liberty, and returned to Africa.

Whether owing to the fact that the slave system was not so thoroughly established then,—that is, had no legal existence,—or the early slaveholders had not then lost their claims to civilization, it was recognized among themselves that no African of noble birth should be continued enslaved, proofs of his claims being adduced. Thus, by virtue of his birth, Shango was enabled to return to his home. His wife, Graci, was afterwards restored to freedom by the same means. She remained in America, and died at the age of one hundred and seven, in the family of her only daughter, Pati, the mother of Major Delany.

Of Delany's pride of ancestry this biographer says further that he did not expect it "to elevate him in America, knowing that custom and education are alike averse to this—scarcely allowing him to declare with freedom from derision the immortal sentence, '*I am a man*' and claiming rights legitimately belonging to its estate." He says further:

> Thus Africa and her past and future glory became entwined around every fibre of his being; and to the work of replacing her among the powers of the earth, and exalting her scattered descendants on this continent, he has devoted himself wholly, with an earnestness to which the personal sacrifices made by him through life bear witness.

In Charles Town, Mrs. Delany had been threatened time after time with violence for persisting in teaching her children to read and write. She finally took them to Chambersburg, Pennsylvania where they could be sent to school. But Martin was forced by the family's poverty to find a job. Dissatisfied with his prospects he persuaded his parents to allow him to go to Pittsburgh, "where facilities for obtaining an education were superior to his home. On the morning of the 29th of July, 1831, we date the first bold and determined move on his part to fit himself for the herculean task which he had marked out for himself. Alone, and on foot the young hero set out for Pittsburgh, with little or no money, and consequently few friends. Crossing the three grand ridges of the Allegheny he soon reached Bedford. Here employment being offered to him, he remained for one month. Never losing sight of his resolves, he now turned his face towards Pittsburg in which city the foundation of his fame afterwards rested."

Rollin says of Delany in Pittsburgh at this time:

> Great efforts were being made by the colored people themselves in Pittsburgh, to advance their educational interests, together with other measures for the recognition of their political rights. A church was purchased from the white Methodists for a school-house—an educational society having been previously organized, Rev. Louis Woodson,[20] a colored gentleman, of fine talents, was placed at the head of it. Under the supervision of this gentleman, during the winter of 1831, his progress in the common branches were such as to warrant his promotion to the more advanced studies. It was commonly said by his friends in school, that his retentiveness of history—his favorite

20. Louis Woodson is a misspelling of Lewis Woodson.

study—was so remarkable that he seemed to have recited from the palm of his hand . . .

With the scene of Nat Turner's defeat and execution before him, he consecrated himself to freedom; and like another Hannibal, registered his vow against the enemies of his race. To prepare for everything that promised success, to undergo every privation and suffering, if necessary to accomplish this object, was now the resolve of the young neophyte. He began in the right direction to prepare himself for whatever position he should be called upon to fill, by a renewed earnestness in his studies. [. . .]

Then no college or academy of note in the United States received within its walls a black student, no matter how deserving, save under obligations, hereafter to be mentioned, not excepting Dartmouth, ostensibly established for Indians, nor the great, independent Harvard of ancient pride . . .

Such was the limited opportunity for a thorough education among the colored people, and so great was the prejudice against them while Martin Delany was endeavoring to acquire his, that it is safe to infer that no colored person, recognized as colored, previous to the establishment of institutions of learning under the antislavery agitation, ever completed a collegiate course. True it is, that a few were educated under the auspices of colonization societies, with no design of benefiting the colored people in this country, but on the condition of their leaving it for Africa.

While pursing his studies in Pittsburgh, his name was solicited and obtained by the zealous Mr. Dawes, agent of the Oberlin Collegiate Institute, at the beginning of that now famous institute. He afterwards declined going, it being then a preparatory school, and his studies being fully equal to those prosecuted there.

Three years later the young Mr. Delany, then 22 years of age, was actively organizing associations for the relief of the poor in the city, and for the "moral elevation of his people." The Temperance Society was one of them. Another was known as the Philanthropic Society. This society, ostensibly organized for relief of the indigent was in reality one of the first great links on the Underground Railroad connecting slaves with friends in the North. Delany was for years secretary of its executive board. The society in one year aided 269 persons to escape into Canada.

About the same time he began to study medicine with Dr. Andrew N. McDowell, the physician who attended Charles Dickens on his Pittsburgh visit. He also studied with Dr. Francis J. LeMoyne and with Dr. Joseph P. Gazzam, both of whom became prominent abolitionists. He did not, however, complete his studies here, but turned to dentistry. In the directories at the time he is listed as a "leecher and cupper." In one, however, his name is added to those of the physicians.

Shortly after his arrival in Pittsburgh, Delany made friends with a student at Jefferson College. The two friends organized a literary society. The name they chose indicated Delany's devotion to African culture for they called it after the ancient Negro capital of Thebes: the Theban Literary Society. To the debates and discussions of the society he attributes the development of his talent for writing and public speaking.

In 1839 he visited New Orleans and Texas. In Texas, General Felix Houston, seeing Delany dress the wound of a man stabbed by a drunken companion, "offered him a good position and protection if he would join him." Delany refused and continued his tour among the slave-holding Indians of Mississippi, Louisiana, Arkansas and Texas.

On his return to Pittsburgh, Delany began in 1843 the publication of one of the earliest and foremost abolitionist newspapers, the *Mystery*.

On March 15 of this same year, Martin Robison Delany was married to Kate A. Richards, daughter of Charles Richards, "the grandfather and father of whom had been men of influence and wealth of their time." Rollin says of this marriage:

> This daughter was one of the heirs to their estate, which had increased in value, as it embraced some of the best property in the city of Pittsburgh, estimated at nearly two hundred and fifty thousand dollars. This was finally lost to them in 1847, simply by a turn of law, in consequence of the unwillingness of attorneys to litigate so large a claim in favor of a colored against white families.

From this marriage eleven children were born, Delany's biographer says:

> In the selection of the names of these children, the specialty (of his pride in African culture) is again evident. If the names given to children generally are intended as incentives to the formation of character, then, when they are sufficiently marked by selections from prominent characters, it may at least be indicative of the sentiments of the parents. If this is admitted then the choice of names of these children gives unmistakable evidence of the determination of their parents that these brilliant characters should not be lost sight of, but emulated by them. While they are strictly in keeping with the father's characteristic, they being all of African affinity or consanguinity, they are nevertheless remarkable amidst such surroundings as American contingencies constantly present. The eldest is Toussaint L'Ouverture, after the first military hero and statesman of Santo Domingo; the second, Charles Lennox Remond, from the eloquent living disclaimer; the third, Alexander

Dumas, from that brilliant author of romance; the fourth, Saint Cyprian from one of the greatest of the primitive bishops of the Christian Church; the fifth, Faustin Soulouque, after the late emperor of Hayti; the sixth, Rameses Placido, from the good king of Egypt, "the ever living Rameses III," and the poet and martyr of freedom to his race on the island of Cuba; the seventh, the daughter Ethiopia Amelia, the country of his race, to which is given the unequaled promise that "she should soon stretch forth her hands unto God."

The Pittsburgh chapters of Delany's life were lived in the most dramatic years of Negro history. This man "of most defiant blackness," of whom Frederick Douglass said, "I thank God for making me a man simply; but Delany always thanks him for making him a *black man*." This man completely identified himself "with a people and a time at once wonderful and perilous." Perilous they were, for Delany was more than once attacked by lynch-mobs during his antislavery activities. On the occasion of an attack on the house of Mr. John B. Vashon, in Pittsburgh, Delany, with a number of older men of the community, called on Judge Pentland and other prominent citizens to protest the outrage. The delegation said that though they were a law-abiding people, they did not intend to remain and be murdered in their houses without a most determined resistance to their assailants, as there was little or no assistance or protection rendered by the authorities. Whereupon Delany was made one of the special black and white police appointed in conjunction with the calling out of the militia by the mayor, Jones McClintook.

Year after year the Negroes of the North sent their best talent to conventions, usually in Philadelphia, for the purpose of placing before the people the true condition of the colored people of the North, and also to devise methods of assisting slaves in the South. To these conventions went Pittsburghers like John Peck and J. B. Vashon. Lewis Woodson and Martin Delany were delegates to the convention of 1839 at Philadelphia. On their arrival they learned that the meeting had been transferred to New York, and on reaching New York they were told that it had been indefinitely postponed.

During the antislavery convention held at Pittsburgh in 1839, Delany said while comparing Jewish slavery with that which existed in America that "Onesimus was blood-kin brother to Philemon."[21] "This extraordinary and then en-

---

21. Delany's comment on Onesimus and Philemon refers to the Epistle of Paul to Philemon, a wealthy Christian of Colossae, Asia Minor, on behalf of Onesimus, Philemon's former slave. Paul, writing from prison, expresses affection for the newly converted Onesimus and asks that he be received in the same spirit that would mark Paul's own arrival, even though Onesimus may be guilty of previous failings. While passing no judgment on slavery itself, Paul exhorts Philemon to mani-

tirely new ground," says his biographer, "was so unexpected and original, that while many approached congratulating him on his able arguments, they expressed their regrets that he ventured to use such weapons, as he rendered himself liable to severe criticisms from the whites." Delany answered that the future which would shortly greet them would establish this as a fact. To the charge of imprudence made against him, his biographer quotes Wendell Phillips, "What world-wide benefactors these imprudent men are—the Lovejoys, the Browns, the Garrisons, the saints, the martyrs! How prudently most men creep into their nameless graves while now and then one or two forget themselves into immortality."

After his editorship of *The Mystery*, Delany assisted Frederick Douglass in his publication of *The North Star* at Rochester, New York. For *The North Star*, Delany traveled, held meetings, lectured, obtained subscribers, and tried to establish an endowment for the paper. It is believed that a story he wrote for *The North Star* at the time of the Free Soil Convention at Buffalo to nominate a candidate for the presidency of the country lost Judge McLean of Ohio that honor, and bestowed it upon Martin Van Buren.

Delany left *The North Star* in Douglas's hands in 1849 and returned to Pittsburgh. He resumed his study of medicine, and on the strength of the teaching of his former instructors, Dr. Gazzam and Dr. LeMoyne, he was registered in the medical college in Harvard. After graduation he made another lecture tour and wrote and published in 1852 *The Condition, Elevation, Emigration, and Destiny of the Colored People of the United States.*[22] He also published a novel, *Blake, or the Huts of America*, which contained some of the first Negro folk songs to be collected. Back in Pittsburgh he practiced medicine and won honor by his skilled treatment of the victims of the cholera epidemic of 1854. He was appointed member of a sub-committee to consider Negro and white applicants to a municipal and private charitable institution. He wrote a paper on "Destiny of the Colored Race in America" while practicing here. This he read at a national emigration

---

fest true Christian love that removes barriers between slaves and free men. The letter was probably composed in Rome about A.D. 61. *Encyclopedia Britannica Online,* s.v. "Philemon, The Letter of Paul to," http://www.eb.com:180/cgi-bin/g?DocF=micro/464/0.html (accessed December 17, 2003). This material about Delany's speech is repeated in chapter 4; chapter 4 also includes a passage in which Jane Grey Swisshelm makes use of the same biblical reference.

22. Delany did not graduate from Harvard. White medical students protested the presence of blacks as "detrimental" to their "interests," and Harvard's three black medical students were dismissed. Delany was forever embittered by this. For accounts of Delany's life and writings, see Frank A. Rollin, *Life and Public Services of Martin R. Delany* (1883; reprint, New York: Arno Press, 1969); Cyril E. Griffith, *Martin R. Delany and the Emergence of Pan-African Thought,* (University Park: Pennsylvania State University Press, 1975).

convention at Cleveland in August, 1854. While a resident of Pittsburgh he worked out an invention for the ascending and descending of a locomotive on an inclined plane without the aid of a stationary engine, but it was never patented.

Delany was elected Mayor of Greytown in Central America, a colony of Negroes, migrants and natives. Instructed to bring with him his own "cabinet of State," Delany traveled for eight months to assemble it, but failed to find the desirable material and abandoned his plans. By order of the American chargé d'affaires the town was bombarded by a U.S. squadron and the young government "disappeared from the stage forever."

In 1856 he moved to Chatham, Canada, and there became an advisor of John Brown of Osawatomie. But he did not involve himself deeply in Brown's plans, having already arranged to leave for Africa as chief commissioner of the Niger Valley Exploring Party in 1859. The result of this trip was a scientific and sociological report which won him a seat at the International Statistical Conference held in London in 1860, at which he achieved international renown.

With the outbreak of the Civil War he became concerned with the role the Negro should play in the victory of the Union troops and the emancipation of the slaves. On February 8, 1865, Delany obtained an interview with Lincoln for the purpose of founding an army of black men, under black commanders. "The sight of which is required," he told Lincoln, "to give confidence to the slaves, and retain them to the Union, stop foreign intervention, and speedily bring the war to a close." Lincoln was impressed. He gave Delany a note to Stanton, Secretary of War, which read: "Do not fail to have an interview with this extraordinary and intelligent black man."

Delany saw Stanton, convinced him of his plan, and on February 27 was mustered into service as a major in the 104th Regiment of Colored Troops. He had his own son appointed as acting lieutenant—this was Toussaint L. Delany, a private in the 54th Massachusetts Volunteers.

On July 15, 1865, Delany was relieved of his military duties, but retained in the service as sub-assistant commissioner of the Freedman's Bureau. His policies in the Bureau laid the basis for Booker T. Washington's advocacy of industrial education for Negroes.

[PART III]

In the *Weekly Advocate and Emporium* for July 23, 1841, an unknown journalist of the time has left an account of the present Hill district, its appearance and its people, under the caption

PITTSBURGH AND ENVIRONS

Prospect Hill—Catontown, Hayti, Arthursburgh[23], Laceyville, and Rice-town.

The progress of enterprise in Pittsburgh and vicinity within the last few years has been truly wonderful. Improvements have taken place so silently, as it were, as to have been scarcely observed by the denizens of the city, although they have been rapid and numerous in execution. The Pittsburgher, however, who may have been absent a short time, perceives at once the changes that may have occurred in every direction. To no quarter, perhaps, would he turn his eye with greater pleasure than to Prospect Hill and the valley southward of it—the locations of the towns above mentioned which have become as *one* city by their growth and proximity to each other.

About twelve years ago, there were not more than about eight or ten houses on the entire hill in the district of those two villages, and they were the farm houses and cottages of those who supplied the Pittsburgh markets with the products of their gardens and orchards. Now we could scarcely begin to enumerate the tenements, many of which are [of] the most substantial and tasteful kind.

The colored population of Pittsburgh were the first to settle down on Prospect Hill, and a colony having been established about twelve years since, it has continued to flourish down to the present writing.

For a while these people had almost sole possession of the hill; but the favorable location attracted the attention of the white brethren who followed in their wake, till at present they number many of our most influential and respectable fellow citizens.

The brow of the hill overlooking Bayardstown is the site of several very elegant mansions; and their commanding position and beauty of architecture, render them conspicuous objects, which call forth the admiration of all those who love nature and art commingled in picturesque effect.

Further towards the south-east, we notice a small Gothic church, which is one of the neatest temples of Divine worship we have in this vicinity. Its white walls and tower render the church a pleasing object, situated as it is on a high knoll, and surrounded with green fields and neighboring woodlands. It seems to impart an air of respectability to the little villages which have sprung up around, ornamenting them meanwhile in its quiet aspect.

There are also numerous other villages which would reflect credit even on the most refined community. Several of the Clergy, members of the legal profession, together with merchants and private citizens, have selected this

23. Arthursburgh was another name for Arthursville.

elevation for their suburban retreats, and have commenced laying off their grounds and constructing their dwelling in accordance with affluence and taste.

Above all, however, the colored people deserve commendation for their industry and enterprise. A large number of them are owners of the houses and lots they occupy, some of the dwellings being of the most substantial kind, brick and frame. In repeated instances they have dug the cellars of their abodes with their own hands and have made brick of the clay upon the spot, and thus secured for themselves a comfortable house, at a comparatively small expense beyond their own labor and perseverance.

We are acquainted with two or three colored families being induced to emigrate to Canada, in the expectation of doing better; but having expended their little all in that while on El Dorado of the colored man, they have returned to their old home, or HAYTI, as some call their town, glad to come back to a land of plenty—literally "milk and honey," as they themselves say, in comparison with the comforts they enjoyed in Canada—accordingly, with renewed efforts, we see them striving to regain what they lost by moving, and from their intelligence and industry, we have no doubt, they will speedily be placed in comfortable if not affluent circumstances.

The colored inhabitants of the hill, moreover, are among the most worthy and respectable, and their example for orderly conduct, sobriety, and the civilities of life, are appreciated and warmly approved by their white neighbors. Indeed many of them prove to be excellent citizens, who seem to take pride in the prosperity of the town originally commenced by them. We hope they will continue to prosper and outlive the many prejudices which have existed against them as to their profligacy and dependent course of life heretofore.

We observe them now crowding to their chapels on the Sabbath, as well dressed and orderly as any people in the land, while the marriage feast and the funeral ceremonies are conducted with the ease and elegance of polished life. Their observance of the rites of the dead have struck our attention repeatedly and won our solemn admiration.

What with schools and religious instructions, and advancement in refinement, may we not expect of the entire community of colored people, if their present town is a criterion by which to judge? Surely all that is adorning to the human character, and society.

We have no estimate of the population of the several towns respecting which we are writing, but suppose it will number at least fifteen hundred, one third of which is colored. The district contains FOUR churches—one Presbyterian, one Episcopal, and two Methodists. There are six or seven schools, two of which are *taught* by a *colored man and woman*.

A number of new buildings have already been erected this season, and others are going forward. In addition to these improvements, the fine strip of property on the ridge facing the Allegheny River has recently been divided into building lots, and in a season or two more we may expect to see the entire brow of the hill ornamented with elegant dwellings like those in the occupancy of Rev. Dr. Upfold, Mr. Loomis, and others. A street has been laid off along this front, and the access to the height, by Coal Lane, recently much improved, is convenient.

We understand that the city has purchased a field about ten acres in the rear of this dwelling, upon which is intended at some future date to erect water works, public gardens and promenades, for the benefit of our citizens.

A proposition has already been made to include the villages we are describing in the bounds of the city of Pittsburgh, but the inhabitants still prefer their *rus in urbe* to any advantages which may be derived from corporate powers.

Taking all things in connection, we may readily claim for Prospect Hill the distinction of being not only the healthy, but certainly the most beautiful site for dwellings, free from bustle and dust of other locations in the immediate vicinity of Pittsburgh. This neighbor, we opine, is destined to become the abode of the intelligence, fashion, and wealth of the "Western Emporium" before the lapse of many years.

The social life of this early American Negro community in Pittsburgh now took on a new quality. In the staid "Victorian" parlors of the 1830s and 1840s, the parlors of the Vashons at Wood and Third streets, or the Hugh Tanners in Arthursville, with their rugs tucked unhygienically into the four corners of the room, women in billowing bombazine skirts, fichus round their shoulders, corkscrew curls dangling at their temples, sat primly on horse-hair sofas to talk with their guests.[24] Men in tight trousers strapped into their boots, frock-coated and Dundreary-whiskered[25], sat stiffly on their slithery chairs sometimes smoking the newly devised "Seegars." On the walls above their heads hung glass cases of shell and feather floral wreaths. They sat round a heavily draped center table over which the new oil lamps spread a circle of mellow light. And they must have talked of the recent lighting of hotels, and shops and city streets, by gas light or, in these days of the kidnaping of Negroes, of the feeling of safety engendered by

24. "Bombazine" is a fine fabric of silk or cotton, which was sometimes dyed black and used for mourning clothes; "fichu" was a woman's triangular scarf worn over the shoulders and crossed or tied in a loose knot at the breast.

25. "Dundrearies" are long sideburns, named after the character of Lord Dundreary in *Our American Cousin*.

the revival of the night watch going about the streets tapping the pavements with his heavy stick to signal a fellow watchman on his beat, and calling the hours— "One o'clock and a starlight night." Or they talked of the ravages of the Asiatic cholera and peered through the heavy, dark-colored curtains into the night lit by burning tar barrels at the street corners and watched the tumbrel[26] carrying the dead to their graves. They must have talked of a question very close to most of them, the demand to shorten the over-long work day in the cotton mills and the iron foundries, a work day of 11 to 15 hours, or the work day of the store clerks of 12 to 16 hours, and the justice of the demands of the "boilers" in the foundries when they struck for six dollars a week, or of the parade of the cotton mill girls with their banners demanding the fulfillment of the Whig promise of "$2.00 a day and roast beef."

When guests arrived from the East, a visiting lecturer or bishop, by either one of the three great coaches, *The Dispatch* or *The Telegraph* or *The Good Intent*, they gathered—the women in shawls and bonnets, the men in high beaver hats and capes—in the inn yard. Horn blowing and great wheels thundering over the cobbles, passengers waving and coachman reining his horses, the big yellow body of the coach with its painted paneled doors swerved into the yard scattering dogs, children, chickens and waiting hosts and hostesses, out of its swaying path. Later at dinner tables, at Rev. Lewis Woodson's on Liberty Street, or at "Father" John Peck's at Penn and St. Clair Streets, linen and silver shimmering in the candle light, William Lloyd Garrison who was to lecture at Temperance Hall, or Frances Wright whose shoulders whitened above her deep lace Bertha,[27] or Wendell Phillips in white stock and tie, sat before the huge pyramid of ice cream that was the usual dessert, or drank their coffee from a deep saucer still spoken of as a dish. And they heard the story of life among the stewards and stewardesses on the dozens of steam packets that tied up every day at the Monongahela wharf, of boilers bursting, and sides ripped by snags, and the grounding and sinking of packets down the Ohio, for these were new things to the visiting easterners. No doubt, then, they took their visitors to see the Monongahela wharf where

> twenty steamboats lie at the landing taking in cargo for Louisville, St. Louis, Nashville, New Orleans and intermediate ports, as the phrase goes. The whole of our broad levee, from the bridge to Ferry Street, is closely dotted with drays and wagons, hurrying to the margin of the river from every point of access, burdened with the valuable products of our factories or with eastern goods. Some half dozen of the steamers are puff-puff-puffing away ready to start. The margin of the wharf is absolutely covered to the height of a man

26. A "tumbrel" is a two-wheeled cart that can be tilted to dump a load.
27. "Bertha" is a wide round collar covering the shoulders.

with freight in all its varieties; higher up on the streets and foot walks, the fronts of the great forwarding horses are blocked up by piles of boxes, bales and barrels, in beautiful disorder. Shippers, porters, draymen, and steamboat clerks blend their hurried voices at once; one is actually deafened with the cheerful din and rush of business. Verily the scene is a pleasant one—to all of whom business has a charm.

If Bishop Brown was a house guest or Theodore Weld, or Lucy Stone, or Abbey Foster, no doubt the dinner talk would be of that strange new sect of Mormons, or of the Millerites and their predictions of the end of the world, or that powerful new force, Mesmerism, as well as the chance of slavery being abolished, and stories of the sheltering of runaways. And this would be followed by hymns and family ballads sung round the low square pianos that were becoming household objects. Family and guests would start for the lecture announced "to begin at candle lighting" or they might walk in the early evening along the promenade on the roof of the Hand Street Bridge for a view of the river. Perhaps they "took a turn out the road" where, as a paper reported,

> A few days ago we went on the Minersville Turnpike and were astonished to see the very large number of carts, two, three, four and six horse teams, constantly going and coming on that road alone; and this is only one of the many roads adjoining, as well as, boats engaged in supplying our cities and manufactories.

They might make up a theater party at Old Drury, though as early as 1833 Negroes were segregated at one side of the gallery, to see the Elder Booth in *Richard III*, or *King Lear*, or James Murdoch as *Claude Melnotte*, or Fanny Wallach, or Charlotte Cushman. If dinner or a concert was formal the ladies wore an "evening demi-toilette of white organdy, embroidered in worsted or silk, extremely elegant." Those of the pattern called "a la jardiniere" were most beautiful when wrought with silk. They presented "the effect of a brilliant parterre of the flowers of every season scattered over the organdy so that a lady wearing one of these dresses seemed to be moving amidst a little Eden." Like figures from *Godey's Lady's Book* in such costumes, and in "bonnets of rice straw such as may be worn at concerts or fêtes champetres," the "most elegant trimming of which was a bird of paradise feather," the ladies, between orations and declamations by the young men of the Theban Literary Society might sing a solo, accompanying themselves on the guitar, the fashionable instrument for ladies of the period. They danced at little cotillions in their homes, or at larger ones at the Eagle Saloon. And they attended bazaars and fairs held in church basements to buy a new altar or a communion service to purchase books and maps for the schools.

The home of Mr. and Mrs. Thomas Arthur Brown on Hazel Street was known nationwide for its hospitality and culture.[28] It was a rest for travelers, and a refuge for fugitives. Brown had been held a slave by his own relatives. Mrs. Brown had been Frances Jane Scroggins. Her grandfather had been an officer in the Revolutionary War. Her mother, Ellen Anne Scroggins, had been a slave. When Frances Jane's father died, the grandfather liberated her mother and the children, but cast them adrift into the world. The mother remarried and the family came north from Winchester, Virginia, in a covered wagon drawn by four black horses. The children rode on a layer of feather beds and were covered with patchwork quilts. Day after day their little caravan wound up and down the mountain roads. At night they stopped, built a fire and ate from a well-filled hamper which the mother had packed. Often they were held up for hours by the patrol while their "free papers" were examined and certified. They settled finally in Cincinnati, and when Frances Jane grew to womanhood she married Thomas Arthur Brown of Frederick, Maryland. The Browns made their home on Hazel Street in Arthursville. They devoted themselves to educating their children and making their home a refuge for slaves escaping to Canada and a rest for travelers from the East.

Brown was a steward on a steamboat running between St. Louis and New Orleans. On one trip the boiler of the steamer burst, the boat sank, and 600 people were drowned. Brown had with him his sixteen-year old son. Weeks passed after the accident before Brown and his son appeared at the Hazel Street home unharmed, in old clothes given them by strangers. The picture of family life recorded by the daughter, Hallie Q. Brown, is a charming one of pre-Civil War culture in American homes. In the Brown home reading and music were everyday experiences. The children were educated at a select school for Negroes in Allegheny and at Avery College under George Vashon, Martin H. Freeman, and Samuel Neale. Miss Hallie Q. Brown tells how "four little books adorned the little center table in the home, the *Bible*, *Pilgrim's Progress*, Jane Porter's *Scottish Chiefs*, and Spurgeon's *Sermons*." She tells of the evenings around the fire, reading aloud from the Bible on Sundays and from *Scottish Chiefs*. Hallie Q. Brown and her brother John finished their education at Wilberforce University. Miss Brown became prominent as a temperance lecturer, writer, and as president of the National Association of Colored Women.

The Brown home was a station on the Underground Railway where fugitives found protection, food, clothing for disguises and assistance in reaching the next station on the road. A Negro family of mother and five children was once successfully hidden by Mrs. Brown from even the rest of her family. Another time a fam-

28. This material about the Brown family is repeated elsewhere in chapter 3 and chapter 4.

ily from Texas was concealed in the home for some weeks. To raise money for this family, the Browns had their pictures taken with the American flag wrapped around them.

Being a religious home, the Brown home was the scene of several events in church history. A room was set aside for visiting bishops of the African Methodist Episcopal Church, and was known in the family as the Bishop's Room. Here slept Bishop John W. Brown on his travels through Pittsburgh. Here, too, slept Bishop William Paul Quinn, the "Pioneer Bishop" of the A.M.E. Church, the first bishop to cross the Allegheny mountains to organize churches in the west.

At a meeting in this home during the general conference of the A.M.E. Church in 1852, Daniel A. Payne was elected bishop, an event said to have been the most important in the history of that church since its founding by Richard Allen in 1816. Bishop Brown in his travels from New Orleans to Canada, in the interests of practically every congregation between the two points, visited hundreds of families of fugitive slaves, and organized hundreds of literary and historical societies and mothers' clubs to bring education and culture to those who had been without such things.

A friend and co-worker of Martin Delany in Pittsburgh was John Vashon. Vashon came to Pittsburgh with his wife and son in 1829 from Carlisle, Pennsylvania, where he had kept a large livery stable and a "public saloon" that was popular with Dickinson College students. John B. Vashon was born in 1792 at Norfolk, Virginia. His mother was a mulatto, his father Capt. George Vashon, a white man of French ancestry, an Indian agent under President Van Buren. Vashon, at twenty, served in the war of 1812 as a common seaman aboard the *Revenge*, cruising among the West Indies and along the coast of South America. Off the coast of Brazil he was made prisoner, exchanged, returned to Virginia and served with the land forces when Negroes were called to prevent the British fleet from ascending the Potomac. In Carlisle, with his friend John Peck, he initiated the formation of a mutual improvement association known as the Lay Benevolent Society. A man of thirty-seven when he arrived in Pittsburgh, he engaged in every progressive movement of the time. For a livelihood he opened a barber shop and public baths, the first public baths for ladies west of the mountains. A city directory prints what is perhaps the first public advertisement for a Negro business in Pittsburgh:

> CITY BATHS
> The subscriber respectfully informs the citizens of Pittsburgh, and strangers visiting here, that his Warm, Cold, and Shower baths, for Ladies and Gentlemen, Nos. 37 and 39, Third Street, between Market and Ferry, having undergone thorough repairs, and being

brilliantly illuminated with Gas Lights, are now open for the season, every day, (Sunday excepted,) from 6 o'clock, A.M., to 11 o'clock, P.M. The subscriber feels grateful for the patronage so liberally bestowed upon him by the public, and will spare no pains to merit a continuance of its favors.

J. B. Vashon

John Vashon's son, George Boyer Vashon, grew to manhood in the Pittsburgh of abolition, antislavery, and the underground railway.

On April 13, 1841, J. A. Thome, of Oberlin College, wrote to the noted abolitionist Theodore Weld:

Mr. Vashon of Pittsburgh (whom you know I presume) has a son of considerable promise. He is now in the Freshman Class and one of the best minds in the class. He is quite a youth—perhaps 18. I hope in process of time to see one or more of our professorships filled with colored men, amply qualified. Such a thing could not fail to exert a very happy and extensive influence. The thought has but lately occurred to me, and though I have never before suggested it to anyone, I fondly cherish the anticipation of one day realizing it.

George Vashon graduated from Oberlin in 1844 with honors and then spent a year in the theological seminary. The degree of Master of Arts was conferred upon him in 1849. For three years he taught with Charles L. Reason and William G. Allen at New York Central College, established by the abolitionists at McGrawville, N.Y. He studied law in Pittsburgh with Walter Forward, at that time a judge, and later Secretary of the Treasury of the United States. On Jan. 17, 1847, the *Gazette* reported:

New York correspondent of the *Philadelphia Enquirer* says: "For the first time in the history of the United States, a colored man was yesterday admitted after due examination, as Atty. Solicitor and Counselor of the Supreme Court of this State. On his examination he evinced a perfect knowledge of the rudiments of the law, had a familiar acquaintance with Coke, Littlejohn, Blackstone, and Kent.

Geo. Vashon, (his name) does not, however, intend to practice his profession here; he merely took out his credentials from our Courts, and intends to practice at the Cap Haïtien, where they will act as a powerful letter of recommendation, and where he can plead without being sneered at.

Mr. Vashon was born and studied his profession in Pittsburgh, his father is a very respectable, intelligent and industrious Colored man, and one who spared no pains or expenses in educating and preparing his son for the legal profession.

The education of young Mr. Vashon was of the most liberal character—such as to draw from his Professors encomiums of praise. His qualifications for legal proficiency were certified to by our most eminent and erudite lawyers. Yet under the present constitution and organization of our Courts, he could not be permitted to pursue the line of life for which he had labored so assiduously to prepare himself. New York has extended the courtesy due to his merit, regardless of the complexion of the applicant.

Shortly after this notice appeared George Vashon sailed for Port-au-Prince, Haiti, where he taught for three years at College Faustin. On his return to the United States he practiced law at Syracuse until he came to Pittsburgh as principal of the one school for Negro children in the city. He contributed poems to various periodicals. He was, according to Martin Delany, "a ripe scholar, an accomplished essayist, a chaste classic poet." He was devoted to Byron, whom he always referred to by his full name, George Gordon Noel Byron. In *Autographs For Freedom*, an abolitionist annual which was edited in 1853 and 1854 by Julia Griffiths, secretary of the Rochester Ladies Antislavery Society, appeared George Vashon's best poem, "Vincent Ogé."[29]

Of this poem Benjamin Brawley says "It shows the author attempting a more ambitious theme than had been used by any American Negro before him, and as having a genuine sense of poetic values. He does not give a straight forward narrative, but uses the rhythmic, discursive, and frequently subjective manner of Byron and Scott, sometimes with surprising effect." Ogé's story has been told by Wendell Phillips in his Oration on Toussaint L'Ouverture. Ogé was a Haitian mulatto, educated in France. In 1791 he took part in the Haitian revolt as a leader of the mulattoes who for years had held a position on the island analogous in part to that of the white slave owners and in part to that of the black peasants. Although they held property, they could not vote. Moreover, they were subjected to special taxes and suffered other indignities of civic and social life.

During the French Revolution of 1789 they sent the revolutionary government a gift of 6,000,000 francs, pledged to contribute to the payment of the national debt one fifth of their income, and asked that all forms of proscription be removed from them. Ogé, a friend of Lafayette, carried back to Haiti the gratitude of the National Convention and a decree of democracy for the inhabitants. The General Assembly of Haiti refused the decree. Ogé was broken on the wheel, drawn and quartered, and the four parts of his body hung in four leading cities of

29. See appendix 3 for the text of two of Vashon's poems, "Vincent Ogé" and "A Life Day."

the island. This was a "prelude to the exploits of Toussaint L'Ouverture." Vashon's work is to be considered with that of the group of Negro poets writing about the middle of the 19th century—James M. Whitfield, James Madison Bell, Charles L. Reason—as precursors of contemporary Negro poets. His other best known poem, "A Life Day," was published in *The Semi-Centenary and the Retrospection of the African Methodist Episcopal Church*, by Daniel A. Payne, published in 1860. In the school in which George Vashon taught in Pittsburgh, Susan P. Smith also taught. The two were married in 1857.

Susan Paul Smith was the daughter of Elijah W. Smith, a famous musical composer and cornetist in the years before the Civil War, who played a command performance for Queen Victoria at Windsor Castle in 1850. Her mother was Ann Paul Smith, daughter of the pastor and founder of the old Joy Street Church, Boston, where the American Antislavery Society found the only available refuge in which to organize. Susan Paul Smith graduated from Miss O'Mears' Seminary at Somerville, Massachusetts. She was the only Negro student in her class and graduated with valedictorian honor. She came at once to Pittsburgh to live with her father and to teach. In Pittsburgh, Susan Smith, then Mrs. George B. Vashon, was active in the direction of sanitary relief bazaars that raised several thousand dollars for the care of sick and wounded soldiers in the Civil War and for housing Negro refugees at Pittsburgh. She was from 1872-1880 principal of Thaddeus Stevens School in Washington, D.C.

CHAPTER 4

ABOLITION YEARS

Retyped by: Sheves / Rewriteman: J. Ernest Wright /
July 13, 1939 / Prefinal
Typist: T. Doloughty / Rewriteman: J. Ernest Wright /
August 6, 1940 / Final

As the frontier passed to Kentucky and Illinois, it left behind a town rapidly becoming big, dirty, recognized, and industrialized. The next fifty years were dramatic with the growth of industry and the problems attending it. In the history of the Negro in Pittsburgh, these years were the heroic age, an age in which democracy-loving citizens joined to protect individual freedom against the growing paternalism of industry, to maintain the democratic traditions of the frontier against the encroachment of financial and manufacturing interests, and finally to maintain the unity of the Republic itself that was threatened by the insurrection of southern slave-owning planters against the industrial expansion of the North.

The town at the forks of the Ohio became a net which caught numbers of people moving westward, some from New York down the Allegheny valley, others across the Allegheny mountains by the old Forbes Road, still others up the Monongahela valley, or from the National Pike by way of Uniontown. Iron forges and foundries gave work to hundreds of these westward travelers who settled here. Boat building and shipbuilding also gave occupations to many. Cotton mills and woolen mills spun and wove the products of southern plantations which came northward by way of the Mississippi and Ohio Rivers.

Frontier days were recent enough that their tradition of independence and freedom had not died. As Pittsburgh lay near the line that marked off freedom from slavery, movements and organizations to aid the fugitive slaves became strong here. Many of the early settlers had come westward to escape taxes, or the stigma of having been indentured servants, or mortgages which had taken their properties, or burdens which had bound them to the rising business and financial interests of Philadelphia, New York, and New England. They had developed a frontier democracy and had defended it in war against the French and Indians. They had helped to establish it in the Revolutionary War by the heroic march of the Tenth Pennsylvania regiment over winter-bound mountains. As the Whiskey Rebels, they tried to maintain it against Hamiltonian encroachment. Jeffersonian democracy found many supporters in Pittsburgh. In the War of 1812, they sent men, boats, and ammunition to Lake Erie for Perry and his men to complete the independence won in the Revolutionary War. Jacksonian Democracy was also strong here. The years between 1820 and 1865 continued the tradition of struggle for human liberty and came to a climax in the freeing of a whole people and in the emergence of the American Negro as another national group.

As the town and its industries grew, and eastern capital was invested, Pittsburgh shared the problems of other towns. Houses became old and crowded. Rents rose. In the rush and pressure of such growth, many people were concerned not only with the preservation of the early freedom and advantages for which they had come here, but with the extension of them. They wanted to fill out and enrich their own lives and the lives of their children. They wanted better houses, better food, better clothing than the frontier had afforded them. They needed easier and quicker ways to travel, streets lighted at night, and safety from rascals and thieves. They wanted a good water supply. They wanted an end to epidemics and panics. They needed more schools and churches. They wanted more leisure and health, more books, more music, more sports and recreation to make their leisure happy and enlightened. They wanted every opportunity for free, healthy, and happy development of a community growing too rapidly to solve its problems in comfort.

The early decades of the nineteenth century were energetic years with the promotion of just this kind of life in the terms of that era: religious revivals, temperance reform, women's suffrage and antislavery conventions, and demands for free public schools. It was a time when working people tried to shorten their long working days, and to raise the wages of girls and women in the textile mills beyond fifty cents a day. It was at a time when men sought to remove property restrictions from the right to vote so that they might have something to say in running of their town, state, or country. These were years when cities were compelled to find ways of dealing with the sick and destitute, with criminals, and with other unfortunates who multiplied as a dense, industrial population developed. Social justice and progress were discussed from lecture platforms and pulpits, in newspapers and magazines. Penny newspapers made their appearance. Clubs, lyceums, and institutions debated issues and planned a more stable and happy world.

Many Pittsburghers felt themselves in agreement on questions of human dignity and rights. In a nation as young as theirs, ways must be assured for all people to move forward together. If part of the people remained uneducated, deprived of health, and of sufficient wages to keep them in health, they retarded progress. If—worse than this—large numbers were kept in lifetime bondage from which they could only escape by flight, then the freedom and progress for which the frontier had been settled was still unattained. No nation could be free so long as one part of it was slave. Freedom was indivisible.

Such sentiments and the closeness of Pittsburgh to the Mason-Dixon line made the city a refuge to Negroes escaping from plantations and chattel slavery heading for Canada and the North Star. Many settled here. Free Negroes also came north, and a number came from the East to a town that still represented the individual freedom of the frontier. There had been a natural growth of the families who had settled in town when it was little more than a cluster of huts around Fort Pitt, and also a similar growth of families of freed slaves in the district.

As the slave owners won victory after victory, the opponents of slavery organized resistance. The Missouri Compromise of 1820, the Fugitive Slave Law of 1850, and the Kansas-Nebraska Bill of 1854 agitated Pittsburgh as they did most cities. The result of these laws was the intensification of every activity that would wipe out the division between the industrial North and the plantation South. Colonization, antislavery, and abolition societies sprang up over night, newspapers were bought up and edited in the interests of the Negro people, slave and free. In their interests, newspapers and magazines were founded by Negro and white editors. Pamphlets were written and published; lecture campaigns were organized.

Pittsburgh came more and more to share the attitude of the industrial North on the question of slavery. Its manufactories, expanding at dramatic pace, needed free labor in the advancing geographic frontier and a unified national economy for which the abolition of slavery was necessary. Each victory of the southern planters to establish slavery in that frontier met more vehement opposition. Every issue of the times was hotly contested—the national bank, the tariff, and ideas of secession. Abolition or antislavery became the banner around which all democratic forces rallied.

In the early years of the movement against slavery the issues were not always clear. Lines dividing colonization from abolition wavered and were often erased, so that at different times different conceptions of each were expressed. But all parties were represented in Pittsburgh and made the city lively with their arguments and activities. Gradually the manufacturing interests became the radical antislavery group. The middle ground was represented by the farmers and the city middle class. The status quo was upheld by the extremely conservative, if not reactionary, commercial and banking interests. There was, at first, an inherited prejudice to be overcome in a community that had been tolerant of slavery for some years. There was the natural inertia of a large group to be broken down, so that Pittsburgh did not become preponderantly hostile to slavery until the Fugitive Slave Law was passed. Slaves were held in the Pittsburgh region, more particularly in the counties to the southwest of the city, until almost the mid-century. In 1833 when slavery was becoming a contested issue, a State Senatorial Investigating Committee reported that the practice of holding grandchildren of slaves was continuing in the region, and that in the country bordering Virginia, numbers of blacks were brought in who had been emancipated on the condition that they serve a certain number of years, usually seven.

The preponderance of public opinion in the district was at first in favor of colonization and against abolition. Colonization proved itself unsound. In 1819, Congress passed a law providing for the return of smuggled slaves to Africa. Thomas Jefferson, Francis Scott Key, Daniel Webster, and Henry Clay favored the colonization of free Negroes with their own consent. But in spite of the favor of these men, and of President Monroe's cooperation with the American Colonization Society in the fifty years during which such attempts were made, only twelve thousand Negroes were sent to Africa. There were reasons for this. Among American Negroes a national life had already begun to take form. America had become the fatherland of thousands of Negroes. They had been born on its soil, spoke its language, and learned its customs.

Colonization was first put forward as a solution of slavery by romantic, philanthropic whites. News of the formation of the first societies spread panic among northern Negroes. They believed they were to be forcibly exported to Africa. Hundreds fled to Canada. However, most of them stood fast, declaring that with the support of white sympathizers they would resist. Negro leaders in Pittsburgh and their followers stood with the three thousand Negroes of Philadelphia who were determined never to separate themselves from the slave population. More and more it was felt that adjustment of the two races must take place here. Frederick Douglass and William Lloyd Garrison opposed the idea of colonization, as later did Booker T. Washington. Those who believed in the idea, nevertheless, continued to organize societies.

The first such organization in Pittsburgh must have died out, for six years after the meeting at the First Presbyterian Church, a meeting was called on Independence day, 1832, at the Reform Presbyterian Church to revive the Pittsburgh

Colonization Society. In May, 1835, an auxiliary society to the Young Men's State Colonization Society was formed. By 1838, more than twenty colonization societies had been established in the Pittsburgh region.

While the colonizers were raising funds and sending willing free Negroes back to Africa, the abolitionists had made their appearance. The name was originally supplied to those who sought to end slavery by orderly persuasion and education under constitutional laws. Seven months after the formation of the American Abolition Society in Philadelphia, the first branch west of the Allegheny Mountains was formed near Pittsburgh in Washington County on July 15, 1834. The following year, an agent from Philadelphia came into Allegheny County.

More radical than either the colonization or the abolition societies were the antislavery societies begun by William Lloyd Garrison. In the mid-thirties, these had spread throughout western Pennsylvania. The first antislavery society was formed at the home of John Vashon at Wood and Third Streets in 1833. In Dr. Williams' Baptist Church, July 1835, the society held a large meeting. The antislavery people became much more aggressive than the colonizers. Opposition became violent between the two groups. Both sides continued to hold meetings to discuss the subject before the community in the public halls of the city, in the churches, and in the classrooms of the university. Colonizers considered the antislavery forces to be too violent, intemperate, and alarming. Abolitionists opposed their aggressive actions, hoping to conciliate the southerners and believing that slavery, where it already existed, should not be interfered with under the Constitution. The abolitionists were called dangerous, visionary, and unconstitutional by the colonizers. The antislavery forces, however, laughed at the weakness and inefficiency of the colonizers. While the lines between abolitionism, antislavery, and colonization were not clear cut, the issue of slavery became more and more acute. From the 1840's on, the colonizationists lost ground. Antislavery sentiment, though it had developed later than the colonization schemes and was at first feeble and incoherent, strengthened as the middle of the century approached. The majority of Pittsburghers were not ardent adherents of either colonization or abolition. Abolition had by the 1850's become the pivotal issue about which the progressive forces of that day centered their activities. It was but one phase of general progress. The majority of whites who supported the movement supported it not merely to free southern Negroes. Conservatives who upheld the status quo saw that abolition was not the only issue. They understood the far-reaching effects on society as a whole, just as today southern bourbons see that anti-lynching activity, if successful, leads to the demand for unrestricted use of the ballot and the right of Negroes to sit on southern juries. Opponents of abolition saw the same trends from 1830 on. The unity of Negroes and whites in Pittsburgh during the abolition years came about because abolition was the banner of those forces, which as election followed, inscribed on that banner their further demands. By the time of the Fremont campaign in 1856, the demands were "free speech, free press, free men, free soil, Fremont."

Education of the public and agitation for reforms were carried on by all possible means. In October, 1838, a convention of all antislavery societies of the Pittsburgh region was held in the city. The following January, a number of smaller societies in Pittsburgh and Allegheny combined to form the Union Antislavery Society. Pamphlets were issued, magazines published, funds collected, and delegates sent to conventions in other cities. To the twenty conventions held in Philadelphia between 1794 and 1829, Pittsburgh always sent delegates. No means was left unused to promote abolition and its related issues.

The press took sides. In May 1837, antislavery forces bought *The Christian Witness* and converted it into an organ for the movement. *The Presbyterian Advocate*, *The Daily American*, and *The Pittsburgh Visitor* were also organs of abolition. On the other hand, the papers of the then Democratic Party generally favored no interference with slavery. When Rev. Lovejoy, an outstanding abolitionist, was murdered in Ohio by a pro-slavery mob, the *Pittsburgh Manufacturer* upheld the actions of the mob. *The Biblical Repertory* (April, 1836) published a scriptural defense of slavery and later issued the article in pamphlet form. But *The Gazette* refused to publish an advertisement for a runaway slave in January of 1837.

Public meetings more and more frequently passed resolutions protesting the extension of slavery. They also called for slavery's complete abolition in states where it already existed, denounced the Wilmot Proviso, the Compromise of 1850, and the Fugitive Slave Law, declared no slaves would be returned from the city, and warned against the passage of the Kansas-Nebraska Bill.

Frequently meetings were disrupted by pro-slavery forces. Often abolitionist speakers were heckled by colonization proponents. When Rev. J. Blanchard, late in 1837, lectured on abolition, the pro-slavery forces attempted to break up the meeting. When C. C. Burleigh, editor of *The Christian Witness*, addressed a meeting in Dr. Robert Bruce's church, disrupters hurled stones and other missiles.

The Methodist Church, which had at first attacked slavery in 1836, took the attitude of saying nothing about it. The Baptists adopted a similar attitude. In 1848, the Methodists split over the issue into a Northern and a Southern Church.

Many instances of fugitives are recorded, also many instances of kidnapings and attempts to restore so-called runaways to false owners. In January 1847, in Allegheny, several white men from Virginia attempted to kidnap a Negro man named Briscoe. They were helped by the police, but Briscoe, with the aid of friends, escaped. In April, another Negro, Daniel Lockhart, was arrested by three men from Winchester, one his alleged owner, Lloyd Logan. But Lockhart, too, was rescued by his Negro friends and escaped to Canada. The alleged owner also was arrested but was released by Judge Lowrie. This same month a traveler was passing through Pittsburgh with four slaves. Negroes and whites together rescued three of the four and set them free.

This year, 1847, was a year of great activity, no doubt spurred by the visits and speeches of Frederick Douglass, William Lloyd Garrison, and other antislavery speakers. At Temperance Hall, Douglass spoke for several days in the interest of antislavery and temperance societies. In November in Pittsburgh, the Circuit Court of the United States, presided over by justices R. C. Grier and Thomas Irwin, tried one of the most famous cases in the country, that of Garett Van Metre of Virginia vs. Dr. Robert Mitchell of Indiana, Pennsylvania. Dr. Mitchell had harbored and employed a fugitive on his farm. Van Metre was suing under the law of 1793 for a debt of five hundred dollars. The judge strongly charged the jury in favor of the plaintiff, and verdict was returned in his favor. So intense was the interest that the courtroom was crowded to suffocation. A protest meeting was held in Temperance Hall, a committee appointed to collect the facts in the case and funds raised to carry it to the Supreme Court of the United States. *The Saturday Evening Visitor* said of the case:

> Judge Grier has given it as his deliberate opinion that common acts of charity—the simple acts of benevolence in supplying the wants of the destitute, are criminal acts. . . . What was proven against Dr. Mitchell, was that some fugitives had taken shelter in a cabin on his lands not that he had brought them there or sent for them to come, but finding them within his old waste cabin, he allowed them to remain, and 'furnished them with some necessaries' . . . We would like to know if there is a farmer in Allegheny County, or any other county, who would turn a set of wanderers out of a useless cabin, or refuse them food, if they behaved civilly. . . .

A year later the case was again tried here in the United States court and a verdict of fifty dollars and costs returned in favor of the plaintiff.

In January 1848, a southern business man had stopped at the Merchant's Hotel. He had with him two slave women. One of these was persuaded by members of the antislavery societies to escape. In July of the same year, a slave who had escaped from Virginia and married and made his home here was victimized by one of those Negroes, not unknown to the city, who were professional slave catchers. The fugitive in this case was asked to accompany the unsuspected catcher on a buggy ride. They were met by the master and some friends who took him prisoner. He struggled and fought until a crowd collected and freed him.

The master was told slave holders should know better than to bring slaves to Pittsburgh. These cases preceded the passage of the Fugitive Slave Law.

In the autumn following the passage of the Fugitive Slave Law, Pittsburgh Negroes who had escaped from slave masters were panic stricken lest they be reclaimed and sent back to bondage. A number were seized and hurried South. Many left in squads for Canada. In September, thirty-five who had lived in the Third Ward in Allegheny left in one group. Within the month, several hundred had left and scores of others were preparing to leave.

The Commercial Journal for January 16, 1851, reports:

FIRST FUGITIVE SLAVE CASE IN PITTSBURGH

Day before yesterday a Mr. Rose arrived here from Wellsburg, recognized a mulatto boy, an apprentice for the last two years to Mr. J. B. Vashon, as his slave and claimed him. Rather than consign the child to bondage, Mr. V., with a fidelity to his principles which does him honor, by means of his own and the contributions of others, paid the owner $200 and the boy is now free.

Apparently the first case to be tried under the law was that of Woodson in March 1851. Woodson, it was claimed, had escaped two years before from the ownership of Mrs. Byers of Kentucky. Witnesses testified that Woodson's name was Gardener and that he had lived here three years. Woodson lost the case and was ordered kept in irons until returned to his owner. A movement was organized to rescue him, but it failed. Woodson had been preaching at Beaver for two years. There he had built a home and also employed himself as a mechanic. He was decoyed to a steamboat landing, seized, put into a small boat, taken out to the middle of the river and put aboard a steamer. At Beaver and in Pittsburgh subscriptions were raised for his purchase. He was finally purchased and returned to his family.

Another case was that of James Wright, who had lived for nine years in Penn Township. He was employed on a steamboat on which his wife was chambermaid. In June 1854, while the steamboat was at New Orleans, Wright was captured by a man who claimed that he was Wright's master and that Wright had escaped twelve years before. He was sold to a Cuban. In September 1854, *the Post* recounted the following story:

Rescue of Alleged Slaves in Allegheny.—A colored woman and four children, said to be slaves, were rescued from their alleged owner yesterday as they were about to start for the West on an express train. A number of persons suspecting them of being slaves sent a waiter (from Allegheny House where they were having dinner) to ascertain their status and made plans to aid them should they be slaves. The woman at first denied, then admitted that she and her children were slaves, but pointed out that their master was taking them west to a free state where they would be given their freedom. Accordingly the waiter passed the word and a number of colored people took charge of the woman and her children despite her entreaties that they be left in the care of the master. Although the master pleaded that they were to be set free the crowd placed no faith in his remarks. There was no disturbance.

On the following day *The Post* related that the gentlemen escorting the women and four children sent word from Cleveland that if they still desired to go with him he would meet them in Cleveland. He stated that they were free by the will of their master and he sent back free papers for the whole family. He said further that he would escort them either to Liberia or Wisconsin as they wished and he would furnish them with $300.

A few days later the *Post* carried an editorial on "the scoundrelism of some pretended philanthropists"—referring to those aiding in the abduction of the above slave and her children. "Our citizens have burdens heavy enough, and taxes large enough without any increases by such a base act as kidnaping free people, and turning them penniless upon the community for support."

Tension and excitement over fugitives grew to great heights and sometimes discharged itself at the wrong target. The Slaymaker Case is an instance. In March 1855 when Colonel Slaymaker's wife was visiting Pittsburgh she was accompanied by Caroline Cooper, a free Negro servant. *The Post* gave an account of what happened:

> A report circulated among the directors of the "Underground Railroad" at this place, that she was a slave traveling in company with her mistress; a delegation of their agents was instructed to spirit her away. Yesterday morning, about 6 o'clock, while she was at breakfast, a crowd of some half a dozen Negroes, headed by a barber named L. Davis, rushed into the room, and, despite her repeated assertions that she was a free woman, seized and carried her off forcibly, using considerable violence in so doing. Disregarding her shrieks, the mob forced her along 3rd Street to Wood Street, where she was secreted. A short time later, one of the proprietors of the City Hotel, went to Dr. Delany, a prominent colored citizen (who is a Director or Conductor on the U. G. R. R.) and by representing to him that the woman was actually free, and never had been a slave, succeeded, through his influence, in having her returned to the hotel.

The *Gazette* gives further details of this story:

After Dr. Delany had examined the documents in Mayor Volz' office he declared that the woman should be set free. Accompanied by officer Frost, he then proceeded to a house near the head of Webster Street, where ten or twelve colored persons were assembled; a consultation was held and the papers examined, when it was decided that the woman should be returned. The party then started down and got the woman from a house somewhere near the intersection of Cherry Alley and Strawberry Alley. Frost was not permitted to go to the house. The woman was then conducted back to the City Hotel and delivered into the charge of Mr. Slaymaker. Dr. Delany furnished Mr. S. with a certificate addressed to "*The Friends of Liberty*," in which he, President of an association or club, (the name, we did not get) declared the woman was free.

It was Mayor Volz who had talked with Dr. Delany. The hotel was exonerated and the headwaiters discharged.

A lengthy letter from a correspondent in the *Daily Dispatch* a few days later provides an interesting first-hand document on the mood and temper of the city population in such crises:

> The Negroes of Pittsburgh—Messrs. Editors: Much has been said of the intolerable and daring insolence of the Negroes of Pittsburgh, in their attempt to liberate a woman whom they supposed to be a slave, in the possession of a Mr. Slaymaker, passing through on his way West; that he (Mr. S.) was knocked down, and the woman taken away in despite of all "entreaties." After a through inquiry into the matter, it was found to be false; in fact, Mr. Slaymaker did not receive a blow from anyone. That the Negroes active in this transaction did pursue a course highly imprudent, if we are to judge from the tone even of those papers which have spoken most moderately on the subject, is much regretted by a large portion of the colored citizens. Without adding falsehood and high coloring to the matter, Mr. Slaymaker in company with a Mr. Sproul, from Maryland, stopped at the City Hotel. The latter gentleman had with him a slave, who was anxious to avail himself of the advantages of the law in this State. This he made known to some friend. The master by some means, thought "things were working," and gave them the slip, which gave rise to the investigation in regard to Mr. Slaymaker's woman. I cannot expect space in your paper to correct the various statements on the subject, but I wish to notice the base, insidious, and sinister attacks on the part of *The Post* and *Union*—their attempt to create political capital by a thrust at the friends of liberty. *The Union* editor, after a mighty charge on the fanaticism of his own race, pours out a tirade of abuse on the Negroes of Pittsburgh, who he says, black boots for their victuals and clothes, and have

their loathsome haunts in Coal Lane. Does the gentleman not know that *there are not three colored families residing in Coal Lane*, and that the only loathsome haunt was a noted one, kept by one of his own race? But *The Union* gives another demonstration, in the case of the Hon. Lynn Boyd, of Kentucky. In this case a strenuous effort is made to array the German and Irish population against the Negroes. The editor seems almost to advise them to mob violence.

Next comes *The Post* with a tissue of falsehoods almost from beginning to end of its two articles especially that referring to an attack on Mr. Boyd, by a mob of infuriated Negroes. There was no mob—there was not even an assemblage of Negroes, either at the St. Charles or at the wharf; nor was Captain Kleinfelter seen by anyone on the stage plank with revolver in hand; nor was there need for such a course on his part, for there were no Negroes to shoot, neither are there any such things in existence as secret oath bound societies for purposes of rescue among them. I flatter myself so much to say that if there were any such I would know of it. I solemnly vow that I know of no such thing in existence. But this editor has his design—the Negroes of Pittsburgh have no press and very few can write for the press, or have their articles published when they do write. Like his contemporary, he aims to create capital, increase hate, and array another large portion of citizens against the blacks; consequently an appeal is made to the commercial interests of the city. Is anyone so blind as not to see the design on the part of those men? We put it to those editors and defy them to prove, by two reasonable witnesses in the city, that there was anything like the appearance of a mob at the St. Charles Hotel or at the wharf.

Reports of the arrival of slave catchers caused great excitement not only among the Negro people but among white abolitionists as well. So determined were joint groups of Negroes and whites that no slave catcher should succeed in the community that guests arriving without clear identification were sometimes suspected. One evening in July 1855, two runaway slaves reached the city. The next morning a stranger arrived at the Monongahela House. In most of the churches the day before ministers had announced the presence in the city of slave catchers. Negro and white abolitionists called meetings. A committee was appointed to call upon the stranger. He proved to be H. B. Northrup, widely known antislavery advocate of New York and rescuer of Solomon Northrup, author of *Twelve Years of Slavery*. Northrup said that it was mortifying to him, who had spent so many years in the cause of antislavery, to be considered a slave catcher. But, he said, at least Pittsburgh is on the right side of the question.

This same year, 1855, Linn Boyd of Kentucky, and late Speaker of the House

of Representatives, with his wife and a Negro nurse had come to the city for a
three-day stay at the St. Charles Hotel. At breakfast the hotel servants surrounded their table to carry off the nurse. A number of people prevented them.
Boyd decided to leave the city at once by steamboat. On the way to the wharf, he
was followed by a crowd of "exasperated Negroes" who tried to complete the rescue. Policemen beat them back. A struggle followed, but the girl was carried to
the "Pennsylvania." At the gangplank, a group of Negro and white abolitionists
attempted to rush the boat but Captain Kleinfelter, with a revolver, held them off.
The papers declared that this attempt "for boldness and success has never been
surpassed in Pittsburgh." The pitch of excitement to which affairs had risen is
voiced by the *Post* of March 14:

> Millions of dollars have been invested in our railroads and canals; and
> now it is proposed to invest millions more in the improvement of the Ohio
> River. The aim of this outlay is to bring through our city and State a large
> share of the travel and trade of the South and West. These efforts to increase
> our prosperity will be useless if our travelers are to be assailed by lawless
> mobs, and forced to fly from the city to escape personal violence, and prevent
> the kidnaping of what they hold as their property under the laws of their
> States.
>
> One such case of lawless violence would deter thousands from visiting
> this city. Shall our property and reputation as a community be given over to
> the control of an irresponsible mob of Negroes, who do little for the prosper-
> ity of the city themselves?
>
> That such mobs injure the business and prosperity of the city, no one can
> doubt. To call this a venal view of the case is as absurd as it would be to call
> it venal to build a railroad or improve a river, in order to attract travel and
> trade this way. We are glad to find that the editor of the *Gazette*, notwith-
> standing his strong antislavery proclivities, takes a similar view of the matter.
> No good citizen can do otherwise. The character of our city should not be
> stained, nor its business injured by Negro mobs. Its business had suffered
> severely enough from other causes in the last year, without adding the curse
> and disgrace of Negro riots.
>
> We hope that the next riot of this kind will be suppressed by the strong
> arm of the law; or be met with plenty of well charged revolvers in ready and
> resolute hands. . . . We are no friend of slavery . . . But to take a young female
> from a comfortable home and kind friends, and cast her among strangers and
> poverty and vice is no achievement of freedom.
>
> Dr. Delany comes out in a flaming proclamation in the *Dispatch* of yester-
> day, denying that the attempt to kidnap in the case of Mr. Boyd was autho-

rized by him. The Doctor is evidently delighted with the notoriety he is gaining by these riots. We take the liberty of ordering tea and toast for Dr. Delany
immediately.

The *Post* of March 12th said:

> Our city is destined to become famous—or at least notorious. Two slave
> riots within as many days is getting ahead tolerably fast. The Negroes,
> through their secret oath-bound society, appear determined to bid defiance
> to all authority, and to usurp the right to carry off any of their fellow beings
> they choose, without consulting whether it is agreeable to the parties inter-
> ested or not. Twice they have abducted free Negroes, and in this case forcibly
> attempting to run off with a person who repeatedly expressed her preference
> to be left with her master and mistress. If this procedure is to be allowed, it
> will not be safe for a colored person to travel through here, unless he is fur-
> nished with a certificate from one of the Directors of the U. G. Railroad—
> such as was given the other day, by Dr. M. R. Delany, to the Slaymaker
> woman—stating that she has privilege to travel.

The location of Pittsburgh, the intensity of feeling, and its growing Negro
population made it an active station on the underground railroad. Organized
about 1815 by friends of the slave, the railroad grew slowly from a loosely knit system of trails and hideouts into a unique network through which the abolitionists
worked well their scheme to rescue runaway slaves. It became know as the U. G.
R. R. in 1830. Passengers on the road stopped here on either of two routes branching from Uniontown. Others met the road here for the first time, having struggled
northward without the aid of the underground organization. Many struggled up
the Ohio River, and others over the hills of western Virginia and the southwestern counties of Pennsylvania. From Pittsburgh, they were guided to Cleveland or
northward along the Allegheny River to Erie, or perhaps to Sandusky, Conneaut,
or Ashtabula Harbor, all terminals of the underground railroad. From these
points, they crossed into Canada. Wheeling Creek, one of the lines through western Pennsylvania, sent up thousands of runaways to farms in northern Green
County. From here, the trail led from West Alexandria to West Middletown,
where farms furnished excellent hiding places as did also the old United Presbyterian Church.

Most popular of these shadowy trails to freedom was the road coming from
Jack's Run on the Ohio that hugged the banks of the rivulet to the headwaters of
Girty's Run. From here, the ex-slaves traversed the Evergreen Road to Bakers-
town. Hidden at Bakerstown during the day by Mrs. Mary William and Mr.
Jones, or by Thomas McElroy, the agent at Bennetts' farm station at Bakerstown,

passengers crawled into covered wagons again at night and continued north to Erie and Canada. On the roads which led through and near Pittsburgh stood many well-known houses where weary fugitives, hungry after the grueling trip and frightened at the thought of capture, huddled into cellars and wash houses to bathe, eat, and rest for next day's travel.

Famous among these stopovers was the home of Edwin Johnson, at 1408 Reedsdale Street. Johnson harbored from four to fifteen Negroes at a time.

"When officers came to investigate," says Mrs. Logan, his granddaughter, "the slaves rushed through the outside entrance of the cellar on up to the attic to hide. My grandfather said it was pathetic how they would moan, 'Oh, please save me, don't let them catch me.'"

High on the bluff, above the Monongahela River, some forty years before Duquesne University rose upon it, Dr. John Ball built a hospital. At this "sentinel on the bluff" runaway slaves found rest and food as they passed through Pittsburgh. Legend tells of a slave who staggered in one night, his hands pinioned behind his back and an iron collar around his neck. Set adrift at the headwaters of the Monongahela, he had floated on a flimsy raft down to the sandbar across the river near the point. He died at the hospital that night.

Where Darlington Road runs through Murdock Street stood the old Murdock house, razed in 1920. Here, too, in the barns and cornfields slaves were said to have found refuge.

Steeped in tradition is the Glen Gormley Inn on Route 22-30, at its junction with the Oakdale road, for here Dr. Pearce, owner of the place and a "transporter" on the Underground, lodged fugitives in his cellar. Pearce worked under the guise of a driver of sheep.

Down the Ohio River, near Aliquippa, Rev. Andrew MacDonald occupied a log manse. Runaways on the route stopped here for shelter. The granddaughter of Rev. MacDonald tells how the slaves were hidden in the cellar of the old house. Wiped out by the mills of Jones & Laughlin, the only reminder of the station is a photograph owned by the granddaughter.

Venango County gives claim to a small station, "two or three miles north of Cooperstown on the Bradleytown Road." Probably more romantic was the home on Benn Farm in Trop Township, Crawford County, on the road to Richmond. John Brown must have directed movements toward this station, for he lived in Richmond Township, now called New Richmond, twelve miles east of Meadville. There for ten years he owned and ran a tannery.

Dodging the "slave catchers" is said to have been practiced by Thomas J. Bigham, editor of the *Commercial Journal*, an antislavery paper. Bigham lived in what is now Chatham Village, Mount Washington. Legend tells how Lucinda, the

Negro nurse in the Bigham family, kept steady watch from the tower of the Bigham House, searching for runaway slaves or guarding against invasion by professional slave catchers.

Tales are told of a tunnel running from the Black Mansion owned by George Black on Western Avenue to the Allegheny River, of cellars and sub-cellars to house the runaways, of help given to Negroes by Major William Wade, industrialist, and of help for the fugitives by Thomas A. Brown.

The abolitionists, chief organizers of the underground railroad, claimed for it greater effectiveness than the colonization societies could claim for their schemes. The latter in forty years had sent less than ten thousand Negroes to Africa. In the thirty years of underground railroad activity, between 1830 and 1860, through eastern Ohio alone forty thousand fugitives were aided to reach freedom in Canada. No estimate is available for the traffic through Pittsburgh.

But the road was "kept bright" here by constant passage. Three rivers made access and egress easy. Pittsburgh's many hills were cut into deep hollows and ravines overgrown with bushes and vines. Many of the surrounding hills were still covered with tall forest trees. Abandoned coalpits and caves in the hillsides offered safe hiding. Food, clothing, and disguises were brought here at night to hidden fugitives. Many houses in the city were fitted with cellars and trap doors. In stables and barns, they were concealed under hay; in coal sheds, they were hidden in boxes and coal piles.

One of the favorite devices for delivering food to runaways was for the station owner to dress as a hunter and go out with a game bag at night. The bag, filled with provisions, didn't come back.

Raccoon-hunting aided greatly in easing the path for underground fugitives. Shadows and darkness made parties of slaves look like groups out for game. Raccoon-hunting was popular in and about Pittsburgh and seldom were these groups led back.

Stations were not always the same. As the Washington (Pennsylvania) *Reporter* says: "They were often changed. In fact any member of the Society (Abolitionists) stood ready at a moment's notice to conceal Negroes near his home at anytime."

Though there was little travel from Pittsburgh southward to abduct or entice away slaves from bondage, there were many instances, as has been noted, of rescue of slaves passing through the city in the company of their owners. But once arrived here on their road toward freedom, they were clothed, fed, sometimes armed with a compass, with a little cold meat and bread, and more often with pistols and knives. They were instructed in the use of special signals to denote arrival at farther stations. They were given passwords or messages written in symbolic phrases. They were taught the various knocks and raps to be used at friendly doors and various calls of animals to announce their arrival at farmhouses.

Toward the end of the operation of the underground railroad an understanding was arrived at with agents who were conductors on steam railroad lines leading out of the city that Negroes provided with specially initialed tickets should be accepted as passengers and not questioned unless slave catchers were known to be on the train.

Many were taken from the city under loads of hay or old furniture, rolled in carpets and rugs, and at times, even nailed in boxes. Many left the city captained by train conductors. Others went singly and disguised, men as women, women as men.

A typical instance is recounted by William Stewart, a prominent businessman of the period:

> On a Sunday morning I was just starting for church when a well-known knock touched my door. I knew at once that church for me was in another direction. I opened my door leisurely, went out and turned to the right towards the East. About a block away, there was a little covered carriage that was very much in use in Pittsburgh at that time. They were called Dearborns. When I left my own house there was a gentleman walking between the carriage and me. We did not speak to each other, but he turned down the first street. The curtains of the Dearborn were all rolled up, and no person but the driver could be seen. It was made with a double bottom, and the slave was lying flat between the upper and lower bottoms. The driver kept going on very leisurely. There was a ferry about where the Fortieth Street Bridge is. We all got on the same ferry, but the driver never exchanged words with us. He was one of our wealthiest citizens and was wearing a fine pair of false whiskers.
>
> After we crossed the river the driver drove on the tow path of the old canal. Finally the Dearborn turned on a road running across Pine Creek below Sharpsburg. There another man came out of the house. The new man took the driver's place, while the other man took another direction, no one having spoken a word since we started. The Dearborn was then driven into a lonely place in the woods, where there was a "station" provided with all manner of disguises. Provided with these, the slave was started on his way to Niagara. After leaving Pittsburgh, they were scarcely ever captured.

At the time the Kansas-Nebraska Bill was before Congress, 1854, a mass meeting was held in the Pittsburgh courthouse, presided over by the Mayor. This meeting demanded that all free soil men should arouse themselves. Resolutions denounced the bill as an outrage of public faith and honor. They denounced also the northern politician who advocated it by extending slavery as new western states were added. A month later the German people of Pittsburgh held their own meeting and vigorously denounced the bill. In March 59 clergymen of the district met in Dr. Riddle's church and signed resolutions against it.

Antislavery sentiment quickly crystallized now in Pittsburgh. The North felt that the slavery question overshadowed all others, and that it "must be settled or it would settle the Union." The breadth and intensity of the issue was shown at a Whig County Convention held in Pittsburgh in June, 1854, at which the slogan was "free men, free labor and free lands." Political notion developed rapidly. Those members of all parties who wished to see fusion on the basis of preserving a Union of "free men, free labor and free lands" began to call themselves Republicans. The *Pittsburgh Gazette* and the *Commercial Journal* called for a meeting in Pittsburgh to organize all such persons into "a Great Republican Party such as is demanded by the suffering interests of freedom." A call was sent out for a Republican State Convention which met at Pittsburgh, September 5, 1855, and represented fourteen counties. The meeting was termed a mass convention and its object was to form with representatives from other states, a national organization of Republicans. At the Republican County Convention held in Pittsburgh Courthouse on August 29, 1855, Rev. Charles Avery was elected chairman. Newspapers commented on the "solid and substantial men" who were delegates from the fifty-three of the fifty-nine districts of the County.

The State Republican Convention met as called for on September 5 in the City Hall. Newspapers declared this the most important convention ever held in Allegheny County. Spontaneously, within the next few months in all parts of the country North of the Mason and Dixon Line, Republican organizations sprang up.

On Washington's birthday, February 22, 1856, there occurred in Pittsburgh one of the most significant events in the history of the American Negro. The Republicans of the Union met in informal convention at Lafayette Hall, perfected a national organization and provided for a national delegate convention of the Republican Party at some subsequent day. This convention would nominate candidates for the Presidency and Vice-Presidency to be supported at the election in November. So was organized that political party which in its earliest stage was the champion of the freedom of a people, and which brought forward the great emancipator, Lincoln.

In the history of the Negro in Pittsburgh the abolition years were the heroic age, an age of epic struggle. Events were the result of deep lying causes. The masses along with professionals, merchants and manufacturers were caught by the fierce current that swept through the times.

Only a half century had passed since the Constitution of the United States had formulated the government of "a new nation, conceived in liberty and dedicated to the idea that all men are created equal." As the abolition movement gathered momentum, it drew into it all the issues of the day—women's rights and universal suffrage; freedom of speech, press and assembly; the rights of working men and women to organize, strike, and petition; prison reform, temperance and moral reform.

It became a great revival of the constitutional struggle "to form a more perfect union, establish justice, insure domestic tranquility, promote the general welfare, and secure the blessings of liberty" to the people and their posterity.

Pittsburgh was congenial ground for the maturing of such a movement. The democratic frontier traditions were still fresh in the minds of many who fought for the abolition of slavery. Pittsburgh lay near the slave-holding states, and it exemplified the industrialization of the North. Here men and women had erected liberty poles in protest against political and social injustices, or in celebration of rights won. When the Declaration of Independence was signed, a dozen mechanics had dragged a thirty-foot pine, stripped of its boughs, to a great hole that had been dug to receive it. With hurrahs and shouts it was set up and flying streamers attached, red, white, and blue. Bonfires were lighted. A keg of Monongahela rye, rolled by a black boy round the hill from the distillery at Suke's Run, was opened and toasts were drunk to liberty, while shots rang out from the long rifles in the hands of the men. When, about the same time, a store of the hated British Tea—two ten-gallon kegs, a box and a bag of it—was discovered at Simon & Campbell's store, it was dragged to a liberty pole and burned. The Whiskey Rebels, Scotch-Irish and Irish farmers, men with a traditional hatred of excise men, had erected a liberty pole outside *The Sign of General Butler*. From its top flew a streamer bearing defiant warning to the eastern financiers and Hamilton's Federalist policy:

> Liberty and no excise.
> Death to cowards and traitors.

Pittsburgh people knew that not only the British king and his mercantile system were their enemies, but also the eastern financiers, the eastern and southern land speculators, and the slave-driving gentry of the Virginia tidewater region. Besides these sentiments there had existed strong sympathy for the French Revolution, its watchword "Liberty, Equality, Fraternity." Men had worn the red-white-and-blue cockade and were proud to be called Jacobins. At gatherings and demonstrations they sang the "Carmagnole" and the "Ça Ira."[1] They clung passionately to the idea of liberty and freedom of the individual.

Hamiltonian Federalism did not long hold power in this "western emporium." Among the Federalists were surviving Revolutionary officers such as Colonel James O'Hara, General John Neville, Colonel Presley Neville, who had belonged to the southern gentry and who were the largest slave holders in the district. To this group also belonged two other Revolutionary officers, Major Isaac Craig and Major Ebenezer Denny, the first mayor of the city. Also in their ranks were Senator James Ross; two wealthy physicians of the town, Dr. George Stevenson, and Dr. Peter Mowry; Abner Barker, the iron merchant, Jeremiah Barker, merchant, justice of the peace and for a time burgess; and Judge Alexander Addison. But against these men a group of Jeffersonian Democrats early won power. A group of Jeffersonians who were neighbors in Clapboard Run—so named from the new type of Clapboard houses that supplanted the earlier log structures—was known popularly as the Clapboard Row Junto or the Clapbordian Democracy. The Clapboard Democrats were Dr. William Gazzam, Justice of the Peace and brigade inspector of the Allegheny County Militia; Dr. Andrew Richardson; Carlton Bates, county prothonotary, a young Virginian who lost his life in a duel; Walter Forward, who became Secretary of the Treasury under President Tyler; and Henry Baldwin, appointed by Andrew Jackson as Associate Justice of the Supreme Court of the United States. It was from these Jeffersonian Democrats, the political radicals of the time, who were called Jacobians, and Republicans, that the earliest expressions of antislavery sentiment came. In 1793 Hugh Henry Brackenridge, one of this group, had published his political satire *Modern Chivalry*. In this first book published west of the Allegheny Mountains, Brackenridge accused many of the men of the district "who for a fine cow would not have shaved their beards of a Sunday" of holding and abusing slaves. Brackenridge on a trip to Kentucky brought back to Pittsburgh and set free a Negro woman who had been kidnaped in the city and sold into slavery. In 1801, Dr. William Gazzam, another of this group, said that he "abhorred slavery and relied upon the constituted authorities to effect the very desirable object of the gradual abolition thereof."

That abolitionism was but one aspect of a world-wide striving for democracy, one phase of an international movement for the freedom of peoples, is clear. Both Negro and white abolitionists drew inspiration from the international struggle for liberty and national independence. Such incidents of the French Revolution as the Haitian revolt of 1798 stirred especially the hearts and minds of free Negroes and slaves. Toussaint L'Ouverture and Vincent Ogé were such heroic examples of struggle that importation of Negro slaves from insurrectionary areas of the West Indies was forbidden. Hundreds of refugees, however, reaching the ports of

---

1. "Carmagnole" and "Ça Ira" were two popular songs of the French Revolution.

Baltimore, Norfolk, Charleston and New Orleans carried tales of uprisings of Gabriel Prosser, Denmark Vesey and Nat Turner.

Abolitionists—Negro and white—were spiritual brothers of the Italian followers of Massini, of Bolivar in South America, of the Greeks at Missolonghi, aided by Byron to free themselves from the Turks because he could not tolerate the idea that "men were proscribed for dreaming of liberty."

Liberty and national independence were the dreams of the Irish under Wolf Tone and Daniel Emmett; of the Belgians, who won their freedom from Holland; of the Poles, who fought for liberation from Czarist Russia in the 1830's; of the German and French revolutionaries of 1830 and 1848. Pittsburgh newspapers, among reports of the improvement of the rivers, of the opening of turnpikes and first locomotives to arrive in the city, of the five leading manufacturers "who grouped themselves together to control prices and wages" and "to break up the small establishments," devoted half or more of their space to Latest Foreign News, to Foreign Intelligence, or to items headed Calcutta, Ireland, French Intelligence, or The Portuguese Insurgents. Letters and resolutions from abroad were printed in support of Abolition.

Sojourner Truth, Harriet Tubman, Nat Turner, Frederick Douglass, Elijah Lovejoy, John Brown—these Negro and white Americans inspired the American Negro in his fight for freedom as the peasant heroes of the Balkans inspired the Hungarians and Jelacic the Croats; or as Jan Keller, the Slovak poet, inspired the Slovaks to rise. These of course were national figures. Abolition in Pittsburgh produced its leaders, too, many of whom were national figures. Rev. E. Smith, who withdrew from the Methodist Church because of its reactionary stand on slavery; Dr. Julius LeMoyne, nominated on the Liberty ticket for Governor of the State, Mrs. Jane Grey Swisshelm, abolitionist editor of the *Saturday Evening Visitor;* Martin Delany, surgeon, lecturer and editor of *The Mystery*, a Negro abolitionist paper of the city; John B. Vashon, veteran of the War of 1812, whose house was attacked because of his abolitionist activities; also William Burleigh and Theodore Weld—all these performed such important labors in Pittsburgh that they became national figures.

Since the roots of the abolition movement reached deep into the economic structure, they found good ground in the industrial Pittsburgh of the half century preceding the Civil War. Civic and industrial growth raised questions of far reaching importance to the rising bankers, manufacturers and merchants—the U.S. Bank, the tariff, internal improvements, the organization of industry, issues that determined their attitudes toward abolition. This growth also raised questions of deep concern to the broad masses of the people and determined their attitude towards the abolitionists. The early settlers had moved westward to escape heavy taxes, or the stigma of having been indentured servants, or mortgages which had taken their properties, or debts which bound them to eastern financiers and business men. As growing industries developed a large class of industrial workers—men, women and children—these problems caught up with the people once more. The growing paternalism of industry, of financial and commercial interests, encroached once more upon economic security and upon social and civil liberties. Houses grew old and more crowded together. Rents and cost of living mounted. Epidemics, delinquency and crime became public problems. The townspeople wanted better houses, food, clothing, than the frontier had afforded their parents and grandparents. They needed their streets lighted at night and safety from thieves and marauders. They needed quicker and better ways of travel from town to town. They wanted an end of epidemics and panics. They needed more and better schools and churches. They wanted more enlightened leisure, more books, papers, music and sports. So they sought ways of dealing with all these problems of a dense industrial population. First attempts were largely sentimental and philanthropic—bible schools, trust societies, temperance and moral reform societies. In 1828, a Negro slave was stricken with smallpox and an epidemic spread. In 1832, when a Negro died of cholera—the first one of thirty people who died within sixty days—a Sanitary Board was hastily organized. But chief reliance seems to have been put in the efficacy of "a day for fasting, humiliation and prayer that God would avert the danger threatening." Social justice and progress were discussed from lecture platforms and pulpits, in newspapers and magazines. Clubs, lyceums and institutes debated issues and sought vaguely to plan a more stable and happy world. Against this background the abolition movement developed through much the same stages—sentimental and philanthropic at first, later as organized and practical, and finally as civil war.

The slavery question took on three forms—colonization, antislavery and abolition—each successive stage more aggressive that the preceding one, and in Pittsburgh each was vividly represented.

Gabriel's insurrection in 1800 brought forward concretely the idea of colonization of free Negroes in Africa. In Virginia the House of Delegates passed a resolution asking that the Governor, James Monroe, "be requested to correspond with the President of the United States [Thomas Jefferson] on the subject of purchasing land without the limits of this state, neither persons obnoxious to the laws or dangerous to the peace of society may be removed." Thomas Jefferson wrote to the U.S. Minister to Great Britain, Rufus King, asking him to determine to what extent Britain would co-operate in sending Negroes to Sierra Leone. The "American Society for Colonizing the Free People of Color of the United States" was organized on January 1, 1817. Bushrod Washington, a southerner, was president. Of the seventeen vice-presidents, twelve were southerners, and all twelve of the managers were slave holders. Within a few days of the formation of the society, a rumor that all free Negroes were to be shipped to Africa spread consternation among northern Negroes. In Philadelphia 3,000 Negroes met with James Forten presiding and declared themselves determined never to separate from the slave population of the country. The Pittsburgh Negro population was not yet large, and no record of such action exists. But Ohio and Pennsylvania became strongholds of colonization societies, whose membership was entirely white.

John M. Snowden, editor of the Pittsburgh *Mercury* defended through his paper against James Wilson, editor of the Steubenville, Ohio, *Gazette* the right of one man to enslave another. His defense brought to the paper replies from many correspondents.

On September 26, 1826 a number of citizens of the city met in the First Presbyterian Church and adopted resolutions approving the American Colonization Society. A constitution was drafted and two nights later the Pittsburgh Colonization Society was formed and adopted this constitution. Henry Baldwin, the Democratic lawyer, was chosen president. Vice presidents were Rev. Francis Herron, D.D., Pastor of the First Presbyterian Church and trustee of the Western University of Pennsylvania; Rev. Robert Bruce, pastor of the First Associate Presbyterian Church, and first Chancellor of the University; Rev. Elisha P. Swift, pastor of the Second Presbyterian Church, and professor of Moral Science at the Western University; Rev. John Black, pastor of the Reformed Presbyterian Church and professor of the Classics at the University; Rev. Charles Avery, Methodist minister, copper magnate and philanthropist; Rev. Joseph Stockton, pastor of, and the first principal of, the Pittsburgh Academy; and Walter Forward, lawyer, state representative and later Secretary of the Treasury. The officers and managers of the society were the church hierarchy and successful businessmen, rising manufacturers, land owners, editors, or holders of other influential positions, men who were not opposed to slavery. Neville B. Craig, another vice-president, was editor of the *Gazette*, which was not a liberal paper. Charles H. Israel, attorney and notary public, was elected Secretary; Mathew B. Lowrie, also an attorney and mayor of the city in 1830, was elected treasurer. Colonization schemes were not supported by the Negroes, by the working class or by whites who believed that slavery should end.

The avowed aim of the colonization societies was expatriation of free persons of color "with their consent," and the obtaining of financial aid from federal and state governments. They gave no explanation of their motives for the concerted effort to remove free Negroes from the country. It soon became clear that the object of colonization was not the emancipation of slaves, nor even the elevation and welfare of free Negroes, but ridding the country of "undesirable and degraded elements," by which was meant free Negroes who were dangerous examples of liberty to the slaves.

Article II of the constitution of the Pittsburgh society said, "the object to which its views shall be exclusively directed is the colonization on the Coast of Africa with their own consent of people of color of the United States, and this society will contribute its funds and efforts to the attainment of that object, in aid of the American Colonization Society." Similar societies were established at Washington, Pa. and at Greensburg. Both places were centers of slave holding communities.

This first Pittsburgh society apparently lived a short life, met infrequently, raised small amounts of money and died out within a few years.

The Pittsburgh *Gazette* in November, 1831 quoted from the Virginia *Petersburg Intelligencer:* "The sentiment is gaining ground in Virginia, that the whole African race ought to be removed from among us. Many people feel unwilling to die and leave their posterity exposed to all the ills which, from the existence of slavery in our state, they have themselves so long felt . . . Others are unwilling themselves longer to suffer these inconveniences—some of our best citizens are already removing, others will doubtless follow unless they can see a probability that some period the evil will be taken away."

This hysteria was the result of Denmark Vesey's attempted break for freedom; it seemed to be strongest among the "best people." A month later the *Gazette* reported that "petitions are in circulation in various portions of Virginia, praying the legislature of that state to devise some means of removal of the *free Blacks*." The *Richmond Whig* is quoted as follows: "We most earnestly call public attention to the subject and trust that the call will be responded to by every section of the state. A simultaneous movement will speedily effect, and at a small expense, comparatively, the removal of a canker on the body politic."

The question of slavery was now one that could no more be ignored than a prairie fire. Its preservation was a life and death matter for the South; its destruction equally important to the industrial economy of northern cities like Pittsburgh. The social conscience of the country became more and more restless under the realization of the thralldom of a whole people within the nation, especially in the light of the world-wide agitation for the national liberation of peoples. The example which several million free Negroes set to those in bondage was a danger, especially when the effect of that example was seen in the rise of Vesey, Sojourner Truth, Harriet Tubman and others.

Pittsburgh papers continued to give space to the agitation of nearby southern states for the expatriation of free Negroes. Early in January, 1832, the *Gazette* reprinted from a Virginia paper the resolutions of the "Committee for Free Negroes,"

Resolved: Free Negroes and mulattos should be removed from this Commonwealth.

Resolved: That as a colony Liberia presents the most favorable aspects and said Negroes and mulattos should be sent there.

Resolved: That the state should appropriate $100,000 for the transportation of said people there.

Resolved: That a board to pass on prospective emigrants should be set up.

Resolved: That as an inducement to emigrate, each emigrant shall be provided at public expense with agricultural implements, clothing and other articles.

But the 1830s was a decade of increased tension and the sharpening of all issues—political, economic, social, moral. In Pittsburgh the adherents of colonization sporadically attempted to promote the schemes of the society for a decade after more realistic and more honest attitudes had developed.

To *The Liberator*, William Lloyd Garrison's abolition paper, John B. Vashon wrote from Pittsburgh, in March, 1832:

Messers. Garrison and Knapp—

Allow me to express the high satisfaction I feel on seeing the enlargement of the *Liberator*. It affords matter for very pleasing reflection to observe this, as being an indication that inquiry is awakening in reference to the condition and rights of a people who have been long and cruelly oppressed. I would fondly hope, that in this land where Liberty is said to dwell, clothed with all her most fascinating enchantments, your noble and untiring efforts in the cause of humanity and natural rights may not be fruitless and unavailing. Why should not this land, which is an asylum for the persecuted of almost all nations, also be a sanctuary of security and repose to the wearied and depressed African? Humanity and justice can assign no sufficient reason.

Permit me, gentlemen, to say that I am impressed with sentiments of deep and lasting gratitude to you, for the able and fearless manner in which you have exposed the wickedness and moral deformity of slavery, as likewise for your views on the character and tendency of the Colonization Society. Your articles upon this subject breathe the spirit and sentiments of every colored man of any intelligence. Why establish a Society for the purpose of inducing

the African to forsake this soil which he has enriched with his labor, and wa-
tered with his tears; which the violence and rapacity of Europe and America
have made his native land? Why plunder him of his liberty, degrade his character, and then entice him into a foreign, and to him a strange land? This is
not justice. Is it mercy? You have shown the scheme to be impracticable and
delusive. No man, who takes a sober view of the question, can entertain a
doubt. But suppose the Society could attain what it is, and has been attempting, viz. the removal of the free people of color, it would then have done more
towards tightening the cords and strengthening the chains of slavery, than ten
thousand laws against freedom, sanctioned and enforced by the whip and the
gibbet. It is well known that the slave has no chance of being informed of his
natural rights, but by his intercourse with those of his color who are free; it
therefore becomes highly desirable for those who wish to see oppression
firmly established, to remove the free people of color. Thus the free African
who permits himself to be allured from his debased countrymen, gives a
bond, as far as he is concerned, that his kinsmen who are in bondage shall
continue meek and submissive as beasts of burden. Let the free colored man
reflect—let him consider deeply, before he puts the seal upon this compact—
the seal is the blood of his countrymen.

You will pardon me, gentlemen, for saying so much on this question as it
is one on which I feel the most deep and lively interest. I join with the friends
of equality and justice everywhere, in wishing that your efforts in this great
and arduous enterprise may be crowned with success.

Yours respectfully,

J. B. Vashon

In July, 1832, the Colonization Society was reorganized at a meeting in the
Reformed Presbyterian Church. Its activities for the next three years are obscure.
But in 1835 an Auxiliary Society for the Young Men's State Colonization Society
was formed. Meantime opposition to colonization had developed, not only
among Negroes, but among those whites who realized its ineffectiveness and its
real motive.

The *Pittsburgh Conference Journal*, a Methodist Church paper, in April 1835,
in a series of articles discussed the necessity of abolishing slavery and published
a set of resolutions drawn up by the Negro people of the city:

The following resolutions contain the sentiments of the free colored
people generally:

Resolved: That we, the colored people of Pittsburgh and Citizens of the
United States, view the country in which we live as our only true and proper

home. We are just as much natives here as the members of the Colonization Society—Here we were born—here bred—here is all that binds man to earth, and makes life valuable. And we do consider every colored man who allows himself to be colonized in Africa, or elsewhere, a traitor to our cause.

Resolved: That we are free men, that we are brethren, that we are countrymen and fellow-citizens, and as fully entitled to the free exercise of the elective franchise as any men who breathe; and that we demand an equal share of protection from our Federal Government with any class of citizens in the community. We now inform the Colonization Society, that should our reason forsake us, then, we may desire to remove. We will apprise them of this change in due season.

Resolved: That we, as citizens of the United States, and for the support of these resolutions, with a firm reliance on the protection of divine Providence, do mutually pledge to each other, our *lives*, our *fortunes*, and our sacred honor, not to *support* a *colony* in *Africa*, nor in *upper Canada*, nor yet to emigrate to Haiti. Here we were born, here we will live, by the help of Almighty, and here we will die, and let our bones lie with our fathers.

The Colonization Society persisted, however. Now it not only promulgated the deportation of Negroes to Africa, but it began energetically to oppose the ideas and activities of the abolitionists. In the late summer of 1835 there was held in the city a meeting of the Friends of Colonization and Opposers of Abolitionism. Among it there were now fewer ministers, but still a number of businessmen, successful lawyers and politicians. Few of the names of the members of the society appear as members of the antislavery societies that were beginning to organize. In the following spring, 1836, the *Gazette* again announced "a large meeting for the resuscitation of the Colonization Society." The call requested that "all those opposed to the dangerous and visionary measures of certain associates calling themselves Abolitionists" should meet at the Young Men's Society Hall at the corner of Fourth and Market Streets, and it was signed by the leading businessmen of the city. A later notice reported that at the meeting ten individuals and firms had pledged $100 a year to support the society. These were Neville B. Craig, S. Caldwell, W. Palmer, Wm. Bell, Jr., the firm of B.F. & J. Bakewell, the firm of Baird, Leavett & Co., Jacob Forsyth, Charles Brewer, Mrs. C. Brewer and John Kratser.

At another meeting that spring resolutions were passed which stated in part:

Resolved: That holding these opinions, and having this information, we feel ourselves bound to put forth our utmost exertion to raise forthwith, in Pittsburgh and its vicinity, the sum of $5,000, by which we shall secure the liberty of 100 slaves and afford each family a lot of ground and a Cottage in the land of their forefathers.

The above resolutions were seconded by an address by the Rev. D. H. Riddle, and further supported by Walter Forward, Esq., and M. Shotwell.

Ordered—that the proceedings of this meeting be published in all the papers friendly to the cause in this city.

On motion the meeting adjourned.
BENJAMIN BAKEWELL, Chairman.
Joseph Laughlin, Sec'y

Persons desiring of making contributions, or by giving their names for that purpose, are informed that they can do so to either member of the financial committee of the society, viz: Benjamin Bakewell, John D. Davis, Samuel Baird, and S. Colwell."

A report of the celebration of the anniversary of the Pittsburgh society was published in the *Gazette* in February, 1837. It said in part:

The Colonization meeting held in the Central Church Wednesday evening was the most interesting one we have ever attended. The addresses by Messrs. Pinney and Skinner, (both of whom had held the office of Governor of Liberia) were replete with facts, proving the wisdom and benevolence of the truly philanthropic enterprises. They were, in our minds, arguments the most cogent. The Rev. T. P. Hunt, who had emancipated all his slaves under the conviction of duty growing out of his embracing its views, forcibly illustrated both by precept and example its benign tendency at the South where it has been the means of awakening extensive sympathy and effort in behalf of the colored race.

"A Colonizationist" wrote to the *Gazette* in the Autumn of 1837:

May I inquire through your columns, how it happens, that so few of the citizens of Pittsburgh take an active interest in colonization? It is believed that throughout the mass of this intelligent community sentiment is decidedly in its favor. Why then so little combined and organized action? Knowing that there was an appointment for a meeting of the Pittsburgh Colonization Society last night at Dr. Merron's church, I attended. I confess it was with surprise that I found so thin an attendance. I write this to express a hope that a much larger meeting of the Friends of the cause will be secured so that some of those who have influence will lend their aid to give effort.

Martin R. Delany stated most forcefully why the Negro people resented and fought against the colonization schemes as having their origin in the southern mass mind and their support in the North among those people who did not want their economic security disturbed. The close parallelism between Martin Delany's paragraph and the resolution passed earlier by the Negroes of Pittsburgh suggests that Delany might have been the one who drafted the resolution for approval.

Our common country is the United States. Here we were born, here raised, and educated; here are the scenes of childhood; the pleasant associations of our school going days; the loved enjoyments of our domestic and fireside relations, and the sacred graves of departed fathers and mothers; and from here we will not be driven by any policy that may scheme against us.

We are Americans, having birthright citizenship—natural claims upon the country—claims common to all others of our fellow citizens—natural rights which may by virtue of unjust laws, be obstructed, but never can be annulled. Upon these do we place ourselves, as immovably fixed as the decrees of the living God. But according to the economy that regulates the policy of nations, upon which rests the basis of justifiable claims to all freeman's rights, it may be necessary to take another view of, and inquire into the political claims of colored men.

Delany says of the Colonization Society:

When we speak of colonization, we wish distinctly to be understood, as speaking of the "American Colonization Society"—or that which is under its influence—commenced in Richmond, Virginia, in 1817, under the influence of Mr. Henry Clay of Ky., Judge Bushrod Washington of Va., and other southern slave holders, having for their express object, as their speeches and doings all justify us in asserting in good faith, the removal of the free colored people from the land of their birth, for the security of the slaves, as property to the slave propagandists.

In his argument Delany relates a curious and striking incident:

We look upon the American Colonization Society as one of the most arrant enemies of the colored man, ever seeking to discomfit him, and envying him of every privilege that he may enjoy. We believe it to be anti-Christian in its character, and misanthropic in its pretended sympathies. Because if this were not the case, men could not be found professing morality and Christianity—as to our astonishment we have found them—who unhesitatingly say, "I know it is right"—that is in itself—"to do so and so, and I am willing and ready to do it, but only on condition that you go to Africa." Indeed, a highly talented clergyman, informed us in November last (three months ago) in the city of Philadelphia, that he was present when the Rev. Doctor J. P. Durbin, late President of Dickinson college, called on Rev. Mr. P. of B., to consult him about going to Liberia, to take charge of the literary department of an University in contemplation, when the following conversation ensued:

Mr. P.—"Doctor, I have as much and more than I can do here, in educating the youth of our own country, and preparing them for usefulness here at home."

Dr. D.—"Yes, but do as you may, you can never be elevated here."

Mr. P.—"Doctor, do you not believe that the religion of our Blessed Redeemer Jesus Christ, has morality, humanity, philanthropy, and justice enough in it to elevate us, and enable us to obtain our rights in this our own country?"

Dr. D.—"No, indeed, sir, I do not, and if you depend upon that, your hopes are in vain."

Mr. P—Turning to Doctor Durbin, looking at him solemnly, though affectionately in the face, remarked—"Well, Doctor Durbin, we both profess to be ministers of Christ; but dearly as I love the cause of my Redeemer, if for a moment I could entertain the opinion you do about Christianity, I would not serve him another hour." We do not know, as we would not serve him another hour. We do not know, as we were not advised, that the Rev. Doctor added in fine,—

"Well, you may quit now, for all your serving him will not avail against the power of the god (hydra) of Colonization."

In and around Pittsburgh, as elsewhere, there were some men who sincerely believed that colonization was the solution to a national problem, men who later became antislavery men. Among these were Dr. Julius LeMoyne and Rev. Charles Avery. Of such men Mr. Delany said:

In expressing our honest conviction of the resignedly injurious character of the Colonization Society, we should do violence to our own sense of individual justice, if we did not express the belief, that there are some honest-hearted men, who not having seen things in the proper light, favor that scheme, simply as means of elevating the colored people. Such persons, so soon as they become convinced of their error, immediately change their policy, and advocate the elevation of the colored people, anywhere and everywhere, in common with other men. Of such were the early abolitionists as before stated; and in the great and good Dr. F. J. LeMoyne, Gerrit Smith and

Rev. Charles Avery and a host of others, who were colonizationists, before espousing the cause of our elevation, here at home, and nothing but an honorable sense of justice, induces us to make these exceptions, as there are many good persons within our knowledge, whom we believe to be well wishers of the colored people, who may favor colonization.

Of Liberia and of the functioning of the colony there he says:

Liberia is not an Independent Republic: in fact, it is not an independent nation at all; but a poor miserable mockery—Colonizationists, the Colonization Board at Washington city, in the District of Columbia, being the echo— a mere parrot of Rev. Robert R. Curley, Elliot Cresson, Esq., Governor Penney, and other leaders of the Colonization scheme—to do as they bid, and say what they tell him. This we see in all of his doings.

Does he go to France and England, and enter into solemn treaties of an honorable recognition of the independence of his country; before his own nation has any knowledge of the result, this man called President, dispatches an official report to the colonizationists of the United States, asking their gracious approval? Does King Grando, or a party of fishermen besiege a village and murder some of the inhabitants, this same "President" dispatches an official report to the American Colonization Board, asking the Board, and immediately decides that war must be waged against the enemy, placing ten thousand dollars at his disposal—and war actually declared in Liberia, by virtue of the instructions of the American Colonization Society. A mockery of a government—a disgrace to the office pretended to be held—a parody on the position assumed. Liberia in Africa, is a mere dependency of southern slave holders, and American Colonizationists, and unworthy of any respectful consideration from us.

... Liberia is no place for the colored freemen of the United States; and we dismiss the subject with a single remark of caution against any advice contained in a pamphlet, which we have not seen, written by Hon. James G. Birney, in favor of Liberian emigration. Mr. Birney is like the generality of white Americans, who suppose that we are too ignorant to understand what we want, whenever they wish to get rid of us, would drive us anywhere, so that we left them. Let Mr. Birney go his way, and we will go ours. This is one of those confounded gratuities that is forced in our faces at every turn we make. We dismiss it without further comment—and with it Colonization in toto—and Mr. Birney de facto.

Under such attacks, the idea of colonization which began in the decade of the 1830's began to give way before a more direct approach to the slavery question.

The colonizers had done nothing to lessen the distress and misfortunes of the Negroes, either slave or free. They had merely tried to shunt free Negroes to Africa to get them and their problems out of the way. They had not worked to repeal oppressive laws in the free states. They had not fought the laws prohibiting manumission. They had done nothing to make slavery a more humane institution. They had made no effort to improve the economic status of free Negroes in the North, to provide education or religious instruction, to protect them from kidnaping, to defend their civil rights. They had, in fact, frequently incited violence against both Negroes and white abolitionists.

When William Lloyd Garrison began publication of *The Liberator* in 1831, John B. Vashon circulated the paper in Pittsburgh and H. C. Howells in Allegheny City. The circulation of *The Liberator* crystallized feeling that slavery was a moral evil, a sin, an injustice. People read *The Liberator* and felt the injustice of slavery, but not much was done about it for several years.

The Liberator not only rejected all colonization schemes, but opposed schemes for gradual emancipation as well. It demanded immediate abolition of slavery. A year after he began publishing his paper Garrison founded the New England Antislavery Society. This national society set up propaganda and organizational machinery, pledged to fight slavery by every means it could use. It published newspapers, issued pamphlets and leaflets, held mass meetings, toured speakers through the country, circulated petitions and to some extent instituted a boycott against products of slave labor.

The year following the organization of the national society an organization was set up in western Pennsylvania. Washington County, strong slaveholding district, organized its society in 1834. At Pittsburgh a year later, in 1835, the first antislavery society was formed at the home of John B. Vashon, at the corner of Wood & Third Streets, according to Martin Delany, who was active in the society. The earliest available record of the society is an announcement in the *Gazette* on June first of that year, that the Pittsburgh Antislavery society would meet in the Protestant Methodist Church and that Rev. Dr. Beman of New York, Professor Nevin of the Western Theological Seminary, and others would speak. This society was, no doubt, in part the result of the work of Theodore Weld, who all through the spring of that year had worked in the Pittsburgh district. Weld did more than any other person for the abolition movement in western Pennsylvania, Ohio and other western states. Weld was one of the Lane Seminary rebels. When the students at Lane Seminary, Cincinnati, had been ordered to dissolve their antislavery society in 1834 and were even forbidden to discuss slavery and the antislavery movement at dinner they withdrew from the school almost in a body and founded Oberlin College. Under the leadership of James G. Birney and Theodore Weld, they went from there "into all the world to preach the gospel."

Birney was to remain in Kentucky, organize a state antislavery society, issue an antislavery newspaper, and work with the Presbyterian Synod for the passage of antislavery resolutions. Weld was to travel through Ohio and western Pennsylvania, where he would organize antislavery societies, procure subscriptions to Birney's newspaper, and reach Pittsburgh. There, in June 1835, he made his famous "extraordinary raid" on the Presbyterian General Assembly. In the autumn and winter Weld abolitionized eastern Ohio, made a hurried trip to Vermont, and in January 1836 was back again in Pittsburgh.

The antislavery societies adopted a moderate enough attitude towards abolition. Their aim was chiefly popular education and development of abolition sentiment. The movement became a moral crusade. The instructions given by the Central Committee to "The Seventy"—these students sent out from Lane Seminary—were "to insist principally on the sin of slavery." But moderate as were these doctrines and activities, they met violent opposition, particularly from the colonizationists and from those who were opposed to interfering with slavery as the right of southerners and their concern alone. They were criticized and attacked in the press. Meetings were stoned and clubbed. Negroes who attended were thrown out of their jobs. Men were arrested and prosecuted under vandal laws for employing Negroes who attended meetings. Houses of Negro and white were attacked and torn down. In the summer following the organization of the Pittsburgh society, an antislavery meeting in Washington, Pa. was broken up by an angry crowd. A town meeting was called and it prohibited the abolitionists from holding meetings and attempting to "intrude their peculiar and offensive doctrines" upon the people of the county. In Pittsburgh, the home of John P. Vashon was attacked and the militia called out to quell the disturbance. Several Negro dwellings were attacked and torn down and two children killed. An Emancipation Day parade on the first of August was stoned, marchers beaten and twenty people were injured. A meeting hall and a church were set on fire.

Papers of the city called the agents of the societies "itinerating stirrers up of sedition." Editorials demanded that the authorities interfere, and asserted that the antislavery men had no more justification for interfering with the southern relationship of master and slave than they had for interference with the growing of cotton.

But the antislavery people carried on their work. The difficulties which they met in securing halls, protecting their meetings and parades from assault, distributing leaflets and petitions raised very acutely the question of civil liberties, liberty of speech, assembly and the press. Other organizations were formed to protect such liberties, and frequently took joint action with the antislavery groups. There were the Friends of Civil and Religious Liberty, The Liberty Association, the Human Rights Association, the Preachers' Antislavery Society, and others.

James G. Birney said,

> It is as much as all the patriotism of our country can do to keep alive the
> spirit of Liberty in the free states. The contest is becoming—has become—
> one, not alone of freedom for the Blacks, but of freedom for the whites. It has
> now become absolutely necessary that slavery should cease, in order that
> freedom may be preserved to any portion of our land. The antagonist prin-
> ciples of liberty and slavery have been roused into action and one or the
> other must be victorious. There will be no cessation of the strife until Slavery
> shall be exterminated or liberty destroyed.

When Rev. J. Blanchard lectured in one of the Pittsburgh's churches, *The
Manufacturer* openly incited its readers to violence. And in December 1837,
when the mail brought the news of the destruction of Elijah Lovejoy's *Observer*
and the murder of Lovejoy, the *Gazette* said,

> The transaction is likely to prove highly injurious to the future prosperity
> of the town of Alton. Northern men will not readily settle in that place.
>
> The citizens of Pittsburgh have, therefore, reason to be grateful that the
> attempts of the *Manufacturer* to get up a mob against Blanchard proved in-
> effectual. . . .
>
> *The Christian Witness* of this city and the *Boston Liberator*, the organs of
> Abolition in the two places, have clothed their columns in mourning for the
> murder of a beloved brother. All this paraphernalia of grief might as well be
> spared, as it is only adding to the evidence of a wild, uncontrollable spirit of
> fanaticism, and insurrectionary design which are encouraged and propa-
> gated by as *heartless, hypocritical,* and *canting a coterie of mendicants* as were
> ever permitted to pass unpunished in any country. With Garrison and Th-
> ompson, the itinerant foreigner and banished criminals to promulgate their
> odious doctrines of hostility to all good government, whether political, social
> or parental, it is not to be wondered at or regretted that the people them-
> selves have interposed their power to prevent their dissemination.
>
> His press had been three times destroyed before the fatal catastrophe,
> as if he disregarded the warning and persisted in a course of conduct that
> the citizens of Alton condemned as tending to destruction of their peace, and
> of the security of their property, *the crime was his own* and he suffered the
> penalty.

Pittsburgh and Allegheny agents of the national society distributed its national publications. An Antislavery Book Store was opened on St. Clair Street,
now Sixth, to carry the bound volumes, tracts and pamphlets, circulars, and
prints. There was also the *Quarterly Antislavery Magazine*, with an annual circu-

lation of 9,000 copies; *The Slave's Friend*, published for children; a monthly publication, *Human Rights: The Weekly Emancipator*. It also carried many of the 100 antislavery newspapers that came from other free states.

Proceedings and documents of antislavery activity are rare. Only infrequent stories appear in the press of the day, which during the 1830's was not particularly friendly to the movement. But it is apparent that education of the public, agitation for some kind of abolition, though vague at first, and organization of articulate sentiment grew more widespread and more specific as time went on. The Pittsburgh Antislavery Society was soon supplemented by the Allegheny Antislavery Society. These frequently joined for meetings and action. They in turn joined with others to form the Antislavery Society of Allegheny County, and all groups of the neighboring counties finally consolidated into the Antislavery Society of Western Pennsylvania.

The term abolitionist as early applied to antislavery men and women was anything but respectable. Mrs. Swisshelm relates that once in passing along the street with a friend, two women who recognized them drew their wide skirts angrily about their ankles so as not to touch Mrs. Swisshelm or her companion, and enabled, "Ugh! Two of those nasty abolitionists." Not until the manufacturing interests stood firmly for abolishing slavery, because they needed free expansion of their industries, did the movement receive full support of the public, and the issue of secession strengthened this support.

In 1839 an antislavery convention was held in Pittsburgh at which ministers and the president of one of the universities of western Pennsylvania were present. It was at this convention that Martin Delany caused a sensation by his argument concerning Jewish slavery, as compared with Negro slavery in America, when he said, "Onesimus was a blood-kin brother to Philemon." The convention was thrown into violent controversy by the statement. Onesimus and Philemon became two of the most talked of men in the antislavery movement.

In November of the same year the Antislavery Society of Pennsylvania split into an Eastern and a Western Division. The constitution of the Eastern Division cut out a clause saying "we will in no way countenance the slave in a resort to physical force to obtain his liberty." The action was so unpopular that many abolitionists refused to have anything to do with the Pittsburgh and Allegheny County society, but it was pointed out that the preamble to the constitution covered the question satisfactorily and it was voted to support the constitution as it stood.

The panic of 1837 was a blow to the antislavery societies. It deprived them of funds to carry out their work. By 1840 many people felt that the national society had outlived its usefulness, and that in light of developing sentiment it was nothing much now but a name. The society split. William Lloyd Garrison remained at the head of what was still known as the American Antislavery Society. But the dissenters formed the American and Foreign Antislavery Society. In this latter organization John Greenleaf Whittier, the Tappans, James G. Birney, Gerrit Smith and later Frederick Douglass took part. The split had come about over the question of political action. Garrison refused to participate with any political party on a platform of opposition to the extension of slavery. He demanded separation of the free states from the slave and denounced the United States Constitution as "a covenant with death and an agreement with hell" because he said it made slavery a constitutional institution in the country.

The new organization, the American and Foreign Antislavery Society, determined to make the most complete use of political action and to organize pressure on political candidates. It used the ballot whenever and wherever possible in the interests of antislavery and influenced large numbers of people to do so. This attitude was reflected immediately throughout Western Pennsylvania, where the various groups participated in the organization of the Liberty Party, the Free Soil, and the Republican Parties. This dissenting group denied that the Constitution was pro-slavery and it opposed splitting the Union.

From now on the antislavery or abolition movement became definitely political. In Pittsburgh, as in other antislavery communities, candidates for political office became antislavery speakers and lecturers. The idea that slavery was a sin gave way to the idea that it was a withering blight on the welfare and the progress of the country, and that it should be destroyed by law. Expatriation of Negroes was fought against more energetically than ever. And a greater insistence developed upon granting free Negroes all the privileges and civil liberties of free men.

As early as 1839, the Friends of Universal Liberty in Pittsburgh held a "large and respectable meeting" and nominated candidates for an Abolition Senate and Assembly ticket. It also drafted an address to The Friends of Human Rights, "urging them to lay aside the party preferences and give their united support" to candidates for Senator and for Representatives, and disclaiming any connection or alliance with either of the political parties already in the field." It resolved, "That John A. Brown, Wm. Marshal and Robert Dickey be a committee to procure tickets and circulate them through the district."

The following year the *Daily Pittsburgher* published a resolution of the New England Antislavery Society:

> Whereas the Government of the United States, by sustaining the slave system is highly tyrannical and despotic; and whereas the policy of the different political parties has given and is giving full sanction to this government; Therefore Resolved, that the United States of America, though a republic in

name, is a despotism in reality; and its great political parties have no claim, whatever, to the appellations democratic, republican, Whig or conservative.

And the Pittsburgher asked, "What have Gen. Harrison's thinking committee to say to that?"

One of the few statements from the Negroes themselves to be preserved in the papers is the letter written by Rev. Lewis Woodson, when a state convention of Negroes was to be held in the city in August, 1841:

Mr. Editor:—Within the last few days I have been asked by several respectable persons, if the colored people intend holding a State Convention in this city any time shortly; if a great number will attend; if they will march in procession through the streets; and if any other than colored persons will participate in the doings of the Convention. From the intimations which accompanied these questions, the manner in which they were put, and out of respect to the persons who put them, I deem it proper through your excellent and liberal paper, to give them a brief and respectful answer.

The colored people do intend holding a State Convention in this city, on the 23rd of this month; the object of which is the improvement of their condition in this state. They will endeavor to improve their condition by the use of no other means than upright men generally employed; such as to pray for the repeal or amendment of all unwholesome laws; to promote the more general diffusion of useful knowledge, to inculcate habits of virtue, industry, and economy, and so forth.

The Convention will be comparatively small. Even if many from any distant part of the state should wish to attend, the scarcity of money will prevent them. Leaving out counties immediately around Allegheny, I do not believe there will be exceeding fifty in attendance.

Such a thing as marching through the streets was never dreamed of—the days of such childish parade are long since passed with us; nor will any other than colored persons participate in the doings of the Convention. The participation of others is not rejected out of any disrespect to them, but because it is natural and right. Every man knows his own affairs best, and naturally feels a deeper interest in them than anyone else, and therefore on that account ought to attend to them.

The Convention will hold two sessions daily, one in the forenoon and one in the afternoon, until it has dispatched its own business. Its doors will be open to all orderly persons as spectators. All who may feel any interest in it, may rest assured that the foregoing is a true description of character of our intended convention; as I have had the best opportunity from the first, of knowing. With a word in reference to the intimations which accompanied the inquiries I shall close.

For the last ten years I have had the honor to be a humble resident of the peaceable and industrious city of Pittsburgh. The kind treatment and liberal patronage of our citizens, has given me a love for her which I feel for no other city on earth. With just pride, and in unqualified terms, have I praised the noble and generous spirit of her citizens, to my brethren in other places; and I cannot now think of the mortification and disgrace I should feel, should she allow her fair character to be tarnished by any laws or violent exhibitions to- wards us. I cannot, I will not think of such a thing; the noble and generous citizens of Pittsburgh will never suffer it to take place. I feel fully assured that they will sustain a lawful and peaceable meeting of a feeble and oppressed people, to consult on the best means of improving their condition.

LEWIS WOODSON

Pittsburgh, Aug. 18, 1841.

The *Manufacturer* said of the convention: "The Convention of colored men that assembled in this city on Monday last numbered about 140 delegates on the first day of the meeting. We understand that the deliberations of the Convention were conducted with much decorum." But what the deliberations were, what subjects seemed important enough to the Negro population of the state to dis- cuss in convention, and what conclusions were reached, or what actions taken, do not seem to have been recorded.

Of an intended meeting of the Western Pennsylvania Antislavery Society in February, 1842, the *Spirit of Liberty* said that it was

> not unreasonable to expect that the approaching special meeting will be *nu- merously attended*; and that the farmer, the merchant and the professional man will, one and all, lay aside, for the time being, their respective vocations and by a formidable and imposing muster, powerfully advance the cause of crushed and bleeding humanity. To induce our antislavery brethren to attend to this important and sacred duty, it is unnecessary to use long and elaborate arguments.

In the Antislavery Lecture Room, at the corner of Fourth and Market Streets, on the evening of February 15th, a meeting was held to arrange for a convention of the Friends of Civil and Religious Liberty on the 23rd. Of this meeting we know a little more than we do of most of these gatherings of men and women con- cerned with the great issues of their day. Since the majority of them lived in the main business part of the city, and the records would have been kept in their homes these records were no doubt destroyed in the great fire of 1845. The newspaper gave them little space. But these groups of men, grave-faced and determined, black and white, in stove pipe hats and knotted stocks above their waistcoats; these women in full skirts, billowing sleeves and Victorian bonnets were making history in their day-by-day activities, constant meetings in the long narrow Antislavery Lecture Room, with its gas lights and coal stoves, to discuss and resolve and draw up petitions.

At this meeting John Mecaskey was called to the chair, and Hugh Arters appointed Secretary. A committee of five was set up to arrange for the approaching convention—Henry Williams, A. W. Ewing, Hugh Arters, S. C. Cole and John Peck. On motion of Rev. E. Smith,

> the friends of Antislavery were requested to provide accommodations for such delegates as may attend the Convention on the 23rd inst., and that may be requested to leave their names and places of residence at the Antislavery Book Store in St. Clair Street, together with the number of persons they can accommodate. The committee decided upon Irwin's Long Room, corner of Market and Fourth Sts., as the place, and 10 o'clock as the time for the meeting of the convention.

On the day set, a joint convention of this group and the Western Pennsylvania Antislavery Society met in Irwin's Long Room as planned. A number of people, Negro and white, held offices and served on committees in both organizations. The President being absent, Dr. Wm. Petit, one of the vice-presidents, took the chair. The meeting was opened by observing a time of silence and then it got down to its several days business. It appointed a Business Committee— John Peck, John C. Clark, E. Smith, E. W. Stevens, Jonathan Catell, John Cammel, K. Williams. It appointed a committee of Enrollment—A. D. Lewis, Joseph E. Cole, Joseph Turner; a committee of Adjustment—"to whom were referred the conflicting claims of W. Allinder and W. H. Burleigh"—Joseph B. Cole, Jonathan Catell, Milo A. Townsend, John Cammel and John Clark.

The Convention resolved that "all who are in favor of immediate emancipation be invited to enroll their names." The list of those enrolled reads: *Pittsburgh*—Benjamin Bown, David Bown, J. B. Vashon, M. R. Delany, John Peck, Hugh Arters, John Mecaskey, A. White, F. Davis, L. Woodson, James Clayton, James Lever, Nicholas Woodson; *Allegheny*—John Wall, Joseph Turner, Samuel C. Cole, John A. Bowman, Margaret Mckain, Mary Lisetor, Jane E. Strange, Ursula G. Lewis, Thomas Lawrence, W. H. Clark, Jacob Sprinkle, John Walker, W. H. Burleigh; *Manchester*—Wm. Petit, E. W. Stephens; *Ross township*—Joseph A. Bowman; *Beaver*—Milo A. Townsend, John Cammel, Joseph B. Cole; *Sharps-*

burg—John Clark; *Brownsville* and *Bridgeport*—Jonathan Catell, John Barr, George Kerr. After these signatures had been set down the meeting closed with prayer.

That evening the session adopted a resolution: "Whereas, In the successful prosecution of the Abolition enterprise in western Pennsylvania an efficient and ably conducted periodical is indispensable, and believing that *The Spirit of Liberty*, under the supervision of its present editor, will not only justify the expectations of its friends, but defeat the machinations of its enemies, Therefore,

> 1st Resolved, That, in the opinion of the society, it is important that *The Spirit of Liberty* be continued, both as it respects maintaining the efficiency of the society's organization and the liquidation of its debts.

> 2nd Resolved, That, we hereby individually, collectively and solemnly pledge ourselves to its support, and promise to use all honorable means to extend its circulation, enlarge its patronage, increase its usefulness, and render it in all respects a vehicle of intelligence worthy of the name it bears and the cause it advocates.

After the Business Committee's "sound report" was taken up, discussed, and laid on the table a third resolution was adopted: "Resolved, That, as abolitionists, we acknowledge with regret, that, in some measure, our efforts have been misguided; for, while we have manifested much sympathy for the slave, yet we have not sufficiently borne in mind the interest and welfare of the free people of color." Once more the meeting closed with prayer, to meet the next morning. Meantime the Committee of Enrollment had reported the following additional names of persons "who took seats in the afternoon and evening": N. W. Fairfield, of Pittsburgh, Elizabeth Smith, Harriet Smith, Elizabeth Brown, Nancy Maclay, all of Allegheny, Charlotte Williams and James M. Saint. The remainder of the sessions concerned themselves with the report of the Adjusting Committee. The question seems to have been the adjustment of the accounts of *The Christian Witness*, which apparently by this time had suspended publication. After a number of resolutions, amendments and substitutes, the convention Resolved, "That all moneys hereafter received upon subscription to *The Christian Witness*, donations or pledges made before the commencement of the *Spirit of Liberty* be divided among all the claimants of the society, in the same way *pro rata* to the claims and all the other moneys not needed to support the *Spirit of Liberty*." Also they resolved, "That the balance of the business Committee's report be laid on the table till the next meeting of the society."

The Convention adjourned *sine die*, M. R. Delany, Secretary *pro tem*.

Two weeks later, on March 8th, according to *The Spirit of Liberty*, "the friends of the oppressed" met in Irwin's Long Room, opened their meeting, as usual, with prayer and then Rev. E. Smith stated that the object of the meeting was "to adopt some plan to bring into more active operation the Antislavery strength of the city."

A committee consisting of R. Robinson, J. Mecaskey and E. Smith was appointed to prepare business for the meeting, and having withdrawn, "after a few minutes came into the meeting" and reported a resolution for re-organizing the Pittsburgh Antislavery Society. The first part of the proposal, to form a new society, was adopted unanimously. But no decision could be reached between the Constitution of the Fifth Ward Society and that of the old "City Society." So the matter was tabled and a committee consisting of E. B. Smith, B. Brown, W. H. Clark, S. Dickerson and T. Marshall was appointed to draft a constitution to be submitted at a future meeting. It was voted to meet the following week, and the meeting closed with prayer.

The Constitution was published a few weeks later, on Feb. 26th, in the *Spirit of Liberty*. Its preamble read:

> We whose names are hereunto subscribed, believing in the inherent sinfulness of American Slavery, that it is a reproach to the Christian, a curse to the Church of Christ, and a blight and a mildew on the face of our beloved country's prosperity; that the duty, interest and safety of all concerned require its abolition without expatriation; that duty and interest are inseparable; that it is always safe to do duty, and that it is our duty to make use of all righteous, lawful and constitutional means in our power for the speedy and entire abolition of the great *moral* and *political* evil, and to protect the nation from the further encroachment of the slave power; and also to do what we can in a lawful and constitutional way to free our country from its baleful influence; do agree to form ourselves into a society under the following constitution.

Article two dealt specifically with the objects of the Society:

> The objects of this Society are to increase and combine the antislavery feeling of the community; to cause the principles of human liberty to be better understood; to free our country from control and influence of the slave power; to effect the entire abolition of slavery at the earliest possible period, without driving the slave from the land of his birth; to elevate the free people of color; and make the colored man the intelligent and firm friend of our country, by enlightening his mind, and extending to him those civil and religious privileges, which the Great Creator has made it the right of every human being to enjoy.

Article Three stressed the lawful constitutional and peaceful means by which these ends were to be accomplished:

> This society will use none but lawful constitutional means for the accomplishment of its objects. It will not encourage the use of forces or violence in any case. Its main dependence—its very dependence is in doing what is right, in the sight of the Great Universal Ruler. It will, under no circumstance, "do evil that good may come."

Article seven provided for membership in the society:

> Any person believing in the inherent sinfulness of slavery and in the right of the slave to enjoy freedom without expatriation, and who will aid the society by contributing to its funds, or otherwise, may be a member.

Little record exists of further activities of the Antislavery Society as such. With the Friends of Liberty, the Friends of Human Rights, the Friends of Universal Liberty, and similar groups, the Liberty Party met in caucus to nominate candidates for state and county offices. Not for another decade did the feeling of the people become unanimous that slavery was an evil, not merely a moral evil, as was felt in the first days of the movement, but a political evil. Then, when it clearly became an economic threat to the progress of northern industry, the disinclination of the antislavery societies to use any but constitutional and legal means broke down. After the passage of the Fugitive Slave Law in 1850, even though for a time public opinion supported the law, events moved too rapidly and violently for passivity and inactivity on the part of those opposed to slavery. Members of the antislavery societies were no longer concerned about lawful and constitutional measures, but sheltered escaped slaves, spirited them on their way to Canada, and even forcibly took them from masters transporting them through the streets, on trains or on river boats.

But before this time arrived one or two events occurred which show the line of progress. In 1843, the New England Society resolved to hold a great series of conventions—one hundred of them—over a period of six months, in the New England and the Middle Atlantic States. From the meetings held in and around Pittsburgh the movement gained its final impetus.

In August of that year the Covenants and Wesleyans announced in the city papers that they were "ready to meet the proslavery tribes of the city" in debate on the question of immediate abolition. And another paper announced that "A correspondent of *The Spirit of Liberty* offers to be one of five to give $5 each, ($25 in all) to Rev. E. Smith to deliver twenty lectures in this county, between now and the election." And the announcement added, "The lectures are certainly cheap enough at $1.25 each." Meetings continued, multiplied in fact. A Negro citizen who signed himself "G," wrote to *The Spirit of Liberty*, leading his letter with a quotation: "As iron sharpeneth," his letter read, "so does the countenance of man his friend."

Mr. Editor—How full of meaning are the above two lines, and how small a degree is the truth contained in them felt, at the present time, by anti-slavery men? What have we, as a peculiar people, done of late against the peculiar institution; strike away our first of August meeting and what have we left? Nothing but a barren waste so far as the city is concerned. Now let us for the future manifest our faith by our works.

It is known to the greater part of the abolitionists of Pittsburgh that we have a place of meeting known as Liberty Hall, and for which rent must be paid, used or not.

Now how profitable it would be, not only to the cause, but to the abolitionists individually to form a *Liberty Association* for the discussion of subjects in a way connected with the great question of the day. Many, I have no doubt, would take sides who are not committed against slavery, and by the "sharpening of iron against iron" would gain information on subjects which perhaps never would otherwise be obtained.

Our elections will soon be upon us, and how unprepared are we for that trying time. That is a day, sir, that tests men's principles, and I make no doubt that many who think themselves well grounded in our Liberty Party, will be seen floating down the pro-slavery current with chips, straws and dead fish, if efforts are not made to prevent it.

In your next paper I hope to have at least a seconder to my proposal. The time of the year is advancing when one or two hours in one evening of the week can well be appropriated to this purpose.

The first of August meeting of which "G" spoke was the Emancipation Day celebration held each year, one account of which survives from the year 1845, in "A Letter by a Colored Citizen" published in the *Chronicle* several days after the event:

Messrs. Editors: The recurrence of the anniversary of a day marked by any great effort in the cause of oppressed humanity, cannot fail to excite emotions of the most pleasing nature in the bosom of every philanthropist. Actuated by such feelings, the colored inhabitants of this city resolved to commemorate, on Friday of the past week, the emancipation of 800,000 of their brethren, in the British West Indies, from the thralldom under which they had been toiling for years. Accordingly, as the day was a beautiful one, they repaired to a pleasant grove in Arthursville, where the Ladies of the Benevolent Society had fitted up a Saloon, in which they vended lemonades, ice creams and other refreshments appropriate to the summer season. A dinner had also been prepared for the occasion, the proceeds of which are to be devoted to the purchasing of a press, etc., for the *Mystery*. Several hundreds, among whom were many white ladies and gentlemen, were present, and took part in the festivities. All was joy and hilarity, and nothing occurred which was calculated to mark the pleasure and harmony in which such a day should be celebrated.

During the course of the day addresses were delivered by Messrs. Peck, Delany, Vashon and others among whom were our white fellow citizens,—Messrs. Kerr, Larimer, and Fleeson. Much might be said with regard to several of the speeches and this, at least, can be said of all—that they were marked by none of that proscriptive feeling, which characterizes too much of the philanthropy of the present day. Resolutions also gotten up on the instant by the Messrs. Kerr and Larimer and calling upon the President, Congress and heads of departments to assist in carrying out the great truths expressed in the Declaration of Independence, were read to the assembly and received by acclamation. That the way to this, the "Universal Liberty" may become the motto of this Republic and that the colored American may no longer feel obliged to refrain from participating in the joy which marks the return of our own National Independence, whilst he participates in that which a day rendered memorable by foreign philanthropy is hailed, are the ardent wishes, gentlemen of [. . .][2]

A Colored Citizen.

The antislavery societies consisted of several groups and classes of people. Most important, there were the Negroes themselves. The Colonization Societies had consisted entirely of white members. The enlistment of Negroes in the Antislavery Society through the leadership of men like Martin Delany, John B. Vashon, Rev. A. D. Lewis, Rev. Lewis Woodson and Father John Peck was one of its chief sources of strength.

Another source of strength was the broadening of the movement into a struggle for maintenance of democratic rights for white people. This aspect of the movement enlisted another element, the working class members. Frederick Douglass said that in his first days in the movement he had not dreamed of becoming a public advocate of the cause so deeply imbedded in his heart. It was enough for him to listen, to receive and applaud the great words of others "and only whisper in private, amongst the white laborers on the wharves and else-

---

2. Text in original ends mid-sentence.

where" the truths that burned within him. Douglass, Garrison, Delany and other pioneers of the antislavery cause could not in the early days hold their meetings even in churches. They were compelled to speak from platforms in the woods, at the corners of public parks, in discarded buildings—blacksmith shops, stables, warehouses. Frequently, says Douglass, they found seated "a few cabmen in their coarse everyday clothes, whips in hand." One of Douglass' companions on his tour refused once to speak to "such a set of ragamuffins," and left the town. Douglass stayed on and everyday for a week spoke in the ramshackle old post office building "to audience constantly increasing in numbers and respectability, till the Baptist Church was thrown open; and when this became too small I went on Sunday into the park and addressed an assembly of four or five thousand persons."

Women too were drawn more and more into the movement. Lucy Stone, Susan B. Anthony, Elizabeth Cady Stanton, Fanny Wright, Abby Kelly Foster lectured frequently in Pittsburgh, demanding equal rights for women, free public education, and abolition of slavery. Women identified their interest with antislavery because they, like the Negro, were denied the right to vote, freedom of speech, the right to hold office, to attend colleges and universities, to hold property. They declared themselves against the prevailing double standards of morality and demanded equal pay for equal work. William Lloyd Garrison, Wendell Phillips, John Greenleaf Whittier, Ralph Waldo Emerson, Frederick Douglass, Martin Delany, the Vashons, Lewis Woodson all supported the Women's Right Movement, as well as the antislavery movement.

The Pittsburgh *Conference Journal* for January 1, 1835 published a "Petition from the Females of Alleghenytown and Vicinity to the Honorable Senate and House of Representatives Requesting the Abolishment of Slavery in the District of Columbia."

> We the undersigned, females of Alleghenytown and vicinity, Pennsylvania, do respectfully petition your honorable body to use your constitutional powers to abolish Slavery in the District of Columbia and the Territories under your control. Believing that it is safe to do so to others as we would they should do to us in like circumstances, and dangerous to violate this rule of intercourse with our fellow men, and believing also that an expression of our desires on this subject will receive due attention from your honorable body, we beseech you by the tarnished glory of our beloved country, by the cries and tears of the slave, by his sweat and blood, and by the fruitless struggles of unprotected and violated innocence to adopt such measures as your wisdom and patriotism shall dictate, for the speedy removal of this sin from all the territories in which it exists under your jurisdiction.

Pittsburgh had no more fiery and unflinching advocate of abolition that Jane Grey Swisshelm, editor of the *Saturday Evening Visitor*, which flayed not only every pro-slavery force in the city, but every person and every movement or institution that impeded social progress or manifested social hypocrisy.

By now the various national groups who were themselves concerned with national independence, like the Germans and the Irish, came out in open support of the struggle of the Negro for freedom. They held their own meetings and passed their own resolutions.

The Pittsburgh Catholic Irish supported the antislavery cause. The Irish and Scots Irish were numerous among the early settlers of the district. They had fought in the Revolutionary army. They were among the Whiskey Rebels who fought the hated whiskey tax imposed by Alexander Hamilton. The Irish and Scots Irish had come to America and to the frontier to find freedom of religion, freedom from tyranny and exemption from heavy economic burdens. These people—whose patron, St. Patrick, the ancient Druids had prophesied would "free slaves" and "raise up men of lowly origin"—felt themselves in accord with the Negroes through their own struggle for national independence. The Alien and Sedition Laws of 1798 had been aimed chiefly at French and Irish immigrants. With the opening of work on the eastern end of the Pennsylvania Canal in the late 1820's, Irish laborers had multiplied rapidly in the city. Everywhere the Irish, like the Quakers, were ardent antislavery men. Frederick Douglass found on his European trips that the Irish, in their fight against union with England refused subscriptions of money raised among the southern slaveholders, because it was "stained with blood." They would never, they said, "purchase the freedom of Ireland with the price of the slave." The bitter anti-Catholic feeling of the 1820's and 1830's gave the Catholic Irish a feeling of brotherhood with the oppressed Negroes. They were referred to in the public press as "dregs and scum of the earth." They were accused of having imported strikes into the country.

When Daniel O'Connell introduced Frederick Douglass at a meeting to demand the repeal of union between Ireland and England, he introduced him as the Black O'Connell of the United States. Nor did he let the occasion pass without his usual denunciation of slavery in the United States. O. A. Brownson had recently been converted to Catholicism, and "taking advantage of his new Catholic audience in *Brownson's Review*" he charged O'Connell with attacking American institutions. O'Connell replied, "I am charged with attacking American institutions, as slavery is called; I am not ashamed of this attack. My sympathy is not confined to the narrow limits of my own green Ireland; my spirit walks abroad upon sea and land, and wherever there is sorrow and suffering there is my spirit to succor and relieve."

In 1842, the Pittsburgh *Mercury* published in its issue of March 16th an

"Address of the People of Ireland to Their Countrymen and Countrywomen in America:

DEAR FRIENDS:—You are a great distance from your native land! A wide expanse of water separates you from the beloved country of your birth. We regard America with feelings of admiration; we do not look upon her as a strange land, nor upon her people as aliens from our affections. The power of steam has brought us nearer together. It will increase the intercourse between us, so that the character of the Irish people and the American people, must in future be acted upon by the feeling and dispositions of each.

America can never be the glorious country that her free Constitution designed her to be, so long as her soil is polluted by the foot-print of a single slave.

Slavery is the most tremendous invasion of the natural, inalienable rights of men, and some of the noblest gifts of God, "life, liberty, and the pursuit of happiness." All who are not for it are against it. None can be neutral. We entreat you to take part in justice, religion and liberty.

We call upon you to unite with the abolitionists, and never cease your efforts until perfect liberty is granted to every one of her inhabitants, the black man as well as the white man.

We are told that you possess great power, both moral and political, in America. We entreat you to exercise that power and that influence for the sake of humanity.

Join with the abolitionists everywhere! They are the only constant advocates of liberty. Tell every man that you don't understand liberty for the white man and slavery for the black man; that you are for liberty for all, of every color, creed and country.

Irish men and Irish women! Treat the colored people as your equals—brethren. By all your memories of Ireland continue to love liberty—hate slavery—cling by abolitionists; and in America you will do honor to the name of Ireland.

Signed: Daniel O'Connell
Theobald Matthew
R. R. Madden
and 60,000 other Irishmen"

When Massini's letter to Wm. Lloyd Garrison, Wendell Phillips and others was published in the *Chronicle* in 1853, the *Gazette* accused the reader who had sent in the letter of drawing unwarranted conclusions as to the meaning of its very direct language. In answer the sender defended Massini in a reply to the *Gazette* in which he said that the Massini had expressed himself "without evasion in right

good Italian," He said, "It is so plain that it cannot, unless willfully, bear any mis-
construction, and the Italian thinks would scorn to see his bold and characteristic epistle obscured by making it a Pickwick perversion about moral force."
Massini had said that the cause of the Italian patriot and the southern Negro are
identical in principle, and must have but one, and that a universal, solution. To
fight this cause, that ballot box, he said, is the only peaceable right, if one has it,
the sword the alternative to him who has it not. He spoke of the 24,000,000
emancipated Italians allied with a like number of American abolitionists in the
cause of universal liberty.

The dominant social institution of the day was the church. The attitude of
the church to slavery, therefore, was important. The decade of the 1840s was the
period of greatest growth in the history of Pittsburgh of both the number of
churches and the size of congregations. This growth itself, therefore, meant
greater influence for or against antislavery activity. The attitude of the church was
different at different times, and as with every other institution, the force of controversy rent every church into two branches. During most of the years of the controversy the church, except the Quakers and the Covenanters, was on the side of
the slave-holder—Catholic, Baptist, Methodist, Episcopalian, Congregational
and Presbyterian. Members of all these congregations held slaves and their ministers defended the system by appeals to the Bible. The abolitionists called on the
church to take the lead in the antislavery crusade, but the "church was given over
to a religion of dogma and ceremony, and instead of leading she opposed the abolitionists with the most cruel denunciation" until the very verge of Civil War.
When the mainstay of her economic life, the industrialist subsidizers and the
pew-renters, called for the destruction of slavery to save the life of northern industry and capital, then the church became antislavery.

During the Methodist Protestant General Conference meeting in Pittsburgh,
in May 1842, a letter to the editor of the *Spirit of Liberty* gave the situation at first
hand, through a letter from Mr. John Clark, a member of the Pittsburgh Antislavery society and the Friends of Civil and Religious Liberty:

> Mr. Editor:—The General Conference of the Methodist Protestant
> Church has now been in session, in this place, since the third instant and a
> very considerable portion of its time has been occupied with slavery; which,
> it is understood, was disposed of by a final vote yesterday; but notwithstand-
> ing several days were occupied in pressing, dodging, shifting, and discussing
> the question, neither could a fair discussion of the real question, viz.; is sla-
> very a *mahem per se*, sin in itself, nor a direct vote thereon, be obtained.
>
> The subject was brought up by the resolution and recommendation of
> nine Annual Conferences, embracing more than one half of the members of

the church in the United States, and some fifteen memorials, from official and private members of the church, all asking in the most unequivocal manner, for efficient action against the moral evil of slavery. But slavery knows no rights—has no conscience—is not subject to the law of reason, or the law of God, neither indeed can be. The resolution which was regarded as making disposition of the subject was offered by a conservative, brother Norris, of Boston, laying the reports of the committee on the table, and declaring that the subject of slavery should not be taken up again, during the present session of the General Conference. This resolution immediately succeeded the adoption, by yeas and nays, of the following: "Resolved, That slavery is not a sin against God under all circumstances; yet in our opinion, under some circumstances it is sinful, and in such cases should be discouraged by the Methodist Protestant Church; this General Conference does not feel itself authorized by the Constitution to legislate on the subject, and by a solemn vote expresses its judgment that the Annual Conferences should be left to make their own regulation on the subject.

On the affirmative were Rev. Geo. Brown, of Pittsburgh, John Burns, of Allegheny, Z. Ragan, of Steubenville, and John Snyder, a Lay Delegate, all of Pittsburgh District, who, you perceive gave the majority to the South in this abominable compromise of moral principle, and whose official instructions given at the request of the first named brother, was "*to oppose the moral evil of slavery.*" Compromise did I say? Is it not an entire yielding of all the slave-holder could ask, and at the same time, offering an insult to the common sense of all but slaveholders? Some of us will this morning present our protest against the action had.

I write in haste, in the midst of interesting conference business.

Yours,

JOHN CLARK.

In the autumn of that year a communication was received by the *Spirit of Liberty* announcing a break with the church made by a group of men who formed a new denomination.

We have been requested to publish the following paper, in doing which we feel that we owe to all concerned, either for or against the measures taken by the Seceders, to say that we are not one of them. We have been urged, for more than a year, to leave the Methodist Episcopal Church, and form an independent congregation, but have steadily refused, and for so doing, have lost some of our friends. But these persons have at last done themselves what they have been wanting us to do.

It will be seen that they have left Methodism in leaving the church; and if they carry out the principles they have adopted, they will deserve the name Wesleyan; and that they have laid the draft for a single church, not for a sect. We bid them good speed in the name of the Lord. And though we have not seen our way clear to be one of this body, we will rejoice to see a church in Pittsburgh take what we believe the right ground on the subject of slavery.

We, whose names are hereunto annexed, being impelled, purely by a sense of duty, to withdraw from the fellowship of the churches of which we have been members, on account of those churches giving countenance and toleration of the enslavement of the African race, who are in this country, which we regard as one of the greatest moral evils ever practiced; to use the language of one whose memory we revere "the sum of all villainies; the vilest system of oppression that ever saw the sun." And as far as the Methodist Episcopal Church is concerned, we have given up all hope of seeing it reformed, so as to exclude slaveholders from the fellowship of the same. We feel ourselves called upon, by these considerations, to form ourselves into a church, and with a single eye to the glory of God, and a humble reliance on his grace, do hereby form ourselves into a religious society, to be called the Wesleyan Methodist Church, and agree to be governed by the following regulation, until Providence shall mark some other course as the course of duty.

The letter was signed "John P. Betker, and others."

In August 1842 the Preachers' Antislavery Society of Pittsburgh Conference of the Methodist Episcopal Church issued their first annual report. This report not only explains the reasons for their organization, but gives also a history of the attitude of the Methodist Church toward slavery.

The society was organized the 21st of July, 1841, in Pittsburgh. It consisted of eighteen members.

The report says:

We united in the society as Methodist preachers, and most of us are traveling preachers, liable to be scattered over the whole conference. Our first and principle object as stated . . . in the society's constitution was "*to increase and combine* the antislavery feeling in the Methodist Episcopal Church against the practice of slave holding and thereby to hasten its entire 'extirpation' from the Church. This great and desirable object, so long held forth in our Discipline, is becoming more hopeless every year—is an old work in our Discipline; it first found its way there at a time when the extirpation of the 'evil of slavery' from the church *was really desired;* and for a considerable time extirpation measures were devising and were trying to be carried into effect. But now this work has lost the greater part of its old company; and instead of being as formerly, *at the head of extirpation measures,* it is now at the head of the *REGULATIONS* of slavery."

For thirty years Methodism existed in the mother country, free from any connection with slavery, and so far as we have evidence, for the next *ten* years in this country in the same way—then the Church changed from *no slavery*, to *slavery opposed*. Next from slavery opposed, to slavery *UNDISTURBED*. And finally from slavery undisturbed to slavery *VINDICATED*. The last and gloomy period commenced about eight years ago; but notwithstanding the gloomy state of things, the Anti-Slavery portion of our church did for several years entertain the hope that our church might yet be aroused from her slumbers and be brought back to the old Anti-Slavery ground, which she occupied against slave holding at the time of her organization, in 1784; and finally, into a regular constitutional way to *extirpate* this *"great evil"* from our entire Church. This design led to the formation of *"the American Wesleyan Anti-Slavery Society"* and also our own society as one of its auxiliaries.

We would not however conceal the fact that our hope of seeing the Methodist Episcopal Church freed from the evil of slavery is far less sanguine now than any other former period—yes, we are almost ready to despair forever. Such is the stronghold that slavery has gotten on the feelings of the great body of our people, and especially our ministers, and the vast and undue advantages in suppressing all antislavery movements in the church, that we can scarcely hope for a favorable change, unless God interposes in some miraculous way, or sends his heavy judgments on the church and nation together. Our official periodicals are not only silent in regard to the abominations of slavery, but are frequently employed to destroy the influence of our most talented and active ministers, who have dared to engage in the antislavery enterprise.

If our brethren are differed with us respecting *measures*, and were disposed to show us "a more excellent way," we would rejoice to cooperate with them. But alas! *Nothing* is proposed but "to wholly refrain." Thus it would seem, that so far as the Methodist Episcopal Church is concerned, slavery, like the *tares*, is to be let alone *until the harvest*, lest the Church be *rooted up*, or in some way be destroyed.

We believe, however, that the antislavery cause is destined to triumph; and should this result be accomplished, not only within the church, but even in *opposition to the Church*, she must of course lose her saving and reform influence and sink disgraced even in the eyes . . . of the World. To guard against any share of responsibility in this disgrace, and at the same time to use all our influence, (as men, as citizens, as Christians, and above all as Methodists, and

METHODIST MINISTERS) against slavery, and in favor of universal liberty, we still feel it our duty, in some significant and public way to stand out before the church and the world in condemnation of all slavery, as well as all slaveholding. And seeing our peculiar situation renders it difficult, if not impracticable, to operate as itinerant ministers in the capacity of a *formal society*; we, therefore, submit the following preamble and resolutions, for the consideration and adoption of the society.

Since Pittsburgh was a Presbyterian stronghold, the attitude of the Presbyterian Church was of particular significance to the antislavery movement here. There were eleven or twelve Presbyterian Churches in the district and also several papers whose editors were members of the church.

In her autobiography, *Half a Century*, Jane Grey Swisshelm says: "In the year 1800, the Convenanter Church of this country said in her synod, 'Slavery and Christianity are incompatible' and never relaxed her discipline which forbade fellowship with slave holders."

Mrs. Swisshelm was a Convenanter. She was born in 1815, and in her autobiography gives a brief, vivid picture of her own early antislavery activity, which must have been about the end of the 1820s, before much is heard of organized, practical antislavery work in the district. "I was still a child," she says, "when I went through Wilkins Township collecting names to petition for the abolition of slavery in the District of Columbia. Here in a strictly orthodox Presbyterian community, I was met everywhere by the objections: 'Niggers have no souls,' 'The Jews held slaves,' 'Noah cursed Canaan,' and these points I argued from house to house occasionally for three years."

As early as 1818 the Presbyterian Church had declared slavery a breach of every precept of the Decalogue and a violation of every Christian principle, the "sum total of all possible villainies." But this was an inactive attitude, an abstract statement unsupported by any action. There was no specific issue to be faced, no action in which to be involved. The church could take a righteous attitude without discomfiture.

In 1832, the Presbyterian Church split over the issue into the Old School, which contended that the Constitution of the United States was a pro-slavery document and the New School, which contended that the Constitution did not sanction slavery and took a positive antislavery position.

The work of Theodore Weld in Pittsburgh and the nearby district has been mentioned. Weld, "eloquent as an angel, and powerful as thunder," spent weeks in the Pittsburgh region evangelizing for antislavery. Weld held his meetings in series, like the "protracted meetings of Finney's Great Revival," usually eight in succession, but sometimes fifteen or twenty. At the conclusion of each meeting he called on converts to abolitionism to rise. Usually the whole audience rose to its feet. In June, 1835, Weld made his "extraordinary raid" upon the Presbyterian General Assembly in Pittsburgh. In a letter to Elizur Wright, Weld wrote that his object in being in the city during the session was first

> to ascertain by intercourse with ministers, elders and others assembled here from almost every state in the Union, the exact position of the slavery question, recent shifts of position, progress of abolitionism, statistics, etc. Second:—to get up one or two abolition meetings and secure to our cause the open advocacy of some men of standing in the church ... During the last year a very large number of professing Christians in all parts of the country, have renounced colonizationism and espoused the cause of immediate abolition, and that these generally have been the most benevolent, conscientious and prayerful portion of colonizationists, and that those who still adhere and are most active in the support of colonization generally constitute the aristocracy and fashionable worldliness of the church—Those who are never found in advance of public sentiment—those who oppose entire abstinence from all alcoholic drinks and stickle greatly for wine and beer, in short, those Christians who join actively in a moral enterprise only when it begins to become popular. This is stated as the general fact. I know well that there are exceptions, such as Gerrit Smith, Mr. Frelinghuysen, etc., but exceptions are not the rule.

Weld was highly successful in his lobbying for "immediatism." As delegates were converted they testified before antislavery meetings, which had been organized by Weld for that purpose in one of the churches. His ministerial converts consisted of more than a quarter of the delegates to the assembly.

Elizur Wright, Jr. wrote to Weld:

> "Anti S. Office, New York,
> 26 May, 1835
>
> I have heard and am delighted with the way in which you are drawing the lines around Pittsburgh, May the Lord be with you, etc.
>
> E. Wright, Jr.

Weld himself was too busy interviewing delegates to the Assembly to attend the meetings he organized, until near the end of the convention. Usually D. C. Lansing or N. S. Beman acted as chairman of the meetings. Weld had induced J. W. Nevin, a professor at Western Theological Seminary, to speak at one of the antislavery meetings. But Nevin finally declined. His letter to Weld shows the institutional control of opinion and activity:

Allegheny, Pa, June 2, 1835

Dear Sir:

I must decline addressing the antislavery meeting this evening, as I consented to do a few days since. I find that a strong repugnance to my taking such a course prevails in the minds of many, and it is apprehended that very serious injury would result to the Seminary with which I am connected, if I should thus stand forth on this occasion as the advocate of a cause so generally held in dislike. . . . I have no right to drag this institution into anything like a party attitude, on this or on any other subject, against the wishes of the body of its friends; and if they honestly think that I would do so by addressing the antislavery meeting this evening, I must so far respect their views as to be silent.

But I wish to be distinctly understood that I have not surrendered, and do not mean to surrender, my right as a free citizen of this country and a member of the church of Jesus Christ, to think for myself on this subject and to bear witness publicly for the truth. The proper authority may, if it be thought proper, command silence; and so long as I retain my place in the seminary, I must hold it my duty to comply with the rule. . . .

If I remain in connection with the Seminary, it will be as the known and decided advocate of antislavery principles, though not with any advantage taken, I trust, of my place in this institution, to enlist its official weight for my help and if on the other hand this liberty be not allowed, I am ready to retire to some other service for the sake of the truth and a good conscience.

As it has been published to some extent that I was to address the meeting, I have thought it proper to explain in this way the reason for my not appearing for that purpose, and to vindicate myself at the same time from the suspicion of acting inconsistently or treacherously to my own principles in failing to do so.

(J. W. Nevin)

As agitation grew, the lethargy of the churches toward the movement provoked criticism from the antislavery societies. A letter to Gerrit Smith from H. C. Howells of Allegheny, Pa., December 25, 1839 suggested that a committee be appointed in New York to receive the funds of those abolitionists, who will no longer sustain the Protestant Missionary Board because "they make no effort for the salvation of the home-made heathen enslaved in this republic nation." He also criticized the ministers, who, he said, had "neglected the blacks."

A meeting of the Old School General Assembly in Pittsburgh, in 1842, was reported by the *Spirit of Liberty* on November 17, which said:

The *dreamseller*, the *Sabbath-breaker*, the *slaveholder*, and his abettors were tacitly invited to seats, and if rumor be true were all present in this motley assembly. . . . At the opening of the meeting, a gag was effectually fastened upon all who would dare to open their mouths for the oppressed. A business committee was appointed, with this proviso, "That no business should come before the Convention, except through said committee." Special care being taken that no one who had not bowed the servile "knee to the dark Spirit of slavery" should have any share in preparing business for its august body.

Rev. Bushnell of Neucorite spoke of slavery in—. "Mr. Chairman, there is another sin, which I know you do not wish to have mentioned—which, I believe, you have taken means, and are determined to keep out of this convention. You know what I mean, shall I name it?" But Rev. Bushnell did not come out and call it openly slavery. Seven or eight DD's had the "appearance of bloody hyenas, ready to pounce upon their prey, and sacrifice him to the Moloch of slavery." Finally Rev. Bushnell said: "Mr. Chairman, it is SLAVERY, and unless this be repented of, we need not expect a blessing." Mr. Smith spoke next. He tried to turn the convention away from Mr. Bushnell's speech toward a revival. Dr. Herron "neutralized all remarks" and spoke with "invidious remarks" against Mr. Bushnell. John Hannen, a respected elder of Allegheny City, tried to return to the subject of slavery. Other matters of discussion took place. Finally Mr. Hannen was permitted to say a little on doing away with slavery.

When Geo. W. Fairfield, Corresponding Secretary of the Western Pennsylvania Antislavery Society, died, the *Spirit of Liberty* challenged the attitude of Dr. Biddle, of the Third Presbyterian Church, who preached the funeral sermon:

We are informed by those who were present, that Dr. Biddle, of the Third Church, in preaching the funeral sermon of which notice was given in our last was very particular to inform the hearers, that tho' engaged in preaching the funeral sermon of the Corresponding Sec'y of the Western Pennsylvania Society, he was *no abolitionist*. Had he given the history of a slave girl he once knew, nearly as white as the whitest lady in the city, it would have saved him this disclaimer. Our informants, say he was careful to inform his auditors, that brother Fairfield was not one of those abolitionists who denounce ministers of the gospel, who do not come out against slavery. We feel that we owe it to the memory of the dead to repel this accusation—this impeachment of brother Fairfield's fidelity. The Doctor had surely forgotten a sermon he heard brother Fairfield preach, in which he delivered his soul on this point. We notice the sermon, for the purpose of calling the attention of our friends to present policy. Abolition has now too many friends to come out against it; and it has too many enemies to come out for it; and a *"go-between"* course is adopted, an apparent, and sometimes a professed friendship for abolitionism, with the distinct declaration, "I am no abolitionist," is exhibited, and thus fair weather is made with both sides—The Doctor's sermon is only a specimen of present policy. To say to our antislavery friends, that we have more fear at present from "go betweens," than any other class of persons. Whenever you meet with a man, especially a professed Christian minister, who would make you believe he is friendly to antislavery, and who takes no active part, does not identify himself with the antislavery movements of the day, watch him. There are *ten* chances to *one*, if he is not seeking his own advantage, and Job-like, will hail with a kiss, and stab to death. Be careful.

Mrs. Jane Grey Swisshelm, editor of the abolitionist *Saturday Evening Visitor*, one of the ablest journalists of her time, wrote of the church when the Fugitive Slave Law was passed.

The church also rushed to the front to show its Christian zeal for the wrongs of those brethren, who, by the escape of their slaves, lost the means of building churches and buying communion services, and there was no end of homilies on the dishonesty of helping men to regain possession of their own bodies. All manner of charges were rung about Onesimus, and Paul became the patron saint of slave-catchers.

Among the many devices brought to bear on the consciences of Pittsburghers, was a sermon preached, as per announcement, by Rev. Biddle, pastor of the Third Presbyterian Church. It was received with great favor, by his large wealthy congregation, was printed in pamphlet form, distributed by thousands and made a profound impression, for Pittsburgh is a Presbyterian city, and a sermon was an out and out plea for the bill and obedience to its requirements. Did not Paul return Onesimus to his master? Were not servants to obey their masters? Running away was gross obedience, etc.

There was no more unity among the Baptists than among other Congregations. The *Spirit of Liberty* commented on the maneuvers of the Triennial Convention meeting in Baltimore in 1841:

. . . Within the last year, many ministers and brethren, and some entire churches of the Baptist denomination have expressed a determination, no longer to *commune* with *slave holders*, or invite them to their pulpits. A paper from the Baptist Antislavery Convention in New York signed by Rev. Elon Galusha as president was sent down to the South during the last year. This paper decisively *condemned SLAVERY*, and declaring that ultimately they must choose not to commune with slave-holders, created no small stir among the inventors and defenders of the patriarchal Institution. A letter was sent to the acting Board at Boston, from the Executive Committee of the State Convention of Ga., requesting to know how they stood on the subject of slavery; the answer was officially *we are neutral*, as individuals, vary, in our opinions. This was in November, last. A reply was soon received that this circular was not satisfactory. The Committee in Ga., say they cannot recognize so wide a difference between individual and official action in the same person. The Board at Boston sent Deacon Herman Lincoln, their treasurer down to the South to reiterate officially what the board had done, and to say what he pleased on his own account, as an individual. Mr. Lincoln went, and freely conferred with the southern brethren. They then stated to the Board what Mr. Lincoln said would be satisfactory, if it had been official, or if it should be sanctioned by the Board. The time of the convention drew near, an explicit demand had been made by the several southern bodies that Elon Galusha be dropped, left off, or expelled from the Board of Managers. The southern delegates came to the convention under the instruction, that if their demands were complied with, they might sit in Convention and pay over their money; if these demands were not met, they were to have no fellowship with the Convention.

On the evening of Saturday preceding the convention, that met the next Wednesday, the whole southern delegation, with five or six leading men from the North had a private meeting, in which they proposed to do something to satisfy the South. There was drawn up and signed, the paper which is called the "Test Act." This paper was signed by more than seventy members of the convention, but without the knowledge of the Abolitionists of this paper, and the action of the Convention under it. The Abolitionists, and we believe many others, complained. They say it means, and was well understood to mean at the *South*, that the abolitionist should be left off the Board of Missions. They say it gives the *sanction of all who signed it to slavery*.

Mrs. Swisshelm summarizes the stand of the Catholic church on the question. The *Visitor* was her own abolition paper.

When the *Visitor* entered life it was still doubtful which side of the slavery question the Roman Church would take. O'Connell was in the zenith of his power and popularity, was decidedly antislavery, and members of Catholic churches chose sides according to personal feeling, as did those of other churches. It was not until 1852, that abolitionists began to feel the alliance between Romanism and slavery; but from that time, to be a member of the Roman Church was to be a friend of southern interests.

The Catholic church at no time spoke out so strongly as, for instance, the Presbyterian church in 1818, when it condemned slavery as "a gross violation of the most precious and moral rights of human nature," as utterly inconsistent with Divine Law, and irreconcilable with the spirit and principles of the Christian gospel. Bishop England, a leader of Catholic thought through the nineteenth century, said publicly that the church did not condemn slavery. Archbishop Hughes, perhaps the most prominent church man during the slavery crisis, though opposed to slavery did not think it should be condemned. The Catholic church was an enemy of slavery "only in the sense that she is opposed even to the calamities of human life, which she has no power to reverse." Catholic laymen, like most other church groups, were divided on the issue. To the other-worldly eye of the church groups, other things were more deplorable than slavery, other interests more dear than freedom. To save one's soul as a slave was more important than to lose one's soul as a free man. Archbishop Hughes wrote to the Secretary of War, Mr. Cameron, in October, 1861: "The Catholics, so far as I know, whether native or foreign born, are willing to fight to the death for support of the Constitution, the Government, and the laws of the country. But if it should be understood that, with or without knowing it, they are to fight for the abolition of slavery, indeed, they will turn away in disgust from the discharge of what would otherwise be a patriotic duty." Bishop England wrote on February 25, 1841 to the *Catholic Miscellany*: "I am not (friendly to the continuation of slavery)—but I also see the impossibility of abolishing it here. When it can and ought to be abolished, is the question for the legislature and not for me."

This seems to be the nearest thing to an official pronouncement available. It sums up to three points—slavery is wrong; it should be done away with; but the abolitionists are too radical and any action should be gradual, and accompanied with the utmost respect for law. None of the first seven Provincial Councils held from 1829 to 1849 makes mention of the slavery controversy or any mention of the Catholic attitude. The bishops were doubtless that the Catholic mind needed no explicit expression on the question.

The press assumed an antislavery attitude very slowly, reflecting the gradual change of attitude on the part of those commercial and financial elements of the population who supported the papers of the city. *The Gazette*, which began as a conservative, Federalist organ, showed a consistent attitude beginning with its support of colonization. During the 1820s, even those Jacksonian papers which supported the political demands of the majority of the people editorialized chiefly from a colonization standpoint—*The Mercury*, *The Statesman*, *The Allegheny Democrat*, *The Commonwealth*. In the 1830s when the antislavery movement assumed the character of a moral reform crusade, the same papers and church papers such as *The Presbyterian Advocate*, *The Christian Advocate*, *The Daily*

Advocate, The Daily American, though outspoken against slavery as an institution did not speak for practical abolition measures. The general tone of the press continued conservative, and opposed the educational agitational tactics of the antislavery forces—the mass meetings, the leaflets, petitions and pamphlets as conducive to strife and threatening the integrity of the Union. To news of the colonization societies and conditions in Liberia they devoted considerable space. The antislavery activities were reported with scant detail.

Shortly after the Pittsburgh Antislavery Society was founded in 1835, however, its members realized that a paper was a necessary means of organizing public opinion in their behalf. Then the several societies of the district merged into the Antislavery Society of Western Pennsylvania, the executive committee purchased the *Christian Witness,* a weekly edited by Rev. Samuel Williams of the first Baptist Church, and made it the first abolitionist paper in the city. It was later edited by Wm. H. Burleigh, the author of a long poem, "Our Country: Its Dangers and Its Destiny," and co-editor in 1840 with R. C. Fleeson of a temperance paper, the *Washington Banner,* and the next year abolition candidate for the state senate.

The editor of the *Christian Herald* for several years during this decade was Rev. Thomas D. Baird, one of the earliest abolitionists in the city. The paper was a church paper, but did at times take an active antislavery stand.

The most radical and provocative newspaper in the city was the *American Manufacturer.* It began March 6, 1830, under the editorship of William B. Conway, who was also the author of a novel, *The Cottage on the Cliff.* The *Manufacturer* was the consistent mouthpiece for the ideas of Fanny Wright, Robert Owen, Horace Greely, Albert Brisbane. The paper supported Jacksonian Democrat principles, and conducted an energetic campaign for religious, political, and social reforms. When in January 1834, the *Manufacturer* proposed, as it had done in years previous, public celebration of the birthday of Thomas Paine, the editor of *The Allegheny Democrat* said: "It is to be hoped for the credit of our city that but few will participate in this abominable festival," and the *Gazette* warmly commended this statement.

Typical of editorial comment of the day is that of the *Aurora,* December 5, 1843:

> A friend asked us the other day, what were our particular views upon the subject of slavery; simply these: we or our ancestors committed a grievous wrong in making these Negroes slaves. We took from them that liberty which was theirs from God, and thereby committed a robbery of Heaven, so far, so good. The abolitionists say, "this being granted, let us repair our sins by immediate cessation from offense"; but shall we commit a greater offense by at-

tempting to repair a lesser one? Certainly not; let us inquire into, would the
American slaves be benefited by immediate emancipation? No!—They are
sunk in grossest ignorance—they are governed by masters' authority; and
controlled alone by their uneducated passions, they would be in a moral and
physical state tenfold more barbarous than at present.

Yet we are urged to take this step by our friends, the abolitionists. But it is
contended, it is our fault these people are thus plunged into ignorance—shall
they suffer for our crimes? It is granted that it is our fault, and they ought not
to suffer for it. Relieve them from bondage as they are now, and they will suffer for our offense. We *must* wait until they are more fit for their freedom,
before we contemplate restoring them their liberty. It is our duty to make
them so. The *Negro race* has *suffered much* at *our hands*—its wrongs claim
redress in *language that must not be neglected.* Let us instead of urging immediate Emancipation, endeavor to persuade our Southern brethren to aid in
preparing their slaves for freedom. Let us extend a portion of the treasure
now *uselessly lavished on itinerant lecturers*, and *senseless tracts*, for the instruction of the slaves. Let us repair first the great wrong of keeping them in
ignorance, that we may next restore them to the freedom which we filched
from their forefathers.

Liberate them now, and you only tantalize the Negro with the appearance
of freedom, *Educate him first—bring him up to the level of his white neighbor
in intelligence*, and he may grasp the glorious reality. Liberate them now, and
you add to the number of serfs and moral bondsmen—give them the light of
learning, and you may add the arms and minds of 3,000,000 of happy freemen, to your country's glory and defense.

The *Aurora* on another occasion said:

The editor of the *Gazette* appears to have set us down for a perfect hater
of the whole Negro race. This is a very great mistake. We are disposed to aid
as far as we can all proper schemes for their benefit. We will do anything except EMANCIPATE! We are not in favor of that plan."

The outstanding abolitionist writers of Pittsburgh were Jane Grey Swisshelm
and Martin R. Delany. Mrs. Swisshelm was first and longest on the editorial
scene. Knowledge of her career is fully recorded in her autobiography, *Half A
Century*, while Martin R. Delany's editorship is but scantily recorded.[3]
Jane Grey Swisshelm entered journalism with a hexameter poem attacking
the four Pittsburgh Methodist ministers who voted for the "Black Gag" law of the

---

3. The journalistic work of both Jane Grey Swisshelm and Martin R. Delany is also highlighted
in the "Press" section of chapter 7.

church in 1840. The verse appeared in *The Spirit of Liberty*. The *Gazette* editorialized in "pious horror and denunciation of the article." A libel suit was threatened. Mrs. Swisshelm consulted "Wm. Elder and John A. Wells, the only antislavery lawyers in the city." Both offered their services gratuitously for her defense. But Mrs. Swisshelm "re-iterated, urged, and intensified the charges brought against these false priests, until they were dumb about their injuries and libel suit."

The Pittsburgh Commercial Journal was the leading Whig paper of western Pennsylvania, edited and owned by Robt. M. Riddle. To this paper Mrs. Swisshelm wrote a letter. Although the letter was published the editor disclaimed its sentiments, "but," he said "the fair writer should have a hearing."

Mrs. Swisshelm's letters appeared once or twice a week for several months. One paper said, "*The Pittsburgh Commercial Journal* has a new contributor, who signs her name 'Jane G. Swisshelm,' dips her pen in liquid gold, and sends her paper with the down of butterflies wings." The *Journal* announced the letters the day before publication, the newsboys cried them, and papers called attention to them. Some endorsed them. Most of the papers, however, abused Mr. Riddle for publishing such unpatriotic and "incendiary rant."

This was the entrance into journalism of the woman whose editorials later were responsible for red lights on trains and vehicles, for the Pennsylvania law granting property rights to married women, for the elimination of Daniel Webster as a candidate for President of the United States and who became one of the most noted abolitionist editors in the country.

The Spirit of Liberty had come into existence in 1842 as the paper of the Liberty Party, whose presidential candidate in 1840 and 1844 was James G. Birney. Mrs. Swisshelm wrote for this paper under her initials for two reasons—her dislike for publicity, and her fear of embarrassing the Liberty Party with the sex question. "Abolitionists were men of sharp angles. Organizing them was like binding crooked sticks in a bundle, and one of the questions which divided them was the right of women to take any part in public affairs."

Of the Mexican War, as one incident in abolitionism, Mrs. Swisshelm wrote: "This great nation was engaged in the pusillanimous work of beating poor little Mexico—a giant whipping a cripple. Every man who went to the war, or induced others to go, I held as the principal in the whole list of crimes of which slavery was the synonym." The general feeling in Pittsburgh towards the war Mrs. Swisshelm records in the incident of Kossuth's speech in Pittsburgh: "When Kossuth was on his starring tour in this country, he used to create wild enthusiasm by 'Your own late glorious struggle with Mexico'; but when he reached this climax in his Pittsburgh speech a dead silence fell upon the vast, cheering audience."

Mrs. Swisshelm recounts a brief history of the abolition press in the city, with some detail of the founding of the *Visitor*, which with Martin Delany's *Mystery*, achieved national circulation in abolition circles:

> The nation was seized (during the Mexican War) by a military madness, and in the furors, the cause of the slave went to the well, and *The Spirit of Liberty* was discontinued. Its predecessor, *The Christian Witness*, had failed under the successive management of William Burleigh, Dr. Elder, and Rev. Edward Smith, three giants in those days, and there seemed no hope that any antislavery paper . . . could be supported in Pittsburgh, while all antislavery matter was carefully excluded from both religious and secular press. It was a dark day for the slave, and it was difficult to see hope for a brighter. To me, it seemed that all was lost, unless someone were especially called to speak that truth, which alone could make the people free, but certainly, I could not be the messenger . . .
>
> After the war, abolitionists began to gather their scattered forces and wanted a Liberty Party organ. To meet this want, Charles P. Shiras started the *Albatross* in the fall of 1847. He was the "Iron City Poet," author of *Dimes and Dollars* and *Owe No Man a Dollar*. He was of an old and influential family, had considerable private fortune, was courted and flattered, but laid himself and gifts on the altar of liberty. His paper was devoted to the cause of the slave and the free laborer, and started with bright prospects. He and Mr. Fleeson urged me to become a regular contributor, but Mr. Riddle objected, and the *Journal* had five hundred readers for every one the *Albatross* could hope. In the one I reached the ninety and nine unconverted, while in the other I must talk principally to those who were rooted and grounded in the faith. So I continued my connection with the *Journal* until I met James McMasters, a prominent abolitionist, who said sorrowfully: "Well, the last number of the *Albatross* will be issued on Thursday."
>
> "Is it possible?"
>
> "Possible and true! That is the end of its first quarter, and Shiras gives it up. In fact we all do. No use trying to support an abolition paper here."
>
> While he spoke a thought struck me like lightning flash, and he had but finished speaking, when I replied: "I have a great notion to start a paper myself."

So Mrs. Swisshelm began publication of *The Saturday Visitor*. It reached thousands of readers scattered in every state and territory, in England and Canada. By five o'clock on the day of publication streets were so blocked by waiting crowds, that vehicles went around by other ways, and it was six o'clock, January 20th, 1848, when the first copy was sold at the counter. Mrs. Swisshelm continues:

My paper was a six column weekly, with a small Roman letterhead, my motto, "Speak unto the children of Israel that they go forward," the names of my candidates at the head of the editorial column and the platform inserted as standing matter.

It was quite an insignificant looking sheet, but no sooner did the American eagle catch sight of it, than he swooned and fell off his perch. Democratic roosters straightened out their necks and ran screaming with terror. Whig coons scampered up trees and barked furiously. The world was falling and every one had "heard it, saw it, and felt it."

A woman had started a political paper! A woman! Could he believe his eyes? A woman! Instantly he sprang to his feet and clutched his pantaloons, shouted to the assistant editor, when he, too, read and grasped frantically at his cassimeres, called to the reporters and pressmen and typos and devils, who all rushed in, heard the news, seized their nether garments and joined the general chorus, "My breeches! Oh, my breeches!" Here was a woman re-solved to steal their pantaloons, their trousers, and when these were gone they might cry "Ye have taken away my gods, and what have I more?" The imminence of the peril called for prompt action, and with one accord they shouted, "On to the breach, in defense of our breeches! Repel the invader or fill the trenches with our noble dead."

"That woman shall not have *my* pantaloons," cried the editor of the big city daily; "nor *my* pantaloons," said he who issued manifestos but once a month; "nor mine," "nor mine," chimed in the small fry of the country towns.

Even the religious press could not get past the tailor shop, and "panta-loons" was the watchword all along the line. George D. Prentiss took up the cry, and gave the world a two-third column leader on it, stating explicitly, "She is a man all but the pantaloons." I wrote to him asking a copy of the ar-ticle, but received no answer, when I replied in rhyme to suit his case:

> Perhaps you have been busy
> Horsewhipping Sal or Lizzie,
> Stealing some poor man's baby,
> Selling its mother, may-be.
> You say—and you are witty—
> That I—and, tis a pity—
> Of manhood lack but dress;
> But you lack manliness,
> A body clean and new,
> A soul within it too.

Nature must change her plan
Ere you can be a man.

This turned the tide of battle. One editor said, "Brother George, beware of sister Jane." Another, "Prentiss has found his match." He made no reply, and it was not long until I thought the pantaloon argument was dropped forever.

There was, however, a bright side to the reception of the *Visitor*. Horace Greeley gave it respectful recognition, so did N. P. Willis and Gen. Morris in the *Home Journal*, Henry Peterson's *Saturday Evening Post*, *Godey's Lady's Book*, Graham's and Sergeant's magazines, and the antislavery papers, one and all, gave it pleasant greeting, while there were other editors who did not in view of this innovation, forget that they were American gentlemen.

There were some saucy notices from "John Smith," editor of *The Great West*, a large literary sheet published in Cincinnati. After John and I had pelted each other with paragraphs, a private letter told me that she, who then won a large reputation as John Smith, was Celia, who afterwards became my very dear friend until the end of her lovely life, and who died the widow of another dear friend, Wm. Burleigh.

In the second number of the *Visitor*, James H. McClelland, as secretary of the county convention, published its report and contributed an able article, thus recognizing it as the much needed county organ of the Liberty Party.

By 1840 the moral and religious enthusiasm of the antislavery forces began to give way to more concrete political notion of the abolitionists. Gradualism became immediatism. The colonizers continued to send occasional groups to Liberia. The antislavery preachers and lecturers had convinced a good portion of the public that slavery was sinful, and greater numbers were interested in practical measures to abolish it immediately. Cleavages among various groups deepened. But Pittsburgh came more and more to share the attitude of the industrial North—that slavery must go.

As the expansion of northern capital demanded abolition of slave labor, hostility towards antislavery activity was rapidly deflected towards slavery itself. Especially in Pittsburgh, whose supremacy in manufacturing, and particularly in the manufacture of iron, was well established, and whose industry and capital were expanding at a great rate, this was true. By 1857 there were 25 rolling mills and 16 foundries in operation. The development of the puddling process in the 1840s and 1850s spurred the iron industry. Steam engines were being produced to the value of nearly $1,000,000 yearly. Two railroads now carried raw materials into the city and the manufactured products to eastern and western markets. The textile industry also was important. In Allegheny seven cotton mills operated.

There was likewise a large glass industry, seven flint glass factories, six window glass factories, five green glass factories and one that made block glass. John Roebling wrote his brother that in the coal business around Pittsburgh "the large capitalists are gradually buying out the smaller ones, thus making the coal business a surer one."

Pittsburgh manufacturers finally opposed slavery because slave labor deprived them of an expanding market. Slaveholders preferred to buy manufactured goods from England at cheaper prices than they paid in the North. But the purchasing power of southern slave owners was low. They had little cash and were compelled to buy on credit, which was profitable to the bankers, who therefore did not oppose slavery.

Pittsburgh investors and financiers also came finally to oppose slavery because the plantation system barred northern capital from investment. The extension of slavery into the opening West threatened to interfere with investments there too. A number of southern states passed laws against the use of steam power. Slave owners put what money they had into more land and more slaves rather than open mines and factories in which slave labor was not practical or profitable, and which would lead to the growth of a white working class.

Pittsburgh manufacturers, like all northern manufacturers, needed improved highways, extension of railroads, canals and other internal improvements to supply their markets. Representatives of the non-industrial South who dominated the national government fought the granting of national subsidies for such measures. Slaveholding southerners thereby incurred the hostility of northern industrialists. Since the slaveholding South opposed the high tariffs, which would protect the imported goods of northern manufacturers, this policy further antagonized the industrialists towards slavery.

Pittsburgh industrial workers likewise opposed slavery. For one thing a large body of unpaid slave labor kept wages down. Northern and southern mechanics, who looked for work in the South were underbid by masters who hired out their slaves, as in the case of the building of the capital at Austin, Texas. The North-South wage differential existed before the Civil War. The differential in the cotton mills particularly affected such Pittsburgh groups as the women workers in the textile mills.

Further, the working class wanted a free west as a field of free labor, and for the possibility of settlement on small, independent farms. A Homestead Act was one of the major demands of Pittsburgh labor in pre-Civil War years. The Homestead Act of 1862, which gave 160 acres to every family head, was passed in answer to a nation-wide demand. Free western land kept the eastern labor market from too great competition and lowering of wages.

Besides these reasons for their determined opposition to slavery, the growing working class was concerned, as much as the intellectual middle class, with the suppression of civil rights. The right to organize into trade unions and the right to strike were being attacked. The right of assembly and petition was denied them.

Colonization had been strongest among church people, professional, industrial and commercial people. The antislavery movement was at first most deeply rooted among the working class and "radical" intellectuals. It did not become a "respectable" movement until after the passage of the Fugitive Slave Law of 1850. Freedom was on the defensive and an abolitionist was an object of scorn, even of bitter hatred in 1834. Slavery was on the defensive in 1860 and an abolitionist was elected to the presidency.

When, in February 1836, the House of Representatives by 129 to 74 decided not to interfere with slavery in the District of Columbia, upon the grounds that such a course would be a violation of public faith, Mr. Darlington and Mr. Denny of Allegheny County voted against the resolution. And the following year, when Pennsylvania revised its constitution, a great debate took place as to whether the Negro population should be given the right to vote.

As early as 1839 a reader of the *Advocate and Advertiser* wrote to the paper a letter on "The Cotton Dynasty," in which he said:

> The COTTON DYNASTY is that which is ruling and ruining us at the present time. As one of the free and independent citizens of the North, I have awaited with impatience and anxiety for the tearing off by some skillful hand of the political plaster beneath which the *real sore* of the laboring community, and Pittsburgh is emphatically a city of working men, is festering deep, and mining all within!

"To relieve this state of affairs," he said:

> Fellow citizens of the North, there is for us but one remedy. It is to break down the Cotton sway . . . Look at it. Who but remembers the threatening tones of the champions of the slave-wrought cotton fields—the war of words—the menace of disunion! And for what? Because, only because that the industry of the Northern Manufacturer was protected from the unequal competition of the *slave* producer of the raw matter, and the *half famished* producer of the fabric. . . . The cotton power, in its merciless exactions, demanded that the tariff be sacrificed to it. The tariff of protection of our own free Northern labor, it seems must yield, that the production of the ground down and half-fed operators of Britain, and that the slaves of the South may be brought into successful competition with the productions of Northern free paid labor . . . Mark then fellow citizens if we quietly, as at present, sub-

mit our necks to the Cotton Dynasty, whose productions are those of unpaid slaves, the depreciated value of Our productions must soon leave us in possession of little more than the name of freeman!

Although the writer was not too clear on the relation of the tariff, manufacturers' profits and the wages of labor, he pointed out that the southern political supremacy with its twenty-seven slave representatives, with "King Calhoun and prime ministers Hayne, Hamilton, and others forced the free laborer of the North down to a level with their slaves" and produced the hard times through which the country was passing in the panic that had begun two years before.

When the Fugitive Slave Law was passed in 1850, public opinion indignantly denounced it. Little pretense was made of obeying it. Four days after its passage a mass meeting of Allegheny County citizens was held in Diamond Square and branded the law as "iniquitous and unconstitutional."[4] This meeting was held on a Saturday night, and Martin R. Delany was loudly called for. He evaded the cries that he address the meeting, saying that some of the white leaders should express their views first. The meeting was adjourned to meet the following Monday in Allegheny. The mayor of the city, a number of ministers, including Rev. Charles Avery, candidates of the various political parties, and delegates from the Workingmen's Congress were present.

Mr. James Callan, member of the House of Representatives, spoke against the bill. "Its object is," he said, "to make you kidnapers; will you be so?" There were loud cries of "No, No!" "Will you be men stealers?" Again cries of "No! No!" "It takes away the two great bulwarks of the nation—trial by jury and the habeas corpus writ. It will brand us with slavery and make us the tools of the South. Agitate! Agitate! Was the maxim of O'Connell, the great Irish agitator, and by its influence the Catholic Emancipation Bill was carried." "I would say to all those that are listening to Joe, 'Agitate! Agitate!' Let not this excitement pass away, and soon this infamous law would be repealed." A set of strong resolutions against the law and against Congress for the passage of such a law were drawn up and approved.

Mr. Ferral was introduced to the meeting by the mayor as a delegate from the Workingmen's Congress. Ferral said he had been deputed by the Congress to express the sympathy of that body with this movement and to read them some resolutions which the Workingman had passed in reference to the subject of the meeting. The Congress had adjourned its meeting so that its members could meet here and swell the outburst of indignation against this barbarous law. Mr. Ferral said: "In this country, whatever evils may exist, you, the workingmen, are to blame. If you knew your own interests—if you were not divided—your will

4. A similar meeting at New Brighton drew up resolutions declaring that the Fugitive Slave Law would be treated with contempt.

would be omnipotent, your power would be irresistible. Be men, then. Record your protest against this law. Remove this blot from our national escutcheons, this damning sin from our land." And there was great applause.

Martin Delany was again called for. Delany explained the vicious features of the bill. Under this bill, he said, the southern slaveholder could come into the town and make its proudest citizen a bloodhound, make him act as his vassal, or suffer imprisonment and fine. It gave the judges constituted by it power to appoint other judges, equal in power and authority to themselves, and such a thing had never before been heard of. "The President of the United States," he said, "holds a high and noble position; but the people are superior to the President. What would you think if he had power to invest another person with privileges equal to his own?" . . . "Under the operation of this bill, too, no colored person can be safe. *Who is to judge whether he is free or a bondsman?* Who is there to swear that I was not born a slave? To a colored man this is an impossibility. Here then am I, a freeman, liable at any time to be taken away and kept forever in bondage. (Voices—'We won't let them take you!') Never Fear! (Laughter) Some will say, 'Let free papers be carried.' But I will never carry parchment in my pocket to prove that I am a man. (Tremendous cheering.) 'Honorable Mayor, whatever ideas of Liberty I may have, have been received from reading the lives of your revolutionary fathers.' No, my course is determined; should the slave pursuer enter my dwelling, one of us must perish. (Excitement). *I have treasures there*; there are a wife and children to protect; I will give the tyrant timely warning; but if the sanctuary of my home is violated, if I don't defend it, may the grave be to my body no resting place, and the vaulted heavens refuse my spirit an entrance." And the account says, there were "loud and continuous cheers."

"About the close of the meeting," says the newspaper account, "when the minds of the vast multitude had been fully prepared to speak out on this question of suppression, Mr. Callan asked leave to submit a resolution which, if not carried unanimously, he was determined to withdraw. But he knew he spoke to clear heads and hearts and would, therefore, offer the following: 'Resolved—That as an expression of the wishes and hopes of this meeting, the faithful page of American history may hand down to posterity some adequate idea of the moral turpitude of his crime, who wields the despot's power and shakes the pillar of justice, of virtue and of equal rights, the only permanent supports of freedom, and the MILLARD FILLMORE—President of these United States is fully entitled to the full cup of public indignation for approving of the Fugitive Slave Bill by his signature.' The above resolutions were received with a vibrant burst of applause and were passed without one dissenting voice." . . . After lasting three hours the meeting adjourned.

The resolutions offered by Mr. Ferral, from the Workingmen's Congress, were lengthy and strongly worded. The last section read: "*Resolved*—That as men and citizens we believe the time has arrived, when our duty to ourselves and to promote humanity's interest calls loudly for the amendment of our state Constitution, by striking out the word 'WHITE,' so that by making all men brothers, in interests, within the boundaries of our commonwealth they may rest assured that we feel resolved not to permit honest old Pennsylvania to come to be a kennel for the slaveholders' bloodhounds. Nor the place where manstealers can find sympathy and assistance."

A few weeks later a mass meeting of colored citizens of Allegheny County was held in the basement of Wylie Street Church. The Rev. John Peck was called to the chair. J. N. Templeton was chosen secretary. Martin Delany, P. L. Jackson, and J. B. Vashon were a committee on resolutions, and H. M. Collins, J. M. Collins, and J. H. Templeton a committee on printing.

The *Gazette* said, a few days after the passage of the Fugitive Slave Law,

> We learn from our colored citizens that upwards of 100 fugitive slaves have already left Pittsburgh for Canada. Forty left Allegheny yesterday evening, after having bade adieu to their friends and families. They almost all lived in the upper part of Allegheny city, and since their escape have intermarried with free persons of color, but they are thus once more compelled to sever all family ties. The escaped slaves have all armed themselves, and declare that they are resolved to die, rather than again be carried into bondage.

The daily papers of the period record numberless cases of fugitives, before and after the passage of the Fugitive Slave Law, also many instances of the kidnaping of Negroes by professional slavecatchers. Of the latter some were fugitives who had established themselves in the city. Some were Negroes who had never been slaves. Such incidents and the trials that resulted from some of them objectified the teachings of the antislavery societies before the public and most effectively roused public opinion in favor of abolition.

CHAPTER 5

CIVIL RIGHTS

Typist: E. Saunier / Rewriteman: J. Ernest Wright /
October 2, 1940 / Final

When the runaway slaves, in their Pittsburgh hideouts, anticipated with every breath an assured freedom, they were merely emerging, had they but known it, upon a northern battlefield whose dimensions and action they could not guess. They envied the freedom of the Pittsburgh Negro, but they did not realize the constantly shifting basis of that freedom in social attitudes and legal sanctions. The historical panorama of the Pittsburgh battleground exhibits a neat paradox: whereas in the earlier years the Negro, denied by law the privilege of equal citizenship, was aided surreptitiously to a greater freedom than his legal status permitted, in later years he was just as surreptitiously denied the civic freedom which city, state, and nation had granted him. Indeed, the whole history of the Pittsburgh Negro shows only too clearly the distance between ethical concepts and social reality.

Before 1780 free Negroes in Pennsylvania had been subject to the same regulations established for slaves. But since Pittsburgh during that time was a frontier community with legal and political administration primitively organized, the laws might as well not have been written into the statutes books so far as general status of slaves in the community was concerned. The number of slaves before 1780 was small, and their civil status was determined more by the character of their owners than by existing statutes. The laws provided, nevertheless, that Negroes—slave or free—should be tried not in the same courts as white men but in special courts. They were forbidden trial by jury and inflicted with harsher penalties than were white offenders. They were victims of special provisions against vagrancy, the same provisions which bound free Negroes to servitude. Heavier penalties were provided against free Negroes who harbored slaves, received stolen goods, or indulged in trade without permission of the master than were provided against whites. The law also forbade mixed marriages. Free Negroes who married whites were to be sold into slavery for life; the white person was indentured to seven years of servitude. A free Negro guilty of fornication or adultery was sold into servitude for seven years; the white offender was whipped, imprisoned, or branded with the letter "A." Free Negroes were forbidden, as were slaves, from frequenting tippling houses, carrying arms or gathering in companies. Free Negroes while traveling had to carry a pass. In other words, freedom was achieved with difficulty because of stringent manumission laws, and was very easily lost.

The act of 1780 for the gradual abolition of slavery fundamentally changed the civil status of the Negro in Pennsylvania. The act technically established legal equality with whites, except that this did not grant the Negro the vote, and forbade him membership in the state militia. The free Negro, however, was not to enjoy political equality for almost another century, until 1870.

Meantime, during the long period of growing crisis culminating in the Civil War, additional laws were necessary for his protection. Kidnaping was the greatest threat to his free movement. In 1788 a law was passed penalizing kidnapers. The practice continued, however, and another legislative act in 1820 set heavier penalties. In 1847 still another act made punishment even heavier. By that year public opinion against kidnaping was sufficiently aroused to make the act effective.

In the earlier years of the nineteenth century, long before the migrations and the great industrial expansion in steel, the Negro in Pittsburgh was comparatively fortunate in his civic position. He escaped, for instance, the injustice and maltreatment which the Philadelphia Negro suffered. Pittsburgh newspapers record no stoning to death of Negro women by white women, no armed disruption of Negro church services, no clubbing or stoning of Negroes at Independence Day celebrations. Pittsburgh at this time was still close to the frontier and was inhabited by many who had matured in the fierce equality of frontier life; the frontier standards of equality and individual rights were still strong, and the Negro, so long as his numbers were few, profited by them. Sincere men early adopted him as a symbol of violated human dignity, and gave aid, though the law forbade it, to slaves escaping their southern masters. Even among men not stirred by such lofty motives, opposition to aiding runaway slaves was half-hearted: after all, the economic property which the black men represented was not the kind that came directly home to Pittsburgh businesses and Pittsburgh bosoms. For many years the city remained engrossed in the larger problem of building its industries and fitting out expeditions for an advancing frontier.

Yet prejudice did develop. Although civil equality had been granted by the Act of 1780, the population for sometime was to a large degree an ex-slave population. For a long time, the Negro remained a menial and was treated as such. He began his progress toward equality from the lowest economic rank; he was hardly yet fitted by education or experience to compete with the white man to whom all opportunities—educational and occupational—had always been open. In the first decades of his history as a free man, he was left without organized assistance largely to shift for himself. He tried his best to gain a foothold in the community, in its economic, political, social, and cultural life, but he was inept, haunted by an actual and a fancied inferiority.

As the number of Negroes in Pittsburgh increased, haphazard kindliness in helping them to adjust themselves persisted, but became more and more ineffective, and by the 1830s the Negroes had become a segregated group that felt with increasing heaviness the white man's civil superiority.

At this time the *Methodist Conference Journal* said of the Negro community in the city:

> Our African or colored population is about 1200 or 1500. They have three churches, two Sabbath and two day schools: Two churches and one day and Sabbath school in Arthursville or Hayti. They have one Literary Society, take a number of newspapers, and pay considerable attention to train up their children in a proper manner—and it is but an act of justice to a majority of these people to state that they are making good progress in knowledge and sound morals, and that they are doing much to educate their children well.

White citizens of Pittsburgh, though they meant well by the Negro, had little thought of admitting him into their civil councils, schools, churches, theaters, clubs, let alone into political assembles where he might exert influence. They adopted, instead, a cumbersome plan of granting separate buildings for Negro instruction, and so tardily were such grants made that for many years Negro education and training were matters of sporadic private effort and philanthropy. More and more during the second and third decade of the century, white churches closed their pews to Negro worshipers until the latter were driven like the children of Israel to wander from one barren little place of worship to another before they could establish comfortable churches of their own. From such simple causes there developed from the very first a public attitude either of patronizing helpfulness or amused contempt for the Negro's social ineptitude. Under pressure of other factors, that attitude deepened to political and economic discrimination and, finally, to social ostracism. As early as 1833, when a new theater was opened in Pittsburgh, the *Gazette* announced:

> To the Gallery: Anxious to add to the comfort of the frequenters of this part of the theater, they are respectfully informed that two boxes from each side have been thrown into the gallery. The two on the left will be reserved exclusively for people of color. The price of which will be the same as admission to the pit. The subscriber hopes the arrangement will prove satisfactory.

One hundred years after that notice, in April of 1930, an article in the *Sun Telegraph* by a Pittsburgh dramatic reviewer was entitled, "Mason and Dixon Line in Theater Irks Negroes." The prevailing idea that Negroes were less skillful and capable, that they were the most poverty-stricken group in the city, that they were incapable of economic progress of culture, slowly froze into a wall of prejudice against which the individual Negro struggled in vain. The efforts of leaders like the Vashons, the Delanys, and the Woodsons, and the presence and activity in the city of such opponents of slavery and proponents of democracy as Reverend Charles Avery, Mr. Burleigh and Jane Grey Swisshelm, Reverend E. Smith accomplished relatively little to help Pittsburgh's Negroes.

Isolation from community life became more physically apparent. The growth of racial prejudice and the denial of civil rights were due not only to the difficulty and frequent failure in competition with a people of longer training and established efficiency, but also to the physical restrictions set down by those who owned the properties of the town and the growing business and industries. Only minor, independent, self-owned businesses—barber shops, public baths, hairdressing establishments, butcher shops, second-hand clothing shops—could be established by Negroes, and therefore only the most restricted business relationships were possible among them or between Negroes and whites. With his meager earnings the Negro could not afford the rents of houses fronting the street; he was limited to the alleys of restricted sections of the city. There he was crowded into an urban squalor which he had not himself created, but which came, illogically, to be associated with him, as though he had deliberately chosen such an environment. He came to be looked upon at best as an unfortunate slum-dweller, and by the many who were irritated at any suggestion of responsibility for his stature he was regarded as little less than a potential criminal for whom harsh measures and further segregation were needed. From their first concentration in one area they became an annoyance to the city government. Those who lived in cellars and shanties—many of them newly escaped slaves who could not find ready employment—through exposure and lack of nourishment in the bitter winters ended inevitably as charges upon public charity. The recurrent economic crises added others to the list. Still others, just as with so many unfortunate whites in similar circumstances, were added to the public charge through immoderate use of alcohol, the most efficient social equalizer of the nineteenth century.

A graphic account of the poverty and its attendant crime in the crisis of 1837 is a story in the *Chronicle* at this period. Although but two cases of Negro privation are listed and neither of these is charged with the civil offenses charged to other cases cited, such conditions as the *Chronicle* describes in conjunction with the fact of African features continued to promote the popular concept of the Negro masses as declassed beings incapable of progress and therefore of too little social worth to be given concern over his civil or political guarantees. The *Chronicle* reported:

THE TIMES AND PEOPLE STARVING

To the human citizens of Pittsburgh and Allegheny cities

A painful crisis has arrived in the annals of our country when the greatest distress for want of money and employment, seems to pervade the greater part of the community and most of our towns and cities, and will soon be felt by most of our towns and cities, and will soon be felt by our farmers in the country. We have lately read of three cases of death by starvation in the once flourishing city of Philadelphia, but in a life near half a century in Pittsburgh, we never till now, knew the painful fact, that there are people and many families in the very greatest distress, and literally starving for want of food. For some weeks past, great complaints have been made by many of the poorer classes, that they could not collect what they had earned, could get little or no employment and could not provide the common food and raiment for themselves and families; but until Wednesday, we did not know of a case of actual starvation for want of food. On that morning we were called upon by a poor and benevolent woman, to visit one of our old acquaintances, and strive to provide for his suffering children, as their mother was dead a few months ago, and the father was then actually dying from starvation. On this painful news, we sent a gentlemen up to his house, in the Fifth Ward; who returned and confirmed all that was reported, and said relief must be at once furnished or it would be too late. We then, in company with two very human and respectable gentlemen, visited the house and beheld what we never expected to see, a man in almost the last agonies of life, with three children, and they had nothing in the house to eat but a little dried meat procured in the morning, and the man had been eight days in bed, and no food, and having been a volunteer to fight the battles of our country in the last war, had failed to get paid his just claims, and being a carpenter by trade, could get no work, and feeling, like too many do in these distressed times, too high minded to make his poverty and sufferings known, he was dying with hunger.

He gave us a plain statement of his case. Our eyes wandered over the poverty and distress around us, and we were struck with astonishment that a human being, in a land of plenty, near a market house, and surrounded by so many kind and humane people, could suffer so long and so much without being known. One gentleman took a loaf of bread, and gave the widow's mite, all the money he had; another took out a $2.00 note, and handed it, promising to be back in the evening with a good supply of necessaries; and this suffering fellow creature has been relieved for the present, and maybe, with good medical aid, raised again.

We left the house, resolved to make his case known upon the house-tops, and this case led to inquiries that truly astonishes us as much as they will our human and benevolent citizens, who have not hitherto known the facts, and we give a few cases, that came to our knowledge within the last two days, and we have no hesitation now to say that there are many families suffering in the same way. . . . [1]

3rd—A Scotch Gardener, who has a wife and four children, and usually made a good living at his business, could not get employment; was recommended to go to the country; went; got work with a farmer during harvest; could not get his pay in money; took part in flour and carried it home 16 miles to his starving family, and now they are in a distressed condition.

4th—A poor aged man living in Allegheny came to the intelligence office with his afflicted daughter—a married woman with a drunken husband, whom she supported with her family for three years, whilst she could procure needle work. Now in distress her husband had eloped, she and her children were starving and she wanted to bind them out that she might hire out and be saved from starvation.

5th—An aged colored man with a wife and two children, after going all over this city to beg a little work, offered to wheel out a large quantity of ashes for 6¼ cents to buy bread for his starving family, came mourning over his fate and asking what he could do to save them and get food.

6th—An aged colored woman came to beg a shirt for her dying husband, who had none to put on, and the colored classes are beginning to suffer very much.

7th—A sober and industrious Welshman had only twenty days work in the last five months.

1. Items 1, 2, and 10 from the list are missing in the original manuscript.

8th—A respectable well-dressed lady went this week with her clothes to borrow $3.00 on them for food.

9th—A poor man in deep distress, stole a coat and sold it for .75 cents to buy bread, and on being discovered, went with the money, and was severely rebuked for not telling his case before he stole; and he would have been relieved. . . .

11th—Some people say, about our suffering poor, why don't they go to the country and get work. Now a farmer has told us that money is becoming very scarce in the country and they don't hire useless hands. A poor young man, a student, who had gone to get work to support life when he could get nothing to do in the city, reports to us that on the Franklin road, where he has seen a great many people go out amongst the farmers and beg work at any price, even at 12½ cents a day, and the farmers having nothing to do, refuse to employ them; they then beg their bread or a meal; and oftentimes lurk about the farmers' houses until dark, when from sheer hunger and necessity they rob their cellars, milk houses, and hen roosts for food.

12th—It is generally believed that the smoke house in Allegheny with about 60,000 pounds of bacon was set on fire by the starving poor to catch what they could in the scramble, as no fire was known about the premises for sometime. This lamentable occurrence is believed by many to be the works of the unthinking starving poor and it is generally believed that nothing but the progress of the great temperance cause and the faithful labor of the noble Washingtonians, prevents many popular outbreaks and mobs by the deeply suffering community, and with these facts and cases before us. We are candid in declaring that we believe there are hundreds of families in daily distress for want of employment, money and food, and that of the 54,000 people who reside in our two cities—two boroughs and 16 small towns within a circle of 5 miles around our city, which at 6 persons to a family, would make 9,000 families, near one-fourth and upwards of 2,000 families—are out of regular employment; and that hundreds of families are at present in distress; and we now for the truth of these facts, as stated, and the names of parties stated, refer to Mr. Harris at his Intelligence Office, and to several respectable citizens whose names are left there—We most earnestly recommend the Mayors of both of our cities to act in concert. And call forth public meetings, and appoint judicious committees in each ward to collect money and provisions for the poor suffering, and to visit and find them out; and relieve every case of real necessity—And to furnish and to give the best advice and assistance to the suffering. And also to recommend to the clergy and human citizens; now to visit and do all the good they can to relieve the wants of the sufferers. For

to be relieved it must be known, for our citizens are famed for their humanity and kindness, and let them now at the beginning of severe sufferings be up
and doing.

—Howard

Early efforts to improve the status of the Negro in Pittsburgh were largely
agenda to the national antislavery and abolition movements. The liberation
granted by the Act of 1780 had begun to drop into abeyance. Although Allegheny
County was one of six counties in Pennsylvania in which the Negro had been
voting until 1838, just when his increasing numbers made his ballot a powerful
weapon, the Negro lost his right to vote in Pennsylvania. With the channels and
agencies through which he could register his protest so limited, private organizations, resolutions and petitions were his only means of action. These he used
with increasing deftness, evolving a series of organizations each somewhat stronger than the preceding one and each merging into a new form once its immediate
object had been attained.

When the First National Convention of the People of Color was held in the
Wesleyan Church in Philadelphia in the summer of 1831 to discuss the advancement of the free Negro in civil life, a Pittsburgh delegate was present. At the second convention held in the same city in 1832, John B. Vashon was a Pittsburgh
delegate. In each succeeding convention Pittsburgh delegates participated. One
of the earliest instances of concerted action on the part of the Pittsburgh Negroes
was the formation in 1832 of The African Education Society. Through the work
of this society the Negro community sought to demonstrate its civil worth and
equip its members to enjoy free civil life. To the Pennsylvania Assembly were sent
anti-Negro petitions with increasing frequency in the 1830s. These petitions
would have materially affected the comparatively large Negro population of Pittsburgh. They asked that immigration of Negroes into Pennsylvania be stopped, or
that laws permitting slavery be once more passed. Schemes were advanced without apology to eliminate the Negro population from the state. Against all such
bills and schemes John B. Vashon, Martin R. Delany, Abraham D. Lewis,
Woodson, John Peck, and other Pittsburgh leaders protested valiantly. They petitioned and drew up resolutions conducting a reasoned propaganda for equal
rights of their people to live as citizens within the state.

These general moves suffered a severe set back when the Constitutional Convention met in 1837 to revise the state constitution. A heated debate developed as
to whether the new document should give the Negroes in the state the right to
vote.

In the autumn of that year, the *Gazette* reported:

Petitions were presented by Mr. Sellers, from Montgomery and Bucks, against extending the right of suffrage to the colored population. On motion of Mr. Konigmacher, all petitions and memorials, were ordered to be laid on the table, and not printed without the consent of two-thirds of the members.

The Resolution of Mr. Magee, of Perry County, for the appointment of a committee to inquire into the expediency of preventing people of color, whether slave or free, from entering into the State, was taken up for consideration, 67 to 35.

That the Negro was only one minority against whom prejudice, social indignity and political restriction had begun to take form is shown by the report with which the *Gazette* continued:

An amendment was offered by Mr. Woodward, from Luzerne County, a leading and influential radical, to have the Committee inquire also into the expediency of reporting a section to prevent foreigners, coming to the country after the year 1840, from holding office, or having the right to vote. Mr. W. spoke at considerable length, and with earnestness in favor of the amendment. He believed the time to be near at hand, when the whole people of the United States must be alive to this subject. The country was over-run in some places with foreigners, ignorant of our government and institutions, but exceedingly active in political strife. This was no party question.

Our country held sufficient inducement to emigrants, aside from political power. To grant this was too lavish a generosity, as though we did not appreciate the legacy of our ancestors. He believed the native citizens could take care of the government well enough, though he would extend to foreigners all other privileges religious and civil liberty, and security to person and property. But as he had doubt of the power of our State to do anything effectually, and at the suggestion of his friends, he withdrew his amendment.

Mr. Cummins charged the gentlemen from Luzerne with having shot his shot and then withdrawing the remark. Mr. W. then renewed it, to give an opportunity for reply. Mr. C. then pronounced an extravagant, and very much out-of-place eulogy upon foreigners. He declared our liberties had been secured by foreigners, and that they had several times saved the government from monarchy, etc. The amendment was again withdrawn, and the debate cut off by the previous question, when the resolution of Mr. Magee was agreed to 56 to 50.

Walter Forward was, during this debate, Representative in the State Assembly for western Pennsylvania, of which Pittsburgh and its vicinity was the very heart, is now, furthermore, with the second largest Negro area in the state, the only populous area beyond the extreme eastern county of Philadelphia. Forward demanded of the Assembly:

> Why do you give a man the right of suffrage at all? Is it because he has or has not the right of protection? Has the black man of property, not an equal stake in the gov't. with you? And is protection not equally dear to him? Does your color give you a larger interest in this matter than it does him?
>
> If the black man be as intelligent, as virtuous, and as patriotic as you, no man can give a reason why he ought not to enjoy the right of suffrage on an equality with you. But, say gentleman, he is an inferior with regard to the offices and duties of life? There is no duty which you do not exact from them, and they are subject to all the obedience to rules and law, that the white man is subject to.

Forward alluded to the colonization societies and if their plan succeeded, and the colored people were capable of self-government, there must sooner or later be an end of slavery in this country; for the institution of slavery among us was, in his opinion, on a false basis, and could not endure.

Speaking further on the suffrage, Forward declared that it was a monstrous injustice to deprive men of their rights, and it was impossible to say what the consequences might be. Was there any more reason why these people should be excluded from its right of suffrage, than they should be excluded from the right of holding property within the commonwealth?

Forward declared to the assembled House:

> If you hold to this doctrine, that these people are incapable of self-gov't because they have been slaves and are degraded, you must recollect that you insult the white men as well as the black, because many of them have been much degraded, and might be supposed to be incapable of self-gov't., besides, you destroy all the hopeful prospects of those most excellent institutions—the colonization societies.
>
> If you establish the inferiority of the black race, you insult some of the white race. Sir, slavery existed among the Greeks and among the Romans and who were the slaves? Was it the Ethiopians or the men of dark skin? No, Sir, it was the white men that were held in slavery, and were not as degraded, and as ignorant as our Negro slaves? Let gentlemen read the history of slavery as it existed in those ancient countries and they will be able to determine this question, as to which was the most degraded as low and lower than our slaves, not the matter of life and death was in the hands of their masters. Many other countries were white men held in slavery, and would say that this race was incapable of self-gov't.

The acrimony of the debate is shown by further quotation from the *Gazette* in January 1838:

> Mr. Earle resumed his speech, and referred to diverse authorities to support his position. He deprecated the idea that the majority has any rightful power to deprive the minority of their rights and disfranchise them at pleasure. Nor could he agree with the gentleman from Luzerne (Mr. Woodward) that foreigners and Irish emigrants ought to be disfranchised. He proved conclusively that Negroes were freemen and citizens—that they have been claimed as such by the American Government when impressed as seamen on board of foreign vessels—and he held in his passport signed by John Forsyth, Sec. of State, of the United States certifying that a black man, who was about to travel in Europe, is a free citizen.
>
> He pronounced it a vile slander on people of Philadelphia city and county, to say that they were so violent, so disorderly, that they would raise a mob, and even endanger the life of a Negro, should he attempt to vote. His colleagues from the county, had slandered the people of Philadelphia, and done them gross injustice—and he had only heard appeals to vulgar prejudices, and arguments in support of slavery from the friends of this measure. His speech was able and argumentative.
>
> Mr. Darlington defended the abolitionists; of which he was one, (and as Mr. Earle had done) appealed to all to say that they had ever known an instance of amalgamation of a member of the Society of Friends with the Negroes—though they take them by the hand as brethren. N.B. It is the duty of the reporter to state whilst Mr. Darlington was speaking, considerable disturbance took place in the gallery, and occasioned great excitement in the hall. The facts of the case were these. The assistant sergeant at arms denied admittance to gallery to several Negroes—and the officers had this morning removed one or two from the gallery. James Forten, Jr., afterwards went into the gallery against the order of the officers, and refused to leave it when they required him to do so—and the disturbance was occasioned by the doorkeeper forcibly removing him.

Mr. Harmar Denny of Pittsburgh presented a "Memorial of the Free Citizens of Color in Pittsburgh and Its Vicinity, Relative to the Right of Suffrage,"[2] which he read in Convention July 8, 1837. The Memorial aroused one of the most heated arguments of the convention. Mr. Ingersoll of Philadelphia thought the petition contained rather harsh language against citizens of other states who merely treated as property and held in bondage certain people of the same color

2. The Memorial is reprinted in appendix 1.

and blood as the petitioners. He thought that nothing should be done to commit the legislature, or involve the state in a momentous problem that concerned the Union. Mr. Sterigers of Montgomery said that the petition was a mere argumentative paper, and that although there were two thousand colored people in Pittsburgh, only one hundred had signed the petition. Mr. Brown of Philadelphia was willing to discount the fact that the petitioners had not used very courteous language, but he did think that when the memorialists said that "impartial observers assert that there is less idleness and drunkenness among those of their color who live in Pittsburgh than among any other class of its citizens" they were using very strong language indeed.

Mr. Cummin of Juniata had another view. He said he had come to the legislature to revise and frame a constitution for the known and acknowledged citizens of the state and not to receive memorials and petitions in the midst of their labors concerning the colored population. The gentlemen of the legislature, Mr. Cummin thought, wanted to be more merciful toward the blacks than He who made them. He who created the heavens and the earth and all mankind made a distinction between the children of men. That argument, Mr. Cummin thought, would stand in opposition to all the learned gentlemen could say in support of the natural equality of the black man. God had made them a base race, and nothing could be put into the constitution of this state that would reverse the decrees of Providence. Mr. Stevens of Adams in concluding said that the state constitution reserved the right of petition to "citizens," and if colored men were not citizens, then they had only that right which subjects have of petitioning those who were placed directly over them.

The Convention also received an "Appeal of Forty Thousand Citizens— Threatened with Disfranchisement to the People of Pennsylvania." The appeal not only set forth the legal basis for their claim but was an impassioned reminder of the services rendered the government which was denying them participation in its functions. It was also an eloquent statement of their constitutional rights and of determination to defend those rights:

> This clause guarantees the right of suffrage to us as freely as to any of our fellow citizens whatsoever for such was the intention of the framers. In the original draft, reported by the committee of nine, the word "WHITE" stood before "FREEMAN." On motion of ALBERT GALLATIN it was stricken out, for the express purpose of including colored citizens. . . . (See Minutes of the Convention 1790.)
>
> The fourth of the said articles contains the following language: "The free inhabitants of each of these States, paupers, vagabonds, and fugitives from justice excepted, shall be entitled to all privileges and immunities of free citi-

zens in the several States." That we were not excluded under the phrase, "paupers, vagabonds, and fugitives from justice," anymore than our white countrymen, is plain from the debates that preceded the adoption of the article.

Take, for example, the following resolution in the House of Representatives Dec. 21, 1803.

On motion, Resolved, That the committee appointed to inquire and report whether any further provisions are necessary for the more effectual protection of American seamen, to inquire into the expediency of granting protections to such American seamen, citizens of the U. S., as are free persons of color, and that they report by bill, or otherwise.

Said the Hon. Chas. Miner of Pa. in Congress Feb. 7, 1828—"The African race make excellent soldiers. Large numbers of them were with Perry, and aided to gain the brilliant victory on Lake Erie. A whole battalion of them was distinguished for its soldierly appearance." In the very year before the adoption of the present Constitution, 1789, the "Pa. Soc. for Promoting the Abolition of Slavery, etc." put forth an address, signed by BENJ. FRANKLIN, Pres., in which they stated one of their objects to be to qualify those who have been restored to freedom, for the exercise and enjoyment of CIVIL LIBERTY.

Are we to be thus looked to for help in the hour of danger, but trampled under foot in the time of peace? In which of the battles of the revolution did not our fathers fight as bravely as yours, for American liberty? Was it that their children might be disfranchised and looked with insult that they endured the famine of Valley Forge, and the horrors of the Jersey Prison Ship? Nay, among those from whom you are asked to wrench the birthright of CIVIL LIBERTY, are those who themselves shed their blood on the snows of Jersey, and faced British bayonets in the most desperate hour of the revolution . . . That we are not neglectful of our religious interests, nor of the education of our children, is shown by the fact that there are among us in Phila., Pgh., York., W. Chester, and Columbia, 22 churches, 48 clergymen, 26 day schools, 20 Sabbath schools, 125 Sabbath school teachers, 4 literary societies, 2 public libraries, consisting of about 8,000 volumes, besides 8,333 volumes in private libraries, 2 tract societies, 2 Bible societies, and 7 temperance societies . . .

But in the name of humanity, in the name of justice, in the name of the God you profess to worship, who has no respect of persons, do not turn into gall and wormwood the friendship we bear to ourselves by ratifying a constitution which tears from us a privilege dearly earned and inestimably prized. We lay hold of the principles which Pa. asserted in the hour which tried men's souls—which BENJ. FRANKLIN and his eight colleagues, in the name of the commonwealth, pledged their lives, their fortunes, and their sacred honor to sustain. We take our stand upon the solemn declaration, that to protect inalienable rights "governments are instituted among men, deriving their JUST POWERS from the CONSENT of the governed"; and proclaim that a gov't which tears away from us and our posterity the very power of CONSENT, is a tyrannical usurpation which we will never cease to oppose. We have seen with amazement and grief the apathy of white Pennsylvanians while the "Reform Conv." has been perpetrating this outrage upon the good old principles, we provide to maintain them on Pa. soil, to the last man. If this disfranchisement is designed to uproot us, it shall fail. Pennsylvania's fields, valleys, mountains, and rivers; her canals, railroads, forests, and mines; her domestic altars, and her public religious and benevolent institutions; her Penn and Franklin, her Rush, Rawle, Wistar, and Vaux; her consecrated past and her brilliant future, are as dear to us as they can be to you. Firm upon her old Pennsylvania BILL OF RIGHTS, and trusting in a God of Truth and Justice, we lay our claim before you, with the warning that no amendments of the present constitution can compensate for the loss of its foundation principle of equal rights, nor for the conversion into enemies of 40,000 friends.

In behalf of the Committee
Robert Purvis, Chairman

The constitution as ratified, however, deprived the Negro citizens of Pittsburgh, and of all Pennsylvania, of the use of the ballot. The Negro had lost his most powerful weapon in his struggle for human rights.

The seriousness of their defeat awakened Pittsburgh Negroes to strenuous opposition. They saw that their lack of protest at the loss of minor rights had cost them their legal citizenship. Only a few years earlier Negroes had been denied the right to assemble, to carry arms, or to serve in the state militia, which they are also denied today, although they had shown long and honorable and heroic service in both the Revolutionary War and the War of 1812.

The Constitutional Convention had brought the issue to its sharpest focus and for the next thirty years it was to become more and more the crux of American political life. The status of the Negro had become an issue which not only the State but the nation was compelled to face. Less than a quarter of a century before, the Negro had only grudgingly been acknowledged as a human personality. The slave, a black "thing" of the African jungle, was not regarded as possessing a human soul worthy of baptism or of any other rights of the church or of the body politic. An early writer had said: "Circumstances by which we have been surrounded in the past, especially in the slave states, have not been such as to develop manhood. The laws of those states ignored it; and to obey the laws, we had to ignore our own Manhood too."

From 1783 to 1789, a Frenchman, J. P. Briscot de Warville, had visited America for Les Amis Des Noirs, a Parisian association organized to study conditions among American Negroes. De Warville's comment helps illuminate the estimation in which Negroes were generally held at the time. It was necessary for de Warville to point out relative to certain groups of American Negroes:

> There exists, then, a country where Negroes are allowed to have souls, and to be endowed with understanding capable of being formed to virtue and useful knowledge; where they are not regarded as beasts of burden, in order that they may have the privilege of treating them as such. There exists a country where the Blacks by their virtues and their industry, belie calumnies which their tyrants elsewhere lavish against them; where no difference is perceived between the memory of a black head whose hair is craped[3] by nature, and that of a white one. I have seen, heard, and examined these black children. They read well, repeat from memory, calculate with rapidity. I have seen a picture painted by a young negro who never had a master; it was surprisingly well done.
>
> The black girls, besides reading, writing, and the principles of religion, are taught spinning, needlework, etc., and their mistresses assure me, that they discover much ingenuity. They have the appearance of decency, attention, and submission.

Variously designated as "blacks" and later as "people of color" the Negro was, by 1840, being given the name which even now is debatable among certain groups as his rightful and dignified title. *The Spirit of Liberty* in August 1842 discussed the use of the word "Negro" and its connotations:

> This is now used as a national epithet, but as a term of reproach. We were informed not long since, by an intelligent colored friend, that he once entered a worshiping assembly without any attention; but the preacher had an occasion to speak of colored men, and he used the term Negro, at the mention of which the eye of a gentleman, who stood close by, was turned on him with an expression of dislike, and every time the preacher said Negro, the eye of this man became more scornful, until our friend, who enjoyed himself well before this term was used, became very unpleasant in his situation, and all from the use of this term; not so much from its effect on him; as on his hater, who stood hard by. The term does not call to the colored man's mind recollec-

---

3. "Crape" means to make hair curly.

tions of the wrongs he suffers, but awake feelings of hatred in the bosom of those who inflict these wrongs. It is nature's law to hate those we injure. This term has a tendency to keep alive that unholy prejudice that exists toward the colored man—a prejudice which is a malumise,[4] and for the reason ought to exist, and the intelligent colored man knows that this term arouses the hate of those in whose bosoms this wakeful prejudice has a home, and must for this reason always feel unhappy when he hears it used.

An instance of this occurred at our first of August meeting, an intelligent colored man declined attending the meeting at night because one of the speakers made free use of the term in the first meeting. The colored friend did not believe the speaker said it out of any unkindness, and yet, such was the effect, that he was not willing to go again. We would advise our friends never to use this term; we have, for the reason above noticed, determination to dismiss it from our vocabulary, as a word not fit for the mouth of any friend to the slave.

It was the persistence of the primitive and unenlightened social concept of Negro inferiority that stood most stubbornly in the way of Negro advance. It was this obdurate theory of human spiritual inferiority that lay at the root of opposition, enmity, suppression and that was consistently attacked by every Negro seeking for civil freedom and by enlightened white men and women who supported him and who were aware that as the crisis of struggle became more acute, it involved their own civil liberties of free speech, free assemblage, free press, freedom of conscience.

The mass white mind could not separate into cause and effect the influx of escaping Negroes from the South and the deterioration of character and the increase of crime in the community. Neither could it relate to this influx of Negroes the rising aspirations and increased efforts to open schools and churches, to attend theaters and concerts, to form literary societies, and to participate unrestricted in social and cultural advance. Unfortunately, aspirations that manifested themselves in attempts to make them practical realities were thought of as presumptuous on the part of a people who not long ago had been considered soulless blacks. Perhaps an even more deep-seated factor in the growth of restrictive prejudice was the resentment against economic competition from the increasing numbers of Negro workmen and their efforts to establish a secure economic base for living even on the meager level accorded them by a community that constricted and confined their cultural aims.

For these reasons, efforts were continued to exclude Negroes from the state,

4. As in original.

to colonize them in Africa, to curtail their political, civil, and social activities. From petty persecution, hostility deepened into lynch law and riots. The attack on Negro tenements in Pittsburgh in 1839 was one instance of the extent to which such enmity might go. Another was the attack on the home of John B. Vashon, of which few details have come to light, but during which Jonas McClintock "displayed his popular ability" when in charge of troops called out to suppress the troubles. The one mention of the "Vashon Riot" so far discoverable in Pittsburgh papers consists of a few lines in McClintock's obituary years later which said:

> On that occasion he made requisition for an ample supply of powder and buckshot, distributed the same to the troops, and then sent word to the civil authorities not to call on the military until "work was to be done." The determination of the commander had its effect, and law and order triumphed.

The obvious purpose of such attacks was to drive Negroes from the community. The method was more direct and brutal than the efforts of the Colonization Societies, but the end in view was the same. Though the Colonization Societies stated their aims to be the transporting of Negroes to Africa with their "free consent," the words were at best a misnomer. A Negro who was compelled to choose between continued slavery or transport to Africa at the expense of the societies had hardly a free choice. Neither could the words "free consent" mean what they imply to free Negroes walking the streets in constant trepidation of violence, or to those denied free entry into schools, churches, and theaters, or to those unrecognized by the courts, or to those denied civilities of every day life in the towns. The more submissive Negroes and those easily intimidated did at times choose "Liberty" to the constant annoyance of those lacking freedom of action.

But the majority stood their ground, claiming their rights and determined to work for the elevation and liberation of their people in those places where they had lived for so many years. Lewis Woodson said:

> Some of us may leave this land from a spirit of adventure, and some from the persuasion of selfish and designing men; but the mass of us will never unwilling and violently be forced away. I am fully satisfied, in my own mind, that we are here by the permission and providence of God, and that here the mass of us are to remain. And if we are faithful to God and ourselves, in the use of all the means necessary to prosperity, He will see to it, that in due time, we, in common with all others, shall enjoy all the privileges and advantages of this land.

The struggle for civil rights acquired a new bitterness after 1838 and national factors gave that bitterness a sharp edge. Agitation was growing over the status of slaves in the South and the extremists in South Carolina were shaping new political arguments. Colonization schemes were being abandoned and antislavery groups were springing up in the North wherever sympathies came to a focus. In Pittsburgh, publication of abolitionist papers widened and deepened the basis for action. Meetings were held, resolutions adopted, debates and arguments promoted in churches and clubs, broadsides and pamphlets were issued, and a steady flow of memorials and petitions sent to the legislature. And still tax-paying Negroes, educated, highly placed Negroes, property owning Negroes, and Negroes who were merely human beings were denied the right to vote.

The question, however, was not a closed one. Negro and white refused to consider it so, and sought by repeated effort to assure the Negro citizen his right to the ballot. On July 24, 1840, the *Daily Pittsburgher* quoted an item from the *Erie Observer:*

> The *Gazette* finds fault with Van Buren's vote allowing free negroes worth $250 the right to vote. That there may be no mistake about this matter we will state the fact as it is: The Federal party was for placing all, White and black upon an equal relation to voting. Mr. Van Buren advocated and voted for a provision, allowing White citizens having resided in the state two months and paid a tax or done military duty the right to vote, and also extending to free negroes possessed of a free hold estate of $250, who were compelled to pay taxes the right to vote. This is the true state of the case which we are fully prepared to show from public documents—*Erie Observer*

Tirelessly the Negro people of the city promulgated one scheme after another for achievement of unhampered existence, for freedom of movement and thought, for a life which could expand in full effectiveness. In August 1843 *The Spirit of Liberty* printed a kind of shorthand report of a county convention which met in the city to consider a number of aspects of the status of the Negro citizenry:

ELECTIVE FRANCHISE—CONVENTION

> Several of the citizens of color having taken into consideration the propriety of holding a County Convention for the purpose of petitioning our Legislature to restore to us the right of the Election Franchise, called a meeting to confer with their brethren throughout the country. A response having been hastily received in favor of the proposed object, a meeting was immediately called, in which all the necessary arrangements for holding the convention were made—Second Monday, in Aug. 1843 at 10:00 A.M. in the Wesley Church, on Third Street, in Allegheny City.
>
> Edward R. Parker chosen Secretary pro tem. The Chairman then called on Rev. A. D. Lewis for prayer.

Resolved—That there be a committee of nine, three from the city of Pittsburgh, three from Pitt township, and three from the city of Allegheny to nominate officers for convention.

Committee:
James Anderson, Lewis McAlfrey, George Spears, Halson Vashon, Chas. Jones, Thomas Norris, George Austin, Edward R. Parker, David Body.

Committee reported following nominations:
President—John B. Vashon
Vice Pres.—Geo. Spears and Geo. Austin, Sr.
Sec.—John N. Templeton, Lewis McAlfrey, and E. R. Parker.

On motion—*Resolved* that a committee of seven, two from each district, and one from the county be appointed as a business committee.

Committee: Martin R. Delany, Lewis Woodson, Thos. A. Brown, James Morgan, Peal Jackson, Samuel Bruce, C. B. Brooks.

Resolved that a committee of three on arrangement be appointed. Committee: John Williams, John Rideout, John Curtis.

Resolutions prepared by the business committee then offered, and adopted.

Resolution 1st—Congratulate ourselves and our brethren generally on the signs of the times, as highly encouraging to our best interests. Remarks by L. Woodson.

Resolution 2nd—Resolved that this Convention will concur with the 4th resolution of the State Convention, held in August, 1841 in the city of Pgh. and that it recommend to our people throughout the State to concur with us, in petitioning the Legislature to alter the Constitution, so as to restore to us the elective franchise.

Resolution 3rd—Resolved that we will petition our Legislature to remove all restrictions on account of color, and that we will continue to petition until our prayer is granted.

Resolution 4th—Resolved that the present condition of our people, so well as present development, and their future prospects, all point to the cultivation of the soil as the best and surest means of their real elevation, and future prosperity and happiness. Tabled until afternoon.

Convention adjourned to meet at 2:00 P.M. by benediction from the Rev. Abraham M. Cole.

Afternoon Session: President called on Rev. Woodson to open meeting with prayer. Resolution laid on table restricting members to 30 minutes, with the privilege to explain.

4th *Resolution* adopted after discussion from P. Jackson, T. Norris, T. A. Brown, L. McAlfrey, L. Woodson, M. Jones, and A. D. Lewis.

Resolution 5th—Resolved that this Convention recommend that our people residing in this county, to pursue those employments so far as in their power lies, that have a tendency to elevate them in the community.

Remarks by M. R. Delany, L. Woodson, J. Peck, J. Mahoney, A. D. Lewis, T. A. Brown and Geo. Parker.

Resolution 6th—That this convention recommend the encouragement of Tradesmen of our own color, where they can be found competent to perform and punctual in their engagements.

Resolution 7th—Resolved that we will do all that is within our power to promote the course of learning within our bounds.

Resolution 8th—That we present the houses in which our public schools are taught as foul, unhealthy and unfit for such use.

Resolution 9th—That there be a committee of three appointed to draft a petition to the next Legislature. Committee: L. Woodson, P. Jackson, and T. A. Brown.

Resolution 10th—There be a corresponding Committee of 7, appointed to correspond with the different counties in the State, urging upon them the necessity of calling County Conventions and getting up petitions to the next Legislature.

Committee: M. R. Delany, J. Anderson, Wm. M. Jones, Wesley White, E. R. Parker, J. Moody, C. B. Brooks.

On Motion—Resolved, proceedings be published in Spirit of Liberty and other papers favorable and that the secretaries compare revising committee. Convention Adjourned.

Secretaries: John N. Templeton, Lewis McAlfrey, Edward R. Parker.

A letter to the press a week later further discussed the proposal that forming the "return to the land" would offer a basis for greater liberty of movement and richer realization of living.

A convention of the colored citizens of Allegheny county was held in the city of Allegheny on last Monday, when, among other things, the subject of farming was brought under consideration; and a resolution was passed, almost unanimously, we believe in favor of it. But we fear that this revolution, like many former ones was passed with more than best deliberation, and therefore, without a proper intention on the part of many who voted in favor of it, of carrying or assisting, it into practice. We were very sorry for this, for we are satisfied, from various reasons which we do not intend now to adduce, that no business is better adopted to improve the present condition of the colored people than farming.

Within the last year we have been frequently asked by our people, heads of families in particular, what are we to do? We are being shut out from the boating business, work is scarce in town, how are we to get bread for our families? Our uniform reply has been, take immediate measures for settling in the country.

But some urge objections to this course, which show that they greatly over estimate the difficulty of making a settlement in the country, and that they are in much need of being better informed. We would be happy to see something done to this end, therefore, we make the following proposition.

Let all who are friendly to farming, or are desirous of becoming farmers, leave their names with L. Woodson, corner of Liberty and Seventh Sts. And when some seven or ten names are collected, let a meeting be called, when, if thought expedient, an organization can be formed, and much further steps taken as may be thought advisable—among other things, a committee might be appointed to collect information, and a course of suitable lectures might be delivered, which would tend to bring the subject in a proper manner before the minds of the people.

One meeting at which it was demanded that the state constitution be amended to grant Negroes the vote was reported in some detail. A letter to the *Commercial Journal* on Nov. 28, 1846, said:

Sir:

Although the inclemency of the weather prevented the meeting of Colored citizens, on last Tuesday evening, from being a large one, still it was quite respectably attended. A spirit of the greatest harmony marked its proceedings; and the interest manifested by all present, showed that they felt deeply the importance of the cause in which they were engaged, and had their disfranchised condition sincerely at heart. After something like an hour had been spent in the appointments of Delegates to attend a County Suffrage Convention, to be held on the second Thursday in December, Mr. Lewis Woodson, arose, and in the course of some very eloquent remarks, suggested the propriety of forming a political union, as an efficient means in securing a redress of those wrongs, under the infliction of which the colored free men of this Commonwealth feel so humiliated and aggrieved. In this, he was ably seconded by Messrs. J. B. Vashon, George Parker, William Jones, and others.

The reasons urged for this project by the very speakers were to the following effect. As the Constitution of Pennsylvania now stands, any amendment of that instrument must, after it has received approbation of two successive Legislatures, be referred to the suffrages of the people for final sanction. At such a stage in its progress, any alteration of the Constitution conferring upon the colored man that right which had been so unjustly wrested from them, must, from the present state of public feeling, meet with a great, and probably, an overwhelming opposition. For, no matter how numerously signed the petitions in favor of this measure may be, in some sections of the Commonwealth it is already evident that the mass of electors of Pennsylvania, are not yet prepared to assist in the great act of justice which is so earnestly prayed for by their disfranchised fellow-citizens. The same spirit which, to satisfy the demands of an unwarrantable animosity and a contemptible prejudice, could, in defiance of every principle of republicanism, aim a deadly blow at the political liberties of forty-thousand tax-payers, may still be sufficiently powerful to prevent a practical recognition of those axioms, in defense of which, the founders of our institutions were ready to lay down their lives. Hence arises the necessity of reforming public opinion upon this matter; and to do so, the employment of lecturers and distribution of tracts present themselves as feasible methods. In furtherance of this, it appears advisable that associations should be formed—associations, which, in their establishment, will beget that union which insures strength, and which, in their very organization, will afford ample testimony, that the restoration of Elective Franchise is not an end proposed by a few restless spirits, but the ardent desire of a host of injured. The establishing of such associations cannot but be highly beneficial in its influences upon the colored people of this state. It will knit them more closely together, will arouse them to increased action, will constrain to exert themselves more earnestly for the consummation they so devoutly wish for, and, (it is not chimerical to hazard the assertion), it will in progress of time, render them, as a class, as fit as any other set of men in the community for the enjoyment of privileges they ask for. Such being the opinion of the meeting, resolutions were unanimously passed, advising the formation of such a union, and appointing a committee to draft an appropriate constitution for presentation to the citizens assembled in Convention. Let every well-wisher to the interest of Pennsylvania, every sincere lover of justice, every truehearted friend of man pray, that the result may fully realize the most ardent anticipations of his colored fellow-citizens.

                                        Z.

The conditions under which the farmers of the decade worked, the futility of
seeking relief through agricultural employment as told in the recent account of
hard times in the city and vicinity, the fact that agriculture was in as great a crisis
from 1837 to 1842 as were the urban industries and small business seemed to go
unreckoned with by the writer of this letter. But that the growing social segregation had its foundation in economic limitation, in the scarcity of work and being
"shut out from" jobs, was taken into account.

The results of the convention of 1843 are not traceable, except in the matter of
continued petitions to the legislature to restore the suffrage. Three years later *The
Commercial Journal* reported discussions in the assembly of a petition from the
citizens of Allegheny:

> Soon after the meeting of the House, Mr. Burnside, from the Judiciary
> Committee, made a report upon the petition of colored citizens of Allegheny,
> praying for an extension of the right of suffrage to them and their brethren in
> the State, that it is expedient to comply with their wishes, and that the Com-
> mittee be discharged from the further consideration of the subject.
>
> Messrs. Bigham, Brackenridge, and Price, of Chester, ably addressed the
> House in support of the rights of colored men, and Messrs. Burnside, and
> Magehan sustained the views of the majority of the Judiciary Committee.
>
> The resolution attached to the report of the majority, was, however,
> adopted about fifteen minutes before adjournment, by the decided vote of 72
> to 13.

Zeta

On the adverse majority opinion the *Commercial* printed a brief editorial:

THE RIGHT OF SUFFRAGE

By the letter of our Harrisburg correspondent it will be seen that Mr.
Burnside, from the Judiciary Committee, has made a report adverse to the
report adverse to the right of colored citizens to vote.

It is "inexpedient," the report says.

The age is becoming too far advanced in humanity and knowledge for
that cry longer to continue,—it is inexpedient to do justice and act our truth.

Falsehood and wrong are inexpedient, not truth and integrity.

Mr. Bigham deserves much praise for his exertions upon this occasion, in
support of freedom.

The *Commercial* steadily devoted space to pointing out unjust restrictions,
relating one incident after another. In the autumn after it had reported the petition of the Allegheny Negroes, it ran a story:

NEGROES IN COURTS

Sometime since we noticed a circumstance of an officer in our Court directing Dr. Delany to take his seat in a particular corner of the room assigned for the use of people of color. The Doctor refused, and left the Court room rather than obey, declaring that the Court had no right to interfere with or molest him, so long as he did not misbehave. A similar occurrence had lately taken place in New York. A colored man, entering one of the Court rooms, was directed by the officer to go into the place appointed for colored persons. He refused and retired. As soon after, the officer received by the hand of a friend of the Negro, the following addressed on the outside, "Public Oppressor: On reflecting on the insult you have been pleased to offer me, I am ready to test the validity of your authority and any time you may be pleased to put into execution. I will be in Court more or less during the week. Perhaps this may lead to a settlement of this vexed question. For our part we would insult no man, whatever might be the color of his skin, whose conduct gave us no reason to doubt his responsibility as a man; and this business of sending a certain class of citizen to a certain corner of a room, while others were allowed to go where they pleased, is a distinction insulting to the last degree. Courts of justice, in all events, should not allow their conduct to be swayed in this manner by the lowest of vulgar prejudice.

The *Journal* seems to have represented that body of public opinion which asked for civil rights and an end of segregation, but stopped short of demanding political rights such as voting and holding office; for in its issue of November 14 of that year in reporting a number of meetings in the city to demand the ballot, it put forward the idea that education was more important in removing such civil limitations than the ballot would be. The *Journal* said:

We have lately seen several notices of meetings of our colored citizens held for the purpose of securing to themselves, if possible, the right of suffrage. We have nothing in this place to say as to the right or expediency of granting their demands. We do, however, feel a great interest in the elevation of that unfortunate race; and are always willing to contribute our mite towards that object. As to the means of their elevation men will differ and many will consider that the granting of the right of suffrage will not tend to their improvement.

Upon one point, however, all will agree: that education is the surest, if not the only means of elevating the condition of the Negroes, for with mental cultivation, we contend will come all the other elements of character which are necessary to the enjoyment of equal political advantagements with the white race. We cannot give entire credence to the opinion that the Negro is intellectually inferior to the Caucasian race.

Before giving our adhesion decisively to such an opinion we would desire to see the matter tested by a fair trial. The Negro has never had an opportunity. In our country he has always been restrained from the arena of scholastic fame; and his efforts at self improvement hooted at as ridiculous or punished as criminal. For a Negro to aspire to giving his child a liberal education was sure to excite scornful comment, not unmixed with displeasure, even in the free States; while the brutal prejudices against the "niggers" closed all liberal professions against them; and custom with a force stronger than law confined these unhappy people to occupations the most menial and debasing. A colored boy some years since, we know not if it is yet the case, could not obtain admission in our colleges. The fastidious youth of a fairer complexion would not consent to tread the halls of learning in company with the dark-skinned Ethiopian.

Notwithstanding all this, we abuse the Negroes for their lack of intelligence. We ourselves fetter their limbs, and then punish them for their disability to walk. We shut out from them the light of science, and blame them for being ignorant. We consider ourselves insulted if they dare approach us as equal; denounce their slightest evidence of self-respect as "Impudence"; and by our laws treat them as inferior beings; yet complain that they do not evince equal mental powers with our own race. Give them a chance, and they will find their own level.

We know not whether the difficulties in the way of educating Negroes are as great as they have been; we think not. The active benevolence of the Liberty men, however much their efforts, politically, has been misdirected, has resulted in the openings of institutions for the instruction of colored youth in all the departments of education; and such of them as have the pecuniary resources, find the other means in some measure supplied. The want of money, however, is a great embarrassment: few indeed of these people having any property and thus another difficulty is presented.

This however may be obviated, as it no doubt will be. As liberal views and more extended ideas of humanity are embraced by the masses of people, our institutions of learning will be thrown open to all, and the last barrier between white and black minds will be utterly destroyed.

We think that the education of their young men should be an object of far greater importance than the giving of the elective franchise to the Negroes. The diffusion of intelligence and morality among them will force granting of all their other privileges or rights. They should begin right. Let them lend all their energies to the task of educating their youth; and in less than another generation the public opinion of the free states will elevate the blacks to their proper position in the political world.

We have been led to these remarks by an incident which occurred to us a day or so since. We met a Negro boy, who appeared to be 16 or 18 years of age, on Third Street. He had a copy of Virgil, a Greek Testament, and a slate covered with calculations and mathematical science in his hands. It is not usual to see articles of this kind in the possession of a Negro, and we inquired of him whether they were his. He informed us that they were. He said that he was studying with another colored man, who had graduated from a college in Ohio and is now, gratuitously, imparting to others the benefits which he there received. The youth appeared to us to be quite intelligent, and made considerable progress in his studies. The perseverance which could induce the poor fellow to pursue his task of self-improvement amid the discouragement by which he must be surrounded is worthy of the highest applause: nor can we speak too highly of the man who patiently and laboriously, self-denying and unrewarded, as the world goes, devotes himself to the instruction of his despised and oppressed race.

There is another department of this subject, Female Education among the Negroes, to which we may take occasion to refer to on some future occasion.

The fallacy of the provision taken by the *Journal* is demonstrated by the civil restriction to which the most highly cultured Negroes of the day were subjected. While traveling through western Pennsylvania the following summer Frederick Douglass wrote in a letter the isolation imposed:

Augustinburg, Ohio
August 20 1847

My Dear Friend:

On Wednesday and Thursday, 11th and 12th August, we held five very interesting meetings in Pittsburgh. The day meetings were held in the open air and were very well attended. The evening meetings were held in Temperance Hall, a large room but by no means sufficient to hold the numbers that pressed to hear. The doorways and windows and yard of the hall were compelled to leave without gaining admission to these. Hundreds remained on the outside of the building from an early hour till eleven o'clock at night. What a commentary on the religion of Pittsburgh it is, that every church in the place was closed against us. All were too holy to plead the cause of our common humanity. The great Christian cause of the age, like early Christianity itself, is too much despised by the world, to be admitted into the house of God. When saving men in our land shall have become as popular as killing men now is in Mexico, we shall not only have churches open to our use but, perhaps, be voted into religious societies as honorary members. On that day, the philanthropic Garrison may possibly be regarded as religious as the pious man-butcher Zachary Taylor.

On Friday morning, 13th, we took the steamboat *Beaver*, from Pittsburgh to New Brighton—the home of our kind friend, Milo A Townsend and our antislavery poetess, Grace Greenwood. A number of our friends accompanied us from Pittsburgh to that place, a goodly number of whom were colored persons. It is usual to dine on this boat between Pittsburgh and Beaver, but on this occasion, strange to tell, no dinner was furnished for the very American reason that a goodly number of persons were colored, and it was deemed probable that some of them might presume to dine, and would thus give offence to the white-skinned aristocracy. So, like the American delegates of the Evangelical Alliance, we concluded to preserve the peace by "going without dinner."

We held two meetings at New Brighton, afternoon and evening, and here, too, the churches were closed against us, and we were compelled to take an upper room in a flour store. Thus making good the proposition, that humanity is received more cordially in the street than in the church. Our meetings at New Brighton were the last we held in Pennsylvania.

Frederick Douglass

A letter from Martin Delany to William Lloyd Garrison a few years later is more acrid in statement. If Douglass and his party were willing to preserve the peace by going without dinner, Delany would never be reconciled to exist in such sufferance. Delany's letter reads:

Philadelphia
May 14, 1852

Mr. Garrison:
My dear sir:

I thank you most kindly for the very favorable and generous notice you have taken of my hastily written book. This, to many, may appear singular, that the author of a work should send words of thanks to an editor for his notice of him, but this favor of yours came so opportune, that it seems like a God-send.

The errors and deficiencies, which you are pleased to pass by unnoticed—justly taking my prefatory apology as sufficient—I have corrected, and will so appear in the next issue, shortly to come out. The corrections you make concerning yourself, I shall add as a note at the end of the work.

I thank those editors of Philadelphia and elsewhere, who have favorably noticed this work, and would add, that the ever good, generous Gerrit Smith has sent me a letter of approval of the work in general.

I am not in favor of caste, nor a separation of the brotherhood of mankind, and would as willingly live among white men as black, if I had an equal possession and enjoyment of privileges; but shall never be reconciled to live among them subservient to their will—existing by mere sufferance, as we, the colored people, do in this country. The majority of white men cannot see why colored men cannot be satisfied with their condition in Massachusetts—what they desire more than the granted right of citizenship. Blind selfishness on the one hand, and deep prejudice on the other, will not permit them to understand that we desire the exercise and enjoyment of these rights, as well as the name of their possession. If there were any probability of this, I should be willing to remain in the country—fighting and struggling on, the good fight of faith, but I must admit that I have no hopes in this country—no confidence in the American people—with a few excellent exceptions—therefore, I have written as I have done. Heathenism and Liberty, before Christianity and Slavery.

> "Were I a slave, I would be free,
> I would not live to live a slave;
> But boldly strike for Liberty
> For FREEDOM or a martyr's grave."

Yours for God and Humanity,
M. R. Delany

Mrs. Jane Grey Swisshelm spoke in her usual castigating way in her *Saturday Evening Visitor* of indignities such as the *Commercial Journal* thought would be lifted by education. In this case the victim was Martin Delany.

Dr. Delany in his paper of yesterday complains of having been refused or rather, we should say conditionally refused in an insulting manner, a passage in a stage coach from Buffalo. The reason for this treatment was that the Doctor was a colored man. We really think that it is time that sensible people should cease to manifest upon such occasions prejudice so narrow. What harm could it be to anyone to ride in a coach with a well dressed, well behaved and intelligent colored man—for all this Dr. Delany undoubtedly is. The most cruel and cowardly thing in this world is a wanton insult to those that are powerless to defend themselves, and whose humility prevents them from giving offence. We have known a man possessing the education or manners of a gentleman to only insult the feelings of these unfortunate people.

The heart breaking effects of intolerance William C. Noll shows in telling of John B. Vashon's experience at the mobbing of Wm. Lloyd Garrison in Boston:

En Route from Philadelphia to Boston
October 21, 1855

John Bathan Vashon of Pittsburgh was an eye witness to the terrible scene which was heart rending beyond his ability ever afterwards to express as, of all living men, John B. Vashon loved Mr. Garrison most; and this feeling of affection continued, for aught that is known, to the day of his death. When the mob passed along Washington Street, shouting and yelling like madmen, the apprehensions of Mr. Vashon became fearfully aroused. Presently there approached a group which appeared even more infuriated than the rest, and he beheld, in the midst of this furious throng, Garrison himself, led on like a beast to slaughter. He had been in the field of battle, had faced the cannon's mouth, seen its lightnings flash and heard its thunders roar, but such a sight as this was more than the old citizen could bear without giving vent to a flood of tears.

The next day the old soldier who had helped to preserve his country's liberty on the plighted fate of security to his own, but had lived to witness freedom of speech and of the press stricken down by mob violence, and life itself in jeopardy because that liberty was asked for him and his, with spirits crushed and faltering hopes, called to administer a word of consolation to the bold and courageous young advocate of immediate and universal emancipation. Mr. Garrison subsequently thus referred to this circumstance in his paper. On the day of that riot in Boston he dined at my house and the next morning called to see me in prison, bringing with him a new hat for me, in the place of one that was cut in places by the knives of men of property and standing.

Fraternally yours,
William C. Nell

As the question of the continued existence or abolition of slavery became ever more bitterly contested, the question of the status of the free Negro was also more heatedly argued. The Fugitive Slave Law was the excuse for attempted legislation to prevent free Negroes from entering the state. But public opinion was not unanimous on the question. In fact, the legislators at no time enacted such laws. The *Gazette* commented in January, 1852:

We noticed a few days since, that a bill had been read in the House of Representatives of Pennsylvania forbidding free colored people from coming into the state. The following is the bill. There are, it is true, precedents for such legislations but that fact cannot and ought not justify it, nor exempt it from the charge of being unjust and cruel and in gross derogation of all the great principles upon which our great government is founded. We trust it will be negatived by a large majority.

Section 1. Be it enacted by the Senate and House of Representatives of the Commonwealth of Pennsylvania, in General assembly, met and it is hereby enacted by the authority of the same that from and after the passage of this Act, it shall not be lawful for any Negro or Mulatto to come into and settle in this Commonwealth; and any Negro or Negroes or Mulatto or Mulattoes, so coming, immigrating or moving into this state for the purpose of settling therein, shall be liable to imprisonment of not less than two or more than nine months upon conviction thereof.

Section 2. That any person or persons employing or otherwise encouraging any such Negro or Mulatto to emigrate into, settle, or remain within this Commonwealth, shall be liable to a fine of not less than fifty or more than one hundred dollars, to be recovered as other fines of like amount are recoverable.

Section 3. That such fine or fines so recovered shall be paid into the treasury of the proper county until demanded by the overseers of the poor of the township to which the offense or offenses enumerated in the foregoing sections of this act shall have been committed, who shall apply it to the use and comfort of the poor in charge.

Section 4. It shall be the duty of the overseers of the poor in the different townships, wards or boroughs of this Commonwealth, to make information and prosecute to conviction all persons violating the second and third sections of this Act; and any overseers of the poor who shall knowingly neglect or refuse to make information as aforesaid, shall be liable to the fine imposed by the second section of this Act.

In 1853 the state supreme court decided that although Negroes had no political rights in the state they could not be deprived of their civil rights. The same year Negroes petitioned the legislature to secure them complete protection while traveling in slave states. Although by the outbreak of the Civil War the mood of the North was overwhelmingly antislavery, and the courts would not sustain the deprivation of legal rights of free Negroes, public opinion nevertheless was so hostile that it still placed many privileges beyond the Negro's attainment.

The Negro was still barred from churches, public meetings, schools, theaters and even street cars. The better types of jobs were strictly limited and apprenticeship to trades was almost completely denied. Although within the eyes of the law he was entitled to the same rights as a white man, chances for equal justice were considerably less and punishment for offenses was both more frequent and more severe. In normal times the Negro was subjected to disdain, contempt, and petty persecution; in times of stress his life was not safe in public places.

In the autumn of 1854 the *Daily Morning Post* related the transactions of a National Negro Convention in which Martin Delany and other Pittsburghers had taken a prominent part, the aim of which was to devise some solution to this most urgent question of the time:

A Grand Scheme for the Colored People

In August last, a National Convention of the Colored people was held at Cleveland, Ohio. It was composed of delegates from most of the states. It was called the National Emigration Convention, and its objects were to consider the political destinies of the black race; and recommend a plan of emigration to countries where they can enjoy political liberty, and form nations free and independent.

The report of the committee takes strong ground in favor of remaining upon this continent, but not in the United States. In the United States it is admitted that the white race has secured the ascendancy, and will ever retain it, and will never admit the Negro race to political and social equality. But this is not considered the country most favorable to the development, physically or mentally, of the colored race.

The committee then proceeds to mark out a grand scheme by which the Negro race may be regenerated, and formed into free, intelligent and prosperous nations. The West India Islands, Central America, and all the middle portions of South America including the whole of Brazil are designated as the regions desired; and that can be obtained as the seat of Negro civilization and empire. These regions and islands are represented as containing twenty-four and a half million in population, but one seventh of which, some three and a half million are whites of pure European extraction; and the remainder, nearly twenty-one million are colored people of African and Indian origin. This immense preponderance of the colored races in those regions it is supposed will enable them, with the aid of emigration from the United States, to take possession of all those countries and islands, and become the ruling race in the empires to be formed out of those wide and fruitful realms. The committee expresses full confidence in the practicability of this great undertaking; and that nothing is wanting to its success at no distant day, but unanimity of sentiment and action among the masses of colored people.

The climate of these regions is represented as entirely congenial to the colored race, while to the European races it is enervating and destructive; and this fact added to the present immense superiority of numbers on the part of the Negroes, is relied on as a sure guarantee of the success of the great enterprise; and that their race could forever maintain the possession and control of these regions.

Other great events, it is supposed, will follow in the train of this mighty movement. With the West India Islands and Central and South America composing free negro nations, slavery in the United States would, they suppose, soon be at an end. The facility of escape, the near neighborhood of friends and aid, it is urged would rapidly drain off from the southern states all the most intelligent, robust and bold of their slaves.

The committee presents this plan as the only mode by which the African race can be regenerated, and elevated to the rank of equals among the peoples and nations of the earth; and it is urged by many arguments.

On one point the committee expresses the most positive and immovable determination. We give it in their own language:

UPON THE AMERICAN CONTINENT WE ARE DETERMINED TO REMAIN, DESPITE EVERY OPPOSITION THAT CAN BE URGED AGAINST US.

In Canada they say that they cannot remain, because the British provinces will soon belong to the United States. To all further acquisitions by the United States southward, the committee is utterly opposed. The whole tone of the report indicates that these projected empires to the south of us would be anything but friends of our republic.

Mr. M. R. Delany of Pittsburgh was the chairman of the Committee that made this report to the convention. It was of course adopted.

If Mr. Delany drafted this report it certainly does him much credit for learning and ability; and cannot fail to establish for him a reputation for vigor and brilliancy of imagination never yet surpassed. It is a vast conception of impossible birth. The committee seems to have overlooked the strength of 'the powers of the earth' that would oppose the africanization of more than half of the Western Hemisphere.

England, France, Spain, Holland and Denmark own large portions of the domain that are to be thus seized and to be converted into Africanized empires; and where are the armies and navies, the arms and munitions of war with which these rich possessions are to be wrested from the European powers? And the South American republics, and the empire of Brazil, have they no strength to preserve their existence against servile insurrection and Negro invasion? The United States too, with its routes of commerce across Central America, its friendly relations with the doomed republics of the South, its intention to annex Cuba, and a little more, will she not bear a part in this grand-comic event? We can assure our colored neighbors that Uncle Sam,

Johnny Bull, Johnny Crappeau, Queen Christiana and the Dutch will all in-
terpose most formidable obstacles to the success of this splendid project.

Nothing but a sudden coup de main could give it any chance of success.
And for that there is no adequate preparation. A few years delay, and Cuba
will be under the Stars and Stripes; and American railroads and canals will
span all the realms of Central America.

We have no motive in noticing this gorgeous dream of the committee except to show its fallacy, its impracticability, in fact its absurdity. No sensible
man, whatever his color, should be for a moment deceived by such impracticable theories.

On the African coast already exists a thriving and prosperous republic. It
is the native home of the African race; and there he can enjoy the dignity of
manhood, the rights of citizenship, and all the advantages of civilization and
freedom. Every colored man in the country will be welcomed there as a free
citizen; and there he can not only prosper, and secure his own comfort and
happiness, but become a teacher and benefactor of his kindred races, and
become an agent in carrying civilization and Christianity to a benighted continent.

That anyone should be turned aside from so noble a mission by the delusive dream of conquest and empire in the Western Hemisphere, is an absurdity too monstrous and mischievous to believe. The committee report was
accepted and adopted, published, and sent forth to the world.

With the outbreak of the Civil War, a series of events in rapid succession profoundly affected the status of free Negroes in the North. Emancipation was declared on January 1, 1863, but it applied only to rebellious states and was based on
a mere presidential decree.

A convention at Syracuse, New York in October 1864, at which George B.
Vashon was a Pittsburgh delegate, made clear the position the Negro people held
in the national life at the moment. Would those things gained by the war be actually realized? the convention asked. Secretary Seward had recently announced
that when the rebels laid down arms, all war measures would cease, including
those that concerned slavery. The convention expressed gratitude to President
Lincoln for revoking a law that prohibited Negroes from carrying mail, for abolishing slavery in the District of Columbia, and for his recognition of Liberia and
Hayti. It petitioned Congress that the rights of Negro patriots be respected, that
the government cease making discriminations in labor, payment of wages, and
promotions in the army. It contended, too, that the right to own real estate, to
bear witness in law courts, to bring suit and to be sued were but theoretical privileges so long as complete political liberty was not granted. It demanded not only

that slavery be formally and completely abolished but asked also for complete franchise in all states, those already in the Union and those that might return later.

Lee surrendered on April 9, 1865, Lincoln was assassinated five days later, and on December 18, emancipation was constitutionally established throughout the country by the Thirteenth Amendment. The Civil Rights Bill of 1866 bestowed American citizenship and legal rights on all freedmen. But the act was declared unconstitutional and the Fourteenth Amendment was necessary to guarantee what the Civil Rights Bill had failed to give. It assured citizenship; it assured certain civil rights by declaring that no state could deprive any person of life, liberty or property without due process of the law. It attempted to give the Negro the vote by reducing the congressional representation of any state that in special elections refused the ballot to adult male citizens.

The man whom Wendell Phillips, lifelong friend of the Negro, called "Jefferson Davis Johnson" entered the White House at the death of Lincoln, and the coalition of southern and northern reactionaries took control of Congress. The battle over the status of the Negro grew furious. The achievements of the "Second American Revolution" seemed about to be destroyed. Men and women who rushed to the South to educate the freedmen and help him maintain the freedom and political and civil rights won by the war were scurrilously labeled carpetbaggers and scalawags.

A delegation led by Frederick Douglass called on the President early in 1866 to ask enforcement of the Thirteenth Amendment, and equal rights for Negroes. This delegation represented Negro conventions and organizations of twenty states. Johnson evaded the issue.

Bishop Payne, at that time compiling *The Semi-Centenary of the A.M.E. Church* said of this visit:

> We are no longer in doubt as to the views of the President in relation to Negro Suffrage. He has spoken plainly and declared his opposition to it. He assigns two reasons: First, that the General government has not the power to grant it. Secondly, that if granted, it would cause a war of races. The reply of the colored delegation so successfully controverts the arguments of the President, that it will be at the expense of right and justice, if his views are adopted by any of his fellow citizens. The well-tempered boldness of George Downing, and the dignified, sagacious and statesmanlike manner of Frederick Douglass, on the occasion of this interview, certainly makes us feel quite proud of our race. Mr. Douglass seemed to blend the genial reserve of Talleyrand and Seward, with the fiery candor of Thompson and Garrison.
>
> We infer, from the President's remarks, that it would not be distasteful to him if we would colonize. "Oh no, Mr. President! We are not going to do that.

We are going to fight it out on this line, if it takes all the generations yet to come." We are struggling for the supremacy of an idea, that it is not only necessary to our elevation, but that of our brethren in Africa; that idea is the unity of races—the brotherhood of man.

In 1866, when the Fourteenth Amendment gave citizenship, an editorial in the Philadelphia *Christian Recorder* voiced the opinion not only of its editor but of Negro leaders like Vashon, Delany, Lewis, Woodson and other Pittsburghers. James Lynch, the editor, said that in the period of readjustment the Negro must use all his "intellect, wisdom, physical power and the aid of friends" to make adjustment. Since the end of the war, his relations to political government, Lynch said, had changed. Though the sky was not clear, the clouds had parted. Colored representatives were in Congress and entered the executive mansion. A delegation was received and counseled with by the most eminent legislators in Congress. Nearly two thirds of each branch of the Congress, he said, had pledged themselves to legislate on behalf of the natural and political rights of the Negroes.

Lynch continued:

There are two ways by which we are to get our rights. The first is to continually present our claim to the nation and the second is to continue to prove ourselves capable of making as good use of all the political privileges which white citizens enjoy as they do themselves. We have proved this already, in our loyalty and sacrifices during the terrible Civil War; but we must add proof to proof, that our very existence may be a living protest against the injustice that would proscribe us.

The colored man who owns a farm and cultivates it well, and carries produce to market, makes a plea for his race far more effectual than the tongue of the most eloquent orator. A colored man standing in the door of his own blacksmith shop, with a leather apron on, is doing as much to elevate the race as the man in public station.

No race of people inferior in numbers or power to another race can live with them on terms of equality, unless they have the same great current of thought and feeling—unless they imbibe the spirit of the age. The present age in America is preeminently a practical and working age. The people's attention is in the work of developing the resources of the country; they are after sinking shafts and hoisting to the surface precious and useful metals, tunneling through mountains, yoking hills together, and spanning streams with bridges. They believe in individual accumulation, and glory in the increasing wealth of the nation. Colored men, now that they have commenced thinking and acting for themselves, must be found in all the different branches of mechanism and labor, in agriculture and commerce.

From this time immediately following the Civil War, efforts to establish civil rights for the Negro people more and more were compelled to consider the fundamental right to economic equality, the equal right with all men to labor at work of their own choice, at wages and under conditions equal to and identical with those of other workers. But for this it was necessary that the Negro have a voice in making the laws which would establish such conditions. And that was possible only by obtaining the right to the ballot. Every Negro in the country was now a free man and citizen, but had not as yet the right to vote.

Before he was given the ballot, however, Pennsylvania, a Republican stronghold, passed laws intended to make effective that clause of the Fourteenth Amendment which promised to guarantee protection of his civil rights.

The *Commercial Journal* reported on March 21, 1867, a bill to make it a criminal offense to prevent Negroes from riding on street cars:

THE NEGROES IN THE STREET CARS—1867

The Bill making it a criminal offense to prevent persons from riding on the street cars on account of color or race came up on a third reading last evening; having previously passed the Senate. The Democratic side attempted to get the bill amended and a filing, undertook a little parliamentary skirmishing. They refused to vote on a call for the previous question, and as less than a quorum answered, a call of the House followed with closed doors. A few of the rebs tried to get into the rotunda, but the Sergeant-at-Arms was slightly in their way. The call of the House showed a quorum present.

On the final passage of the bill, they again refused to vote and less than a quorum answered. The names of the recusants were read, and were declared to be in contempt of the House under Rule 57. They were quietly informed by the Speaker that unless they purged themselves of the contempt by recording their votes, the Sergeant-at-Arms and his assistants would proceed to oust them without the bar of the House, and that they would be deprived of all rights and privileges as members of the Legislature until they were purged.

Seeing the fix that they had got into, and after keeping the House in disorder for two hours, they came down and one by one, with diverse lame explanations recorded their votes, not wishing to have the contents of such parliamentary guns fired into them. The bill passed 50 to 27. Just before the previous question was originally called on the passage of the bill, Mr. Boyle offered an amendment. Col. McCreary, temporary chairman, decided that the amendment had not been offered until after the call and therefore was out of order. Mr. Boyle and his friends insisted with a good deal of spirit that it had been offered in time. "Hence those tears."

After Col. McCreary had left the chair, the skirmishers attempted to wriggle out of an awkward predicament by pretending that the Col.'s ruling had been unparliamentary, arbitrary and in disregard of the rights of the minority, but it was all sound and fury, signifying nothing. A poor excuse may sometimes be better than none, but it was not in this case.

How immeasurably stupid such factions, such opposition to any measure intended for the colored man's amelioration appear in the light of present American sentiment. So wide, deep and determined is it that all loyal class barriers, all ancient prejudices are being rapidly swept away by it, yet the Democracy of Pennsylvania would imitate the folly of Dame Partington who sought to stay with her broom the waves which the furious storm drove into her sea shore cabin.

The suggestions of enlightened statesmanship, the sanctions of Christian morality, the lessons of history are all lost on them. Like the Bourbons, they never forgot anything, and never learned anything.

Such was the mood of the era into which the struggle had now passed; the era which began with the guaranteeing protection of civil rights, yet in which was waged a fight for the equal use of public conveyance. An incident which occurred in July of the same year further illuminates the civil scene of that decade. The *Commercial* reported an:

Interesting Court Proceeding

Motion in the Court of Common Pleas to admit a colored lawyer to the bar—remarks by Hon. P. C. Shannon, Judge Stowe and others.

On Saturday last in the Court of Common Pleas, before Judge Mellon and Stowe, Hon. P. C. Shannon moved for the admission to the Bar of George B. Vashon, Esq., (a colored person) and in making the motion he stated to their honors, that Mr. Vashon was born in Carlisle Pa., graduated at Oberlin College as a bachelor of arts, and pursued the study of law for three years under the tutelage of the late Hon. Walter Forward. Mr. Vashon afterward moved to New York, where after proper examination he was admitted in the Supreme Court to practice as an attorney, solicitor and counselor in the several courts of that state. The examination of Mr. Vashon as to his abilities and qualifications took place before Justices Strong, McConn, and Edwards of the Supreme Court, and was conducted by the Hon. James T. Brady, Joe S. Bosworth Esq., and H. H. Warner Esq.

After an absence of over two years in the West Indies, Mr. Vashon had settled in Syracuse, New York, and was there engaged in the practice of his profession, until his removal to this county. At present he is the Principal of

Avery College in Allegheny City. Judge Shannon in conclusion referred to the excellent scholastic attainments, and good character of the applicant; and as the Supreme Court of the United States had recently admitted a colored person to their Bar, he presumed that now there would be no objection here; but he believed that the Supreme Court of the District of Columbia had refused a similar application. He believed that the District Court of this county had some years ago refused to admit.

James H. Hopkins Esq. stated that his application should be referred to the committee. His Honor Judge Shannon replied, he thought not. It was unusual to do so unless some objection to be made to the character or qualifications of the applicant. In this case the whole objection related, it would seem to be the man's color. This appeared to be the only difficulty. Mr. Hopkins added in reply the course he advocated was the usual and proper course; and he did not wish to see special and unusual privileges extended to a colored person, over and above those extended and allowed to white persons. He wished in this matter all treated alike.

After some remarks by Hon. John M. Kirkpatrick, and a good deal of conversation among the members of the Bar present, who seemed to take a lively interest in the proceedings, the court concluded to grant a rule to show cause why Prof. Vashon should not be admitted to the bar of Common Pleas.

The whole affair has created much animated discussion and will be watched with deep interest. The main question is this—will the court now that the matter is squarely before it, rule that Mr. Vashon is a citizen of the United States. Viewed—from a Pennsylvania standpoint? Shall he be refused admission to the County Court of Allegheny while he was an attorney of the Supreme Court of New York?

The *Gazette*, too, commented on the Vashon incident:

COLORED QUESTION, AND THE PITTSBURGH BAR

The very full attendance of members of the Bar in the Court of Common Pleas on Saturday, was sufficiently indicative of the interest felt in the application made on the Saturday previous, for the admission to the Bar of Geo. B. Vashon a colored resident, claimed to be sufficiently learned in the law to entitle him to recognition as a practitioner. It was understood it seems that the rule was granted to be argued on Saturday, but this was a mistake. In the *Gazette* report of the granting of the rule, it was stated that it would come up for disposition in regular course on the argument list, and such was the arrangement. . . .

We learned that the question of citizenship as regards to color will not be touched. This will take away much of the importance which at first seemed to attach to the proceedings, as all that remains to be inquired into is as to the qualifications of Mr. Vashon, or as to his right to admission on the strength of the certificate of the Supreme Court of New York.

It is held by some that a person who practiced law ten years ago, and not since, might very properly be refused admission to the Bar on the ground of disqualification. Should this view prevail, and we are inclined to believe it will, Mr. Vashon's admission on the certificate he claims to hold, will be refused, unless after under going examination before the committee, he is considered qualified to practice. The Court will be governed in its action by the declaration of the Committee, to whom the matter will be deferred.

Mr. Vashon was refused admittance to the Pittsburgh Bar.

Discussion waxed furious on the question of Negro equality. In oyster bars, on street cars and railways, over dinner coffee in the prosperous homes and at supper in more modestly placed families the battle was fought. No new arguments presented themselves; all the old ones were brought out and polished up for new service. The *Gazette* comment in December of 1867 is typical:

EQUALITY

A Democratic Journal which professes intense horror at which it designates "Negro equality" portrays the demoralization of society among the whites in the principal northern towns. It says:

"Murder is perpetrated in open daylight; theft occurs in crowded streets in sight of a multitude too busy in the pursuit of trade's gain to go to the rescue; arson kindles its fires on the fruits of honest toil; the libertine finds entrance into society where the purest are endangered; wives glory in their infidelity; husbands make no apologies for their adulteries; mingling in all the fashion comes to gild with wealth crimes which should be and really are black as hell. The corruption of what is called 'society' was never worse in any country in the world, than it is today in America."

That is decidedly hard on the whites. It is greatly to be hoped the blacks will not insist upon an equality with them in these particulars.

In 1870 the Fifteenth Amendment to the Constitution climaxed the series of laws that established the status of the free Negro. It granted the right to vote to all citizens regardless of race, color, or previous condition of servitude.

By the three amendments to the Constitution the Negro had received theoretical citizenship and theoretical suffrage. These amendments developed in the national conscience a point of intense awareness of the Negro, a heightened realization of his position in a growing industrial civilization. A larger white group within the country was constrained to examine its relationship to a tremendously enlarged group of black citizens. The enlargement of the already existing group of free Negroes by the addition of three and a half million newly freed slaves was bound to affect the economic, political, and civil standing of the free Negro. And as business and industry entered its postwar development and began to dominate social and cultural activities the precept became more and more clear that to maintain progress the Negro must participate in the growing industry and business with an ever increasing degree of equality. The right of employment became a paramount issue on which to base the enjoyment of all other rights and privileges.

In Pennsylvania the suffrage was made fact by law of 1870, recorded in *Purdon's Pennsylvania Statues* as follows:

> Persons entitled to register and vote: compensation of assessors in Philadelphia. So much of every act of assembly as provided that only white freemen shall be entitled to vote or be registered as voters, or as claiming to vote at any general or special election of this Commonwealth and the same is hereby repealed; and that hereafter all freemen without distinction of color shall be enrolled and registered, according to the provisions of the first section of the act 1 of 2 approved by April 17,1869, entitled "An act further supplemental to the act relative to the elections of this Commonwealth" and shall where otherwise qualified under existing laws, be entitled to vote at all general and special elections. Provided this act shall in no way reduce the compensation of the assessors of Philadelphia, which shall be $1000, as now established by law. (1870, April, 6, P.L.53 10)

A new state constitution in 1873 further guaranteed to the Negro the vote denied to him by the 1838 constitution. But already in 1870, Pittsburgh Negroes had under the act of that year, voted for the first time since 1837. Guarantee of the right to vote would seem to have given the Negro a legislative key that would open all doors closed to him during the first half century of American Democracy. But for another three quarters of a century he continued to live out a rather dreary history under the shadow of prejudice and segregation, and suffered denial of elemental civil rights. In spite of progress—economic, political, and cultural—the Pittsburgh Negro, sharing the lot of the Negro anywhere in the North, lived year by year under civil and social restrictions hemmed in by taken-for-granted taboos, tricked in politics, proscribed by industry and by civic agencies, held in the penumbra of the white man's culture.

Two years after his ballot had been restored, that is in 1872, the *Post*, a Democratic Pittsburgh paper, under the caption: "Colored Men—What They Can and Can't Do," said:

As the Republican party claims to be the special friends and champions of colored men's rights, we append a few specimens of the "equal rights" which the colored men enjoy in this Republican county of Allegheny.

- He cannot be admitted to the orchestra, dress or family circle of the opera house.
- He cannot purchase a sleeping birth on any of the seven railroads that go out of the city.
- He cannot take dinner at the Monongahela House, Hare's Hotel, or any no. 1 restaurant.
- He cannot send his children to the 3rd ward Allegheny School.
- He cannot join the Lincoln club except as a waiter.
- He cannot make the riffle when he runs for 3rd Allegheny Council man.

Once assured that his people were legally free, and that he was a full-fledged citizen of the re-United States, with the ballot in his hands and polling places open to him, the Negro had a tendency to relax his vigilance during the half century following the war which established these rights. The pre-Civil War leaders who had carried the abolition movement to its successful, if bloody conclusion, were dead, or too old to maintain their early militancy. The idea gained ground that the legal battle having been won, application of the law was assured. The theme of living during the last three decades of the nineteenth century was "educate our people," and "train our people for industry." Those who entered politics in the next half century—and many did—were satisfied with their own rewards. Social life broadened among the middle classes to include ever larger numbers. Club life developed. Fraternal societies grew in number and scope. Small businesses multiplied. Churches increased. Musical and literary societies became more numerous. The Negro community acquired a superficial self-sufficiency. Many of the needs of the people could be met within the Negro community. Those that could not were largely cultural luxuries and might without too much sacrifice be dispensed with rather that enjoyed at the expense of sufferance, discomfort, or rebuff. Pride of family and an exclusive social life within the Negro community assured the leaders of a certain amount of social authority and political power over Negro votes.

But the post-war scene was different basically from that of the ante-bellum days. From 1870 the Negro population increased at a greater rate than any other period before that date. Moreover, the increasing number of Negro men found places, not so much in the rapidly growing industries of the city, but as coachmen and servants, or in lowly occupations such as draying and hauling, refuse collection and janitoring. The Negro workman was, however, beginning to take his place in industries, and could not be held aloof from the growing labor tension of these years. One after another the strikes and lockouts that marked the growth of the industrial monopoly found the Negro worker involved, and in turn involved his civil liberties even more than they did those of white workers. The issue, nevertheless, did not focus sharply until the years following the First World War.

For such reasons Negro pressure for observance of the law of 1887 slackened, and during the year once more the law lost touch with social reality. Fewer and fewer cases involving the constitutionality and the operation of the law came into the courts. The most pertinent part of the act of 1887 was tested in the famous case of the Commonwealth v. George. The decision in this case was that any proprietor of a place of public accommodation or amusement who sets aside a part of his establishment for separate service to Negro patrons could not be prosecuted under the act unless that part was not equal in service to that maintained for white patrons. As time went on, the operation of the law was largely ignored and complete civil rights became a purely theoretical condition.

———

In the crisis and depression that struck in 1929 civil rights once more became a dramatic issue. Unemployment, evictions for inability to pay rent, arrests during picketing and peaceful assemblage, demands for relief and jobs on C.W.A., F.E.R.A, P.W.A., and W.P.A., discrimination in types of jobs, wages and conditions of work on public jobs, brought the fundamental issue of economic discrimination against Negroes strongly into the foreground.

The depression also brought a general resurgence of activity in the ranks of labor, particularly the drive to organize the workers in the steel industry of the Pittsburgh district. In sections where union meetings had been violently broken up for years, workers now had won the right to peaceful assembly and other civil rights denied them since the great steel strike of 1919. The success of the campaign was accompanied by the election of labor men to public offices. Negro workers, because of their strategic position in the industry, flocked into the unions, and the growing consciousness of the political role and significance of labor raised issues besides those of simple trade unionism. Foremost among these was the general question of civil liberties for all workers and for Negro workers in particular. The depression had intensified such violations. Discrimination existed on relief roles. Furthermore, minor riots over the use of the Warrington, the Paulson, and the Avalon public swimming pools in Negro neighborhoods and the pools in Beltzhoover, and on the North Side raised the question more sharply in the social community than it had been raised for years.

The Beaver Shanghai episode of 1933 represented on a larger scale than some of the other incidents the degree to which treatment of the working class Negro

approached lynch law in the first years of the depression. Although the case arose
in Beaver County it aroused more resentment and activity among the Pittsburgh
population, dense as it is, than in Beaver County. A mass arrest of thirty Negro
men and women had occurred at Industry, a town in Beaver Valley, one of the industrial areas just beyond Pittsburgh. Unable to pay the fines levied, they had
been herded into the Beaver County jail overnight. Next day the thirty men and
women were loaded into three trucks, hauled more than 100 miles to a point below Waynesburg in Greene County, just beyond the West Virginia border, ordered out of the trucks in a driving rain, and ordered to "get goin" into West Virginia.

Accompanying this geographical segregation in the city, undercover pressure
has been brought to keep the Negro physically localized. Struggles have arisen
not only around the right of Negroes to swim in public pools, but around the
right of Negroes to teach in public schools; and around their right to enter professional training fields like the Medical School of the University of Pittsburgh,
and the practice teaching units in the School of Education. The Pittsburgh Negro has had to fight for the right to intern in the hospitals of the city, to train and
serve as nurses in those hospitals, and to attend settlement classes and activities
even in the most densely populated Negro districts. He has, by long struggle,
won the right to work in some places and at some occupations of his own choice
and for which he is highly qualified, but often as not the opportunity by subtle
manipulation has been denied him. Secret quotas bar his entry into many fields.
A national insurance company maintains a separate office and a separate white
staff for its Negro clients; despite repeated requests they have refused to hire
Negro agents for their Negro clients. The same company offers only two types of
insurance to Negroes (at higher than normal rates), whereas whites may choose
among thirty varieties. Within recent years a Negro attorney who purchased a
home in one of the residential sections of the city was compelled to move out of
the district by repeated breaking of his windows and other depredations upon his
home; his "neighbors" preferred an indirect way of stating their convictions.

The campaign for equal rights has been carried on in Pittsburgh and Allegheny County through three agencies. By political action, by legislative enactment,
and in the courts both Negroes and progressive whites who see the Negro problem as a question of basic democratic rights for all American citizens are breaking
down obstacles.

As the Pittsburgh Negro has learned vigilance in guarding his hard-won
rights, more agencies have been involved. The Urban League of Pittsburgh has
successfully fought for the right of Negroes to work in occupations of their own
choice and for what they are trained. Through conferences with employers, by
showing the role of the Negro in a particular industry, his aptness, his past con-

tributions, the dependence of that industry, large or small, upon the Negro as a consumer, the Urban League has opened new fields, and has done much to break down discrimination and restriction.

The National Association for the Advancement of Colored People has financed court cases that could not have been fought without its aid. The International Worker's Order, the Tenants' League, and the Workers' Alliance have joined in the struggle for equal rights for Negroes in the labor field, in fraternal insurance, in public health, in housing, and against discrimination on relief rolls, and on WPA jobs. They have been on guard against evictions during the depression, against high rents, meat frauds, discrimination in food prices in stores on "the hill," and have campaigned for employment of Negroes in stores serving them.

An early entrant into this economic field was the American Negro Labor Congress, organized in Chicago in October, 1925 "to lead the struggles of the Negro workers and farmers against terrorism, lynching, and mob violence, police brutality, segregation and all forms of race hatred; for equal work; for better working conditions, for the organization of Negro workers into trade unions on the basis of complete equality." The work of the Labor Congress naturally was strongest in industry. It called for admittance of Negroes into trade unions, with full participation in all offices and affairs, and for organization of Negroes into unions where none existed. It organized Inter-Racial Labor Conferences for the unionization of all Negro workers. While the Congress did good work among the Pittsburgh Negroes, it antagonized many people by what seemed its excess of militancy; hence after its last convention in 1930, it was metamorphosed into the League of Struggle for Negro Rights. The new League organized a demand for Negro teachers in Pittsburgh public schools, conducted rent strikes, picketed businesses in Negro neighborhoods which refused to employ Negroes, and protested evictions. In cooperation with the Unemployed Council, it stopped the deportation of Negro workers to Ohio and Negro relief clients to Georgia—Negroes who had settled in Pittsburgh but had insufficient time to establish legal residence. Its program, however, was somewhat aloof from the everyday needs of the people; it was considered too radical by most Negroes, and it too died out.

The League of Struggle for Negro Rights was superseded by the National Negro Congress, a broader organization which stressed the need for education among middle-class Negroes and white collar professional workers as well as among unskilled labor. It has won these groups to its programs and through them has brought organization and direction into the movement for equal rights and for organizing education and action against the worst features of oppression, the most intense form of race hatred, and many of those aspects of a depression-torn era.

The Equal Rights Act of June 11, 1935, officially designated as P.L. 297, is the peak of these efforts. It is entitled "An Act to Amend Section 1 of the act approved 19th day of May 1887 entitled An Act to Provide Civil Rights for all People Regardless of Race or Color, amplifying or extending provisions of said act and increasing the penalties for violating thereof." Included in the places named are inns, roadhouses, hotels, barrooms, parks, drugstores, bath houses, theaters, music halls, gymnasiums, libraries, schools, colleges, trains and resorts. The *Literary Digest* cites an instance of one attitude with which the law was received: "Some hotel men have said flatly that they would not obey the law and there would be trouble if white waitresses were called to wait on Negro diners." The *Digest* also said: "The manager of one of Pittsburgh's largest amusement parks said: 'This bill is a terrible thing. It was passed purely for political reasons. We will positively not allow Negroes to enter our dance halls or our swimming pools except when there are Negro picnics. If there is any trouble, and there is the possibility that there will be, we will carry it to the courts immediately, and I don't think there is a jury that will find us guilty.'"

A Negro attorney says of the bill: "Quite significantly enough it constitutes a Declaration of Rights not only for Negroes in the state, but for all other minority groups as well. If the trend of the times, as some estimate, is towards reaction and oppression of minorities, it may yet be cited as much by Jews and aliens as by Negroes." The bill was introduced in the State Legislature by Mr. Hobson Reynolds of Philadelphia. It was in danger of being recalled when Representative Homer S. Brown of Pittsburgh, through a direct appeal to the Governor, saved it and pushed it through the Legislature. Although the bill was intended to establish equal rights for Negroes in the state, it in no way mentions the Negro. Its declaration that all persons within the jurisdiction of the Commonwealth shall be entitled to full and equal accommodations, advantages, facilities, and privileges of any places of public accommodation, resort, or amusement, subject only to the conditions and limitations established by law, and applicable alike to all persons sets a uniform high standard of equality. As a criminal statue the bill proceeds to specify and particularize on the general statement. The same Negro attorney quoted before says:

> It declares a public policy that will carry over into civil law. Quite clearly the bill is not legislation in favor of class or group, but, in the words "applicable to all persons," secures the right of the individual, Negro or White, citizen or non-citizen, native or foreign born, to the privileges named. It establishes the right of individuals as against a whole class, and is obviously advantageous to all minority groups. In this respect it resembles the 13th, 14th, and 15th amendments to the Constitution of the United States. The act is stronger than previous acts in it that it remedies the weakness of early acts

passed after the Civil War in which equality of accommodation was distinguished from identical accommodation. By making equality of accommodation synonymous with identical accommodation, the present act can be considered an amendment to the Act of May 19, 1887.

In Pittsburgh several cases have been brought into the courts testing the constitutionality of the Equal Rights Act and establishing precedents for the rest of the state.

The first case in the state in which the constitutionality of the law was involved arose when three city workmen—two white men and their Negro coworker—cleaning snow from the streets in East Liberty, asked to be served lunch at a nearby restaurant. They were at first refused. The proprietor then offered to serve the white men if the Negro left. The newly passed act was cited to compel service. The proprietor declared his indifference to the act and his sovereignty over his business. The NAACP took the case to court. The proprietor was found guilty, but the defense asked for a new trial on the grounds that the Equal Rights Act, under which he was convicted, was unconstitutional. The case came up in April 1936, listed as No. 37 in the criminal court of Allegheny County. In October 1936 the case was finally decided; the constitutionality of the act was fully upheld.

The Brentwood school case was another such case. Since the Brentwood High School had not enough pupils enrolled to maintain itself, it offered to take graduates from the neighboring Baldwin Township. Baldwin Township had no high school to which eighth grade graduates could be sent. When the Negro students from Baldwin Township applied for admission at Brentwood they were refused. The Brentwood Board declared they had not intended the verbal contract to apply to Negro students. The Committee for Legal Redress in the Pittsburgh Branch of the NAACP took the case to the Common Pleas Court, fought it, and secured a mandamus against Brentwood which opened the high school to the Negro students.

Still another Pittsburgh case set a precedent for the state. In October 1936 case No. 1058, Stokes v. the Borough of Avalon, was called. The Avalon Borough Council had passed an ordinance assigning Negroes certain days for use of the municipal swimming pool. Here, too, the NAACP took action. An injunction declared the Avalon Council to be without authority to pass legislation forbidding anyone the use of institutions supported by the expenditure of public money. The borough declared the pool was not a public enterprise. They were, however, finally enjoined from enforcing the ordinance. The precedent has since been followed throughout the state.

In January 1938 information was made against the owner of a Pittsburgh skating rink who, having rented his rink to the American Youth Congress, refused its use when told that Negro members of the Congress would attend the skating party, and "guaranteed violence" if any Negro skaters appeared. A grand jury indicted the owner, but a visiting judge threw the case out of court, with the statement that it was a test case and never should have been brought into court. The costs and fine were placed on the plaintiff, who, unable to pay, spent 24 hours in jail until the fine costs could be collected from Negro and white friends.

The more expensive restaurants and hotels continued to openly segregate or refuse service to Negroes even since the passage of the Equal Rights Act of 1935; a recent national convention solved the problem of housing Negro delegates only by quartering them among private families. More important than these individual violations of the letter and spirit of the law, however, is the laxness exhibited by white citizens and echoed among some middle-class Negroes when they reason on such violations that the Negro does not and should not want to go to such places anyhow, that such places are too expensive, and that the issue of the right to eat or sleep in such places is raised not by the Negroes concerned but by the "radical" and "communistic" groups who are out to make trouble, who use the Negro's inequality as an excuse. Such evasions tend to nullify the legal equality which the Negro has gained in Pennsylvania only after years of brilliant struggle.

All in all, the question of formal civil rights for Negroes in Pittsburgh, despite the long years of struggle, have never been a truly paramount issue. The tragic and bloody pattern exhibited in other cities and other states has been mercifully avoided. Progress toward a legal assurance has been reasonably rapid and complete. The division however, between principle and social fact remains as clear today [1940] as it ever was in Pittsburgh history. A new and perhaps more tenuous battle ground has been laid out; organic inclusion of the Negro into the life of the city now depends on the vitalization of a social attitude for the Negro and the white citizen. The Negro in Pittsburgh has lived by a genteel social assumption that was not based on social fact. Victim of two contending forces, he has suffered from a debilitating duality throughout the whole of his Pittsburgh existence; the unity of a fully rounded personality has been denied him, and he has been forced by habit or intelligence to acquire two codes, two emotional languages, and two social horizons. A recent Negro graduate of the University of Pittsburgh said, "The moment I step out of my home in the morning, I begin to live by a different psychology." Such a shift to an alter ego, automatic and unconscious, results in the development of a split social personality bearing, frequently, much misery in its wake. Not a few middle-class Negroes in Pittsburgh today contend (as comfortably as they can) that deprivation or infringement of civil rights among Pittsburgh Negroes has never been a problem of great concern; they add, moreover, that years ago, when they were younger, before the great migrations, discrimination and segregation were practically unknown. Others contend that this attitude is one of somewhat uneasy defiance; that those who speak so are conscious of living comfortably in a northern city, and that they do not wish to further be disturbed. Habituated to the dual code by which they live, it is said, they are willfully blind to the fact that in its whole Pittsburgh record the Negro has never enjoyed the full, taken-for-granted rights of American citizenship.

The Youth Council of the NAACP have recently adopted as their pledge:

We believe in the advancement of Negroes, not in a spirit of racism, but as a contribution to a common American culture.

We believe in fundamental social and economic change, leading us into a new cooperative commonwealth, dedicated to freedom, equality, and security for all.

We believe that to struggle for the rights of Negroes, is to fight fascist terror, and to help in building the new society.

We believe in preserving and extending democracy, as a bulwark against fascism, an aid to social change.

We therefore, pledge ourselves to fight, relentlessly with the ballot, in the courts, with education of public opinion, and the enactment of legislation;

Through the NAACP, for equal opportunities in all spheres, for protection and extension of civil liberties, and against the insane fury of the mob.

CHAPTER 6

THE NEGRO WAGE WORKER

—•◦•—

Rewriteman: J. Ernest Wright /
April 24, 1939 / Pre-final

It hardly needs to be said that the Negro wage worker constitutes the largest group of the Negro population in Pittsburgh, as it does anywhere else. That the wage worker is also the basic group and the barometer of the Negro's welfare may not be so readily admitted. Yet as the fortunes of the Negro worker rise and fall, so rise and fall the well being of the people—not the Negro people alone, but the whole people. The prosperity and security of a people is as great as that of the least of its people. If the greater number of a people are ill-fed, ill-housed, ill-clothed, one can hardly say that the people are prosperous or secure. The lowest wage paid will be the standard by which is judged what constitutes a high wage. A standard of living is a comparative thing, high only in comparison to the lowest. Security and freedom, too, are comparative aspects of good fortune, great only in comparison with the meager security and freedom of the least fortunate.

The industrial status of the Negro in Pittsburgh is determined chiefly by the state of heavy industry concentrated here. Its almost fabulous development began just at the time when the newly freed Negro slaves became a factor in industry as an available supply of free labor. And, unfortunately, at the same time there began to develop one of the greatest obstacles to Negro progress—the idea that the Negro worker was a competitor of the white laborer, and more vicious still, that he is even inferior as a human being.

This chapter is very rough and contains several disjointed subsections. For the published edition, these sections have been rearranged to present smoother transitions, where possible.

216

The Negro wage worker has never lived and worked out of the shadow of the southern plantation. The influence of the industrial revolution upon the growth of the cotton industry reached beyond the southern slave worker to the worker in the North. The feudal plantation system which impoverished the Negro and held him in bondage also debased him by developing in him a sense of subservience and in his white masters and the majority of their northern compatriots a theory of his inferiority under the weight of which he has lived and worked ever since. The debasement of the spiritual or social attitude of a whole nation in this respect has not yet been remedied. In this respect, the profits to northern cities such as Pittsburgh which results from slave labor in the South weakened the support of the abolitionist movement and retarded his rise toward civil and social equity.

The contribution of the Negro worker to the advance of American labor has been grudgingly admitted, if at all. His role has been strategic in every industrial crisis since his acquisition of an industrial status that began at the close of the Civil War. In Pittsburgh the Negro worker has been a major factor in such situations. That his significance as a factor in the progress of labor is equally important to his struggle for social equality and civil justice has not been seen clearly enough and he has not therefore always used his position to take full advantage of American life. In addition to these things, he has had the early antagonistic attitude of trade unions to struggle against. In this field, as in so many others, the economic crisis of the nineteen thirties has taught both Negro and white wage workers the most valuable lesson they have to learn—identity of interests as an economic class. And as the working class of America moves forward, it moves more and more as a united body of Negro, white, American, Italian, Jew, Hungarian, man and woman, youthful worker and more mature.

One of the chief obstacles to the progress of the Negro wage worker was the growth of the prejudice-inspired conception of the "Negro job." This concept had its origin in the early years of Negro freedom. In the beginning of the nineteenth century, when the iron industry was young and booming, and when the War of 1812 had boosted the growth of cotton and woolen mills in Pittsburgh, white men flocked to the iron foundries and forges, and white women to the cotton mills. The Negro worker filled the gaps left—the men as draymen, coal venders, barbers, valets, and caterers, the women as domestic servants and seamstresses. Even for the earliest professional workers—ministers particularly—occupation in one of the these trades was necessary to make a living, as it was for the Rev. Abraham D. Lewis, "Father" John Peck, and the Rev. Lewis Woodson. This situation was a carry-over from the plantation system of slavery, which impoverished the Negro, held him in bondage, and debased him by developing in him a sense of subservience, and in his white masters a theory of his inferiority. This debasement of the spiritual or social attitude of the community has not yet been remedied.

For decades afterwards the majority were employed in domestic and personal service as was George B. Vashon, perhaps the outstanding leader in the city of his day.

————

The Negro worker was not a component part of basic Pittsburgh industry until the World War.[1] He had, it is true, been found in isolated cases in the mills in the actual manufacture of steel. Early in the history of industry he had found frequent occupation as janitor and as chef in the mess halls which were at one time a feature of the industry.

On March 3, 1875, the Negro industrial worker made his appearance on the Pittsburgh scene. For several months union puddlers of the Pittsburgh Bolt Company had been on strike. A company official announced, "We brought puddlers from Europe here during the former strike and we could do it now, I suppose." But a cheaper and easier method was discovered. The *Pittsburgh Leader* of February 28 said: "A short time ago the Pittsburgh Bolt Company sent representatives to Virginia, and some other firms are doing likewise. An executive of theirs said an abundance of colored puddlers could be had."

In publishing the news that Negro puddlers would be brought in from Virginia, the *Leader* warned against violence,

> If there should be any attempt to interfere with the Negro puddlers who have been imported into our midst, it would not be met with the same public indifference as that which attended and followed the Italian massacre. The old republican feeling would be stirred to its depths, the old abolitionists would emerge from their hiding places and the assault on Negro rights would be avenged.

The day after the arrival of the puddlers, a crowd of 400 men and boys stormed about the mill. The twelve police detailed to guard the plant refused the request of the mill officials to disperse them, claiming they had no such authority unless violence occurred. Sheriff Hare was called, but before his arrival, the strikers, through threats and letters of warning, had compelled all workers except the Negro puddlers to quit work. Upon receiving a signed order from their chief, the police dispersed the crowd. Meanwhile, Mr. Kavlor, President of the company had obtained from the Governor an order for the Washington infantry to stand by, ready to move.

The Pittsburgh Bolt Company incident was typical of certain phases in the

1. This refers to the First World War.

history of Pittsburgh labor for years to come. But gradually the Negro worker was able to throw off the forced, ignominious role of competitor and strikebreaker and to join the ranks of organized labor in general.

This subservience on the part of the Negro worker, the white employer's idea of the Negro job, and the prejudice of white workers against Negroes on skilled jobs militated against the entrance of the Negro worker into early trade unions. In the tremendous expansion of industry between the Civil War and the Spanish American War, it was to the advantage of the increasing merger of companies into corporations and the growth of monopolies to keep wages down, hours long, and out-put on the increase. To do this it was necessary to keep the various organized groups of workers apart, to forestall organization.

The Negro worker did not quickly become a component part of basic Pittsburgh industry; that position was achieved only with the World War. Early in the history of the industry he found frequent occupation as janitor and as chef in the mess halls which were at one time a feature of the industry. He was, it is true, found in isolated instances as worker in the mills. Negro puddlers exclusively were employed in Park's Black Diamond Mill in Lawrenceville. Negro rollers were employed by Carnegie Steel Company in the old Clark's Mill. Yet until 1907-08 only two out of every hundred steel workers were Negroes. Within the next ten years the 2,250 so employed increased to almost 7,000. Many of these, however, who called themselves steel workers did not actually work in the production of steel. In the Homestead plant of Carnegie Steel Company twelve percent of the workers were Negroes.

Negro employment in steel production reached a peak of ten percent of the total—in actual numbers less than 5,000. These workers, moreover, did chiefly the unskilled jobs. Semi-skilled and skilled work fell to them only when it was distasteful to white workers, or too dangerous, or during labor troubles. The 5,000 Negro steel workers constituted eighty percent of the Negroes employed by the manufacturing and mechanical industries. In no other manufacturing industry did Negro workers exceed two percent of the total force. The Negro worker, therefore, could not become a factor in trade unionism until he established himself in the basic industries.

Pittsburgh industrial policy was typical of that of the era—to use cheap foreign labor wherever possible, isolate it from native-born labor, and keep one eye on the newly available black labor from the South. Slav and Italian workers were taken up more quickly into native white labor groups and the white community generally, although they too met opprobrium and prejudice which expressed itself in terms like "Hunkie" and "Wop." The "Hunkie" and the "Wop," nevertheless, were more readily taken on as apprentices than were the Negroes. They were allowed to work at skilled jobs, and were therefore absorbed more quickly by the growing trade unions.

The Negro worker, who came in increasing numbers into the region, faced another situation. If the policy of the earliest unions was indifference to the increasing masses of unskilled workers, it was openly hostile to Negro workers, skilled or unskilled. Only after Negro workers had been used to break several more of their strikes did Pittsburgh steel workers admit the Negro to the union.

In 1881 the Amalgamated Association of Iron, Steel and Tin Workers declared Negroes eligible to membership. First at Richmond, Virginia, the chief source of supply of strikebreakers for Pittsburgh, and then in the Pittsburgh plants themselves, where it was possible, separate Negro lodges of the Amalgamated were set up. Negro workers were skeptical. They felt white unionists were merely insuring themselves against further Negro strike breaking.

The Knights of Labor took all white and Negro men and women into their ranks. They were strong in the Pittsburgh region for some years, more particularly, however in the steel and mining suburbs of the city.

The Knights were quickly replaced by the American Federation of Labor, which had held its first convention in Pittsburgh in 1881, five years before it adopted the name by which it has become known. Yet the American Federation of Labor in its first half century of existence meant chiefly disbarment of Negroes from union protection and benefits. This attitude of the unions has proven itself so shortsighted a policy that within the past few years it has changed basically. The policy of exclusion has not always been openly stated, but it has nevertheless been definitely practiced. Twenty or more unions had clauses in their constitution discriminating against Negroes. Many more used round-about ways of barring Negroes from membership or from the enjoyment and exercise of equal rights. As late as 1931 eleven international unions affiliated with the A.F. of L., and thirteen unions not affiliated, excluded Negroes.

Instances occurred where Negro workers were taken into steel unions, as in the Lafayette Lodge at the Butler Street plant of Carnegie Steel Company. Here they struck with white workers in 1901. They left with the white officials of their lodge to work at a plant down the river. There the white union workers refused to work with them. The Negroes returned and enlisted as strike breakers.

In 1925 only 518 Negroes in Pittsburgh belonged to trade unions. Of these 478 were in the building trades. The Lathers Union Local 33 was the only mixed union which had Negro apprentices. Of 22 members in 1925, three were so enrolled. The only Negro metal lather in the city was asked to affiliate. Negro plasterers could not join the white union, nor could they establish their own local.

At the time of the World War thirty Negro plasterers, discouraged by dis-

criminatory policy of the union in their field, requested of the national organization permission to set up their own local. They were told that a charter could not
be given without the consent of the older, white local. The Negro secretary was
allowed five minutes to present his request to the local, and no action was taken.
The brick-layers and the carpenters permitted but did not encourage Negro
membership. Electrical Workers made membership virtually impossible. No
painter has been admitted to any white local within District Council #1, of Pittsburgh. One local, number 18, in 1925 was composed of 65 Negroes. There were
no Negro members among elevator constructors or sheet metal workers.

The hoisting engineers accepted Negroes and elected them to office but did
not have Negro apprentices. The International Association of Bridge Structural
and Ornamental Iron Workers admits Negroes on parity with white numbers.
The Negro members of the Pittsburgh local brought transfer cards from other
cities. The plumbers have consistently excluded Negroes from membership.

The reasons given by the painters for their policy of exclusion are typical of
the prejudice Negro workers must face and of the lack of understanding of trade
unions among union members themselves. The reasons given were: arguments
between Negro and white members at meetings; the Negro wanted the distinction of being the only Negro member and therefore would not encourage others
to join; collecting dues from Negroes was difficult; and the Negro member violated rules more frequently than white members.

Negro employment in these Pittsburgh industries became noticed in the
1890's but the Negro continued to play his old role of strikebreaker. After a settlement, however, Negro workers sometimes were retained, and were occasionally
given skilled jobs as black smiths, foremen or first and second open hearth helpers. Occasionally, also, they held jobs as draftsmen, mill wright, roller, civil engineer, or chemist. In one mill, for instance, 100 Negro workers, or one-third of the
total, were in skilled and semi-skilled jobs. The hod-carriers, the building trades,
the laborers and the cement finishers unions have had the largest membership. A
Negro was business manager of a hod-carrier local and a former organizer of the
A.F. of L. The great majority, nevertheless, kept the hardest and most dangerous
jobs in the mills. Many of those workers on jobs classified as semi-skilled are so
ranked not because they possess a technique of manufacturing process but because they have learned, in a few weeks apprenticeship, to control a particular
machine. Generally they are paid a mere fraction more than the unskilled worker.
Negro labor in the industries, therefore, works preponderantly for an unskilled
wage.

By August 1923, the Negro reached his peak of employment in Pittsburgh
industry. In eleven plants of Carnegie Steel Company over six thousand were

employed. In four plants of Jones & Laughlin there were about three thousand; in the Pressed Steel Car Company, 1700; at Westinghouse Airbrake 465; and at Pittsburgh Plate Glass, 4 plants, 350.

Because of the closed door to many of the unions in various industries, the Negro worker has played a determining part in strikes in Pittsburgh industry. The policy of exclusion from unions actually hastened his entrance into the mills. Almost every strike between 1875 and the middle eighties was marked by importation of Negroes. In 1876 the Parke Brothers Mill in Lawrenceville imported six hundred strikebreakers. The Black Diamond Mill in Lawrenceville, the Moorhead Mill at Sharpsburg, the Clark Mills—one after another imported Negro workers in this capacity. A serious battle occurred when the Elba Works attempted the same practice.

The steel strike of 1919 was the first major strike in which Negroes were involved in large numbers. About 800 were employed in the Homestead district. Of these only 8 joined the union and struck. At Duquesne 344 were employed. Here none struck. At Clairton out of 300 employed, 10 joined the union and struck for six weeks, then decided to return to work. At Braddock 600 Negro employees neither joined the union nor struck. Constantly Negroes were transported from plant to plant to defeat the strike.

At this time the Pittsburgh Urban League initiated the placing of eighteen Negro welfare workers in eleven plants employing the overwhelming majority of Negroes engaged in the steel industry. When William Z. Foster began the organization of the mills, the industrial secretary of the Urban League and other Negro leaders suggested the use by the strike committee of Negro organizers. But the impression grew that labor leaders were merely making a gesture toward Negro labor and that they looked forward to eliminating the Negro worker from the mill when the strike was won. Only a handful of Negroes in the region answered the strike call.

A not uncommon attitude toward Negro labor is represented by the reply of a manufacturer when questioned on the Immigration Restriction Law. He said restriction of aliens kept out many discontents who only fomented trouble in American industrial life. His industry, he said, could get along very well without foreign labor because it had learned to use the Negro, who is less susceptible to radical dogmas and who, because of his southern heritage, is more easily disciplined. It was once predicted that introducing the Negro worker to machine production would not waken him quickly to economic class consciousness; his plantation psychology would persist. This has not proven true. The depression has brought Negroes into Tenants Leagues to fight evictions, into demonstrations for relief, into meat strikes, and into movements to compel the hiring of Negroes in small businesses patronized largely by Negroes.

When the crisis [of the depression] struck, unemployment became wide-spread among the Negro people. Breadlines, food baskets, doubling and tripling of families in already crowded houses, Hoovervilles, and hunger marches were the lot of hundreds of families in the Hill, the Strip, Manchester and Woods Run. Although only 8.4% of the city's population, Negroes made up 17.4% of the city's unemployed. This number was almost half of the employable Negroes. The larg-est group of unemployed Negro workers are domestics. Among professional and white collar workers unemployment is far greater than among whites. Among the unskilled more men than women are unemployed. Negro men make up one-third of the total unemployment. A report issued by the Urban League says that unem-ployment can go down in history as one of the few institutions not guilty of dis-crimination and limitation on a racial basis.

The migration of southern Negroes from 1914 to 1923 profoundly affected la-bor policy. The restriction of foreign immigration had decreased the supply of cheap labor in the North. The enlistment of workers in the A.E.F. during the World War intensified the shortage and the war boom opened occupations hith-erto closed to Negroes. In fact, some industries were unable to continue without the aid of Negro workers. Migration became a boon to northern business. Steel mills and mines became terminal points of several routes bringing streams of people from southern farms and cities. From Alabama, Georgia and Tennessee, from Texas, Arkansas and Oklahoma; and from the tobacco fields, sugar farms and rice swamps on the eastern seaboard thousands of Negro workers made their way to Pittsburgh. Among these thousands of migrants were substantial laboring men who later sent for their families, single men who soon married, single women who had heard of domestic service opportunities, and widows with children to be educated. And inevitably there were "floaters." This great migration thrust upon Pittsburgh and other northern cities problems for which their white and Negro communities were unprepared.

Mill and mine operators welcomed these thousands as a supply of cheap la-bor. They did so by various devices. They printed appeals in southern papers: "Let's go North where there are no labor troubles, no strikes, no lockouts; two weeks pay; good houses; we ship you and your household goods. All colored ministers can go free; will advance you money if necessary; scores of men have written us thanking us for sending them; go now while you have the chance."

The southern states grew alarmed at the great numbers leaving for the North. Intimidation was employed in many forms to keep black workers in the South. For a time the mass movement slowed up. A Carnegie Steel official in Pittsburgh said, "When the immigration failed to bring colored labor to the mills in suffi-cient numbers the companies sent agents South and brought thousands of black workers back." Southern states then passed laws forbidding agents to enter the state. A tactic was employed. A northern Negro was sent into a southern town, apparently to visit relatives and friends. Inconspicuous and cautious, he moved about drawing men into casual talk at barber shops and on street corners or by feeding them in restaurants. He was well-supplied with bills of large denomination. These he flashed at stores, at churches, at socials. The surprise they caused and the questions asked were the effect calculated upon. The explanation was simple—the visitor worked in the steel mills for $10.00 a day. He worked six and seven days a week. When the astonished listeners asked what were their chances of earning such wealth they were told to see the Rev. So-and-So: he could tell them. And shortly afterwards groups of men and women surreptitiously left for the northern mills.

Workers in cities like Birmingham found getting out of town comparatively easy. But the majority of those who came north for jobs were rural people. Sharecroppers who were constantly in debt, workers in rice swamps and turpentine camps were easy prey for the northern agents. These found escape more difficult than did those employed in cities. Even from small towns it was hard to leave. Railroad agents refused to sell tickets; conductors refused to allow Negroes to board trains for the North. When laws were passed forbidding the activities of agents, distribution of free tickets to northward bound workers was considered too risky. A new plan was adopted. Meeting places were assigned at railroad sidings or switches outside the towns for groups of a hundred or more. Men who that day had "plowed a mule" and had no time to return to their cabin for clothing; men in overalls, bareheaded, unshaven; men in the broad flapping straw hats of sharecroppers; men with their personal possessions tied in sheets were crowded into Jim Crow cars so densely that many of them stood all night jolted against each other or over their bundles and belongings. But they were thankful for escape from the peonage of plantation, swamp, and camp. Arriving aching but high-spirited at the Pennsylvania or B. & O. station in early dawn these crowds were met by the messengers of particular firms and taken direct to employment offices to be signed up. If they arrived at night they were met by small hotel owners or house owners eager to take them as roomers and boarders. Friendless in a strange town, often without a change of clothing, but with enough money given by the agent to carry them through their first few days, and unacquainted with northern ways they became easily exploited victims, crowded into rooms to sleep by tens and dozens, given cots in bath rooms or halls, or a shakedown on the floor. After one day's work they were allowed an advance of fifty percent of a day's wage to meet their expenses.

Hundreds were herded into barracks on company ground. Garages and stables were hastily converted into living quarters, tippling houses were bolstered for use. The men were fed army-like in groups, or if lucky enough to live together in houses, they bought dearly at the company stores, their purchases deducted from pay checks.

Meantime married men sent back South for their families which, carefully watched since the disappearance of the father or eldest son, had to steal from town to town until they could freely board trains for the North.

In barracks and houses where these people slept eight or nine to a room, epidemics of flu and pneumonia killed them by scores. Vice and crime were inevitable. Discontent and disillusion soon appeared. Instead of the promised ten or twelve dollars a day, they received three or five. In many cases the money advanced by the agent was deducted from pay envelopes. In the period of unemployment immediately following the [First] World War, these workers became especially bitter. But for the most part they remained passive, expressing themselves only in the half-seclusion of barbershop or restaurant.

Many who had been industrial workers in the South made their way back, but the croppers, rice workers, and turpentine workers chose to "stick it out" rather than go back to the old life.

Following this mass of industrial migrants frequently came professional and small business men. Preachers, half of whose congregations had migrated, followed their flocks, as did teachers in Jim Crow schools, undertakers and small business men.

———

When A. Philip Randolph rose to demand of the A.F. of L. convention at Atlantic City in 1935, "Why should a Negro Worker be penalized for being black?" he raised a question that found dramatic answer in the organization of the C.I.O. For in the C.I.O. the Negro wage worker has begun to gain his rights. This recognition has in turn stimulated a resurgence of a movement for similar rights in the A.F. of L.

The report of the special committee of five to investigate discrimination in the unions had been suppressed, although four of the five committee men had signed it. When the convention upheld the right of affiliated unions to ban Negroes from membership, John Brophy of the United Mine Workers resigned from the committee. Brophy called the committee "merely a face saving device—rather than an honest attempt to find a solution of the Negro problem in the American labor movement."

When the C.I.O. began its drive for the unionization of steel, a conference was called in Pittsburgh, at the Elks Restaurant on the Hill. The Steel Workers Organizing Committee called the conference, to which came steel workers direct from the mills and lodges, along with outstanding leaders from other fields—

A. Philip Randolph, T. Arnold Mill of the National Urban League, Bishop J. W. Walls of Chicago, Dr. J. C. Austin of Baptist Church, Rev. T. J. King of Ebenezer Church, Pittsburgh, R. L. Vann, editor of the Pittsburgh *Courier*, Dr. Charles Wesley Burton, Vice President of the Chicago National Negro Congress, and Miss Thyra Edwards.

The conference established a program for unionization of Negro steel workers, and made such special demands of Negroes in the industry as equal pay for equal work, no discrimination in hiring and firing, and condemnation of all Jim Crow practices. To accomplish this the conference set up committees in every locality to help steel organizers. It planned mass meetings to hear reports of the conference. It campaigned through the pulpits, the radio and the press, urging all Negro steel workers to join the union. A chosen Sunday was devoted in all churches to support the steel drive, and special activities were promoted among women and youth.

The result has been that there are now five Negroes in trade unions to every one in 1935. This means that practically all workers in the building trades, the American Reduction workers or refuse collectors, and building service employees are members. It is a commonplace now for groups of Negro workers on the job, in restaurants, or club rooms, at bars or on the street to discuss their union policies and activities.

Besides trade unions, other agencies are active in adjusting Negroes and jobs. The Center Avenue (Negro) Branch of the Y.W.C.A maintains industrial secretaries to supervise and promote the welfare of Negro workers. The Pittsburgh chapter of the Urban League has brought into local practice a national policy of organizing a Worker's Council. This Council consists of 150 members, union and non-union, from various trades. Its object is to discuss labor problems and to increase participation in trade unions, such as the Electrical Workers, where the color barrier has not yet been broken. One of the chief purposes of the Council is to see that Negro workers receive proportionate employment with white workers in industry. On the new Housing Authority Projects in the Hill, for instance, the Council has succeeded in having a proviso made that all contracts should have a minimum of four and a half percent of the pay roll of the building trade mechanics employed go to Negro workers, and that 29 percent of the laborers' payroll should be similarly dispensed. To insure such apportioning the Council has established a contact committee to work with building contractors. The Council also stresses its industrial education program of meetings, speakers, and discussions.

The shifting of the roles of the Negro steel worker is shown recently by his participation in strikes to preserve jobs, maintain wages, shorten hours and to increase safety or otherwise better conditions of work. The 1937 strike at the Jones and Laughlin Mill is an excellent instance. Here the Negro workers in the union participated one hundred percent in the strike. Many of them spent twenty-four hours a day on picket lines. When the strike was declared, they swarmed into the Amalgamated Association to participate in the strike. The same situation occurred at Aliquippa. Even earlier than these strikes, in the one conducted in 1931 by the United Mine Workers, the Negroes gave full participation although they were aware of discrimination in mine jobs.

With the opening of trade unions to full Negro participation, the basis of Negro life in Pittsburgh as everywhere is becoming more stable. Political rights, civil rights and social rights are increasing. The Negro is finding assimilation easier into the family of nationalities that is Pittsburgh. His political activity is greater and clearer. Until recently Negro leaders have exerted their control through churches and fraternal organization. They are asking support from C.I.O. and A.F. of L. groups. To gain and keep this support they must stand for progressive measures; hence the rights of larger, less favored groups are more easily maintained.

Such a situation strengthens the economic basis of Negro life. It is possible for the Negro worker to earn more, to maintain steadier employment for his nationality proportionate to that maintained by other nationalities. It makes possible a higher standard of living for the largest group among the Negro population and contributes through increased spending power to more stable and remunerative business for the middle class business and professional groups.

HISTORIC RISE OF THE CIO

That record shows the President discouraging the big strikes which broke out after the enactment of Section 7a,[2] encouraging strikebreaking in effect in the great San Francisco general strike, aiding Hearst against the Guild in the Dean Jennings case, curbing organization in the auto industry through the Automobile Labor Board. Its is only after the rise of the CIO and the great protests of the farmers and the middle classes that he sought to ride the whirlwind by his campaign of 1936 and "we have only just begun to fight."

Even after that, the President faltered and floundered on several occasions. The National Labor Relations Act was passed without his active support, contrary to general belief. Many crucial social measures, such as the anti-lynching

2. Section 7a of the NIRA (National Industrial Recovery Act), passed in 1933, was a landmark piece of New Deal legislation that provided workers the legal right to join unions and bargain collectively.

bill, never got his approval. In the Little Steel strike, this attitude was summed up in the well-known Rooseveltian words: "A plague on both your houses!"[3]

With the mass migration of Negroes to the North in the years between 1916 and 1923, and the surge of Negro workers in the heavy industry of Pittsburgh, the Negro worker became a major factor in trade union growth and activities. The subsequent opening of union rolls to Negro membership has made profound changes in the class composition of the Negro people, and has made staunch allies of former competitors.

The attitude of the trade unions of 50 years ago has proven itself shortsighted and within the last few years has changed basically. But it has taken years for trade union leaders to see the disastrous results to the rights and privileges for protection which their own organizations [created] by excluding the Negro worker from the unions. This exclusion hasn't always been an openly stated policy, but has nevertheless been a definitely practiced one. Since the earliest organization was among the skilled workers, unskilled labor—both Negro and white—suffered through being led to shift for itself, unorganized and undirected. More than this, unskilled labor, both white and black, was used to break the strikes of the skilled workers.

The Negro industrial worker came upon the Pittsburgh scene in the ignominious role of strikebreaker. The story of his break with such forces, his development into loyal, stalwart, and resourceful unionist is the honorable story of struggle against great odds, of escape from a position forced upon him into one for which he struggled consistently against misdirection and opposition.

The general policy in industry has been to segregate the Negro from the white worker in the trade unions ever since Negro puddlers were imported from Richmond to break a strike in 1875. In the greatest of Pittsburgh industries—steel—workers had seen several more of their strikes broken and then they were admitted only in Jim-Crow lodges.

Shortly after this, Negro workers were taken into the Amalgamated at Richmond, Va., which was the principal source of supply of Negro strike breakers for the Pittsburgh district. It was not long then until organization began to develop among the Negro workers in the Pittsburgh plants. Still, wherever it was possible, separate Negro lodges were set up. In 1887, a separate local, the Garfield Lodge, was organized in Pittsburgh.

The Negro workers declared that the white unionist had acted merely to insure themselves against future strikebreaking and not out of interest in general welfare and security. This feeling was strong for years; in fact, it is not dead yet.

3. The "Little Steel Strike" of 1937 was so named because it was directed against Inland Steel, Bethlehem Steel, Republic Steel, and Youngstown Sheet & Tube, companies collectively known as "Little Steel" because they were not part of US Steel. The strike was quite violent.

With the growth of the steel industry in particular, and with the growth of heavy industry generally, there have been attempts to encourage Negro workers to join separate unions. These, however, are known to be ineffective unless strong in numbers. There has been some advocacy among Pittsburgh workers of Chandler Owen's idea of a United Trades Union for Negroes patterned after the United Hebrew Trades. So the history of the Negro unionist in Pittsburgh industry has been a long, sad story of color discrimination, even against competent skilled workers except at the times of strain, when organized and unorganized groups have been put in opposition to each other and when the existence of the unions has been threatened by strikes. At such times Negro labor has been solicited.

Since the Negro worker has become a component part of the basic industries of Pittsburgh, his place in the union ranks has been recognized as of extreme significance. The Negro worker himself has raised the question. Industrialists, as the possible role of Negro labor became clear, attempted to organize the Negro worker into social units which would carry out recreation programs, educate him to take pride in pleasing his boss, and stay away from union organizers. This policy met with fair success.

But the responsibility for lack of organization of Negro workers lay squarely with the white unions themselves. A union with a membership of nearly 5,000 had five Negro members. An official of an even larger union expressed astonishment that there were white people interested in the Negro question.

Employment in steel mills and plants throughout Pittsburgh is limited mainly to unskilled types of labor. This is true of most steel centers. In fact 95% of Negro workers in steel mills are unskilled. In most of the plants these Negro workers are without technical foundation. Again the inability of Negroes to secure apprenticeships because whites are unwilling to teach Negro apprentices hampers their progress and keeps the Negro in the unskilled labor class. In one plant there are five firemen employed but Negroes are not considered for any other type of work. Another plant hires Negroes as janitors only. They are never hired as a "matter of policy" at the Armstrong Cork Company. Many other employers refuse to consider Negro laborers also. There are instances when preference is given foreigners before considering even diligent, ambitious Negro workers. Discrimination is also practiced in one plant where Negroes are hired in the summer as workers at the furnaces and replaced by foreigners in the winter.

Hundreds of Negroes are employed in some of the larger steel mills in Pittsburgh. Usually they are considered as assets to the plants. In these plants, almost 100% of the group are common laborers.

CHAPTER 7

Church, School and Press

———— ·•◆•· ————

Typist: B. Shawcross / Rewriteman: J. Ernest Wright /
July 17, 1939 / Pre-final
Mrs. Paul Jones, Herron Jr. High School
Mr. James M. Albriton, Probation Officer

The devotion of the Negro people to the church is grace returned by a child to a beneficent mother. The church, from the days of Richard Allen's and Absalom Jones' Free African Society of 1787 to the Emancipation Proclamation of 1863, ministered to every need of the people. The early church led a people from bondage. In the early years of freedom, it fed them their portion of the milk and honey in the Canaan of the northern cities of the early 19th century. It shed and clothed them with skill and knowledge, teaching them to read and write so that they might dwell more easily in spirit with the inhabitants of their country.

To the slave on the plantation or in the rice field, religious gatherings were occasions for his common hopes and sorrows to find expression in communion with his fellows. To many this early formless church took the place of family life broken by slavery, of the schools and every social experience forbidden by the system under which they worked. In religious fervor he could for a time forget the grueling labor of the sun-scorched fields, the child and mother sold "down the river," the hunger, the squalor of the huts. And he indulged his dreams of freedom. He sang of his sorrows in EGYPT and his aspirations for CANAAN. Not only in prayer and song did he express his deepest feelings, but in an ecstatic rhythm of clapping hands, swaying bodies and stamping feet that became a religious dance like that of the daughters of Israel. Poetic sermons and exhortations, shouts and sorrow songs became conspiratorial means of communication, by code and symbol, of information of escape and revolt otherwise difficult of communication. God was the emancipator, Canaan the free land, Jordan the boundary between bondage and freedom.

Little wonder then that the church was and has remained so important to the Negro, a power over his development into a national American group. The first act of many a fugitive after his long, dangerous flight and his first step onto free ground was to throw himself on his knees, kiss the earth and, breaking into tears of happiness, shout hallelujahs to God his emancipator.

In freedom the Negro banded together to sing his gratitude and pray for protection from capture. Through these prayer meetings in homes, first steps were taken towards establishing a permanent church. And in such meetings the first attempt to fit himself into freedom was made by teaching reading and writing, by discussing common needs and ways to satisfy them. With the founding of specific congregations, the church continued to be the outlet for surplus energies unused in day-by-day living. It still performed the most vital social functions for a people restricted in expression in most spheres. No wonder the church has won such devotion from his people as it has. With freedom and growth of the community, the aspirations of the Negro grew. And the church largely made possible their satisfaction. Not only did it develop religious doctrine and give moral guidance, it also established all means of social communication and expression, choral music, literary societies, dramatic clubs, bands and orchestras. Through the doors of the church for many years the Negro found his chief entry into the world he wanted to inhabit.

The difficulties under which the early churches were founded and maintained were great. Small congregations that had grown out of cottage prayer meetings moved into any discarded building available. Many churches in Pittsburgh began in such quarters as store rooms, market houses, or vacant rooms over feed stores. As white church buildings were discarded Negro congregations moved in. White congregations lent vestries, basements, Sunday School rooms, and chapels. White pastors at times served Negro parishes until they were established, particularly in the case of Episcopal, Roman Catholic, and Presbyterian Churches.

The first Negro church in Pittsburgh was Bethel A.M.E., organized in 1822 by Bishop William Paul Quinn, the pioneer Bishop. This was but six years after the union of several churches in Philadelphia which brought the A.M.E. Church into being under the bishopric of Richard Allen, and only a quarter of a century after the organization of the first Negro church in America. Bethel was the first Negro church west of the Allegheny Mountains and was for years one of the greatest Negro churches in America. Bethel was the mother congregation of other congregations and missions. Five of these are still flourishing—Brown Chapel, St. James A.M.E., Chartiers Street, Trinity and St. Paul's on the South Side. Since its organization, outstanding ministers of the Negro church in America besides Bishop Quinn have been in charge. Three have been raised to the bishopric—two in America and one in the British M.E. Church. So significant was the conduct of Bethel in the growth of the A.M.E. Church west of the mountains that constant contact with elder churches in the east was kept up.

Bethel also helped organize education among Pittsburgh Negroes. The first Negro school teacher, Lewis Woodson, taught in this church in 1833. Later John M. Templeton taught here, assisted by Prof. Wesley D. Gasaway, the father of Rev. J. Gasaway who pastored the church in 1897.

Bethel apparently sufficed for the religious needs of the Pittsburgh Negro for the next fifteen years. Then in 1836 a group of men and women met in prayer meetings at the home of Edward Parker, on Arthur Street. A little later preaching services were held in the home of Obediah and Charlotte Maloney on Roberts Street, a block away. And in the Maloney home that year, John Wesley African Methodist Episcopal Zion Mission was founded. The congregation soon dedicated a one-story building on old Linton Street and this building became affectionately known as "Little Jim." In 1850, the present building was constructed at 40 Arthur Street. This same year, 1836, across the river in the town of Allegheny another group of Negro people were holding prayer meetings in two other homes, those of Edward Parker and George [. . . .][1] Then three years later, in 1839, Rev. David Stevens began holding meetings on Second Street, Allegheny, from which developed a second A.M.E. Zion congregation. Rev. Charles Avery, who followed the frugal and persevering development of the little congregation, frequently preached for them. In 1846 he erected the building, Avery Mission, in which the present congregation still worships. Rev. David Stevens lifted the first shovel of ground for the foundation. Rev. Charles Avery, who had made a fortune in the iron and copper industry, turned to religion, entered the Methodist ministry and became a philanthropist.

Other difficulties beset the early church. Pastors could not give full time to their parishes. To make even a modest living they were compelled to follow a trade. "Father" John Peck conducted a barbershop and hairdressing saloon; Rev. Lewis Woodson shaved and pomaded the Thaws and the Nevilles to supplement what Bethel Congregation could pay him. Theological training was expensive for the average aspiring Negro minister, and few seminaries were open to him. Many congregations, therefore, suffered from well-intentioned but untaught preachers who substituted religious emotionalism for sound doctrine. The earliest Pittsburgh churches, however, were happily free from such disadvantages. Rev. Lewis Woodson was a man of culture whose letters to men like Theodore Weld on abo-

1. Name is missing in original.

litionist activities have strength and grace. Rev. John Peck and Rev. Abraham D. Lewis were also cultured men. At a general conference of the African Methodist Episcopal Church in 1844, Bishop Daniel A. Payne introduced a resolution to draft a course of study for prospective preachers. It was overwhelmingly voted down. Next day Rev. Abraham D. Lewis, referred to as "an aged father of Israel," rose in the conference and demanded its passage to extend "light and learning." The resolution then was generally accepted. More than once early ministers studying at a seminary lived for days on bread and molasses, and walked miles between towns to establish and service missions. In the early days of Bethel, "Father" Collins, an elder, walked twice to Philadelphia and back to report and get aid for his church. Ministers and congregations built their churches with their own hands, made pews and installed them, made their pulpits and choir lofts. The women embroidered altar cloths and made vestments.

A second African Methodist Church in Allegheny, now known familiarly as Brown Chapel, typifies the early history of the Negro church. Brown Chapel grew out of house-to-house prayer meetings. In 1837 regular meetings were held in a building which had been a blacksmith shop. Ten years later the congregation moved to a building on the "Commons" which was burned in 1856, took refuge in a stable on the site of the present post-office, and after several more removals anchored at their present home as late as 1902. The growth of Brown Chapel, too, resulted from Negro and white efforts. Here, too, went some of Rev. Charles Avery's beneficence, and that of R. H. Monosine.

African Methodism was, during these years, in its infancy. Congregations were small and poor. Visiting preachers traveled on foot, taking shelter in sheds and stables. On visits to Brown Chapel they lodged at the home of Brother Buroe, the second steward who was allowed free rental of one of three houses owned by the church. They were fed at a restaurant run by Brother Moses Howard. At the three services held morning, afternoon and evening of each Sabbath, the women wore Quaker bonnets and large white handkerchiefs tied round the neck and fastened at the wrist. The word of the Lord was preached with great fervor, shouts, and hallelujahs ringing throughout the congregation.

Harris' Pittsburgh Directory for 1837 gives a separate section to "African Churches" of which it said there were three churches for colored folk—a brick structure in Arthursville, a brick structure in Miltenberger's Alley between 8th Street and Strawberry Alley, and a frame structure on Front Street near Smithfield, all under the A.M.E. order. A Sunday School in Miltenberger's Alley, the *Directory* says, "contains nine regular females and six male teachers. Has seventy-three girls, forty-seven boys—under the direction of James Shaw." Another school was taught in the church in Arthursville. A "List of Regular Ordained Elders and Preachers in Pittsburgh" gave the names of Rev. Thomas Lawrence, Station Elder; Rev. George W. Boler, Local Elder; Rev. Samuel Collins, Rev. Samuel Johnson, Rev. Abraham D. Lewis as Local Deacons; and Rev. George Coleman, Rev. Jas. Coleman and Rev. Charles Peters as Local Preachers. Thomas Norris was Steward.

Four years later the Church on Front Street (now First Avenue) was named as the African M.E. Church credited with forty-five members and a flourishing Sabbath School of about one hundred scholars. Rev. Thos. Lawrence was pastor, his dwelling house in Arthursville.

Rev. Lawrence also pastored the Second African M.E. Church in Arthursville, a congregation of eighty members. The Wesleyan Methodist Church, with thirty-two members also in Arthursville, conducted a Sabbath School composed of children of both Arthursville Churches. Rev. Leonard Collins was pastor, his dwelling house in Allegheny. Rev. Collins was also pastor of the Wesleyan Methodist Church situated in Garrett's field in Allegheny with a congregation of one hundred and eleven members, and a small Sabbath school. This year seven Negro ministers were listed with their addresses.

Methodism took hold upon the Negro population for several reasons. The growth of the African Methodist Church in the first half of the nineteenth century was but one phase of the growth of Methodism in the United States. Many of the early settlers were Methodists for the same reason that the Negro was drawn into Methodism—they were evangelized through great revivals. There was therefore a Methodist base for proselytizing the Negro. Also, the Methodist Church was highly evangelistic, with zealous ministers. Methodism as a form of church government was a tightly drawn system and it appealed to the Negro; in part this was a copyist attitude of the Negro toward the white congregations.

By the time the Pittsburgh Negro population became considerable, about 1856, northern churches began to close their pews to Negroes. The result was a rapid growth of Negro congregations.

Presbyterians and Episcopalians, being less evangelical and more conservative, grew less rapidly. Besides, they comprised the wealthier and the more fashionable congregations.

After the Civil War there came a change. The Baptist congregations increased rapidly. For one thing the Baptists had established themselves in the South as the Methodists had in the North, and Negroes began to move from the South into Pittsburgh even during the war. The Baptist Church furthermore, was more easily established. No leader or higher potentate was necessary. Any group might get together because they were at odds with a previous organization or set of ideas, or because they wanted to exercise certain freedoms not permitted in the Methodist and other churches. All that was needed was a just cause, and they wrote their constitution for a new congregation. New migrants could thus easily form a Baptist congregation without waiting for permission and episcopal formalities. Another reason for the spread of Baptistry was that bishops had limited power, unlike Methodist bishops.

A Pittsburgh newspaper announced March, 1848: "The Soiree of the Colored Baptist Church came off at Temperance Hall on Tuesday, Wednesday and Thursday evenings this week." So far as can be determined, this is the earliest mention of Negro Baptistry in Pittsburgh, an institution which in the next half-century became the dominant religious group in the city. Which church gave the soiree, whether it later developed into one of the now known churches is not known, but the soiree shows that Baptistry began among Pittsburgh Negroes in the pre-Civil War period. Ten years later the *Gazette* records: a "hopeful revival of religion in progress at the Baptist Church under the care of Rev. Gerkes who is justly held in high esteem among his people."

With the founding of the Metropolitan Baptist Congregation in Allegheny in 1868, Baptistry began its quick stride forward. Macedonia has been called not only the first Negro Baptist Church in Allegheny County, but the first west of the Allegheny Mountains. One account attributes its founding to the dismissal of sixteen Negroes from the white Sandusky Street Baptist Church. Another legend attributes the founding to the use of china communion cups by white congregation and tin cups for Negro communicants.

The Hill District is served by the largest Baptist church in the city—Ebenezer, founded 1875. Ebenezer was organized in the white Fourth Avenue Baptist Church where they met for some months and then began the typical peregrinations to a small hall off the Hill to the old Fifth Avenue Market House, to the old Silver Palace, and finally to the site of the Fifth Avenue bank, where in 1862 they bought four lots and erected the first church building owned by Negroes in western Pennsylvania. In recognition of their achievement, the Congregation took the name Ebenezer—"Hitherto Hath the Lord Helped Us." Because of a disagreement over open communion, the pastor and three hundred members broke away from Ebenezer in 1891. Ebenezer was the first Negro Baptist Church in America to subsidize fully a Negro missionary in a foreign field.

Other Baptist congregations have grown around Macedonia and Ebenezer. In the Hill District there is Central Baptist and Macedonia, and in the East End there are Carron Street, Mount Ararat, and Rodman Street Baptist congregations; and in Lawrenceville, Shiloh and Good Hope.

The predominant white church in western Pennsylvania, from its frontier history, had been the Presbyterian. The Negro did not become part of this denomination until immediately following the Civil War. On January 9, 1868 the *Commercial* said:

For several months the colored people of this city who believe in Presbyterian Doctrine—and the number is large—have been holding stated meetings in the Sixth Presbyterian Church (Rev. Prof. Wilson, past.) on Franklin
Street. The services have been conducted from Sabbath to Sabbath by Ministers of different Presbyterian Churches, and students from Theological
Seminaries, and the attendance has grown to what should be the nucleus for
a prosperous church. The Ohio Presbytery at its last session appointed a
committee to consider the claims of these colored people to an organization.

The committee must have done good work for the *Commercial* announced,
in less than a week:

The first colored Presbyterian Church of Pittsburgh was formally organized yesterday, Jan. 12, Sunday—the exercises being held in the Lecture
Room of the Sixth Presbyterian Church. A few weeks ago, some thirty colored worshipers signed a petition to the Ohio Presbytery for the organization
of their own church. This was referred to the special committee which
passed on the idea. Messrs. Hezekiah Anderson, and Elias Edmunds were
elected elders and ordained by Drs. McKinney and Wilson.

The Congregation became Grace Memorial Church, on the Hill. Bidwell
Presbyterian is on the North Side, and Bethesda in the East End of the city—the
only three black Presbyterian Churches in the city.

St. Benedict's is the only Roman Catholic Church in Pittsburgh for Negroes.
In 1890 a group of twenty-five or thirty people held their first services and organized St. Benedict's Mission in the home of Dr. Olschul, which he had given for
the mission. The first priest to officiate was Father McDermott, the actual pastor
Father John Griffin. In the church on Overhill Street, built by the parish, school
was conducted for a time by Mother Catherine Drexel of Philadelphia, for about
twenty-five pupils. But since the number of Catholic Negroes in Pittsburgh has
never been large, the life of St. Benedict's has been a struggle. The school closed
in 1912 because of lack of funds. The church itself closed for a time in 1914, when
there was little money and no regular priest and the only activity was Sunday
Mass for a period of three months.

One Episcopal church exists among Negro Pittsburghers. St. Cyprians followed the course of earlier churches. Under white and Negro priests and the
Laymens League, it shifted from spot to spot, from vacant halls over feed stores to
chapels of white churches, to a Sunday School room in Allegheny, and for a year
gave up services altogether. The church changed its name to St. Phillips and finally in 1923, merged with St. Augustines of the North Side to form Holy Cross.

The new church took over St. Pauls, the church building of a white congregation, where a congregation of about six hundred now carries out its parish activities.

As the Negro community expanded, the usual denominations proved insufficient for the developing religious needs and ideologies. New denominations made their appearance, a sign that the Negro was going along with the religious currents of the time, and that as much as ever the Negro turned to the church for satisfaction of social needs. The Hill district is typical. Until 1920 no period of ten years had seen the founding of more than two new congregations. But between 1920 and 1930 fourteen new churches sprang up on the Hill. At the end of that time there were forty-five churches in the Hill's two wards. Of these, seventeen were Baptist, and six were of the Methodist persuasion. A survey made in 1930 lists Seventh Day Adventists, the Christian Missionary Alliance (a mixed Negro and white group), the Bible Institute (also a mixed group), Spiritualist, Holiness, Church of God and six "others."

It is these "others" which come and go, which wander from one temporary anchorage to another, which appeal to small groups of uneducated, underprivileged people for whom a larger world offers no accommodating niche. They are included in the eighteen listed "storefronts"—those pathetically furnished, crudely painted, quaintly captioned homes of fervid religionists "seeking God in a grain of sand." The Church of the True Vine Fire in God Baptist, for instance, denies the idea of Hell, and preaches heavenly joy on earth. The latter is to be achieved, in spite of leaking housetops, empty cupboards and purses, by bright apparel and jubilant music. Weekly, in summer months, the men and women of this faith don their bright-colored garb—women in white dresses, red or blue sashes, poke bonnets and broad white hats trimmed with chenille ball braid; men in uniforms pieced together from gold braided trousers, epaulettes that never match, plumed hats, and flashing swords—rear or stage properties. A woman beats a bass drum; a girl shakes a tambourine. One man blows a trumpet; another plays a triangle. Cow bells, dinner bells, rattles or guitars make music unto the Lord.

Tabernacle No. 2, of Pittsburgh, was the second tabernacle of the Church of God and the Saints of Christ to be established in Pennsylvania. In 1897 it was organized by Prophet Wm. S. Crowdy. This church observes Saturday as the Sabbath and gives tithes in the form of one tenth part of its labor, which it offers on the first day of the week. Baptism is by immersion only, and washing of feet is observed regularly. Singing is an important feature of worship, but no musical instruments are used. The Jewish calendar is accepted by which April is the first month, and by which the Passover is celebrated.

The role of the church in Negro life has been summed up by two leaders of these people. Martin R. Delany, that early champion of the welfare of the Negro, in writing *The Condition, Elevation, Education and Destiny of the Colored People of the United States, Politically Considered*, said:

> The colored races are highly susceptible of religions; it is a constituent principle of their nature, and an excellent trait in their character. But unfortunately for them, they carry it too far. Their hope is largely developed, and consequently, they usually stand still—hope in God, and really expect Him to do that for them, which it is necessary they should do themselves.

Delany wrote of the church in its most militant age, when it championed its people's rights to freedom, to full human dignity and full participation in a civilized world. But the phenomenal expansion of the church after freedom was proclaimed—when the Negro, recognized as no longer a chattel but a human personality with spiritual and human aspirations—was too rapid for the available pastoral supply. Yet thousands of Negroes continued to follow the leadership of half-educated ministers and were appeased for "the lack of many a thing they sought" by church revivals, wholesale baptisms in the Allegheny river, and all the sublimating poetry and mysticism of church services. Although the church progressed mightily in numbers and acquisition of properties, its social and spiritual progress did not keep pace, so that James Weldon Johnson's words in *Negro Americans—What Now* were possible: "The Negro Church is the most powerful and potentially the most effective medium we possess. The whole church needs another Reformation, a sloughing off of outworn creeds and dogmas and an application of its power to the working out of the present day problems of civilization and of social and spiritual life."

Within recent years the Negro church in Pittsburgh is, with the national church, taking new paths. Waking to the truth of Martin Delany's and James Weldon Johnson's ideas combined, it is giving its members realistic, worldly guidance through the troubled maze of present-day life. The bread of life which it offers its communicants is not only the mystical wafer.

In youth movements such as Boy Scout and Girl Scout troops, in dramatic and choral societies, and in symphonic orchestras and literary clubs, it seeks to maintain cultural stimulus. In Interdenominational Youth Conferences, it seeks broader contacts and points of view. In promotion of National Negro History Week and Commemoration of Lincoln-Douglas Day, it refreshes the minds of its members with the historic traditions of a people. It is still a center for lectures and mass meetings where the trained leaders of a people bring discussion of social, economic, and political issues. And bringing abstractions close to the homes of its adherents, it opens community centers for education, recreation, and health clinics.

EDUCATION

Negro education, like politics and religion, moved along a tortuous, stony path in its beginnings. Snatching at frugal bits of learning gleaned from scraps of printed paper picked up on the street or studied on boxes and crates along wharves and in storerooms, words dug laboriously from first primers and spelling books or hymnals, the Negro started slowly to piece together bits of knowledge which started him on his way to freedom of the mind.

Slavery in and near Pittsburgh had never precluded education of the Negro. On the contrary, in 1796 Pennsylvania law required sufficient education of slaves to enable them to fulfill citizenship qualifications. Older slaves, however, who had grown to maturity before this law became effective, had grown up illiterate. But the drawback came when in the first twenty years of the 1800's the plantation shadow began to spread across the North.

Fugitive slaves had been forbidden by law to learn. Hundreds of those southern men and women found refuge in Pittsburgh. Most of them, old or young, were illiterate. But they were eager to read and write, so eager that more than one learned by carrying about scraps of paper, or by memorizing the appearance of the words of hymns which they knew by heart.

The first schools, like many other institutions, grew around the church. But in 1817 no Negro church had been organized in Pittsburgh. Rev. Herron, however, the white Presbyterian minister, and two of his parishioners, James Wilson and Nathaniel Smith, realizing that existing prejudice excluded those eager Negro people from the white schools then established, opened a school for Negroes in a carpenter shop at the corner of Smithfield Street and Diamond Alley. True to the philanthropic and pious spirit of the time, religious education was thought most important; and because readers and primers, geographies and histories were too expensive, the Bible was the one text used. But here above the carpenter shop 100 pupils, of both sexes and all ages, learned reading, writing and religious lore.

Like the first churches, the schools had difficult times. The Negro community could not afford buildings and had not yet produced teachers. This first school shifted from place to place. Mr. M. B. Lowrie, later an active abolitionist, took the pupils into his own school on Hay Scale Alley. Later it was held in the discarded Presbyterian Church. A report issued in 1822 pictures this first attempt to reach toward culture and learning. It says in part:

> When the directors call to mind the condition of the colored people of this city a few years ago, and their then situation with the present, they have cause of thankfulness for the success which has attended their instruction in

the Sabbath School. Then very few were able to read, now nearly every person of color from three years and upward can read or is in a state of progression toward that desirable attainment. Men and women, some forty, fifty, sixty, and seventy years of age, some on crutches and some wearing spectacles, who at the commencement could not distinguish one letter from another, in eight, ten or twelve months, have learned to read quite intelligently in the Bible.

Ten years later Pittsburgh had a population of over 12,000 people. About 700 of these were Negroes. Free public schools had been made compulsory in Pennsylvania in 1834. Negro children, however, were excluded from these schools. But in Pittsburgh there were now a number of cultured Negro families, men and women esteemed for their activities in the progressive movements of the day, families related or associated with the leading families in other cities who were active in the advancement not only of the Negro people but in the general reforms of the period—colonization, abolition, temperance, women's rights, general conditions of working men and women, health and diet, religious reform, and abolition of crime and delinquency. These people naturally wanted educational opportunities for their children. In the Pittsburgh *Gazette* for February 10, 1888 appeared the following notice:

> At a meeting of the colored people of the City and vicinity of Pittsburgh convened at the African Church, on the evening of the 16th of January, 1832. J. B. Vashon was appointed Chairman, and Lewis Woodson Secretary.
>
> The object of the meeting being stated by the Chairman, after some further deliberation, the following preamble and Constitution was adopted.
>
> PREAMBLE
>
> Whereas ignorance in all ages has been found to debase the human mind, and to subject its votaries to the lowest voices and most object depravity; and it must be admitted that ignorance is the sole cause of the present degradation and bondage of the people of color, in these United States; that the intellectual capacity of the black man is equally susceptible of improvement. All ancient history makes this Manifest and even modern examples puts beyond a single doubt.
>
> We, therefore; the people of color of the city and vicinity of Pittsburgh and State of Pennsylvania, for the purpose of dispersing the moral gloom, that has long hung around us have under Almighty God, associated ourselves together, which association shall be known by the name of the Pittsburgh African Education Society. . . .
>
> The meeting elected as officers: John B. Vashon, President, Job B.

Thompson, Vice-President; Lewis Woodson, Secretary; and Abraham D. Lewis, Treasurer. Richard Bryans, Wm. J. Greely, Samuel Bruce, Moses Howard, and Samuel Clingman were named the Board of Managers.

All papers in the city, friendly to education are most respectfully requested to give the foregoing an insertion.

The Constitution of the society empowered it to purchase books and raise money to buy ground and build schools for the Negro youth. It also permitted them to build a hall for the use of the society.

Attempts to provide education for the Negro bore little fruit until 1837. At that time another notice appeared in the *Gazette*:

PUBLIC SCHOOL MEETING OF COLORED CITIZENS OF PITTSBURGH

According to previous notice, a meeting of Colored Citizens of Pittsburgh was held in the African Methodist Church on Monday evening, 6th Inst. The meeting was organized by appointing Rev. Thomas Lawrence, President, and Thomas Morris, Secretary. After the object of the meeting was stated by the chairman, the following preamble, resolutions were adopted, and ordered to be published.

WHEREAS it is with deep felt satisfaction, we have heard that the joint meetings of school Directors in the city, have determined to organize a public school for the instruction of our youth which school both they and we desire, should go into operation as soon as possible; and have requested us to furnish the Board of Directors in each ward, with number, age, residence, name of parents, friend or guardian of the Colored children, residing in each ward respectively.

THEREFORE RESOLVED, that J. B. Vashon, and A. D. Lewis, for the West Ward; Richard Bryan, and Samuel Bruce for the North Ward; Thomas Norris, and Charles Peters, for the East Ward; Samuel Johnson and George Gardiner for the South Ward, to ascertain the number, etc., of children in their respective Wards, and make returns of their enumerations on Wednesday evening next. On motion, Resolved that the thanks of this meeting be tendered to the joint meeting of School Director, in this city, for their attention to this subject which is of such vital importance to our rising youth. Meeting adjourned to meet the following Wednesday 24 evening.

Thomas Lawrence, President
Thomas Norris, Secretary

At this time the delegates to the State Constitutional Convention by means of an amendment turned thumbs down on the Negro right to vote. In the discussion the question of Negro education came up. Many saw no use in educating the Negro if he was not to become a citizen. In spite of this feeling the resolutions of the past few years had results for in 1838 Negro children attended their own public school for the first time.

Beginning in a small church in Miltenberger's Alley, with one teacher who acted as principal, the pioneer school in Pittsburgh lived a hand-to-mouth existence, moving from place to place as circumstance required, located usually in churches, once in a church basement, and once even in an engine house. The city had passed a law requiring a school, but had not provided for a location.

The first teacher and principal was John N. Templeton, a graduate of Athens College in Ohio, and a leader in Negro education for twenty years.

When the school outgrew its small room on Miltenberger's Alley and moved to a church on Wylie, Mrs. Mary J. Burles was hired to assist Mr. Templeton and she replaced him after his death in 1851.

During the years from 1852 when Abel Dobson, a white teacher, became principal, until the Central Board of Education of Pittsburgh was organized in February 1855, the school declined in number and provisions. During part of this time Dr. Martin R. Delany, author, lecturer, and nationally known as a promoter of Negro progress taught the school, with Miss E. L. Peck as assistant. At a meeting of the board in March 1855, Mrs. Calvin Sackett who had succeeded Dr. Delany offered to teach for five hundred dollars per year and so, after a brief shutdown, the school opened again in the Wesleyan Church.

In January 1856, there came to the school a woman destined to become a national figure in Negro education and a woman who from her arrival in Pittsburgh became one of the foremost leaders of her people, Miss Susan Paul Smith. The year after Miss Smith took up her duties, George B. Vashon succeeded Mr. Sackett as principal, and Miss Smith and Mr. Vashon were married. Miss Mary Strange and Miss Emily Burr also taught after the resignation of Susan Vashon. Mr. Vashon gave up his post in 1864.

Isolated, completely segregated, deplorably furnished, its pupils and three teachers cramped into two small rooms, the school had struggled to give service to those children of Negro parents who could afford neither private tutoring or instruction in private schools. The situation demanded action after thirty years of inattention, so at a public meeting of the "colored citizens of Pittsburgh," a committee of Mr. Knox, Mr. Little, and Rev. Underwood was appointed and in March, 1867 met the Central Board of Education to protest and ask that conditions favorable to decent education be established. Lots were purchased on Miller Street between Center and Reed and a two-story building was built of brick and roofed with shingles. The school was equipped with the most improved type of school desks and a hall furnished with settees. A playground 100 feet square was maintained. Dr. Jacob B. Taylor was appointed principal, July 1867, to be succeeded the next year by Daniel W. Atwood. Mr. Atwood was assisted by a competent staff of teachers. In February 1869, the curriculum was extended to include singing, gymnastics and drawing.

Across the river in Allegheny City, another public school had begun about the same time as the Miltenberger's Alley venture. The Negro Public School of Allegheny City also led a normal life, classes meeting in a church basement, a carpenter shop, the Temperance Ark, and the Universalist Chapel on Montgomery Avenue. Matilda M. Ware, teacher at the time, stayed with the school for twenty-nine years. It moved into a location on Webster Street the same year as its brother school. Two hundred and fifty seven students attended classes in 1867. They were taught by a staff of three teachers: S. A. Neale, principal; Mrs. Jane Miller; and Mrs. Amanda J. Cooke.

While struggling for his rights to schooling in the primary and secondary fields, the Pittsburgh Negro was already turning his facilities for learning in the higher levels. One of the landmarks in Negro education and cultural development was the foundation in 1849 of the Avery Mission Industrial College. Rev. Charles Avery, partner in the Eagle Cotton Mill, and pioneer with the Howe's and the Hussey's in development of the copper regions of Lake Superior, a man of wealth and a philanthropic Methodist minister, gave stocks and property for the incorporation of the College. For a time George B. Vashon was president of Avery College. The Honorable Henry Highland Garnett, one-time minister to Liberia, was one of its principals. The Hon. T. Morris Chester, and the Hon. Moses B. Hopkins were graduated from this school. Martin H. Freeman, who earned his A.B. Degree at Rutland College, Vermont, taught as a professor at Avery for a number of years. He later went to Liberia to teach, and was succeeded at Avery by George B. Vashon.

Mr. Avery left a fund to maintain twelve scholarships at the later University of Pittsburgh for young Negro men residing either in the United States or the British provinces of Canada. The scholarships, still in existence, provide four years of study.

In 1854 the State Legislature reorganized the system of public school education. The Act passed provided separate schools for Negroes and mulattoes, to be established in districts where twenty or more children resided. Then in February, 1869 an Act of Assembly said "the Central Board shall continue and maintain one high school for the education of pupils of both sexes, and one or more distinct and separate schools for the exclusive education of the children of color."

On April 9, 1872, an Act of Assembly was passed repealing part of section 54 of the Act of 1869 consolidating the wards of the city of Pittsburgh for education. That part of the act was repealed which authorized or required sub-district school boards to exclude from the schools of their respective sub-districts "persons of color."

Since 1874, when separate schools for Negroes were abolished, Negro children have attended the public schools of the city. An Act of Assembly June 8, 1881, further provided that: "hereafter it shall be unlawful for any school director, superintendent or teacher to make any distinction whatever, on account of, or by reason of the race or color of any pupil, or scholar, who may be in attendance upon, or seeking admission to, any public or common school maintained wholly or in part under the school laws of this Commonwealth."

Accounts of progress in the seventies and eighties are meager, perhaps because of the merging of Negro with the white in common schools. High school graduates were rare. The years near the turn of the nineteenth century saw Negro education branching off into other fields. Miss E. F. Crawford's school for shorthand and typing in 1897 saw students trying their hand at commercial work in the rooms of the Young Women's Friendly Institute on Sheridan Avenue, East End, which had been founded by Mrs. Francis R. Bolling. Next year the *Pittsburgh Press* mentioned the graduation of three Negro girls from the cooking school maintained by the Central Board of Education at the Grant School—Grace Barney, Estella Wells, and Marie Kilcott. This same year, the Mission of St. Benedict the Moor maintained a parochial school on Overhill Street with two Negro teachers—Miss Eloise Walker of Butler, and Miss Sadie A. Hamilton, a Pittsburgher.

In the 1890's Thomas Ewell conducted Ewell's Evening School, a preparatory school of English studies at 6229 Penn Avenue, East Liberty.

As early as 1880 in the minutes of the Board of Trustees of the University of Pittsburgh for October 12, there appeared an item: "Last year a precedent was made by the courtesy of some members of the Board and a number of colored pupils were admitted to the Preparatory Department free of charge." In the "Afro-American Column" in the *Pittsburgh Press*, June 13, 1897, mention is made of John Cloverdale Gilmer graduating from Western University of Pennsylvania and the "distinction of being the first colored man ever to receive such an honor in this Institution. The degree of Bachelor of Arts will be conferred."

In 1908 and 1909 a total of nineteen Negro scholarship students enrolled at the University of Pittsburgh through the benefits of the Avery Fund. In 1924, eighty-seven Negro students were reported at the University and in 1931, one hundred in all local universities. The low rate of increase is attributable to the depression of 1929.

In recent years Negro students have enjoyed full educational advantages in primary and secondary schools of Pittsburgh. The lower percentage of graduates compared with the percentage of white graduates is due largely to the lower eco-

nomic grouping of the majority of Negro students. Of the grade school enrollment in Pittsburgh, 12 per cent were Negro students; of the High School enrollment, 6.5 per cent; of the trade school enrollment 5 per cent. During the five
years between 1930 and 1935, 1,494 Negro students graduated from Allegheny
County High Schools, fourteen schools of which reported no graduates during
this period. Of the total number of graduates just given for the five-year period,
Westinghouse High School graduated 320, Schenley High School 267, and
Peabody 113. In 1935 the graduating class in nine High Schools totaled 123—
Westinghouse 54, Schenley 31, Fifth Avenue 14, Allegheny 6, Peabody 5, Oliver 4,
South Hills 6, Langley 1. The total with the February graduating class reached
235 for the year.

Eleven city schools report more than twenty-five per cent of their pupils are
Negroes; nine more than one third; two with more than one half, and one with
nearly nine-tenths. In spite of the fact that about forty-four percent of the pupils
in those schools are Negro, there was not until 1937 a Negro teacher in any of
them. After this time Negro teachers became members of the Pittsburgh staffs,
but the ratio of Negro teachers to Negro students is still low. To bring about a
balance between Negro and white teachers Pittsburgh schools should hire between two hundred and fifty and three hundred Negro teachers.

Such an increase would be a decided advantage to the Negro student for he
still lacks the advantage of Negro teachers acquainted accurately with the history
of the Negro. The Negro students likewise lack the benefit of courses in Negro
history. Moreover he reads in texts by white authors a distorted and incomplete
record of the history of his people.

In the professional schools, especially at the University of Pittsburgh, the
Negro student is at a disadvantage. The school of medicine refused Negro students. The school of education admits Negro students but the Board of Education bars them from practice teaching although they are permitted to observe
classroom methods.

The textbook has replaced the hymnal and the scrap of paper as the Negro
student's guide. The student has weaned himself away from education in his
church alone, and has become part of the municipal school community.

THE PRESS

Dodging threats of tar and feathers and the danger of presses wrecked by an-
gered whites, men in Pittsburgh and Philadelphia started their first Negro newspapers in the abolition and antislavery years of the early nineteenth century.

The first papers published in the interest of the Negro were edited and
printed by white men. Wm. H. Burleigh began editing *The Christian Witness*

which had been purchased by the Antislavery Society. This was the first antislavery paper in the city. Burleigh had taught in Prudence Crandall's School for
Negro Children, and with his brother had founded *The Unionist* to support the
school. He, like most editors of antislavery papers, was also interested in temperance, peace movements, woman's suffrage, and labor problems of these years.
Burleigh later edited *The Temperance Banner* in Pittsburgh. The ventures lasted
six years.

The editor of these papers, who disliked controversy and wished to devote
his life to quiet editorial work and purely literary writing, was drawn into the progressive reform movements of his day when he realized their urgent nature. This
man who loved peace and quiet wrote with fire against the evils of his time. He
denounced the war with Mexico as the design of the slaveholding powers, and for
this and other opinions he narrowly escaped mob violence.

Burleigh was a staunch champion of freedom of speech and of the press. It
was in the interest of these principles that he began the publication of the *Witness*. Since the appeal of the press was limited in those days, lectures reached
greater masses of people, and were very popular. Burleigh was a very active lecturer.

Among Pittsburgh editors Jane Grey Swisshelm was perhaps the most fiery
and fearless advocate of all reforms which centered around antislavery. Mrs.
Swisshelm had lived in Louisville for several years. There she had devoted most
of her time to teaching Negro children. This activity aroused such opposition
that citizens threatened to burn down her house and tar and feather her if she did
not cease. She returned to Pittsburgh and began publishing and editing the *Saturday Evening Visitor* in 1847, founded by a legacy which she had received from
her mother. On the masthead of her paper Mrs. Swisshelm printed from the
Bible, "Shall I not visit for these things, Saith the Lord."

Mrs. Swisshelm particularly scored the practice of slave catching in the city.
She attacked the decision of a federal court judge in a fugitive slave case. She was
threatened with a libel suit, but persisted in her attack until she made the judge
appear ridiculous, and won the support of the Pittsburgh public. Mrs. Swisshelm
said among the many things printing on this subject in the *Visitor*:

> Anyone who for a twenty dollar fee would aid in tearing a man from his
> family and consign him to the condition of brute beast ought to be held with-
> out the range of human sympathy. We would not let such a bigot sleep in our
> barn or take a drink at our pump.

The Spirit of Liberty ran a brief career in the 1840's in the interest of the Liberty Party and the election of James G. Birney as an antislavery and women's
rights candidate. Under her name Swisshelm published some scorching verses in

which she named and condemned those Methodist ministers in the neighborhood who at a conference of the church in 1840 had been responsible for passing the "Black Gag" rule. This rule forbade Negro Church members from testifying in church against white members in those states where they were also forbidden by law to do so in the courts.

In July 1849 Mrs. Swisshelm wrote in the *Visitor*:

> *The Christian Herald of the African M.E. Church*, is the title of a new paper started in our city, of which we have the first number, A. R. Green, Editor, One dollar per annum. If we could really wish our colored brother success; but we have sectarian papers. They of necessity teach brethren to devour each other. This paper is an evidence of the intellectual equality of the races.

Charles P. Shiras edited *The Albatross*, another abolition paper. Of this paper and its importance *The Bangor Gazette* in 1848 said:

> We confess that when friend Shiras was forced to haul down that beautiful and swift bird *The Albatross* there was no more heart for us in Pittsburgh. We almost gave it over to the coal trade. . . . If ever a man's paper deserved to succeed it was the *Albatross*.

The editor of the *Gazette* said that perhaps the town was afraid to manifest too much sympathy for the Negro lest it attract southern attention.

At this time Martin R. Delany was bringing to a close the publication of *The Mystery*, which he had begun four years before. In spite of attempts by the city's Negroes and efforts by Pittsburgh papers to put it back on its feet, the paper, which did well crusading for Negro rights, had to close its columns.

Most of the news in *The Mystery* was quoted by papers all over the country. Delany's description of the great Pittsburgh fire in 1845 was given space on many front pages.

Delany had run a rocky road as had his colleagues. Through the press he had charged a colored man with selling out some of his race by assisting slave-catchers. Sued for libel, Delany had been convicted and fined, but prominent Pittsburgh attorneys and judges had appealed the case and caused Governor Ritner to remit the fine. Slave hunters had sued him again on the same grounds but this time Delany had been acquitted. In spite of his popularity with citizens of Pittsburgh, Delany's paper came to the brink of bankruptcy and finally faded into oblivion with other Negro journals.

For many years after these early papers the Negro population of Pittsburgh had only the regular newspapers of the day to make public their activities and attitudes. And sadly enough, these years were years when the prevailing stereotyped conception of the Negro was maturing. Jim Crow, Sambo, and Rastus types, or the doings of such types were chief items of interest. The crimes, the eccentricities of such characters as "General Andrew Jackson" were reported with amused unction. But the work of Susan Vashon in organizing fairs to raise funds for the rehabilitation of Negro soldiers returning from the Civil War, or of Martin R. Delany in the cholera epidemics was given no attention. Among the reports of civic, professional, or artistic activities there is little or no mention of Negro choruses or bands, literary societies or social clubs, political or civic activities.

The inadequacy of reporting dealing with Negro life in Pittsburgh was in part remedied in 1890 by the appearance of *The Meteor*, a four-page, six-column paper edited by Daniel Mahoney and Nelson J. Miles. The paper had a county-wide circulation, and ran until 1894. From this time on several papers lived short lives. *The Western Enterprise* was issued for a time under the editorship of T. B. Littlejohn. It ceased publication on February 1, 1897.

In the preceding November the *Pittsburgh Press* had begun publication of a column, "Afro-American Notes,"[2] written by Dr. John W. Browning, a pharmacist, who had come to the city from Montgomery, Alabama. The *Press* for January 24, 1897 announced that with that issue copies of the paper would be exchanged with Negro journals outside the city. After about eight months of editing his column, Dr. Browning died and the column was taken over by Abram Hall, who continued the work until 1932. Mr. Hall's column became one of the chief repositories for items on Negro history in Pittsburgh.

In 1907 the Baptists of Pittsburgh issued *The Pioneer*, which lasted two years, and in 1919 there was in existence a *Progressive Afro-American*, a weekly periodical.

Such newspapers had their effect, but they all died out, and up to 1910 no Negro paper in Pittsburgh had worked its way into journalism as a permanent organ. But in this year Robert L. Vann and his colleagues went to press with the *Pittsburgh Courier*, adding its pages to news and expression of opinion on the Negro in America.[3]

At first merely the counsel for the incorporation and publication of the *Courier*, Mr. Vann soon bought up the stock and by enterprising editing quickly pushed the paper into the top ranks of Negro journalism. In 1923 the *Courier* set up its staff in Attorney Vann's Fourth Avenue law office. In 1929 the paper moved into its new $54,000 building on Centre Avenue.

The *Courier* is read by 70,000 people and has three editions—city, southern

2. In the original manuscript, the title of the column was written incorrectly as "Afro-American News"; it has been corrected for the published edition.

3. The *Courier* was founded in 1910 by Edwin Harleston, a guard at the H. J. Heinz food-packing plant. Within a few months, Harleston resigned, and Vann became editor.

and eastern. It is a successful, well-managed business, and gives employment to about 80 skilled and professional workers. Although its editorial policy has not been consistently progressive, the *Courier* has become one of the most influential Negro papers in the country.

The *Competitor* was edited by Mr. Vann during its 1920 appearance. He was aided by Emmett J. Scott, Walter Buchanan, and Alice Dunbar Nelson. It was a general literary magazine, to which among others such writers as R. R. Moton, James Weldon Johnson, Mary Church Terrell, R. R. Wright, Jr., Walter S. Buchanan and Kelly Miller contributed.

A few other provincial papers have been published in Pittsburgh, chiefly political mushrooms, such as the *Crusader*, edited for several years by Ivory Cobb; the *Citizen*, edited for a short time by Roger Lawes; and one or two church papers. Of these *The Vanguard*, edited by Dean Wilson during the 1920's for the Baptist congregations, and the present non-denominational church paper, the *Triangle Advocate*, edited by Finley Davis are examples.

CHAPTER 8

The Later Community

Typist: Brooks / Rewriteman: J. Ernest Wright /
July 23, 1939 / Pre-final

The snow that fell over a murky city on New Year's Day 1863, fell on a city rejoicing over the proclamation which, in accordance with President Lincoln's promise of the preceding October, declared free all slaves of those men still in rebellion against the Union.

Beginning at dark, from the hills above the Monongahela, a salute of a hundred guns was fired, continuing into the night. Parades with bands made jubilee in the streets. A half century of passionate, vehement effort had found its reward. As the *Post* said, defeat of the Rebellion was assured, the Union would be saved, and a people freed. Democracy in the United States would no longer be an ironical norm.

The *Pittsburgh Christian Advocate* began a column and a half editorial by saying "This is a memorable day in our world's history. It is the most brilliant New Year's Day that has dawned upon the republic during the eighty-six years of her existence. It is a day destined to be cherished in the most sacred memories of millions through coming centuries." The *Advocate* called the proclamation "one of those moral revolutions, which occur from time to time, and form great epochs in the history of our world." The *Advocate* felt the international significance of the proclamation.

This Revolution is not one of a year and a half, but of decades; not of the United States alone, but of all states and nations in Christendom. What means this struggle? Simply that the world is in transition from spiritual and political despotism to spiritual and political freedom. It is the genius of the age struggling for the advance of an enlightened Christian liberalism. Humanity is making some of its grandest struggles for true liberty. The shaking has reached all nations. It has effected a reduction of class legislation in Great Britain. It has given constitutional enactments to France. It has abolished serfdom in Russia. It has originated a constitution for Austria. It has regenerated Italy. It has resurrected Greece from the slumbers of ages. It is now harmonizing constitutional theory and practice in the United States, taking away our shame before the world, and adjusting an old and bitter quarrel with the God of nations. Slavery is but a great multiform system of oppression which is perishing before the triumphant march of enlightened Christian liberalism.

The *Evening Gazette* said, "The blow is struck this day which will restore this nation to unity and peace. More than three millions of human beings pass from bondage to freedom." And it quoted the *New York Evening Post*: "The seed is sown; the die is cast; the hammer has fallen. The Nation is forever committed to universal freedom not only in the minds of the slave, but on its own records, in the sentiments of its people, and in the sight of the world."

When Lee surrendered, the Thirteenth Amendment had given constitutional freedom to the Negro. A year later the Fourteenth gave him citizenship. In 1870 the Fifteenth put the ballot into his hands. Pittsburgh celebrated each successive step with parades and mass meetings. It seemed that the Negro had a clear way ahead; now that the southern slaves were freemen a whole people was united in freedom.

A convention at Syracuse in October, 1864, at which George B. Vashon was a delegate, was fully conscious of the position the Negro people held in the national life at the time. Would these principles for which the war had been fought be actually realized? Secretary Seward had recently announced that when the rebels laid down arms all war measures would cease, and this would include those concerning slavery. The convention expressed gratitude to President Lincoln for revoking a law that prohibited Negroes from carrying mail, for abolishing slavery in the District of Columbia, for his recognition of Liberia and Haiti. It petitioned Congress that the rights of Negro patriots be respected, that the government cease making discriminations in labor, payment and promotions. It contended, too, that the right to own real estate, to bear witness in law courts, to bring suit and to be sued were but theoretical privileges so long as complete political liberty was not granted. It demanded not only that slavery be formally and completely abolished but asked also for complete franchise in all states, those already in the union and those that might come in later.

In 1866, when the Fourteenth Amendment gave citizenship to the Negro, an editorial in the *Philadelphia Christian Recorder* voiced the insight not only of its editor but of Negro leaders like Vashon, Delany, Lewis, and Woodson in Pittsburgh. James Lynch said in his editorial that in the period of readjustment the Negro must use all his "intellect, wisdom, physical power, and the aid of friends" to meet it. Since the end of the war his relations to political government had changed. Though the sky was not clear, the clouds had parted. Colored representatives were in Congress and entered the Executive Mansion. A delegation was received and counseled by the most eminent legislators in Congress. Nearly two-thirds of each branch of the Congress, he said, had pledged themselves to legislate in behalf of the natural and political rights of the Negro. Lynch said:

> There are two ways by which we are to get our rights. The first is, to continually present our claim to the nation, and the second is to continue to prove ourselves capable of making as good use of all the political privileges which white citizens enjoy, as they do themselves. We have proved this already, in our loyalty and scarifies during the terrible civil war, but we must add proof to proof, that our very existence may be a living protest against the injustice that would proscribe us.
>
> The colored man who owns a farm and cultivates it well, and carries produce to market, makes a plea for his race far more effectual than the tongue of the most eloquent orator. A colored man standing in the door of his own blacksmith shop, with a leather apron on, is doing as much to elevate the race as the man in public station.
>
> No race of people inferior in numbers or power to another race, can live with them on terms of equality, unless they have the same great current of thought and feeling—unless they imbibe the spirit of the age. The present age in America is pre-eminently a practical and working age. The people's attention is in the work of developing the resources of the country; they are after sinking shafts and hoisting to the surface precious and useful metals, tunneling mountains, yoking hills together, and spanning streams with bridges. They believe in individual accumulation, and glory in the increasing wealth of the nation. Colored men, now that they have commenced thinking and acting for themselves, must be found in all the different branches of mechanism and labor, in agriculture and in commerce.

This was the note on which life began in the post-Civil War period for the five thousand Negroes living in Pittsburgh. By 1880 the number had increased to approximately seven thousand.

The movement of free Negroes increased rapidly by voluntary migration and through political colonization schemes. The "Local Affairs" column of the *Post* in 1870 announced that "The Third Ward in Allegheny is over run with imported colored men," and a few days later, "The Eighth Ward is over run with imported Negroes." The *Post* conducted a steady campaign against this colonization.

> Simon Cameron has agents who bring in Negroes from Maryland, Virginia and the District of Columbia to vote for Hartranft in Pennsylvania.... It is estimated that several thousand blacks have been forwarded to the cities and southern counties of Pennsylvania, in pursuance of contracts made for that purpose. They have gone in detachments, under the lead of scamps who have been well drilled as repeaters, and some of them have figured in similar expeditions elsewhere. They are coming from smallpox localities. It has increased rapidly, and assumed a graver form, as reports and action of the Board of Health show within the last few weeks, since this political emigration commenced.

The *Post* voiced the opprobrium that faced the Negro in Reconstruction years, in the vocabulary that was general at the time.

> All their howl about Colonization was occasioned by the National Convention of Colored Delegates now in session in this city. We know that weeks past, and before the Odd Fellows arrived, strange squads of colored men have been here, apparently railroad laborers, looking decidedly free, acting suspiciously, and giving contradictory accounts of theirs for the benefit of the 'organs' who feign to think that all the strange colored men are 'Odd Fellows,' we may state, that one hundred and fifty of these 'coons' arrived there yesterday, and yesterday morning twenty-three of these 'fresh gentlemen of color,' left this city on the 7:10 AM Day Express, Allegheny Valley Railroad on route for Manorsville, Armstrong County. When questioned as to their object they were exceedingly reticent giving no information except 'they were from Virginia and hunting work.' Those who think that all this is a joke, may realize are many days that such jokes may lead to the penitentiary. That they were here to vote for Hartranft was acknowledged by one of the gang, and not denied by the Ring.

The *Post* continued:

> We have letters from Maryland, District of Columbia, and Virginia stating that car loads of Negroes have been shipped to Allegheny County, it is thought for the purpose of voting. Thus to offset the loss anticipated by the German vote, it won't win. We give notice the first Negro who attempts to vote, who is not legally qualified, will be in jail in less than fifteen minutes.

From Frederick county, Maryland, a correspondent wrote the *Post*,

> There are about two hundred Negroes from this and an adjoining district
> in this county, now working in Allegheny City and Manchester, Pennsylvania.
> They are registered voters in this county, have not been there six months, but
> will vote at the State election if not stopped.

The Negro continued to be the human focus of the democratic tradition
within the reunited republic. As reconstruction brought the displacement of
masses of Negro people not only from the plantation to the southern cities, but
from the South to the northern cities such as New York, Philadelphia, Chicago
and Pittsburgh, brought the problems of the South in modified form to northern
areas. The great folk epic continued through the early chaos of freedom—a whole
people engaging with surprising psychological unity in mass action for the various advantages of a new state—first of all jobs and self-maintenance, then for education of the great illiterate masses and industrial training for thousands who
wanted to be equipped to take their new places in the labor market of a fast-in-
dustrializing world. At the same time these people faced the disillusionment of
the loss of the newly won franchise and curtailment of the civil rights implied by
citizenship. Mass concentration in the black ghettoes of northern cities created
tensions demanding adjustment in devious ways. A divided white mass mind,
tackling the problems of the post-Civil War years, the expansion of the country,
the intensification of industry, the political accumulation of power in the hands of
powerful lobbies for finance capital. Many issues that had centered around the
abolition movement were not yet settled—education for the masses of the people,
especially in the South and the new West; easy money and credit for the farmers;
votes for the women of the nation; transportation to make accessible larger markets; adjustment of incoming nationalities from Europe; shorter working days;
safer and healthier conditions for working men, women and children; and a just
share in wages of a tremendously increasing profit of industry. And the epic
movement of the Negro people into the northern cities created special aspects to
each of these problems.

Confronted with a divided white mass mind, social misunderstanding which
regarded him as a competitor in industry, as a "ward of democracy" rather than
as an ally in maintaining it, the Negro developed an intense group consciousness,
which expressed itself as race pride rather than national feeling. Mounting one
barrier after another to assimilation into the American community, he had thrust
upon him the realization that he was a separate part within a larger, superior unit.
The best he could do was to take up Booker Washington's philosophy of one as
the hand but separate as fingers. And he instituted numberless self-help programs and compromised on a bi-racial mode of existence. Not until the World

War made him a considerable factor in industry did the labor and economic aspect of his status come more realistically to the fore. Then also, the effect became more apparent on the national social mind of the advance of the black minority. Negro and white leaders came to see "the Negro problem" not as a problem of race but as a problem of national democratic advance. More and more clearly the status of twelve million Negro people was understood as a human problem, and the keeping of one-tenth of the national population in an arrested condition of progress came to be understood as a denial and paradox of practical democracy. Self-contained progress proved itself impossible. It crumpled with the depression. A resurgence of the pre-Civil War alliance of Negro and white liberal elements become inevitable and the complete liberation of the Negro people from economic, political, social, and cultural handicaps was recognized as one of the greatest needs of progressive democracy.

The most notable feature of the quarter century following the Civil War was the prodigious expansion of industry. The growth of the Kloman forge into the gigantic United States Steel Corporation was typical. Industrial growth developed a new physical and social world. It created millionaires and multi-millionaires—the Carnegies, the Phippses, the Olivers, the Fricks, and the Thaws. And it expanded the working class to include not only the Germans and Irish who were already here in large numbers and continued to come, but the Italians and later the Poles, Hungarians, and other Slavs.

The city expanded geographically, reorganizing its government to consolidate control for the Republican machine. With increased territory, expanded and improved transportation was needed—horsecars were replaced with cable cars but because of steep ascents and sharp turns these gave way to electric cars. Inclines scaled the cliffs of the city. Public utilities increased. The telephone came into use. Natural gas and a new water supply were provided. A public park, new schools, new papers, musical organizations provided education and recreation.

On this tide of industrial and municipal development came new social problems and situations. Not the least of these was the place of the national groups developing within the community—their role in the creation of community wealth, the apportionment of the created wealth to their economic and cultural needs, the transfusion of cultures—European and native American. These groups were at first recognized only as a supply of cheap labor to carry out projects of an expanding community. Foreign labor agents brought thousands of Italians, Poles, Hungarians and Lithuanians to the steel areas, where they worked under the eye of patroness and labor spies, and bought in company stores. As they became restless and less docile in the industrial scene, attempts were made to replace them by Negroes. The increase in Negro workers gave a basis for the growth of a Negro middle class which could support a greater number of professionals—doctors, dentists, lawyers chiefly. The professional and semi-professional workers organized recreational and cultural clubs, musical and dramatic groups. All phases of Negro life expanded.

By the 1890s the Negro community had taken on much of its present form. Between the Emancipation Proclamation and the year President McKinley took office, 1892, the population had almost doubled. Within that decade it made a further increase of almost 175%. By 1900, then, the Negro population of the city was over 17,000. Thousands of new arrivals had restricted themselves largely to the Hill, to the Strip and to the North Side. But after the beginning of the new century, the more well-to-do began to move eastward to East Liberty, Homewood and Brushton. Already there had developed characteristic segregation of national minorities: a little Ghetto, a little Italy, a Black Belt, little Syria and little Athens. The rapidity with which the Negro population continued to increase and become congested into particular regions is shown by the Fifth Ward on the Hill. There in 1900 the Negro population was 811. By 1910 it had reached 6,000. By 1920 it passed 10,000.

With numerical and geographic expansion came occupational expansion. By 1900 three hundred Negroes conducted businesses employing three thousand Negro helpers. Chief of these were barber shops, restaurants, hotels, excavation and hauling businesses. When a Negro in 1897 had secured a position as shipping clerk in the Union Foundry and Machine company, the news was thought sufficiently significant for reporting in the "Afro-American Notes" of the *Pittsburgh Press*. Ten years later, 58 percent of the male workers were employed in domestic and personal services. Of women 90 percent were similarly employed. There were one hundred seamstresses or dressmakers, and 127 employees on the city payroll as laborers, messengers, janitors, policemen, detectives, and postal clerks.

Among the 17,000 Negroes in Pittsburgh in 1897, there were four practicing attorneys, six physicians, and 25 preachers. There were also a few music teachers but no professional singers or performers.

Since in Pittsburgh the social attitude is colored by that of the South, doctors and lawyers are generally restricted to practice among their own people, although whites are also among their patronage. About one-third of the established physicians and dentists in 1918 reported such patients. Of the 57 Negro physicians now practicing in Pittsburgh, only three are on the staffs of the 35 hospitals serving the county and city, and those three are in the out-patient departments of two of the clinics. No Negro physician has been graduated from the Medical School of the University of Pittsburgh since 1914 although the university claims to serve chiefly the western Pennsylvania district.

Eleven of the Negro lawyers of the city belong to the Robert N. Terrell Law

Club, organized to promote fellowship among Negro lawyers. It is a quasi-social and study organization which meets at homes of its members. Negro lawyers belong to the Allegheny County Bar Association, the American Bar Association and the National Lawyers Guild.

The Negro businessman has faced the same conditions in Pittsburgh as throughout the rest of the country. His trade is confined, with but few exceptions, to the impoverished black belt. It is compelled to consist on restricted capital. It cannot compete successfully with large-scale undertakings. One of the first attempts to develop business and trade by the Negro community was a cooperative store opened during the 1880's. Within the following ten years four or five small hotels were opened. Most businesses were barber shops, restaurants, and more recently beauty culture parlors and undertakers, businesses which have almost complete control of Negro patronage in communities where white concerns in the same field practice segregation. The growth of Negro population in the eighties formed a basis of patronage for small businesses conducted by Negroes. The opening of a drugstore on Wylie Avenue in 1899 was "a move in a commercial way which should be applauded and patronized" according to the "Afro-American Notes" column of the *Pittsburgh Press*, which added that success for the new business depended on the appreciation of the race. At the end of the first decade of the twentieth century Negro business had expanded to include barbers, restaurants and hotels, grocery and poultry shops, tailors, pool rooms, hauling and excavation businesses, printers, pharmacists, undertakers and livery businesses, caterers, and eight miscellaneous enterprises such as an insurance company, stationery and book shop, a photographer and a real estate office. These enterprises gave employment to fewer than six hundred Negroes of the twenty thousand in the city. By 1935 Pittsburgh, fourteenth city in size of Negro population, was last among fifteen cities in the country with a population of 50,000 or more in the number of retail stores operated by Negroes. Eighty-one retail stores were operated by 84 active Negro proprietors and firm members. In six years, 1929–1935, 46 percent of those were wiped out.

The largest enterprise conducted by Pittsburgh Negroes is the Diamond Coke and Coal company, organized in Homestead in 1890, by a Negro river engineer. In the boat building business he built 21 river steamboats. The company owns a mine, docks and steamboats and employs one thousand men.

The Brown Gas Log Company, organized in 1913, sends eight and ten salesmen throughout the United States and Canada. Their products have reached Japan and Argentina. They manufacture the Boy Scout Camp Fireplaces for the country.

In 1920, at the height of the southern migration, the Steel City Bank was founded. At the end of five years the management reported resources of $1,110,290.65

and a surplus and undivided profits of $31,468.55. In five years it had done business to an amount exceeding $7,000,000.

Four years after the Steel City Bank opened its doors, a second institution—the Modern State Bank—was founded. It carried two thousand commercial and savings accounts. Capitalized at $50,000, with total deposits of $52,810.18 and assets of $115,999.00, it was unable to meet clearings or reserves required under the state banking laws and closed its business after four years operation.

To attain that "economic efficiency which is the foundation for every kind of success," the Pittsburgh Negro sought to counteract discrimination in trade and business by developing "race" financial enterprises. In 1896 the Afro-American Building and Loan Association was launched with a sermon at Good Hope Baptist church. Attorney W. H. Stanton presented the organization with its charter, said to be the first ever granted to a body of Negroes in Pennsylvania. The association had 58 members and had sold 128 shares of stock. Two years later 222 stockholders were enrolled; 36 had withdrawn, 56 had forfeited rights. Cash receipts amounted to $3,000; cash loans on real estate to $2,000. By 1905 one house had been bought. In 1899 a Ladies Savings Fund Society was formed. By 1905 three real estate companies had been incorporated. A syndicate established four drugstores within four years. The *Pittsburgh Leader* in January, 1911 said our fellow race people are fast evidencing the fact that the better citizenship is known not only by moral and intellectual advancement, but by material advancement as well. During the past ten days five colored men bought valuable home properties in Pittsburgh, and a fact worthy of comment is that all of them paid cash for their properties. A house on Oakland Avenue, price $7,600; a house on Lang Avenue, Belmar districts, $5,200; one on Fayette Street, North Side, $4,500; a house on Amanda Street, price $3,700.[1]

---

1. At the conclusion of this chapter, the original manuscript says: "A section on social agencies will be inserted here. Also, a section on cultural activities. Then transition will be made to the politics and a concluding section of one or two pages will draw the politics and the book itself to a close."

CHAPTER 12

FOLKWAYS

——————◆•◆•◆——————

Typist: Marian Holmes / Rewriteman: J. Ernest Wright /
May 2, 1939 / Pre-final

Typist: E. Saunier / Rewriteman: J. Ernest Wright /
November 20, 1940 / Final

There exists in Pittsburgh a Negro way of life as individual as the Italian, the Jewish, the Polish, or native-white way of living. It has become traditional, integrated, and it colors the larger community. It shapes the religion and politics, the press, the sociabilities, the arts, the method of livelihood. It is a unique body of folkways and racial lore.

It appears most sturdily and articulately where people live most densely and are most free of superimposed and restrictive elements from other folkways, where it is spontaneous and unselfconscious. Out of it the future culture of a people will emerge. From it the artists of a people will create, when they become deeply conscious of it and understand it as the life pattern of a distinct nationality. Still largely unobserved, unrecorded, and unstudied, it has persisted through a long past, involving more, perhaps, than is usually thought or acknowledged of African folkways. It has been affected by American ways and the ways of other nationalities which it touches. In sayings and street songs, in beliefs and practices, and in that deep vernacular spoken by a large group and as indigenous to that group as Yiddish to the Jew or French to the French, there is a racial wisdom, imagery, and myth, the moods, confidences and distrusts created from social and economic suppression. These sayings and vernacular of a people, their beliefs and superstitions, the street songs, the food served in little restaurants are

Originally "Folkways" appeared as two separate texts, labeled chapter 9 (pre-final) and chapter 12 (final). Here they have been brought together as chapter 12.

often looked upon askance, repudiated and scorned by many who wish to prove their racial equality by copying white ways of living. These people do not realize that the greatest cultural service the Negro can perform is to bring his national characteristics into the most articulate expression possible, so that its characteristic features will vitalize American culture.

Negro life in Pittsburgh as elsewhere is highly organized, in the church, fraternal and secret societies, civic and social clubs. The large membership in fraternal and secret societies can be explained not only by the social, sickness, and death benefits offered but by the fact that a people, unable to participate sufficiently in the general political and social structure, through these organizations can exert among themselves those powers denied elsewhere. Restricted in the freedom to excel in many fields, they find in such societies these restrictions removed, and freedom granted to excel in whatever pursuits such organizations offer. In them large numbers of people find opportunities for achieving eminence, a desire and a need deep-seated in every human being. In these groups a man may become a Grand Patriarch, a Grand Sword Bearer, a Noble Grand, or a Grand Pursuivant, and in the auxiliaries a woman may be a Daughter, or a Worthy Councillor. To talk of and to deal with Grand Special Communications, Decorations of Chivalry, Royal Purple Decrees, is to touch glamour and achieve exaltation.

Annual sermons, picnics, dinners, boat rides, and balls have become social traditions. The annual Memorial Day Dinner and the annual Armistice Day Dinner are not only social events pleasant with conversation at flowered tables, but also benefits for hospitals and homes for the aged. The Armistice Day Dinner was in its early days a lavish affair of gleaming tables, flowers and banners, music and sociability. Churches, clubs, and sororities took tables at which they furnished their own service, and thousands of dollars were raised for charitable work. It is still in less lavish form a Pittsburgh tradition.

The Pittsburgh Jabberwock is held each spring by the Delta Sigma Theta Sorority to create college scholarships for Negro Youth. Stunts, plays, dances by competing social and civic clubs are awarded prizes.

Although fraternalism and secret societies are on the wane among established Pittsburgh residents they still form, in their better aspects, a definite part of the social pattern in the Negro community.

On the Hill at little bars, over sloe gin or beer, across wooden tables where chittlerlings or hog jowl and turnip greens are the specialty, or at street corner or from window to window confidences, one overhears a colorful, native vernacular. At first it is strange and as foreign as Eskimo. Yet it is so persistent that visitors and travelers soon come to understand it, just as one comes to understand his mother tongue. To many it has become a mother tongue, if perhaps only a step-mother. Some go out deliberately to acquire it, but usually one breathes it in gradually just as one breathes the odor of beer or general stuffiness, or the incense burned in front rooms and in the many spiritualist churches that dot the Hill. It comes rhythmically and vividly from black lips, and often from white. It explodes and crackles and sings and hums. It is created and dies and rises from its own ashes in new forms, brilliant with racial imagery, prismatic with race moods.

The folkways of the Pittsburgh community are not and have never been the folkways of Harlem. They are not those of South Chicago. They are certainly not those of the South. They partake of the nature of all these. They have of course a universality. They are certainly distinct in many ways from those of the white community. And in more than one respect they are true to Pittsburgh. What the Negro thinks and talks about is not altogether what the Slav, the German or the Swede thinks and talks about, or what the native white thinks and talks about. What the professional man and woman think, and how they spend their leisure, what they read, their vocabulary—all these differing one way or another from the thoughts, leisure, vocabulary, beliefs, sayings, of the laborer, the steelworker, the dweller on the Lower Hill. Through any mood, action, thought or attitude, however universal, there will at times appear a variation, a quality, an element more characteristic of the Negro in Pittsburgh than of any other person. Here the Negro way of life is as characteristic as that of the Italian, the Jewish, the Polish or the native-white way of living, whether it is expressed in the Negro church, the Negro press, the social life, the arts, the folk-sayings, the charms, beliefs and superstitions, the racial wisdom and imagery in speech, the legends and myths, the vernacular of the people, the very food they eat, the anniversaries observed by the community, the traditional customs and observances of the people.

In a paper read before one of the literary societies of the city, Mr. A. Hall, a journalist who has lived in Pittsburgh for sixty years and has known the community in many aspects, who knew some of the oldest members, some of the most active members, survivors of the oldest pre-Civil War community has sketched that life in some of its aspects. The Billy Lee he mentions is said to have been the servant of General Braddock on his disastrous expedition into the western Pennsylvania wilderness to claim it for Britain. Lee is said to have carried the wounded General from the field of battle and to have been bequeathed by him at his death to the young Major George Washington. This may be one of the legends of the people. At any rate Mr. Hall says:

> Ever since Billy Lee lent his color to the very complicated, exciting and important international proceedings, which took place during the early settlement of what is now the Pittsburgh district, others of our racial group, in one capacity or another, have graced the festal scene, until now they are

almost as numerous as are said to be the leaves at Valambrosia. Like the grain of mustard seed, that was hid in the bushel measure of the bible, they have increased and multiplied in number until they now approximate a population in excess of 50,000 persons. Their activities, which at the first were largely confined to menial pursuits, have broadened out to include many of the handicrafts, quite a few of the professions. An encouraging quota are engaged in commercial vocations and several have attained honorable mention. Dunbar tells us that "Slow moves the pageant of a climbing race," and that is a fact which, while it applies to us as a people, is equally true of all the races which go to make up our composite nationality.

We are citizens of no mean City, and if we will let our minds run back to a period before the War of the Rebellion, when, in what is now called Old Pittsburgh there flourished such genteel families as the Pecks, the Moles, Jones, Robinsons, Mahoneys, Dunlaps, Woodsons, Rideouts, Collins, Murrays, Halls, Johnsons, Parkers, Letts, Billows, Goldens, Baileys, Turfleys, Arnetts, Knoxes, Simpsons, Dorkins, Palmers, Googins, Capertons, Hills, Tapers, Grandisons, Washingtons, Gibsons, Whites, Tocas, Gaithers, and many others whose names evade me; while across the Allegheny there were the Wilkersons, the Masseys, the Pulpress, Jenkins, Waters, Delanys, Neales, Blaneys, Grays, Doughertys, Dimmeys, the Scroggins and a host of others that have passed from my memory; while in the Birmingham or South Side section, there was Shep Waters, the Jacksons, the Hances, the Dixons, the Clarks, and Barretts, we shall find that despite the advent of jazz music and the short skirt, and without the aid of natural gas, electricity, the telephone, women's votes and prohibition, there existed a social circle, an aristocracy based on decency, honesty and clean living, which was immeasurably to be preferred to the race conditions, of whatever kind that exist here today. In those days the social life of our folks centered chiefly around the church, for they were essentially a God-fearing people, the sewing circle and the mutual aid society. Dancing, especially in public places, was tabooed, and card-playing was one of the unpardonable sins. At most of the parties given, "spinning the plate," "pillow," and romping through "Weevily Wheat" were the amusements, and the fellow who brought his girl to the fair with a horse and buggy was almost in a class by himself, caused all the other beaux to have a fit of jealousy and furnished the fair sex with a two-week-affair of that day and time, which provoked the greatest spirit of rivalry, were the dinners or suppers served now and then by those who posed as social leaders; and on such occasions they used to virtually put the big pots into the little one, create a great deal of fuss and feathers around the house of the hostess in preparation of the feast, and the table, brave in its show of white napery, and glistening with delftware or china, would often fairly groan under its weight of substantial and dainty food; for then as now your people and my people, to whatever other shrine they paid obeisance, always paid the highest honors to the culinary art. If a young man called regularly three or four times on a young woman, and was known to have been her escort to and from church, prayer meeting, sewing circle and the few and far between parties and receptions, which were given, he was regarded as her steady company, and the gossips and match-makers began to name the date for their marriage. Parlors were conspicuous by their absence in those days, in the homes of most of our people, and what was called the sitting room, was often ornamented with a big lordly looking teeter bed, fairly regal with its piled-up feather ticks, downy pillows and deftly-patterned quilts and counterpanes. The stoop at the front door, served all the purposes of a porch, when the weather permitted its use; and when the courting had to be done indoors, the tallow of wax-candle, with the aid of the snuffers, had the same reckless fashion of going out, at a convenient time, that gas or electricity has now during the sparking period. While everybody knew everybody and could be counted on in a time of trouble, sickness, or death to render any assistance and extend every ounce of sympathy at their command. Still, there were cliques. The Virginians, district of Columbia and Maryland folk consorted together; the North Carolina people thought themselves made in a special mould; those from Kentucky just knew they were what the doctor ordered; while the free Negroes, who drifted in from Ohio and New York, didn't take a back seat for anybody. But these little clannish differences were after and attended by all of those in health, and when the grim reaper—death—invaded a household and bore away one of its inmates, the demise of almost any race person assumed the proportions of a personal loss. The prevailing sentiment was "Each for all, no man for himself."

That was the atmosphere in which the race men and women, and the race boys and girls of an early day laid the foundation, blazed the way, created a sentiment and opened the opportunity for those of us who have since come upon the scene to make progress. Many of them were illiterate, so far as school education is taken into account, but common sense abounded and out of the necessities of their civic, business, mental and moral condition, they early learned the wisdom of assuming a virtue if they had it not. They awoke the appreciation and secured the esteem of the dominant race, and handed it down to their progeny as a precious legacy. Then came the Civil War, with the status of the Negro as the bone of contention and, to use a biblical phrase—"The evening and the morning was the first Day." What has since transpired, affecting us as a people in this community, includes so many changes, and involves so many issues, that to go into it now, even casually, would be presumptuous on my part, and would be a gross invasion of the time allotted other speakers. In conclusion, permit me to quote:

> We stand upon life's earnest stage,
> And onward is the motto of the age,
> The Past has left us, the Future lies hidden,
> Let the Present engage our attention unbidden.

The end of the Civil War saw a world different from that described by Mr. Hall take shape with fairy-tale rapidity. The old tension of slavery days gave way to a more easy way of living. Men and women no longer walked the streets in fear of kidnaping. Families no longer lived from day to day in tense uneasiness lest concealed fugitives be discovered in their homes. Life did not, however, become easy and altogether pleasant between one year's end and another's.

There was a great deal of ugliness to life between 1870 and the present. With prosperity came recurrent panics and depressions. With one issue after another life grew tense and relaxed. But national and local issues were different. The great question of freedom had been settled affirmatively. There were new subjects to talk and think about. There were new things to do. But from the Civil War to the present, it had taken on more aspects of life as America as a whole lives it.

The 1870s were hard times to live through, for Negro and white. The great wave of industrial prosperity that swept up with the war burst with the failure of Jay Cooke and Company into the chaos and misery of panic.[1] Life was difficult enough for the masses of white men and women who were thrown out of work; it was worse for the majority of the Negro population who from earliest morning lined the streets waiting for soup kitchens to open to get a pail of soup and a half loaf of bread, for families of eight, nine or a dozen. No help but private charity was available. Starvation, even death from exposure, was frequent. Coal was scarce. The water supply was polluted. Epidemics of typhoid, diphtheria, and small pox occurred one after another, sweeping thousands—rich and poor alike—into homemade graves. Houses where the pestilence struck were roped off. Women who had recovered from smallpox or diphtheria went from house to house ministering to the stricken. There were too few doctors to tend the sufferers, too few undertakers to bury the dead. At night carts rumbled over the cobbles attended by weeping men and women who buried their dead with their

---

1. Jay Cooke was a powerful Philadelphia banker who was instrumental in financing the Union cause during the Civil War.

own hands. Pest houses were hastily erected. All through the night at street corners barrels of tar were kept burning; it was thought they would disinfect the pestilential air.

But life went on.

Not all classes of people found life the same. To some these years were the Gilded Age. To others they were panic years. To in-between groups they were just other years, recalled now as the years of their youth or the early life of their parents, who have told of incidents and manners of the day that show the broad social changes taking place. While working men and women were receiving their wages in nails and trading in those nails for groceries and clothing at the stores, great new fortunes were being made by Pittsburgh iron and steel men and by men who were striking some of the richest oil fields in the country.

"A month in Pittsburgh would justify anyone in committing suicide," Herbert Spencer said in the 1870s. Pittsburgh was the blackest and grimiest city in the United States. Against the windows of cabs, soot and cinder spattered like rain, housewives waged an unending fight with chamois and hot water upon windowpanes in order to see into their neighbor's back yard or on their neighbor's front steps.

Pittsburgh was a city of horses, and as characteristic as its smutted atmosphere was the ammoniac air drifting out from stables in the summer heat, seventy-five of them in the downtown section. At these stables many Negroes found employment. Equally characteristic were the old wells in the stable yards, and the granite dippers that hung on posts or the pump shaft. Trees and hitching posts and mounting blocks lined the curbs.

River packets that tied up at the Monongahela wharf gave employment to Negro men as stewards and deck hands and to women as stewardesses. At night the flicker of feeble gas flames under glass bells on iron posts were lighted by men with ladders, and partly dispelled the darkness for a circuit of some ten feet. And to inmates of Pittsburgh homes, sitting in the light of their hanging lamps, often came the sound of the crier's bell and his call of "Child Lost—Child Lost." The 1870s were the decade of Charlie Ross, the Lindbergh baby of that era.[2]

The streets were noisy with horse-cars and newsboys, with drays and cabs, with shouting, swearing Irish laborers. Down Liberty Street trains ran to the station near the point, clanging their brass bells to warn pedestrians from the tracks. Along these tracks one often had to wait until a dray pulled out from loading at a storehouse, or one has to skirt its rear and trespass on the tracks, and often to duck a great half-beef swung out from a freight car door.

2. Charlie Ross was the "Lindbergh case" of the nineteenth century. Kidnapped from his Philadelphia home in 1874, the four-year-old boy was never found despite numerous ransom notes and the willingness of the family to pay.

Pittsburgh in the 1870s was a drinking city of bars and chop-houses and oyster grills, their doors flanked by busy loiterers, busy in afternoon leisure talking of Jay Cooke's failure, or the Indian wars in the west. Newell's, the old hotel located on Fifth Avenue, which lasted into the present century, was a gathering place famous for its oysters. At Newell's, Negroes were hired as waiters, bootblacks and doormen. Oil men, politicians and horsemen met at Newell's to buy and sell their respective wares and to loiter through mid-day eating hours. Here more than one Negro property owner or investor got a "tip" from a business man that started him on his way to a competency, or was placed on a political committee. Newell's hadn't the chic of the Union Depot dining room, nor its half-worldly, half-domestic atmosphere; but there you met people who enlivened the life of the city. At Newell's over beer or hot toddies were exchanged stories, horses, and city wards. Oysters were consumed, leases signed, liaisons established. The young bloods gathered here; a few daring young ladies sat here and smoked. Show people came after the theater. Newell's was one of the city's bright spots.

In the slang of the day, one of the "tony" places was the dining room on the second floor of the four-story Union Depot. It was reached by broad red carpeted stairs with metal treads, in flights of seven or eight, from the top of which one looked down the winding well. It was one of the aristocratic resorts of the city. Here, Negroes hurried with great silver trays, called not trays waiters "waiters."[3] Typical of the place and time were the white stoneware pitchers of ice water. Iced milk was the most called-for item on the cards. The Hotel was run by Colonel Unger, a tall, straight and genial gentleman. Mrs. Unger was short and fat, and is remembered by more than one present-day Pittsburgher as rushing through the red velvet halls, clutching in her hand a parrot case. Here were served the "better class" passengers on a stop-over between Philadelphia and Cincinnati or the booming towns farther west. Here too lunched the "better class" citizens of Pittsburgh and Allegheny, meeting friends in town for lunch or business appointments. Dandies in coats buttoned high on their chests, and wearing the popular drooping or up-curving mustaches of the time, visiting politicians, an occasional artist or musician appearing in evening recital at Library Hall, all caned and derbied and boutonniered in the fashion of those summers, handed bustled, waterfalled ladies up the rich carpeted stairs. Outside they opened fringed parasols for ladies in polonaise and bonnet, to step into shining open carriages driven by Negroes; or they closed the doors of handsome cabs and raised their derbies in gentlemanly salute.

Other establishments where Pittsburghers gathered in those days of the city's adolescence were St. Charles, the Central Hotel on Smithfield near the post office, where local ball players such as Al Pratt, the popular short stop, might be

3. Language here is reproduced as in original.

met and chatted with (the leagues were going full tilt in the 1870s); and the Red Lion, beside the river at the foot of Sixth Street, famous for its stable yard, in which horses were sold at from fifty cents to a hundred dollars. The Home Hotel near Ninth Street was a temperance house, barren and sad and run by an angry manager. The Earl House was patronized by Alleghenians, as was the Central Hotel behind the present Carnegie Library, an eminently respectable hostelry, where Pennsylvania Railroad officials and newly arrived young merchants like Henry Buhl, Jr. made their homes. Then there were Mrs. Morgans, beside the Sixth Street bridge, where one went as a special treat for ice cream; and Hubley's, quiet, sedate, decorous, furnished with the plain elegance of Brussels carpets, lace curtains and white marble-topped tables. Here "Sandy" Washington, a leading member of the Negro community, was head waiter, and here too Negroes were served. Reinaman's Restaurant too was popular, through not so good as Hubley's or Mrs. Morgan's.

Pittsburgh's population was 86,076; that of Allegheny 53,180. The population was, of course, predominantly English. Roughly one-third were foreign born. Of these, about one-fifth were British, Scottish, Welsh, and Irish. The Germans made up about one-tenth of the total. A few hundred French and Belgians worked in the glass industries. About 130 Slavs had just been imported by manufacturers.

There were three distinct Negro communities in those days—the Hill, Allegheny, and Minersville. In Allegheny a small group of families clustered round the Avery College center, had their own social and cultural worlds and visited frequently over Pittsburgh or farther out in Minersville. Minersville was a community of families who had bought lots out near the Ewart farm. The district was often referred to as "The Orchard" because of the many fruit trees covering the hillsides. Those who went visiting there would commonly say "We're going out to the orchards." Here lived the Stantons, the Washingtons, the Highgates, the Roaches, the Barkeses, the Smallwoods and others, in the country where Morgan, Wandless, and Berthoud streets now run. From here Negro children walked several miles to the Miller Street School, passing on their way the Minersville school, until Jack Smallwood, a politician of the time, initiated a successful campaign, joined by Rev. Terry and other people in Allegheny, for unified schools.

Within the Negro community as in the white community there was a growth of semi-skilled and skilled workers. Many members of the most successful families were still barbers, cooks, valets, stewards on the river packets, and in this horse-and-carriage period many were coachmen and liverymen. But as the years went by they were able to buy property; a few families bought a considerable amount of property and became prosperous. An "exclusive" group developed that held themselves aloof from families coming into the city from the southern states. They developed their own manners and customs. These were the families who gradually moved from homes in the alleys out onto the streets by purchasing their own homes. They accepted into their "social set" only those who could point to parents and grandparents and say they were "old families," who had "character." In other words, as in all communities, social castes induced genteel snobbery.

This period was the American counterpart of the Victorian age, and American houses were furnished with Victorian stuffiness. Homes of the "comfortably off" people were crowded and stuffy. Carpets were nailed into the corners with straw laid unhygienically beneath them. A regular Saturday brooming raised clouds of dust such as Christian encountered in the Interpreter's House. Against walls and in corners were ranged the stiff hideousness of horsehair chairs and sofas, from the slithery surfaces of which sedate gentlemen and ladies might, if not careful and adept in the "social graces," be catapulted like packages from the end of a chute. In living rooms and parlors, iron stoves raised high their funeral-urn tops of polished brass. Every parlor had its center table, ornately carved and topped with chocolate-colored marble. On this table reposed—actually reposed, for its was seldom disturbed—a copy of Martin Tupper, *The Poetry of Ossian,* or *Friendship's Offering,* and the inevitable green or red plush family album. Over this general furnishing of the parlor of the 1870s was scattered into odd spaces and corners examples of spatter-work, designs made in skeleton leaves, flowers of shells and feathers, wreaths of wax flowers in glass frames or under glass bells, Landseer engravings, pious mottoes in faded grasses or in double cross-stitch, alum baskets and beaded moccasins that Uncle William had brought back from his trip across the plains. Every parlor had pairs of chromos—"Wide Awake" and "Fast Asleep," or church engravings of "Mercy at the Wicket Gate" or "The Three Graces."[4] But even these were not enough. The ensemble was festooned and draped and covered and swathed with portieres, lambrequins,[5] pillow shams and doilies that, when you rose from a chair or a sofa, you carried it with you stuck to your clothes.

If there was a piano in the home this ebony piece of furniture bore its pleated front-silk copies of the "Battle of Prague" and "The Last Link is Broken" more often than it carried a Mozart or Handel sonata.

At the corner of the fireplace stood that symbol of domesticity of the seventies, the hassock, for tired feet or listening children. And within arm's reach on the edge of the mantelpiece stood that product of odd moments of leisure, a jar of pills, twisted bits of paper to light the lamp with, a father's pipe. And, arch

4. "Chromos" is short for chromolithographs, pictures printed in colors from a series of lithographic stones or plates.

5. Portieres are curtains hanging across doorways; lambrequins are akin to valances.

achievement of decoration and culture, somewhere in this welter of furnishings there stood a Rogers group, preferably "Weighing the Baby."[6]

Home life in the seventies moved under a surface broken by political and financial excitement. In ball rooms and in parlors people danced the polka, the waltz, the mazurka. Men had their portraits taken in studio, plush album poses— hand inside the coat, only the top button fastened. Dundreary whiskers rippled silkily onto their chests, and the fobs affected the monocle.

A descendant of one of these families says:

> The social life of those days was conducted on a very high scale. Both Pittsburgh and the North Side, then called Allegheny, had their social sets and the requisites to belonging to them were first of all parents or family background, character. If you came from certain families you were accepted into these circles. People of good standing were highly respected and were not supposed to do anything that was unbecoming, for that would disgrace the family name or record. That was considered very important. If a young man wished to take a young lady out to any kind of social affair, they had to consult the parents first. If he was not the proper type he was refused the honor.
>
> In spite of political and financial excitement the decade was one of increasing physical comforts, and in general of buoyant optimism. Every youngster could think of himself as a possible future president or a millionaire. From rags to riches was one of the dominant American myths. The age was an age of social aspiration. People wanted wealth, leisure, and power. And it was an age of "correctness" and politeness, "genteel" in behavior and thinking.

The Negro community still lived chiefly within the church. And the gentility of the age was perhaps stronger within the Negro community, more intense perhaps than among the white population, because the Negro was "on trial" socially. "There were not many dances," a Pittsburgh woman says, "because for a long-time dancing was not popular with the older people." This was probably due to the very high regard for the church and religious customs. At parties there would be games such as dominoes and checkers. But card playing was for many years tabooed. But among the better class of people dancing became popular in the later 1880s and the 1890s.

In such a milieu a dozen or so families moved according to an elaborate social

---

6. John Rogers (1829–1904) was an American engineer, machinist, and sculptor whose works of art became popular as "accurate records of the period." Thousands of his "Rogers groups" were produced by machine and sold into American homes. *The Columbia Encyclopedia,* Sixth Edition, s.v. "Rogers, John," http://www.bartleby.com/65/ro/Rogers-J2.html (accessed December 19, 2003).

scheme. There was a definite card etiquette. It was important to know whether to leave your card or not, and if left, which corner to turn down, what might be inscribed upon it and what might not. Calling hours for the ladies were strictly from two to five in the afternoon. In the evening they might call with their husbands after seven. "At homes" were established and taken-for-granted affairs. Nice distinctions in age were observed. A young girl was Emily or Carolyn until she reached her teens; then she became Miss Emily or Miss Carolyn. New Years Day was the great day for formal calls among Negroes and whites, especially for gentlemen to call on the ladies. Lemonade or wine and cake was served. The "Greenleaf Social Club" was an exclusive Negro club that gave formal parties, banquets, and dances in winter, picnics and hay-rides in summer. Their affairs were "invitation only." The guests were very select, and from the best families. There were gala affairs, charming pageants in which the women who became our grandmothers were young people gowned in the robe imperatrice made popular by the Empress Eugenie,[7] or they carried their evening silks bunched and draped over that quaint monstrosity, the bustle, and for evening parties and receptions, they powdered their hair with gold dust.

Their partners in the bright crowd that gathered, the gentlemen of the decade, were attired in black broadcloth generally, or tight doeskin trousers, meticulously uncreased—for a crease in those days was held in universal distaste as a sign of the store shelf. The gentlemen pomaded their hair and wore stove pipe hats indiscriminately, merely as matter of choice for very formal evening affairs, and if their whim dictated, even for morning wear. And any assemblage offered the most amazing display of luxuriant and variegated beards. But beards and bustles and uncreased trousers or empress robes, pomaded hair or gold dusted chignons, the whole assemblage smelled wonderfully of sachets.

Pittsburgh in the seventies was a hospitable, hearty city. Houses of those who could afford to entertain were filled constantly with guests, especially for supper. Invitation was by person most frequently. And after supper—the evening meal was not called dinner until the eighties—there were games, charades, tableaux, or Twenty Questions. Private theatricals, pantomimes, singing and backgammon sped the evenings. Supper in the seventies was usually at five, dinner at one. Breakfast was a hearty if not heavy meal. It was this period which saw the introduction of oatmeal, commonly called "grits." And such a beginning was followed by steak or grilled kidneys, fried potatoes, eggs, toast, marmalade, biscuits and coffee. Usually straight through the winter there was buckwheat cake and sau-

7. In the first half of the nineteenth century, Empress Eugenie popularized the "Empire-style" evening dress, which flared out enormously because of the crinoline skirt: "a mechanical device to magnify the wearer and also to emphasise the triangularity of the skirt." See C. Willett Cunnington, *English Women's Clothing in the Nineteenth Century*, (New York: Thomas Yoseloff, 1958), 186, 221.

sage. Oleomargarine and butterine were just making their appearance on Pittsburgh tables, following the establishment of the early meat packing industries. Wines were not commonly drunk at meals. In fact, more than one Pittsburgh bookcase or statuette of Power's "Greek Slave" concealed a bottle of Bourbon and ice water for that after dinner interim when the men "repaired to the library." It was not uncommon for the men to do the marketing, a basket on one arm and a cane hanging from the other. In fact no "well-bred" man dared go out without a cane. It was cause for anguish in more than one minister's family at Christmas lest the father be presented by his congregation with another gold-headed cane.

Pittsburgh in the seventies picked up the popular jokes, songs and slang of the day. It was the era of "The man on the Flying Trapeze," of "Dad's a Millionaire." One can scarcely believe that mature, strong, and otherwise sensible men sang and whistled such songs as "I'm Tired Now and Sleepy Too" on the streets of Pittsburgh. Other popular songs of the day that regaled the ladies and gentlemen who gathered round the parlor piano in the evenings were "Down In The Coal Mine," "Little Robin," "Tell Kitty I'm Coming," and "Lilly Dale" survived as one of the most popular songs of the decade.

In this era of Pittsburgh's social life the phrase "You're welcome" was not considered polite rejoinder to expressed thanks. The phrase sanctioned by best usage was not at all. But in more jocose moments of salutation on a shopping expedition, a call, on a tennis lawn, or in a theater foyer one was usually greeted by a friend's "Ah, There, My Size," or "Ah There My Complexion." The masterpiece of jocoseness, however, was the chestnut bell. This 1870s phenomenon, in shape like the nut for which it was named, dangled from a tiny chain on the gentlemen's waistcoat or from the ladies' shoulders. When the wearer wished to check a tall story or a piece of annoying badinage, or otherwise gently to razz his companion he jiggled the chestnut bell and exclaimed "Ah, chestnuts." If a little stronger admonition was called for it was expressed by the slogan, "Pull Down Your Vest and Wipe Off Your Chin."

With the 1880s, the churchly piety of the community began to sanction dancing. Parlor and public halls were gay with the two-step, the polka, the mazurka, the schottische, the quadrille and the Virginia reel. Lafayette Hall on Fourth Avenue was a popular resort until it became disreputable. It was rented for church and lodge and bazaars and fairs, for balls and for public lectures.

As the century drew to its close, a kind of end-of-the century gaiety took hold of the people. Dancing was established as a perfectly respectable pastime. Card playing had broken out in spite of churchly taboo. In the nineties the Negro community began to follow the custom of the white community in taking summer vacations out of the city. Theater going, also, had been sanctioned in the mid-eighties. The grandparents and the older parents of families of today could see at the Academy of Music a great panorama of "Pilgrim's Progress." The Grand Theater and Library Hall were the two family houses for theatrical performances of the higher grade. To either of these gentlemen took their wives, sisters, and sweethearts. The Bijou had just been rejuvenated and opened with glitter and ceremony. At Library Hall pretty Emma Abbot played regularly a week's stand. Christine Nileson too appeared here. Here too Carncross and Dixie's minstrels put on their very elaborate shows, Carncross as middleman, Dixie as end man.

Pittsburghers, like everyone else in the eighties, "adored" Lotta.[8] They also "adored" the young John Drew and Maurice Barrymore in "The School for Scandal." They saw Charlotte Cushman play her farewell to the stage as Nancy Sykes and Meg Merrilees. They sat excitedly through the shocking can-can introduced from Paris and thought of by most people as fit only for rowdy nightlife crowds. They watched the glamorous Mary Anderson, who preceded Mary Pickford by forty years as Our Mary, do Perdita and Parthenia. Edwin Booth gave performances of Iago, and Joseph Jefferson turned away crowds from Rip Van Winkle. Kate Claxton stirred pitying tears in Two Orphans. And Olga Nethersole entranced her audiences in La Cigale.

Between Minersville, The Hill, and Allegheny visits were made largely on foot. Pittsburghers began early in the 1880s to use horses and buggies in everyday life—businessmen for driving to work in the mornings, families for recreational driving in the evening. But as most Negroes were barbers, coachmen, or hod-carriers, and most of these occupations averaged seventy-five cents or a dollar a day, they did not own horses and carriages for sometime. And so, as one Pittsburgher relates, when wealthy families were away from home, or when the carriage was not in use on the coachman's day off, he might come around with the family carriage and take his family or his friends for a drive. This was considered "a grand fete." But for picnics which were held in Baum's Grove or at Friendship Grove at the corner of Negley and Penn Avenue young men hired buggies to drive their sweethearts, and families hired carriages.

Through the 1880s and 1890s every church organized its literary society, or oratorical society. Contests, inter-church debates, and spelling bees were popular, and prizes were awarded. Closely associated with the churches, also, were the big picnic dinners, which was the custom of the older people to hold once a year. To these, baskets filled with food were brought—hams and chickens, pies and cakes, fruits and jams. Cloths were opened on the ground, people spread their coats and jackets on the grass, sang grace and feasted.

In the 1880s croquet became popular and in this sport, too, it was the custom

8. Lotta Mignon Crabtree was a child dancer in the mining camps of California in the 1850s. She earned a fortune from enchanted, and besotted, miners who tossed coins to her and her mother; she went on to become the belle of Broadway.

for coachmen and maids, when the families for whom they worked were out of town, to invite their families and friends to play croquet on the lawn, at the homes of their "masters." For men quoit pitching was popular. This could be indulged in their own yards, in vacant lots, on spare ground in the neighborhood, or on the quieter streets and alleys.

Bicycle riding also became popular, the men taking to the high "bone-shakers" with the huge front wheel over which they were often pitched head first if they struck a pebble or a rut in the road. Only a few women took up bicycle riding.

The gayest feature of the end-of-the-century decade was the cakewalk. Hardly a dance or ball or bazaar or fair was held that did not have as its climax this colorful, graceful feature. Arm-in-arm the dancers or cake-walkers marched. Women in rose satin trains, hair in pompadour, scarves fluttering, sometimes carrying parasols, gold chain bracelets dangling heart-shaped lockets at their wrists, men in high hats, boutonnieres in their lapels, canes under their arms or twirling like drum majors' batons down the room, around the sides, meeting again, coming down center, the lines dividing and turning, crossing and threading, weaving intricate figures as they followed their leaders under the gas lamps, or the newest electric lights. The "Afro-American Notes" of the time says:

> The cake-walk has come to stay. Far from being a source of amusement solely among colored people, it has finally invaded the parlors of the leaders among white social society in various portions of the country, and several enterprising professors of dancing have been quick to announce their ability and readiness to teach persons intending to compete in cake-walking the necessary pose and stride, all of which goes to show that while walking is common to most of us, cake-walking is one of the fine arts requiring the service of a professor in order to perform it with grace and skill. Its origin is shrouded in mystery, but more than a century ago, it was a divertissement among the French Negroes in Louisiana. It is probably a close imitation of some of the old French country dances, with such eliminations and additions as only the fun-loving minds of a volatile Creole could suggest. It resembles several of them in form. From New Orleans it spread over the entire South and thence the North. It was found a convenience to the plantation Negroes. At a cakewalk a man might legitimately show his preference for a woman and thus publicly claim her for a wife. In effect the cakewalk was not different from the old Scottish Marriage which required only public acknowledgment from the contracting parties. So this festival became in some sense a wooing, and acceptance or rejection, and a ceremony. This explains its popularity with the blacks, outside of its beauties, with the accompaniment of music

which is competent at all times to command Negro support. Cakewalking has improved, as do most things that are constantly practiced. It has lost its old significance in the South. Negroes now get married, when they do at all, in the white folks' fashion. It has however become a pantomime dance. Properly performed it is a beautiful one. The cake is not much of a prize, though the Negro has a sweet tooth. At the summer resorts along the seashore the guests take to cake-walking quite as readily as they do to shore rides and quite often the judge for the occasion is chosen among the colored folk of the hotel or boarding house. It is not assumed that the colored people are better pedestrians than are other people, but it is a fact that surrounded by their friends, inspired by lively strains of music, and spurred on by the consciousness that there are rivals watching their every movement, they amble, glide, and strut along with a grace, ease, and dignity which no amount of dancing school coaching could ever teach them to do. All of them hail to the cakewalk! It means erect bodies, graceful poise, easy and courtly gesture, for all of which there is ample room among all classes of society in the country.

In the past decade of the old century, caste and social rank was intensified in the community. It attempted to organize. The "Afro-American Notes" in the *Pittsburgh Press* said on January 24, 1897:

SOCIAL LINE DRAWN

An organization among Colored Society folks, to which only Pittsburghers to the manner born will be eligible, is quietly talked of on the streets. The organization, (It might be called, possibly, the SONS AND DAUGHTERS OF PITTSBURGH) will admit to membership no person not born in the city, and thus forever sealing the admission into the select society of Pittsburgh. And why should not Pittsburgh have an exclusive Colored set of her own making? Boston, Chicago, Philadelphia, Louisville, Cincinnati, Atlanta, New Orleans, and other cities have such organizations.

Social clubs multiplied rapidly in the 1890s. There was the Four Hundred Social Club of 30 members, The Monday Night Social Club of 30 members, The Twin City Social Club, The Frederick Douglas Club with 200 members, The Frances Harper League, The Riverview Athletic Club, The Walker Social Club. There were besides these more than a dozen lodges of Odd Fellows, Masons, Pythians, and other organizations. The Odd Fellows had a hall on Arthur Street that seated 300 people, another on Irwin Avenue that seated 200, Cole's Hall on Frankstown Avenue in the East End seated 400, and the Masonic Hall at Fulton and Wylie seated 100. These halls were used for all kinds of entertainment on a scale that they could accommodate. When conventions met or larger meetings were held larger halls were rented in various parts of the city.

Newly rich families spent money recklessly. Their doings were discussed in the papers and by word of mouth among servants in their employ. About this time society news began to occupy considerable space in the papers. What women wore at the races on Brunot's Island, or the opera, what wines were drunk at the Peacock's balls, that Mr. So-and-so ran a special train with fifty guests from Pittsburgh to San Francisco to break the record for which Mr. Blank had spent $100,000 a month before, that Mr. Somebody who had just made a fortune in steel was giving automobiles as gifts to his friends, and Mr. Newly Rich Somebody Else smoked dollar cigars encased with a band engraved with his newly designed coat of arms. Hamburg grapes were bought at five dollars a pound and seats in the last row of the gallery at the theaters sold for three dollars to see Sara Bernhart or hear Emma Calve in "Carmen." In spite of chronic unemployment and poverty, many people had plenty of money, especially if they were engaged in business, associated with the booming steel industry recently organized as the United States Steel Corporation, or in businesses patronized by the newly rich.

The social life of these years is vivid in the memories of men and women of late middle age in the 1940s. Among certain elements life took on a flashing color and devil-may-care dash. There was a sporting crowd that made and lost money easily through contact with the white sporting world of the time. Frank Sutton's place at Sixth and Wylie was a rendezvous for these people. At Sutton's Hotel and Saloon, Bert Williams would come on his Pittsburgh appearances, or Cole and Johnson. Here Jack Johnson met the local sports fans, fighters, and promoters. The Colonial House at Logan and Wylie was a quieter eating house run by Mr. Robb. It boasted a large Negro staff, an excellent chef, and was frequented by wealthy whites and theater people who wanted to get color and jokes. Here Eva Tanguay was a frequent visitor. Here new dances were invented and picked up by white performers and the "fast" whites who already were dramatizing Negro life in their own way.

This was the golden age of the Lower Hill in its more brazen aspects, an age when sporting women walked down Wylie Avenue "with a thousand dollars worth of clothes on their backs," wearing diamonds in their ears and on their fingers and wrists worth more thousands, carrying or leading pedigreed bull-dogs worth $300 or $400. In the many cardhouses run in the districts, high stakes at crap and card games were won from visiting white salesmen or white theater people by this gaming, sporting element, men and boys who were waiters or bus boys at downtown restaurants where they made contacts with their white customers.

Burke's Hall was another of the "spots" of the time. At Burke's on Thursday afternoons, girls who were maids in white families danced with "gigolos" of the time, and the best-dressed boys of the Hill. Here too inventive liveliness of the dances produced new steps that were carried to other places and to the stage, to vaudeville and musical comedies. Burke's, of course, was considered by "refined" Negroes as no place to go, as a place only for "kitchen mechanics."

Farrell's across the street was thought more respectable. Farrell's was run by a white man, E. K. Thumn. Farrell's set a standard of Negro deportment. In the pool-room on the upper floor only Negroes who were "dressed up" could play. But men who worked around the wharfs in overalls, or down at Newell's as waiters or janitors went into Farrell's by a side door to the basement to shoot pool. Or they could change clothes there, and then "cleaned up," they might join the players on the upper floor. Many men who drove wagons about town, and the many roomers who had no home life and came direct to Farrell's from work, took advantage of this service. Farrell's was a kind of club where mail could be left or called for.

Wylie Avenue in these first years of the century was a neighborhood famous for street fights and gang depredations. The old political fights of the eighties continued as a rowdy tradition. Bruisers were active chiefly to prevent voting. A man who knew this life and neighborhood tells how before starting out on their excursions they deftly weighed their collection of guns to see which fit their hands the best. Wylie was visited by gangs from other parts of the city, too, like De Rosa's gang from East Liberty. It was the battleground of Kid Bates' gang. Kid was a remarkably quiet fellow, but his gang was notoriously dangerous. There were also the Terry Boys, who appeared at most of the Hill dances and were not to be played with.

At times of industrial difficulties this notorious aspect of the Lower Hill was intensified. On days when men were idle or laid off, they drifted to the Hill from other sections of the city, clustered at the street corners and saloon doors, eyed the passers by or the other idle, disgruntled men, and asked, "Where are these bad Niggers I hear about." Or a Hill man would walk up and ask of a stranger, "Buddy, what you looking for?" "I'm looking for one of these tough guys I hear live on the Hill." "Well, you've met one." And they would start down the hill headed for the wharf. That evening's *Press* or *Leader* would contain one of the usual accounts of the fights between Hill Negroes. But no editorial would comment on the homelessness, joblessness, strained nerves and frustrations that made such scenes possible.

About this time, an old resident of Pittsburgh says, there occurred a number of disturbances on Sundays. Gangs like the Red Onion Gang objected to Negroes walking up the main street of the Hill, and thought they should keep to the alleys on their way to Bethel Church. One Sunday a river man was stabbed to death. Then several Negro men and a few of their white friends met on a quiet August evening at the head of Wylie as if by accident. Here they made a quiet demonstration of shaking hands, walked together down Wylie to Sixth, and the street was safer after that for the average pedestrian. Such a state of affairs is denied by some families who lived in the neighborhood, but agreed to by others. The story is told by one of the men who participated, the story is told for what it is worth.

Folkways have changed little since the generation of 1910. For ten years or so after the First World War, the Hill assumed in a minor way some of the aspects of Harlem. "Night spots" sprang up in small nightclubs where Negro musicians played and sang, where drinks were served and one kind or another of high pitched amusement was pursued. Some of these were frequented by whites who made anything pertaining to the Negro a cult and thought of Derby Dad's,[9] Paradise Inn, or the Devils Cave as places "to see Negro life" or "life on the Hill." In some of these, good music could be heard, and there was a folk life, but in these "spots" whites were not welcomed. Such "spots," however, have almost disappeared in the last few years.

Negro life in Pittsburgh as elsewhere is still highly organized, in the church, fraternal and secret societies, civic and social clubs. Fraternal and secret societies appeal not only by social, sickness, and death benefits offered but by the fact that a people, unable to participate sufficiently in the general political and social life, through these organizations exert powers denied them elsewhere. One Negro says,

> In them, large numbers of people find opportunities to achieve eminence, a desire and a need deep-seated in every human being. In these groups a man may become a Grand Patriarch, a Grand Sword-Bearer, a Noble Grand, or a Grand Pursuivant, a most worshipful Grand Master, or Thrice Potent Grand Master, and in the auxiliaries a woman may be a Daughter Grand, or a Worthy Councilor. To talk of, and to deal with Grand Special Communications, Decorations of Chivalry, Royal Purple Decrees, and such things is, for many members, to touch glamour and to achieve exaltation.

Twenty years before the Civil War, fraternal life had been organized in Pittsburgh. The Negro Masons paraded each year on St. John's Day, at mid-summer. They held banquets, with their band playing, and conducted other festivities. The Odd Fellows, also, had organized lodges. Early lodges of the fraternal organizations noted as effective committees of correspondence among the Negro

---

9. The original manuscript misprinted the name of this establishment as "Derby Dan's"; it has been corrected to "Derby Dad's" for the published edition.

communities throughout the states, more effective even than the churches, for they frequently took more decisive practical action, whereas the churches trusted largely to prayer and supplication. The original Grand United Order of Odd Fellows admitted Negroes to membership, but barred light-skinned men. In New York City the Negro membership objected to this and a number of brown-skinned men went to London to secure a charter. The white membership thereupon sent a delegation to London to forestall the granting of the charter, but it arrived too late. On their return to New York, white membership withdrew from the lodge and took the name of the Independent Order of Odd Fellows. The two names persist to the present. The Knights of Pythias were organized among Negroes later than the Masons and the Odd Fellows. In the 1880's the Grand United Order of the Woodmen of the World and the Grand United Order of True Reformers developed large memberships in Pittsburgh. By the 1890's fully a score of lodges were active in the city: The Mount Moriah Lodge, No. 36, F.A.A.N; the Sheba Chapter, No. 13, N.R.A. Masons; The Cyrene Consistory; the Cyprian Lodge, No. 13; The Morning Star Lodge; The Naomi Court; The Lily of the West and others.

Annual sermons, picnics, and dinners have become social traditions. The yearly sermon preached to the Elks, the Odd fellows, the Masons, the Pythians, the True Reformers, the Woodmen, the Rebeccas, the Eastern Stars are attended en masse by the respective organizations. On a Sunday morning in spring, when marching weather is good, each lodge meets at its hall. The men in full blue and white regalia, plumed hats, clanking swords, glittering epaulettes, and golden insignia march to church, their gold-tasseled flags and silk banners flying in the sunlight, their bands playing. Women in white dresses, white and violet capes thrown over their shoulders, wearing cordons of gold-lettered ribbon, carrying flowers and flags and banners also march to church for their yearly sermons.

The annual Elks Jubilee is another spring tradition. At Elks Restaurant on the Hill and at the Elks Hall in East Liberty, fraternal conclaves, dances, parades, sermons, and card parties enliven the days and nights of the jubilee.

Each summer the lodges hold a union picnic at West View Park, with the usual basket spreads, programs of parades, games, sports, and dancing. Olympia Park is crowded one day each summer with thousands at the Baptist Union picnic. All day the miniature railway, the merry-go-round and the roller-coaster carry laughing, shrieking crowds. Families spread their basket lunches on the tables. Games, races and dancing make the day and night lively.

The Armistice Day dinner is a benefit for the Home for Aged and Infirm Colored Women. For many years this dinner was held in the old City Hall above the Market House. The dinner was looked forward to by the entire community as an occasion for old friends to meet, talk of the past, reassure themselves of each other's health and well being, and speak of those who had died since they had last met. The Old Ladies of the home were guests of honor. They were brought, wearing their "best bibs and tuckers," in machines supplied by the churches. The hall was festooned with streamers and decorated with plants and flowers. The old ladies from the home displayed their quilting and needlework. Each table was in charge of a social sorority, a club, a church group, or a civic organization. The traditional turkey dinner was served—mashed potatoes, peas and beans, cranberry sauce, celery, jellies, pickles, slaw, hot rolls, pie, cake, ice cream, and coffee. The Armistice Day dinner, during the past few years, has grown smaller, is now held at the home on Lemington Avenue, and has changed its tone somewhat. It is still, for the occupants of the home, a link with the past, an event to look towards as their future shortens. *The Pittsburgh Courier* said of the 1940 dinner:

> COMMUNITY ANTICIPATES HAPPY
> DAY WITH THE CHARMING OLD
> LADIES OF THE HOME
>
> Annual Autumn Tea and Musicale at
> Home for Aged and Infirm Colored
> Women Will Claim Interest of
> Many—Dinner and Program
> from 2 until 7
>
> The local community anticipates a pleasant afternoon at the Home
> for Aged and Infirm Colored Women in Lemington Avenue,
> Sunday, September 22, when the management will hold its annual
> Autumn Tea and Musicale. Dinner will be served two until seven.
> The delightful old ladies who grace the home look forward to this
> annual festive occasion with great eagerness. They welcome
> visitors, especially the large number that crowd the home on such
> occasions. They meet many of the friends of the old days. Some
> have grown up from children. Others have become old like
> themselves . . . some they have forgotten. But every smile, every
> gesture of friendliness warms their hearts and they live again in a
> busy world just for a day.
>
> The committee makes a point to have a grand dinner. There is a
> variety of delicious main courses and entrees from which to choose
> . . . a delectable assortment of pastries and puddings and ice-cream.

The annual Mardi Gras of the Lucy Stone League raised money for scholarship students in the universities and colleges. The old Labor temple on Miller

Street was gay with streamers, colored lights, and refreshment tables. On the stage a coronation throne was set for the king and queen. The Mardi Gras was the traditional masked ball, pierrettes, clowns, milkmaids, cowboys, devils, peasant girls, gay with whistles, rattles, bands, and confetti. The gallery was packed with spectators. The Grand March ended with the crowning of the king and queen. Dancing went on until morning. At decorated booths one bought peanuts, pop-corn, ice cream, hot-dogs and pop.

The former glory of Frog Week has largely departed. But for years Frog Week was a national social event. It was preceded by days of preparation for house guests, of preparing frocks and gowns, of planning luncheons, dinners, break-fasts, picnics, and card parties. Then cars arrive from all over the country—Chicago, Louisiana, New York, Denver. But the spirit of Frog Week is best given by an account in *The Pittsburgh Courier:*

"HOPPIN" WITH THE FROG:

It's a great privilege to be in Smoketown these Frog Week days: The sun is shining, the town is jumpin' with the gayety that usually abounds during this much talked-about week.

I sailed forth Sunday for the opener. The salutation to the week was mag-nificent. Frog George Gould emceed to masterly fashion the Symposium at the Y.M.C.A. Bill Curtis poured forth a full tide of eloquence that held his listeners at rapt attention. Young Luther Johnson painted portraits of song as his dad matriculates his magic flash bulbs and takes beautiful photographs. The fine musicianship of Mrs. Johnson is reflected in the piano and the larger crowed, colorful in the bright hues of summer, applauded vociferously.

There was a scarcity of visitors, in fact, the out-of-towners were conspicu-ous by their absence. Perhaps it is too early in the week as most arrive Mon-day and Tuesday. But Sunday I scanned the crowed for strange faces and I saw very few.

However, the old timers were there and some of the young timers. But I'll go into that under topic THRILLS FOR ME, ahem!

After the "Sym" the crowd gathered at Loendi and I hope I never smile again if it wasn't chattery and comphish![10]

THRILLS FOR ME!

BOBBING UP like a rare opportunity came C. D. Lowndes of Chicago, one of the first Frogs. C. D. looks grand, the years have caressed him as it

---

10. Spelling is as in original.

were, and he is in fine fettle. Sallie Fisher Clark of Dee Cee, whom we look forward to seeing every Frog Week, was among the visitors. She is house guest of the George H. Goulds. Sallie came to the Loendi in the evening in a long, princess gown and she is getting streamlined, believe me. Other old timers here for the obsequies of despair were Bill Lovett, also a Frog, and Eugene Cheeks of Cleveland, Arthur Dixon and his lovely wife of New York.

The Joe Boldens have a charming group of relatives here. Mr. and Mrs. Rexford Bolden of Roanoke, Miss Josephine Bolden of Salem, Ralph Coleman of Roanoke.

Mrs. Bolden is an AKA and teacher in Vecay[11] and Josephine is a recreation worker in Salem. There is a lovely Miss Charlotte Coleman of Roanoke and, bless my soul, if Booker Bolden, one time of this town and now of Roanoke, isn't here in all his smiling glory greeting the homefolk.

Perhaps by coincident, biggees tipped mightily in our town the past weekend.

Big Bill Lindsay from Chicago spent Saturday. Jo Finley Wilson, Czar of Mikdom, breezed in and breezed out Monday in a blustering cloud of Willkie-for-President enthusiasm. Maurice and Myrtle Dander drove over from the Big Town and W. G. Munns, their hosts, and all of us are threatening them like the Nazis the Jews if they do not remain the entire week.

In the meantime, THE ALPHA PHI ALPHAS gathered their creative minds around a Cotton Ball, and brought the socially fashionable a most entertaining and enjoying event. Perhaps I shouldn't say entertaining but when one looks at dozens and dozens of pretty girls garbed in colorful, cottons ala decolletes . . . it is most entertaining!

I think Pittsburgh has the most beautiful girls in the world, but that is another question.

The Alphas' invitations were quite unique . . . in the shape of the Greek letters "A.P.A." in the fraternity colors, black and gold with a tiny wad of cotton suggesting the type of party! The design was the creation of newly initiated Louis Fenderson of the poetic mind whose words of love have bestirred many a feminine heart.

Following the dance, somebody said 'breakfast' . . . and into the vast unknown the brothers and their lovelies disappeared. I was invited, but the invitation failed to carry an address . . . but who cares! The early dawning was made for the young. Family Style . . . and Bring us more of 'Em.

The Frog picnic was in family style, in fact, if you didn't have a family, you

11. Spelling is as in original.

were out of bounds. The younguns were numerous. They took charge of everything and for once, the fathers and mothers retired to the sidelines and looked on with beaming faces.

It was the best picnic the Frogs have given in many years. It was close-up, chummy, and friendly. It was an outing like you read about—tables laden with good things and everyone insisting that you dine. It was a happy display of good will with the Frogs passing out gobs of ice cream and cold drinks and the kids dancing the jitterbug for hours and hours.

I remember when Jack Denning and Billy Edwards Jr. were babies, and lo, and behold; they swung their partners in great glee.

It was amusing and "illuminating" so he'p me, to see the young generation taking hold of things. The Frogs should organize them, get them in line to follow in their footsteps, because they are the future Frog Week carrier-oners, believe me.

After the closing of the "Miss Pittsburgh" contest Friday night at the Roosevelt, there will be just two more events and Frog Week of 1940 will be over.

Champagne for Twenty-Five!

Dawned Thursday and Bob Williams (Robert to you) bid us to Loendi for 'lunch,' he said. Six-thirty and no minutes, we arrived, and lo! there was his wife, Norvella, home from Virginia, where that naughty broken ankle has kept her confined for many a day and week and month. She comes here now and then to look the town over and then retreats to her lovely home 'neath the shade of the Blue Ridge Mountains.

It was a party for Norvella, and what a party. Cocktails and champagne, five courses of delectable food and then several hours of merrymaking. Incidentally, Norvella mentioned that she and Bob had been married 32 years, giving us a new low-down upon the age of the handsome host.

The Sun Has Set UPON ANOTHER FROG WEEK.

And, we here in smoketown, pause and relax!

For six days and nights we have been going. Parties, parties and this thing and that finally landing at Loendi, the center of interest the entire week. And let me tell you "furrinere," without Loendi, we would be lost for that smart some place to go, so, give the institution a big hand!

Beginning where I left off last week Wednesday! It was the night the Matrons and Maids were hostesses to a beautiful party at Cottage Inn. M.&M. affairs are always up to the minute, and this 1940 event might be considered more streamlined in its loveliness. I don't know when I have seen more charming gowns, and the men, contrary to all conventions, came together along in everything under the sun. They just refuse to forego comfort for style and something should be done about it. But what?

But despite their "scenery," the party was most enjoyable. There was an abundance of frozen punch, a literal shower of roses, pleasant chit and chat of happy friends. President Mary Gould beamed upon the committees and members who officiated and au revoirs were reluctantly said.

Dawns Thursday . . .

AND WE MOTORED out to Olympia Park to hear Andy Kirk and Pha Terrell and June Richmond and Mary Lou Williams . . . and to watch the interesting group of youngsters who jittered and had so much fun. The breezes were cool and it was so pleasant we walked around the park several moments after the music had ceased. Sam Milai and Charles Richmond saw that everything ran smoothly.

Friday the Saturday Card Club

HELD FORTH AT LOENDI. Twelve tables were in play. A delicious luncheon preceded the serious business of card-playing, and then on to victory came the champions. The prizes were gorgeous. Perhaps you do not know that Ella Christian is the "chooser" of this club's prizes, and this year her choice was superb. Jewel Blow won first, a silk bedspread; Helen Phillips, second, lace covers; Agatha Simms, a compact; Hallie Woodson Brown, collar and cuff set. Mrs. Ira Lewis is president of the club and the members include Mrs. Rhona Truman, Mrs. Mary Gould, Mrs. Wilhelmena Butler, Mrs. Ella Christian, Mrs. Kathleen Douglass, Mrs. Ella Powell, Mrs. Gladys Garrett, Mrs. Gladys Curtis, Mrs. Jessie Vann, Mrs. Betty Butler.

Friday We Chose "Miss Pittsburgh"

Miss BEATRICE WILLIAMS is "Miss Pittsburgh"!

Beautiful "Bea" was chosen from twenty girls to go to Chicago to compete in the "Miss Bronze America" contest. Miss Edith Mae Mille is "Miss Alternate" and the third winner is Miss Marian Whitlock.

The contest was most spectacular and all of the girls looked marvelous. Judges Billy Howe, Lionel Hampton and Maurice Dancer declare they "enjoyed" every moment and I believe them.

Bea will leave Pittsburgh, Friday night. She will be accompanied by her mother, Mrs. Stanley Williams. While in Chicago she and Miss Mills will be the guests of the Afro-American Emancipation Exposition Commission. They will live at Poro Mansions, 4401 South Parkway, where arrangements have been made for housing and meals. They will be in the big town until the 26th, when "Miss Bronze America" will be chosen, and may Pittsburgh win.

SATURDAY SUPPER CLUB

THE MOST exquisite appointments marked the initial event of the Saturday Supper Club at Loendi Saturday evening. Less than fifty guests were invited to this exclusive affair, a supper dance.

Small vases of flowers centered twelve tables in the dining room. Flowers and ferns also decorated the parlors. Cocktails and hors d'oeuvres were served in the card room, then a luscious dinner interspersed by dancing proved most delightful. A photo of the members appears on these pages.

Of the Loendi Club *The Pittsburgh Courier* gives a history:

Loendi, the oldest and finest social and literary club in this city and one of the most outstanding in the country, was founded in 1897 by George Hall. Its social and literary objectives have attracted the most influential men and women in the country. Although, strictly a men's club, it has invited prominent women to speak at its banquets and symposiums, the fulfillment of its idea to serve the literary and social interests of its members. For years and years, Loendi has been the traditional "spot" for all things worthwhile. It has remained exclusive, though democratic. Joining its ranks has been looked upon as an achievement, and its membership boasts the finest men of the city.

Loendi's list of speakers and honored guests run the gamut of big names. Among these who have either been guests of the organization, or have spoken at some of its outstanding affairs are Judge Terrell of Washington, D.C., Mrs. Butler Wilson, Mrs. Lena Trent Gordon, Judge George of Chicago, Judges Josiah Cohen, Marshall Brown and Schafer of the Common Pleas court here; William H. Lewis of Boston, Dr. Emmett J. Scott of Washington, D.C., the late Booker T. Washington, Tuskegee, Ala., Charles Anderson, Geo. C. Hall, Bert Williams, Joe Louis, Dr. John Brashear, Rabbi J. L. Levy and countless others.

ILLUSTRIOUS PRESIDENTS

The club has progressed through a number of illustrious presidents. In years gone by, the parties and banquets at Loendi Club were not only the talk of Pittsburgh, they were the talk of the country.

Setting a standard for excellence in social affairs, Loendi Club achieved a reputation which has lasted down through the years.

Some of the former presidents who contributed to this illustrious and enviable record were George C. Hall, W. H. Patterson, Atty. Wm. H. Stanton,

Eddie Johnson, Captain C. W. Posey, Samuel Pangburn, Ollie Jones, James Peck, John Henry, John W. Anderson, Sylvester Jones, William E. Hance, Sr., Eugene Lewis, Robt. L. Vann and many others.

To these men, the club was all possessive and all enveloping. They maintained the high standard and the enviable principles upon which the organization was founded. To them goes the credit for developing and perpetuating the principles and ideals of the club.

The boat-rides of the Coobus Club,[12] of Frog Week, and of Holy Cross Church are summer classics of entertainment. The Homer Smith, the Washington, the St. Paul and the Senator, all decks crowded, a dance orchestra on second deck, bingo parties in play, bar and restaurant crowded, slot machines running, calliope playing, have swung out from the wharf, made the trip down the Ohio to Rochester or Rock Springs and back.

Social clubs bloom like the flowers of spring, springing up, lasting through a life of colorful gayety. Some are hardy perennials, blossoming into activity from season to season; some are passing annuals, flowering through a season or two only. There are the Sevilles, a young man's club that gives dances by invitation only. The Pierettes, Les Modernes, Le' Gai Femmes are young women. The Swelegants is a mixed social club. The Ducks, The Drakes, the Frogs' Wives, the Matrons and Maids, the Turf Riding Club, the Entre Nous, the Junior Debs, the Gay Hill-Toppers make the winter season lively with card parties, luncheons, and dances.

At the University of Pittsburgh, two men's fraternities—the Kappa Alpha Psi and the Omega Psi Phi—and two women's fraternities—the Alpha Kappa Alpha and the Delta Sigma Theta—go formal for Christmas and New Years or Pre-Lenten and Easter affairs. A number of business women have also organized a business sorority, the Zeta Phi Betas.

On the Hill at little bars, over sloe gin or beer, across wooden tables where chitterlings or hog jowl and turnip greens are the specialty, or at street corner of window-to-window confidence one overhears a colorful, native vernacular. It is so persistent that visitors and travelers soon come to understand it, just as one comes to understand his mother tongue. To many it has become a mother tongue, if perhaps only a step mother. Some go out deliberately to acquire it, but usually one breathes it in gradually just as one breathes the odor of beer or gen-

---

12. Coobus Club is a nickname for the Cooperative Business Club, an organization that fostered business development in the Hill, and also provided entertainment in its building. Frank Bolden, interview with author, July 25, 2002.

eral stuffiness, or the incense burned in front rooms or in the many spiritualist churches that dot the Hill. It comes rhythmically and vividly from the lips. It explodes and crackles and sings and hums. It is created and dies and rises from its own ashes in new forms, brilliant with racial imagery, prismatic with race moods.

"Jive," it is called in its own vernacular. And in this vernacular you are asked, "Are you hipped?" if the speaker wants to know whether you understand. If you are a smart person here, you are "a hip cat"; if you are a smart woman, you are "a hip chick." Here you "feed the joy box" by dropping a nickel into the electric victrola; a "Jew baby" (mulatto) dances with a "tea kettle blonde" or a "fast back"; a "chalk" (white woman) or a "gray stud" (white man) may look on from his corner, that is, may "case a pad." A man of no accounts is a "frone guy," a woman of similar standing a "frone frail." In this jive a man who is broke is "beat to my socks."

If a guy has "lead," he speaks of it in strange denominations; a "rough"— twenty-five cents; "deuce"—a dime; a "cropek"—five cents; a "lamb's tongue"— a dollar bill. Change under a dollar is "scratch," and a five dollar bill is a "fin." If you are "holding," you have money; if you want to borrow you say "let me hold." If you want to say "give me," you say "knock me back," or if you are going to get something you are going to "knock myself back some." Those who put on airs are "hinkty," and if you put up a false front you are "staffin." If a thing is perfect, it is "solid" or "my solid sender." If a thing is charming or "swell" it is "ready." If you ignore an acquaintance, you "play him cheap." If you are out to spend a lot of money, you are going to "jump up," or "kick up a little light sport." When you get high, you "blow your top," but if you do it on "reefer" or "gaga" (marijuana) you "bust your conk." And while you are having the time of your life you may be greeted with "kill your fine self." Much talk is "cheap beating," "beatin' up your gums" or "layin' your gamble." If you are waiting for someone, you are "stickin' pat," if you are leaving you are "cuttin' out" or "blowin'." Home is "pilch," bed is a "pad." Food or eating is "scarf." To "cop a nod" is to take a nap. "Dig you," says the friend who will see you later.

Every type and character has his name—a ready woman is "a soft"; a desirable one, "a mellow chick"; a play girl, "a killer-diller"; a white person, a "pink toe"; a woman worn down by life, a "beat broad"; a playboy, a "Lochinvar"; a sponger, a "solid drag"; an older person a "gay ninety"; a drunk, a "creampuff"; a policeman, either a "nab," "bluebird," or a "Johnny Nab." A beggar is "double trouble." A prostitute is a "stink." A conjure woman or man is a "doc mojo." A white woman is a "pink." A "joker" is a no good guy; a "rug cutter," a habitual attendant at rent parties; a "weed sucker," a smoker of marijuana. Smoking this drug is "blowin' gage." A cigarette is a "pimpstick." You "weave" when you pray;

you pray to "the big Jeff," and you get down on your "double deuces" to do so. A "freeby" is a free drink, a free dance, or anything else that may be free. To be "weak" is to be a fool. "Fast Mail" means a woman is waiting for you.

The depression and WPA have contributed to this vernacular—"a G-man" as a WPA worker, "international pay day" as welfare relief day, "wrapping paper" for relief check, "ocean paper" for WPA check, a "sitting squawk" or "Quawker" for stool pigeon, "tick-tock man" for time keeper, "Georgia Buggy" for wheelbarrow. If you are "usin' a spoon," you are digging with a shovel on a WPA project. If you are out of a job, you are "working for Pat and Turner."

This vernacular is not merely picturesque. It raises the daily lives of the people and shapes itself from the imagination and vitality of its creators. It grows inexhaustibly—one phrase is discarded and another is born day after day, the rest of life expressed in vivid imagery.

Small trades are plied on the Hill—not only at street corners—from stationary push-carts whose stock consists of an old grape basket full of carrots, a dishpan filled with tomatoes and a couple of dozen bananas but by men who push through the streets all forms of fantastic vehicles, and charm the buyer into purchase by rhythmic songs. The "Pie Man," for instance, a bulky sturdy ancient, his brown trousers strapped tight about his ankles, a white apron and peaked white cap giving a touch of the Chef, carries his chip basket from door to door calling:

> Pie Man! Pie Man!
> Here comes the Pie Man.
> Lady! Lady!
> Come and get your pies.

A tall, thin bent man whose trousers end at the calves of his legs and are held round his waist by a dangling rope, pushes a cart he had made from a discarded baby carriage and square shallow mortar box. To those families who have neither the storage space for coal nor enough money at one time to buy enough to store, and to those who buy a dime's worth of ice every other day, he delivers both, side by side in his home-made cart. And he calls:

> Coa'-ca—Coa'-Coa' Ice!
> Coa'-ca—Coa'-Coa' Ice!
> Coa'-Ice—Coa'
> Coa'-Ice!

The watermelon man who appears on the streets only when the fruit is in season, also has his songs.

Watermelon today!
Watermelon today!
Plug 'em an' try 'em
Before you buy 'em.
Big-fat-watermelons.

This he varies after a number of renditions with another call:

Watermillons! Watermillons!
Red to the rind! Red to the rind!
Red to the rind and the rind red too!
Get your letter from home!
Get your letter from home!

The rind man is unique. When a dance is on at the Savoy he is sure to be found in the neighborhood. His territory is chiefly Center Avenue between Elmore Street and Chauncey Street the neighborhood. Here he peddles his bacon rinds. Cut into strips and fried, and sold from a large chip basket, to create thirst just as pretzels are eaten at bars. And his song is:

Skin man! Skin man!
Get your skins from the skin man,
Big skins, little skins,
Fat skins, skinny skins,
Get your skins from the skin man.

Numbers have taken hold of the Hill as thoroughly as any other part of the country. Thousands play them daily—Negro and white, men, women and children, church members and reprobates, executives and menials. At one time, two figures dominated numbers playing on the Hill—Woogie Harris and Gus Greenlee. The legacy they have left since their retirement is hundreds of stations, concealed in restaurants, fish shops, and news stands. The system by which they are played is elaborate. Besides the hundreds of stations, many sub-stations exist, and for those who do not or cannot get to the station, "writers" are sent out on regular routes to write up customers. All slips are written in triplicate—one for the customer, one for the sub-station and one for the central office. Pick-up men go to sub-stations to pick up the slips and the money collected from the writers. Writers get a percentage of the write up and another percentage of any hit made on his book. Each sub-station gets a percentage on its turnover. A deadline is set at which all numbers must be in the main office—an elaborate organization of adding machines, counting machines, clerks, stenographers and accountants. The deadline is necessary protection against foreknowledge of the number to turn up that day, either from last minute consultation of stocks, or by a phone call to the stock exchange. The central station pays off all hits; the hit money goes back to the sub-station and from there is delivered on the route by the writers, or is called for. Operators are called bankers and if a number is played particularly heavy a banker will replay it by sending out writers not known to other bankers. As a side-line bankers print and distribute their familiar green and orange tip cards that hang in so many newsstand windows on the Hill. Special tip envelopes are also sold for as high as a dollar each in which numbers are printed as a result of juggling figures on the law of chance or average. Spiritualists are also consulted to whom fees as high as $5 are paid for likely hits. These people usually protect themselves by predictions of what combination will hit within ten days. Combinations consist of three way and six way numbers, indicated by "boxing," or enclosing a number with a three-sided bracket and writing the amount to be played on each number beside it.

At one time a carnival man won great attention by allowing himself to be "buried alive" for sixteen to eighteen days in a coffin on the ground owned by the Carney Post of the American Legion. A tube was run down to the coffin for air, and those who wanted a tip paid twenty-five cents to call down and be answered by the man who existed in a "state of catalepsy" or "suspended animation."

Many people claim to make a living playing the numbers by these various devices. "Run Downs" are popular—that is numbers of three digits in which the last one is changed for each play—123, 124, 125, 126. Or a hundred numbers may be played at one cent apiece. Long run downs of penny numbers are popular.

Among those inhabitants of the Hill, the Strip, and the North Side who often find wages insufficient to meet the living expenses, house socials are still frequent. Once a week, so long as a crowd "holds," and less often as it falls away, these affairs are held to meet rent or other obligations. On known paydays at department stores, and mills, or on WPA projects, crowds gather in little rooms lit with a single 25-watt red bulb. Strangers are not usually welcome. A piano player is engaged from 9:00 p.m. to 4:00 or 5:00 a.m., usually for all he can eat and drink; liquor, "cut" or bootleg, is sold. Chitterlings or barbecued pork sandwiches are served in the kitchen.

"Reefers" can be had for fifteen cents or a quarter, depending on their strength. The night is passed in slow-moving, close dancing under the dim light. Partners are seldom changed. "Muggin" is the order of the night. Upstairs there is the usual crap game or the Georgia Skin game. Fights and brawls are common. The favorite instrument is a three-inch blade switch knife. An average take-in at such affairs may range between fifteen and twenty-five dollars.

When life becomes gray and tight, and one day after another uncertain in what it will bring; when illness could be warded off or cured if only one had a better equipped purse that would allow medicines; when the future seems dark and the past inescapable, it is a human impulse to turn to folk remedies, charms, and divinations that developed in the childhood of the human race, seek some hope of relief from present stress. This accounts for the prevalence of spiritualists, crystal gazers, the Black Art and remnants of voodooism. On the Hill, even these aids, however, demand cash; and since constant recourse to their powers costs more than a ten-cent or twenty-five cent dream book which can be taken from the drawer or from under the mattress and consulted daily, dream books sell by the thousands. Lurid and plentiful they lie or are hung in shop windows, in grocery stores, novelty shops, pawn shops, restaurants, or news stands, offering cheap solace and anesthesia.

The practice of folk medicine is common. Burns and scalds are treated by "blowing." A child with rickets is measured with a string tied in knots at each joint and the string is burned. This is repeated at intervals and on the last day of treatment the child is tossed from the woman who treated it to its father. An old tooth, once extracted, is buried to cure toothache; potatoes or other perishable goods are rubbed on warts and burned or thrown into the river to decay, and in sympathy the warts are supposed to do likewise. Or a parcel of pebbles of the same number as the warts is rubbed over them and thrown into the river.

Belief in luck determines what must be done or what must not be done in many matters. Many of these practices are not special to the Negro, but are shared with many groups. He does, nevertheless, practice them or believe them. There are lucky days on which to begin things or end them. Lucky numbers ensure success in one venture or another; unlucky ones warn against evil or misfortune. Luck, too, is associated with many crooked or twisted objects—a stick, a spoon, a finger, even a hunchback or cripple. One must not walk under a ladder, or allow a post to separate one from his walking companion. Belief in triples dictates that if a dish is broken, luck will be bad until the number is raised to three. If on leaving the house you return for something forgotten, you must return three times to avoid ill luck.

Spittle is still believed to possess lucky power. Shopkeepers spit on the first takings of the day. A bargain may be met by spitting as well as by taking a drink. Children spit on their palms and say "spit, spit, tobacco, spit. Tell me where my lost ——. is." If the first Monday morning visitor is a woman, that is a bad omen; you must lay your hat on the floor beside a chair and spit in it.

Housewives and shopkeepers believe that if the first visitor or customer of the day is a very black person, luck comes with him or her. Many are those who carry and believe in the power of the amulet—the rabbit's foot, the lucky penny with a hole in it, the lucky band. And before his return to sea, a Negro sailor has been known to explore the Hill for a baby's caul as a protection against drowning.

Perhaps the great movement of southern Negroes into Pittsburgh brought the practice of voodoo and conjure to the city. At any rate, in more than one house or back store-room these ancient rites still hold—vivid, even fearful to many participants.

That conjure and voodooism are distinct cults is not always recognized; and on the Hill, far from the southern springs that were the immediate source, they have both been modified, and new rites, formulas, and practices have been devised by fusing both. From a conjure woman who has a large clientele formulas for "fixing" people, for keeping a man, and for the "withering conjure" have been established.

To "fix" somebody: Go to the cemetery. Dig some dirt from the east corner. While digging say, "I am digging this for the Father, the Son, and the Holy Spirit." This must be done at midnight. Take home a handful of this dirt, mix it with red pepper and salt, and put it in either one of two places. If the person to be "fixed" lives in the house with you, put it under his mattress; if he lives in another house, put it beneath his front steps. He will be tormented the rest of his life, and will never be able to face you.

To "fix" some one as a means of protecting oneself from intended harm: At midnight, sprinkle salt and red pepper in three equal amounts into the coal fire. Each time you say, "in the name of the Father, Son and Holy Spirit," and you name the person. To keep a man (1)—Through the toe of a man's worn socks you put two needles; put two also through the heel. Fold the sock from top to toe and place it under the head of the mattress upon which he sleeps. To keep a man (2)— Get a little silk bow from inside his hat and roll it in the top of your stocking. As long as it stays there he'll follow you. To keep a man (3)—Clip several hairs from the head of the man you want to keep. Hide these under the inner sole of your shoe. He'll follow you as long as you keep them there.

For the withering conjure: Take several long hairs from the tail of a black horse. Take two thigh bones from a black cat. Dry these and powder them. Clip the horse hairs very fine and put with the bone powder. Put as much of this mixture as you can take up on the tip of a spoon and drop it in any food or drink. Whoever eats it will contract the withering fever. There is absolutely no cure.

Annual initiation ceremonies into "The Order of the Serpent" with all the ritual dances, music, and incantations are held on St. John's Eve. By signs, emblems, and symbols, initiates are recognized. Rumor has it that only descendants of African chiefs learn the innermost secrets of the Order. The general population is evasive on the subject, though the number of patrons of the several "doctors" is large among both Negro and white. Voodoo bags and Lucky Bags are easily obtainable in the Wylie Avenue neighborhood, at a general market price of $5, though the price varies according to the credulity of the purchaser and the ready money in his pocket. A voodoo bag is made of heavy twilled muslin, about 2 inches long, an inch wide and a quarter inch thick, tied at the top with white thread and topped with four rattlesnake rattles. It is filled with aromatic powders and spices, pepper predominating. A "lucky bag," which sells for the same price as a voodoo bag, will ward off demons and evil spirits, and will bring luck in business, social affairs, and especially love.

At various stores, if you know how, you may buy the ingredients for voodoo prescriptions—serpents' tongues, frog livers, bats' hearts, toad skins, various powders and potions. After the proper incantations have been woven about it, a cat's tooth left in the house of an enemy will ensure his torture by neuralgia.

On the outer fringe of the voodoo doctors are the male and female herb doctors. These are the usual intermediaries between the voodoo doctors and the applicant who wants advice. Knowing the penalties of practicing medicine without a license, they are wary. Their practice in no way competes with the masters of the mysteries, but supplements their work by imitation and discipleship.

Out of these habits and customs, these beliefs and sayings, will grow the future culture of the people just as it has emerged from spirituals and work songs and the older folklore. And from this material artists will create their poems and novels, paintings, and their songs when they become deeply conscious of it and understand it completely as the life pattern of a distinct nationality.

CHAPTER 13

ARTS AND CULTURE

———•◆•———

Typist: W. Funkhouser / Rewriteman: J. Ernest Wright /
February 26, 1941 / Final

From the days of the Theban Literary Society of the 1830's, organized by the Vashons, Pecks, Delanys, Woodsons, and others of the earliest Pittsburgh Negro families, to the Aurora Reading Club and the Saturday Night Club of present-day Pittsburgh, a current of interest in ideas, books, music, drama and, to a lesser degree, painting and sculpture has animated Negro life in the city. And to American Negro culture Pittsburgh has made definite contributions. Henry Ossawa Tanner is usually cited as the outstanding example. But J. B. Vashon, his son George Vashon, Rev. Abraham D. Lewis, Rev. Lewis Woodson, Mrs. Susan Vashon and Miss Matilda Ware, Martin R. Delany, Samuel Neale—these and others established cultural traditions.

Purchase of books and magazines, attendance at concerts and theaters, training in the arts, or advanced study in the humanities and the sciences have not always been easy, or possible, for large numbers of people. Economic handicaps and the existence of the color line in theater and concert hall have few restrictions. Unwritten rules in musical, literary, art, and historical societies, and unexpressed but understood disfavor among their memberships have kept doors closed to Negroes in some of the most highly developed activities of the white community.

A century ago Bishop Daniel A. Payne said to his friend Lewis Tappan that abolitionists were unprincipled agitators. The bishop declared that slaves should be educated before they were freed, so that they might be prepared to enjoy freedom when they achieved it. Lewis Tappan answered, "Don't you know that men cannot be educated in a state of slavery!" Just as strongly many Negroes say today that since the Negro achieved freedom, economic and civic restrictions have not been conducive to cultural maturity. Pittsburgh's primary concern was with industry. Its religiosity and the age-old blue law mood of the city have not been the kindest atmosphere for intellectual and artistic life among any groups that make up the city population—native whites, foreign-born white nationalities, or the Negro. Yet of all these groups the Negro has felt the heaviest handicaps.

Access to national Negro culture, however, has been made possible by constant appearances in the city of Negroes eminent in intellectual and artistic life. The Urban League, the Y.M.C.A., the Monday Night Forum and the Negro fraternities and sororities at the University of Pittsburgh have brought to Pittsburgh lecturers such as Dr. Max Yergan, William Pickens, George Carver, W. E. B. DuBois, T. Arnold Mill, Mordecai Johnson, Charles Wesley, Emmet J. Scott, Alain Locke, Walter White, and Negro women leaders like Alice Dunbar-Nelson, Lucy Delany, Mary McLeod Bethune, Mary Talbot, Alice Jesse Faussett, Louise Thompson, Thyra Edwards, Nanny Burroughs, Crystal Byrd Faucett. Poets and writers Countee Cullen, Langston Hughes, and James Weldon Johnson have lectured and read their poems. Marian Anderson, Roland Hayes, and Paul Robeson draw great crowds. Shirley Graham has spoken on her opera "Tom-Tom." Hazel Harrison, pianist; Camille Nickerson, specialist in Creole music; Lillian Evanti, soprano; James Rosemond Johnson, Louis Vaughn Jones, violinists; W. C. Handy, Helen Hagan, pianists; Florence B. Price, composer and pianist; Carl Diton, pianist and composer and singer; and many others are familiar to Pittsburgh audiences.

Between the Civil War and the Spanish American War, the community laid a basis for a broader social and cultural life than had been possible up to that time, and began a slow transfusion of culture between Negroes and whites. Freedom, citizenship, the ballot, erasure of the color line in public schools, these, with expansion of the population, geographic spread within the city, occupational expansion in the Negro community itself, the growth of a middle class, an increase in the number of college and university graduates, and a growth in the number of skilled and professional workers all resulted in an expansion of cultural activities. Development of women's clubs, of literary, dramatic, musical, civic, and social clubs showed that the Negro people were participating in the general movements of the times. One of the earliest and oldest existing groups to make organized efforts to promote cultural life in the community was the Pittsburgh branch of the Frances Harper League, which was formed in 1893 by Mrs. Rebecca Aldridge and Mrs. Sadie Hamilton, in order to organize the limited leisure of a group of very busy women so that they might devote part of that leisure to reading and discussion of ideas. The club programs promoted discussion of public questions, of music and the other arts, and of various crafts.

In this last decade of the nineteenth century and the first years of the twentieth century, many clubs sprang up. Most of them lived a short life. A few have survived. The Wylie Avenue Literary Society of the 1890s had three hundred members who met monthly to listen to lectures on Temperance and similar subjects. As the Homewood-Brushton Negro community grew, the Homewood Social and Literary Club, the Emma J. Moore Literary and Art Circle, and the Booker T. Washington Literary Society of Carson Street Baptist Church were formed. The "Afro-American Notes" in the *Pittsburgh Press* reported topics for discussion: "Why not Live for Five Score Years," "Etiquette in Public Conveyances," "Responsibilities of Christian Brotherhood." Miss Gertrude Gordon, columnist on the *Press*, spoke on "Institutions of Correction." Mr. Robert L. Vann, later editor of the *Pittsburgh Courier*, spoke on "Benefits Derived from Literary Work."

Within a short time there existed the Four Hundred Social Club, the Hesperia Club, the Gilt Edge Social Club, the Rosebud Social Club, the Twin City Married Ladies Circle, the Laman Social Club, the Columet Club, the ladies Magnolia Circle, the Volunteer Social Club of Allegheny, the Four Whitecaps Progressive Club, and many others. In 1903 the State Federation of Colored Women's Clubs was organized and most Pittsburgh organizations affiliated. In 1907 more than twenty-five Negro women's clubs were active. In 1914 the majority of them affiliated with out-of-town groups to form the City-County Federation of Colored Women's Clubs. About 1912 the Pittsburgh Literary Union was formed by representatives of nearly every lyceum and literary club in the city to organize programs and activities for the year.

In 1897 the Loendi Club was organized among Negro men in Pittsburgh. Its object was the advancement of the Negro in the city, and socially, the entertainment of men of wide reputation and ability. It purchased a $10,000 property on Fullerton Street, which is maintained as its present headquarters. It is the oldest and most exclusive men's club in the city.

The Aurora Reading Club was organized in 1898 at the home of Mrs. Hallie Lovett by a group of busy women who realized that only some kind of organization of their time would allow leisure for intellectual and cultural activities. The present membership consists largely of the daughters of the charter members. The club has devoted its meetings to discussions of topics and books of the day. In 1912 they discussed "The Indians of the Great Northwest," Kipling, and "The Recessional." In 1926 they were discussing the "Life of Washington Irving" and selections from Irving, and Cornwallis and the Colonial Congress, "Successful Negro Business Women," and "Colored Colleges." The 1937 program offered such subjects as "The Supreme Court and Its Responsibilities," "Present Unrest in the Labor Movement," "The Far Eastern Situation," and "The Awakening of China."

The So-Re-Lit Club (Social, Religious, and Literary), organized in 1911, typifies much of the work of women's clubs in Pittsburgh. Their dinners and lawn fetes raised funds for work in Shadyside Hospital and philanthropic homes, for annual contributions to the National Association for the Advancement of Colored People, the Y.M.C.A, the Community Fund and other agencies. The club has also presented speakers and lecturers.

For some years the Tuesday Study Club met at the Wylie Avenue Branch of Carnegie Library. An early notice says it was

> composed of a number of intelligent and earnest minded ladies of the race, whose forays in Literature are directed by Miss Howard, the Librarian. . . . A review of "Portrait of a Lady" was an intellectual treat. An address on "Tolstoi and His Writings" was interesting and ably compiled. The Club Prophecy created considerable amusement, it showed that Dan Cupid had been quite busy.

The Saturday Night Club is a recent organization of men and women of professional, college and university training who meet for critical study of technique of the modern novel and drama, discussion of books on the race question, and the appreciation of poetry, music and painting.

The Pittsburgh chapter of the National Association of Negro College Women discussed "Music and the Appreciation of it," "The Problem of the Unmarried Mother and What We Can Do about It in Our Community," "Charm as Depicted by Proper Dress," "The Place of the Negro in Social Work," and "The Negro in the Field of Art." It also conducted a Race Relations Forum and a Psychiatric Forum.

Early in November 1847, the *Pittsburgh Post* ran a short item about a "Negro Tragedian" which said "The Negro Tragedian had a large audience on Friday evening. . . . They say he performed his part well." This earliest mention of the Negro in Pittsburgh theater is not clear. Dramatic reviewing in Pittsburgh in those days was at a low level. Obviously the appearances of a Negro tragedian was news but apparently of insufficient consequence to name the actor.

A few months later, in January, *The Daily Commercial Journal* reported that "Mr. Jones, the colored tragedian, is to give one of his unique and pleasant entertainments next Monday night. Other young colored men are to appear on this occasion, and new recitations are to be given by Mr. J." The *Dispatch* was a little more specific:

Jones, the well known colored tragedian assisted by another young man designs giving his imitations of celebrated players at Philo Hall this evening. The Duquesne Band will add to the attraction by their music. Jones' exhibitions have been well attended and we understand that his talent in that line is great.

Several days after the performance, the *Commercial Journal* reported that

> Mr. Jones, the colored tragedian, had a very good house the night before last. The Duquesne Brass Band were present on this occasion. They play excellently well, and with a little more experience will be one of the best bands in the city or in the country indeed. The musical talent of the Negro race has often been remarked; and the proficiency of this band, composed entirely of colored men with their brief practice and many disadvantages, is another proof of the fact.

This seems to be the extent of notice given to Negro theatrical life in Pittsburgh for many years. No doubt the Negro acted as seldom on Pittsburgh stages as on those of other cities. Negro characters appeared in plays. Slavery, of course, was the subject of drama, and minstrelsy had brought the Negro as comedian to the stage. But for years Negro characters were played by white actors in black makeup. Such characters were chiefly slaves, ex-slaves, or servants. The first performance in Pittsburgh of *Uncle Tom's Cabin* was given at the Old Drury on January 28, 1854, and was repeated in November as a "spectacle." Later Mrs. Stowe's *Dred*, another spectacle, was produced there in a version specially written for the occasion.

The Fugitive Slave Law and the controversy it aroused was the theme of a play announced in the *Post* in 1856:

> We are to have on Monday evening next Mr. Jamisson's new play of *The Fugitive Slave*. It would naturally be supposed from the title that this play was one of the trashy Uncle Tom batch of bastard dramas, but we are credibly informed that it is one of brilliant literary merit, abounding with graceful measure, beautiful figures and high thoughts expressed in poetry. Let everyone who has a desire to see American dramatic literature take a stand in our own country, rejoice the heart of the author-actor by their presence on Monday evening.

But the Civil War and freedom began to release the dramatic talent of the Negro, as it released the expression of so many other aspects of Negro life. About 1870 Mr. George Gross, a resident of Allegheny, went to England for a time, returned, claimed that he had studied acting there, and organized a dramatic group, and in a hall in old Germantown or Dutchtown presented such melodramas as *Ten Nights in a Bar Room.*

The theater has been as difficult of access to the Negro actor in Pittsburgh as it has in any other American city. But in dramatic reading, where the individual can express himself without the elaborate sets, costumes, and technical equipment of the theater, Negroes who might have turned to the stage have found a well paying profession. In the last decade of the nineteenth century, Thomas Ewell opened a School of Elocution and Dramatic Arts in the East End. Mrs. Susie Lee, Vensuella Newsome Jones, and Miss E. Marie Coleman have trained readers who have performed for clubs, churches, and fraternal societies.

Interest in dramatics resulted in 1898 in a production of *Macbeth* by the Lend-a-Hand Club of Allegheny. But community annals record nothing more of this kind until twenty-five years later when Richard B. Harrison, teaching and coaching for a year in Pittsburgh, produced *Damon and Pythias* at the Pershing Theater, and *The Merchant of Venice* with himself as Shylock, at Schenley High School. A short time later Vensuella Newsome Jones produced *A Mid-Summer Night's Dream* outdoors and again produced *Damon and Pythias.*

In these years American Negro drama was hardly formed. Little repertory was available that portrayed Negro life from a realistic point of view. Training in the acting, directing, and technical production of standard plays was too difficult for the average Negro either in dramatic schools or the professional theater. Dramatic clubs were chiefly social clubs.

Dramatic activity, like so much else, grew within the church, organized both for recreation and to raise church funds. Out of the clubs which performed in the churches or in available small halls grew most of the amateur groups in Pittsburgh. The Carron Street Players of Carron Street Baptist Church, and the St. Benedict's Roman Catholic Church still exist as church groups.

A score of amateur groups have been active, among them the Entre Nous, Nightingale Arts, Imperial Arts, Blue Ribbon, Pen and Masque, Olympian Players, Enco[1] Art Players, the Talley Amateurians, The Urban Players, Latimor Players and others that have come and gone.

Miss E. Marie Coleman, who has taught elocution and dramatics for some years in Pittsburgh, says:

> For fifteen years there was a great deal of amateur dramatic activity in Pittsburgh. And there have been good possibilities for development of Negro dramatics. The community has been interested. People wanted dramatics, especially young people. Audiences were easy to find for plays that were done. Seventy-five and one hundred dollar houses were usual at twenty-five

1. Later in the chapter, this art league is referred to as "Emco."

cents a head. Even at fifty-cents admission we could crowd the school auditoriums and library auditoriums. And that was over a broad range of territory,
in the East End, at Homestead, at Carnegie, Pa. and at Braddock. But efforts
were too scattered to realize the full possibilities of Negro drama.

There was a variety of repertory, most of it plays with a lot of fun in them
because that seemed to be what the people liked and it was easy to get young
people out to rehearse them. Most of the plays were given to raise funds for
churches or the proposed hospital or the various homes. Sometimes groups
were asked to give particular plays, like the pageant "America Yesterday and
Today," which the auxiliary of the Livingstone Memorial Hospital asked for,
or "Uncle Tom's Cabin," which one of the churches wanted to give when it
was being given around the city by white groups. Some members of the
church became indignant over a church giving such a play.

Then of course there was "Scrap," which Mr. Lett of the Urban League
wrote for the National Convention of the Urban League. It was given for a
definite reason. It dealt with the difficulties facing Negro youth when they get
out into the white world and look for jobs.

There hasn't been much interest in drama for the sake of drama. The object of the Negro Drama League was to stimulate such interest. That was why
we invited speakers from the University of Pittsburgh, Carnegie Tech Drama
School, Duquesne University, and the Pittsburgh Drama League to discuss
the subject with our audiences. That was why the Negro Drama League entertained the cast of "Green Pastures" in co-operation with the *Pittsburgh
Courier* at the Negro Y, when we had 800 people to welcome them.

But Pittsburgh audiences haven't accepted Negro drama very freely when
it has been tried. There isn't much argument about it now because none is
being produced. Pittsburgh Negroes did not like "Green Pastures." They
went to see it. They liked Richard B. Harrison and the rehearsal group. But
most of them thought it was a mockery of Negro religion They were proud of
Ethel Waters, too, and her acting in "Mamba's Daughters." But they thought
it was too bad that she couldn't find a better vehicle."

Out of the Metropolitan Baptist Church Dramatic Club grew the Olympian
Dramatic Club with a membership of twenty-five in 1923. "Our aim from our
foundation" says the founder Lynn V. Hose, "[is] the production of plays dealing
with Negro life, written by Negro authors. But we faced the usual two difficulties,
lack of repertory and an indifferent or a hostile public. However, with the appearance of Ridgely Torrance's 'Rider of Dreams' and later with Randolph Edmond's
plays the Olympians were able to break new ground with scripts that suited their
purpose."

In 1931 five dramatic groups combined to form the Negro Drama League. For three years the League held annual competitive performances. These performances brought forward the question of Negro drama by Negro players.

The League stated its object on its first program:

> These Players, organized from the membership of the Negro Drama League, have for their purpose, primarily, the stimulation of intelligent dramatic appreciation, with the hopes that the same may lead ultimately to the presentation of plays conceived, written, acted and produced by their own membership. They seek thus to offer to the interested members of the Negro Drama League, the opportunity for the development of Dramatic expression and talent. This effort should have the support of you, your friends and community.

The Negro Drama League's first evening of plays consisted of Elisabeth Hall Yates' "The Slave" by the Olympian Dramatic Club. The productions were for the benefit of the Davis Home for Colored Children. A Negro and white jury of award presented a loving cup to the winning group.

With the evenings' presentation by the Olympian Players of "The Slave," the question of Negro characters in drama, and presentation of realistic themes of Negro life in the theater were debated in *The Pittsburgh Courier*. The Olympians, like other Negro dramatic clubs, performed largely in Negro churches, and had been refused performance of "The Slave" in one church "because of its too great realism." The correspondence concerning their Drama League performance of this play is an interesting documentation of Negro culture in Pittsburgh. A correspondent wrote the *Courier* on April 20, 1932:

> Dear Sir:
>
> As a future citizen of America and the Negro Race, I wish to make known my reaction to the initial appearance of the Negro Drama League at Fifth Avenue High School, Friday, April 8, 1932. Knowing that you were one of the honorable judges on this occasion, I felt my reaction would be more seriously considered by one who attended the performance and is greatly superior to myself in qualifications to comment and criticize. I may also state at this point in my discourse, that I am not a member of any of the clubs represented on that occasion: thus my opinion is truly unprejudiced and unbiased in its scope. In addition to not being a member of any of the clubs, none of the members of the club which won the trophy are my enemies, which score as another factor preventing me from being rated as "jealous." Let it be further understood that I am not condemning your stand taken as a judge, because I do not know which way you voted so I hesitate to say anything on that I don't know.

Without further deliberation on the matter, I now present my frank opinion of the four plays presented that evening. I feel that "Rain" was the more superior from a dramatic standpoint as well as the general theme. I learned, however, through personal discussion, that one of its greatest criticisms was the extreme sentimentality of the production on a whole. The too-often-used curse words of Tim Baird was also recorded as a second major criticism, although it was obviously natural for a character of his appearance (in the play). I am not a personal friend of the person who portrayed Allie Baird, but I feel that her acting alone would merit a trophy; not forgetting however, that she was given honorable mention. All the characters in this play acted their parts supremely well and they deserve congratulations for that fact, if nothing else.

The play which stood out next in my mind from a dramatic standpoint was "The Slave," which as you know, received the prize. But it was far from being next in its general theme and atmosphere. The greatest and worst criticism I heard and agreed with, was the extremely noticeable over-acting of Mr. Roderick, the publisher. The second worse criticism was the only too-natural and seemingly degrading acting (if such it may be called) of Fern to have money at the cost of the honor of her race. Again, I would say about the characters in this play as I did in "Rain," that they all portrayed their parts very well. Let it be clearly understood, that it is not the characters of this play I am criticizing, because they only acted, I feel, as the play was written and intended to be produced. But it is the club's very poor choice of a play I condemn, knowing that it was to be a public affair thus assuring them there would be white people in the audience, since a few of the judges were white. Perhaps they were broadminded white people but who really knows? The majority of the audience didn't, I'm quite sure. The broken English constantly used and that "lazy nigger" phrase surely did wring my heart strings. When, Oh, Race, will you ever awaken to your ignorance in doing such things as this?

Another incident in this play which hurt me, occurred when Ms. Fern called Mr. Roderick the publisher and changed the harsh truthful phrases in his book just to satisfy his wife's greedy desire for money and clothes: Or in other words, he sacrificed the Honor of his Race for the petty, material things in life: I ask you reader, what price is the Glory and Honor of your Race? Is it MONEY and a low social standing? No! No! No! Let it not be that, to me it is the demand for equality and respect from all mankind. Oh God, when will my people see their mistakes and seek to amend them? I pray Thee, awaken them to a sense of Love, Honor, Fellowship and Duty to Thee, and to their race.

To me, this play only renewed and imbedded into the minds of the white people present, the readiness and willingness of the Negroes to do anything for money. Also the fact that we, as a Race, are only far enough advanced to enjoy and be able to produce such things as that: A poor point for Pittsburgh, I say. I am heartily in favor with all the opposers of the Amos 'n' Andy radio program, yet this production to my mind was equally as inferior if not more so since it was members of the Negro Race ridiculing themselves to the public. It made our heroic step taken to banish the Amos 'n' Andy program by submitting personal letters and signatures to your paper, seem to be a momentarily false pride—which I don't think it was in most cases.

The master of ceremonies announced after the program words to this affect: "tonight's performance marks the beginning of a New Era in drama among the Negroes in Pittsburgh." A New Era! New to our foreparents perhaps, not to us who call ourselves "modern intelligent, 20th century Negroes striving for advancement and equality!" Far be it from new. Oh, Race! my heart within me burns, when I think this step caused Pittsburgh, backwards her Race pride to turn. Frankly speaking, as I aforestated I would, I am truly ashamed of this first decision taken in drama among the Negroes of Pittsburgh. When I read of the future successes and affairs of the Pittsburgh Negro Drama League, I will always remember with shame and scorn the play which won the first prize for Negro Drama in Pittsburgh.

But alas: I must cease this, before the monotony becomes unbearable. I only wish my readers will forgive me for my perhaps too severe opinion, but the Almighty knows it is only the truth unadulterated and unbiased that I want the world to know. Pittsburgh, may it not happen again.

E.E.C.S.G.

To this letter a reply was published on May 3:

My dear E.E.C.S.G.:

After smiling through your lengthy criticism of the Negro Drama League's prize-winning play, "The Slave," I have been forced to classify you as belonging to the McKinney school of reasoning which is very unfortunate, indeed, especially if you are yet young. I am a member of the Olympian Dramatic Club, the club that presented the play entitled "The Slave." As a member of that club I feel that it is my duty to offer refutation to your unjust and narrow-minded criticisms.

First of all, you object to what you consider overacting on the part of Mr. Roderick, the publisher. That was not overacting, merely stressing a point. The southern white man has no respect or love for touching Negro property for fear of contracting a disease or soiling his lily-white hands. You know that and so did this actor.

I agree with you on the point that Fern wanted money regardless of race pride or honor. But she was ignorant; she was uneducated. Fern had learned the power of gold; she knew that it would materialize her dreams. What did she know of race pride or honor? Born in the South and not enjoying the enlightening advantages of an education she was a victim of circumstances and environment. She was not responsible for her lack of race pride. Fern represented the ignorant mass of Negroes who are impeding our progress: that mass to whom talk of Negro advancement and progress is like Abyssinian dialect.

Of course, we know it was to be a public affair and yes we expected white people to be present. But what of it? Are we a race, to allow the likes and dislikes of white people to determine our actions? Whether they were broadminded or not should not make any difference to us. If it made them color and feel uncomfortable to see themselves portrayed as cruel and unsympathetic toward Negroes why should you worry? If it made them realize that the Negro is rising to assert his rights why should we feel ashamed? As a dark race we have respected the white man's presence already too long. If we expect recognition, if we expect consideration from the white man then we must face him squarely and have our say. Talking among ourselves in a club meeting or convention and then smiling at your Mars Tom will never advance us. Think it over.

About that "lazy nigger" phrase to which you objected. It can be heard on every street corner, in every dance hall and in almost every Negro home—yes, I've even heard it used among college students! Certainly that was not the first time your heart-strings were so painfully wrung from the effect of that phrase. I'll wager that you use it yourself! You are only wasting your words and emotional energy when you raise a cry to God pleading to Him to awaken your Race. Why not set the example by first awakening yourself. If you are desirous of seeing your Race advance then step to the front and lead. Don't call on God and expect Him to do the work. That is probably the Negro's most detrimental characteristic. He prays and prays but does nothing for himself. Rather thank God after you have helped to do the work.

You feel that Mr. Lawrence turned traitor to his Race when in despair he desperately told the publisher that he would accept his offer. But consider the motive, Mr. Lawrence did not sell his Race's honor to satisfy his wife's greedy desire for money. He sacrificed his life's ambition for his love for his wife. And what act could be more noble? Remember, deep and true love has often changed the course of history.

If, as you think, the play has renewed and imbedded into the minds of the
white people the readiness and willingness of Negroes to do anything for
money; then it has also aroused the pride and race spirit and shame of the
Negro. It has instilled within him a determination to launch an extensive
clean-up campaign that will result in the development of a new and educated
race of Negroes. No longer will our progress be obstructed by the ignorance
of Fern, but in her place will arise a broad-minded, educated militant Mr.
Lawrence type of youth who will turn her back upon gold and sally trium-
phantly forth for the sake of the pride and honor of the Negro race.

Edward W. Brown

About this time Rese McClenden wrote in the *New York Times*:

There have been any number of efforts to build a Negro Theater, but each
effort always ended in failure. The reason chiefly has been due to the fact that
all groups in the field believed that the use of an all-Negro cast constituted
the creation of a Negro Theater.

Now what makes a Negro Theater is not so much the use of Negroes as
the selection of plays that deal with Negro life, faithfully presented and accurately delineated. Any other approach is doomed to failure.

The recent company at the LaFayette is a case in point. This company
presented a series of plays that included "The Front Page" and "Sailor Beware." After three weeks the company gave up. The reason is that there is no
Negro audience of sufficient size to support a theater in Harlem. In the immediate sense that is true, but this does not mean that a substantial audience
cannot be tentatively presented "Waiting for Lefty." Over 4,000 people
turned out, by far the largest audience of people that ever attempted to see a
play in Harlem. This piece was not written for Negroes, but a few changes in
the script made it highly adaptable for our purposes. It proved beyond a
doubt that a theater can be developed that will cater successfully to Negroes.

It proved also that Negro Theater operated by Negroes as a cultural experiment, based upon a program of social realism could be established on a
permanent basis. Such a theater could in the course of time alone create a tradition of any national group. It is possible within such a structure to develop
not an isolated Paul Tebessen, or an occasional Bladsoe or Gilpin, but a long
line of first-rate actors. With this belief, the Negro People's Theater, which
was organized about six weeks ago on a temporary basis, has decided on a
permanent form. This announcement has created wide interest among other
theater groups and elicited immediate praises of support. The Group Theater, the Theater Alliances, the New Theater League, the Theater Guild, the

Theater Union, the Theater of Action and others have unreservedly endorsed it.

The result of the controversy over the Olympian's production of "The Slave," Mr. Hooe, director of the play said, "was a step in the direction indicated by Mrs. McClendon. The Drama League was thrown into a controversy among its own groups over the question of dialect plays, plays dealing with Negro life and whether the League should or should not present Negro plays. The result was that the second annual competition, April 1933, was devoted to plays with Negro themes; Ridgely Torrance's 'Rider of Dreams,' Paul Green's 'Your Fiery Furnace,' Mathew's 'Trette,' and a script written by a member of the group and dealing with prejudice in a southern jury."

The third and last year of competitive performances sponsored by the League was devoted to plays by white authors. "In order to please everyone, we had decided to alternate with successive year," the league members said. This last year's productions were John Galsworthy's "First and Last," Werlinger's "Real People," and "The Valiant." The League conducted symposiums on drama, exhibited models of stage sets, started a class in stagecraft, and entertained the cast of "Green Pastures" at the Center Avenue Y.M.C.A.

At this time, too, contact was begun with white groups. The Olympian Players and the Drameontra Players exchanged performances. The San Drama Players at Sandusky Street Baptist Church and the Olympians also exchanged performances.

The Negro Drama League had been founded in part because the Pittsburgh Drama League had refused admittance to the Olympian Players, either to membership or to their competitive festivals. In 1935, however, the Olympians broke down the color bar in the Pittsburgh Drama League for the first time in twenty-five years, entered the annual competition with "Breeders" by Randolph Edmonds and won the popular acclaim prize. In 1938 the Olympians won second place in the radio competition of the Federation of Non-Commercial Theaters with the same play. In the Federation's 1939 contest they won first place with "Lov'd Does You' Understand?" an anti-lynch play.

Mr. Lynn Hooe says of Negro drama and dramatics activities in Pittsburgh:

Any amateur group in Pittsburgh that is independent of an organization which demands certain types of plays, and that is therefore free to experiment with repertory and methods of production has never been able to do these things because money has always been such a problem.

The theater is still too much just entertainment or a means to raise money for clubs and churches—that's the first and only attitude toward theater among Pittsburgh Negroes. Plays like "The Cat and the Canary" or "Gas-light" go over big. They are melodramatic and can be given spectacular pub-licity that will attract crowds. Some one not long ago suggested we give "Hedda Gabler" or "Craig's Wife." But another member of the group said such plays are above the level that our people can understand. Even in the legitimate theater the main thing that attracts the Negro is a well-known name or personality.

In the autumn of 1935 the Negro Drama League conducted the Little Theater off Court Square, in the auditorium of the Chatham Street Y.W.C.A., where monthly performances were given.

Next year this venture and the Negro Drama League were dissolved and the Emco Art Players and the Olympians joined the New Theater, a group of non-professional white players who had rented a theater on Miller Street in the lower Hill district. Here a training school for the theater was operated by professional theater workers.

New Theater with mixed Negro and white casts presented Odet's "Waiting for Lefty," Paul Peter's "Revues," Alice Ware's "Mighty Wind A'Blowin," "Union Label," and Irwin Shaw's "Bury the Dead" throughout western Pennsylvania, and at Youngstown, Ohio, for discussion forums, clubs, fraternal organizations, trade unions, and mass meetings.

For three years the Urban League sponsored the Urban Players, who gave the first radio broadcast of the Negro play by Negro players, Paul Green's "The No Count Boy," and who made one attempt to present Negro drama dealing realisti-cally with contemporary Negro life. The play "Scrap" was written by the Indus-trial Secretary of the League and dealt with the difficulty Negro youth faces when it leaves school to find a place in industry.

Sporadic productions have been given of musical revues. The *Courier* spon-sored a revue with Ethel Waters as guest artist at the Nixon theater. The Urban League presented a revue at Syria Mosque. The Livingstone Memorial Hospital Board sponsored a patriotic pageant "America Yesterday and Today" at Greenlee Athletic Field. Other church pageants have been numerous.

The most recent phase of Negro theater history in Pittsburgh is the effort of the Center Avenue Branch (Negro) of the Y.M.C.A. to develop a Negro Theater as part of its community activities. Here the Olympians, the Race's and the Latimor Players for two years gave in the gymnasium monthly presentations of one-act plays.

MUSIC

Of the arts, music has been most widely practiced and most fully developed by the Pittsburgh Negro. It was fostered by the church in choirs, religious and secular quartets, choral groups, and in concerts by Negro artists. The growth of American Negro music has consequently had its Pittsburgh phases. The early plantation shout and breakdown came north to Pittsburgh with the fugitive slaves and persisted almost to the present. As minstrelsy and later as musical comedy Negro music dominated the theater for some decades. The sorrow songs or spirituals had their Pittsburgh exponents. Ragtime, jazz and swing have in succession enlivened nightclubs, cabarets, dance halls and radio. Bands and dance orchestras have flourished. And most recently choral groups and a symphony orchestra have assembled highly trained musicians.

The church has exerted an indelible influence on musical taste, composition, and performance. Pittsburgh choirs have improvised spirituals and still do so occasionally. The rhythms, harmonies, and improvisations of work songs and of the un-concertized spirituals have carried through from their originals to jazz and swing, both in composition and performance. The introduction of music into the Negro schools in 1869 and the teaching of music in public schools after segregation was abandoned have developed an ideal range of musical ability and appreciation. Increased attendance of Negro students at musical institutes and conservatories has refined and matured such ability and appreciation.

Precisely how music was made and what kind was made in the early community there is little way of knowing. Casual mention of "the famous old choir of Wylie Avenue Church" is about the extent of comment[2] except for a notice or two of a brass band that played for some festivities. Whether Pittsburgh congregations, like those in Baltimore and Philadelphia, opposed the first choirs because they sang by note we cannot tell now. According to Bishop Payne, many of the "old people" of Philadelphia Bethel "particularly some aged sisters who professed sanctification, were so greatly offended" by the first concert or "vocal soiree" held there in 1841 that they said "The devil has got into the church" and "they left Bethel and never returned to her communion." Excitement was so great that the bishop had to preach a sermon in defense of sacred music. At Baltimore Bethel Church, however, a choir was in popular favor in 1843, although instrumental music was not introduced until 1848 or 1849 with a concert of sacred music accompanied by instruments. The songs were composed by the pastor

2. "The extent of comment" probably refers to comment in the local press, especially the column "Afro-American Notes," which appeared weekly in the *Pittsburgh Press*, and which covered local events, including many musical recitals and performances.

and the music composed by Dr. Fleet, a musician of Washington, D.C. The accompanying instruments were a piano, flute, guitar, and bass viol. A little later a second concert was held "accompanied by seven—musicians. And Bishop—this concert of stringed instruments not—the violin could be used with great effect in the service of the Lord."

Organs were not used in churches until the Civil War years. The organ was not introduced into Bethel at Baltimore until 1864. No choir was organized in the churches in Washington, D.C. until 1843, and organ music was not introduced into Washington until 1864. Opposition to choral and instrumental music in the church came from those "who cared only for those 'corn field ditties' which could produce the wildest excitement among the thoughtless mass. Such persons are usually so because they are non-progressive, and being illiterate, are consequently very narrow in views of men and things. A strong religious feeling, coupled with a narrow range of knowledge, often makes one a bigot." This, too is the statement of Bishop Payne. He adds that "the membership of our church in the enlightened city of Boston was so intelligent that they regarded the introduction of the choir and the organ as an advanced step in their religious public worship (in 1867)." Although a choir had sung in the New York church since 1830, there was no organ until 1861, and even then it met strong opposition.

When choral music was first sung in the churches, some of the ministers or even members of the congregation wrote words and music. For one Children's Day, Rev. Benjamin T. Tanner, then editor of the *Christian Recorder* and senior bishop, wrote words and music for five numbers. Dr. Tanner's was called "Our Father's Church." Bishop Payne wrote the words for an "Easter song," to which Rev. Levi Coppin wrote the music. Coppin also wrote "Consecration of an Infant Daughter." Elder William G. Alexander wrote three pieces, "Personal and Home Consecration," "Consecration Home," and "Reveal Thyself to Me."

From descriptions of early residents and from accounts of church services it is apparent that the praying and singing bands of which Bishop Payne disapproved in his ministerial travels were as characteristic of Pittsburgh as of any other vicinity. The bishop was intolerant of such music because he thought it unfitting for worship. Musicians and students of folklore realize now that the music of those praying and singing bands influenced later music and were themselves folk music of that period. The bishop says:

> I have mentioned the "Praying and Singing Bands" elsewhere. About this time I attended a "bush meeting" where . . . after the sermon they formed a ring, and with coats off sung, clapped their hands and stamped their feet in a most ridiculous and heathenish way. I requested the pastor to go and stop their dancing. At his request they stopped their dancing—they remained gig-

gling and rocking their bodies to and fro. This they did for about fifteen minutes. I then went and taking their leader by the arm requested him to desist
and to sit down and sing in a rational manner. I told him also that it was a
heathenish way to worship and disgraceful to themselves, the race and the
Christian name. In that instance they broke up their ring; but would not sit
down, and walked sullenly away. He replied: "The spirit of god works upon
people in different ways. At camp meeting there must be a ring here, a ring
there, a ring over yonder, or sinners will not get converted." Among some of
the songs of these "Rings," or "Fist and Heel Worshipers," as they have been
called, I find a note or two in my journal which were used in the instance
mentioned, As will be seen, they consisted chiefly of what are known as
"corn field ditties":

"Ashes to ashes, dust to dust; If God won't have us, the devil must."

"I was way over there where the coffin fell; I heard that sinner as he
screamed in hell."

To indulge in such songs from eight to ten and half-past ten at night was
the chief employment of these "Bands." Prayer was only a secondary thing,
and this was rude and extravagant to the last degree. The man who had the
most powerful pair of lungs was the one who made the best prayer, and he
who could be heard a square off. He who could sing loudest and longest led
the "Band," having his loins girded and a handkerchief in hand with which
he kept time, while his feet resounded on the floor like the drumsticks of a
bass drum. In some places it was the custom to begin these dances after every night service and keep it up till midnight, sometimes singing and dancing
alternately—a short prayer and a long dance. Some one has even believed it
the "Voodoo Dance." I have remonstrated with a number of pastors for permitting these practices, which vary somewhat in different localities, but have
been invariably met with the response that he could not succeed in restrain-
ing them, and an attempt to compel them to cease would simply drive them
away from our Church.

Pittsburgh has disputed with several cities the claim of having afforded the
social milieu from which came the first musical entertainment of the Jim Crow
type which rapidly developed into Negro minstrelsy.

The Ethiopian melodies popularized by Thomas Dartmouth Rice, "Daddy
Rice," and the various burnt-cork singers known not only as minstrel companies
but as opera troupes were not produced by the Negro people, and did not grow
out of the life of the Negro. They reflect the nineteenth-century white man's patronage of a people achieving, in the years in which such entertainment was
popular, the first marks of national cohesion. And by their "gentle" and "kindly"

treatment of such national aspirations they hoped to "keep them in their place." Although northern whites, Pittsburghers as strongly as any, strove with fiery and courageous enthusiasm to help the black slave achieve freedom, once he was free they were loath to grant the full achievement of those ideals of human equality, economic, social and cultural, which had actuated the abolitionist movement. At first the free northern Negro was helped into humble jobs, to form humble churches, to sing humble songs, but then he was in large part disregarded and then actually opposed in his own attempts to achieve political, economic, social and cultural progress.

The social and cultural status of this newly cohering black nationality is symbolized by the names given to him in literature and music for some time, names which the American Negro justly resents—darky, pickaninny, Rastus, Sambo, Bones. The name which T. D. Rice chose for his song and dance act and for his prototype of the Negro as delineated in arts for many years afterwards, the name Jim Crow, has come to designate every obstacle to American Negro life. This type devised by Rice and popularized by the minstrel troupes survives today as the stereotype conception, fostered not only by white writers, singer, and artists, but unfortunately by many Negroes.

Pittsburgh, during the decades when this stereotype was being popularized, was at its busiest. In the 1830s and 1840s, it was a transportation center through which thousands of travelers passed daily by stage, covered wagon, and river boat. Through its tree-lined streets omnibuses rattled over the big cobbles, guided by top-hatted drivers. At its stone-paved river wharves hundreds of white steamboats were tied. Up and down their gang planks Negro wharf laborers and deck crews rolled hogsheads of sugar, barrels of potatoes or whiskey or oil, and carried sacks of wool or cotton. Smoke curled from the funnels, the engines beat heavily, wheels churned the water, bells clanged and whistles piped. And to ease the backbreaking, arm-wrenching labor, which the Negro workers were glad to get, they sang. Their songs were strongly accented to make the heavy movements easier, co-ordinate them with each other, and to work in groups more easily. And the words were creatively picturesque because this was the chief creative activity the singers found. From this heavy labor came the movement, the dress, the music of the Negro wharf laborers and the deck hands, derisively called mudsills and roustabouts. But the real river- boat songs were in great part disregarded by white entertainers who devised caricatures of them to amuse white audiences.

Robert Peebles Nevins account of the first performance of Rice's Jim Crow act, this performance being credited to Pittsburgh, is characteristic of one aspect of Negro life in Pittsburgh in 1830.

A Negro attendant at Griffith's Hotel on Wood Street was called Cuff. He was one of those unfortunates compelled to eke out the wages he earned carrying baggage to the steamboats by such fantastic means as holding open his mouth for boys to pitch pennies into, from three paces away. Rice, a crafty showman, took Cuff to the theater, borrowed Cuff's clothes, and when the curtain rose jigged onto the stage as an impersonation of the well-known Pittsburgh character, to sing his Jump Jim Crow. The act created a sensation. It spread to every American city and to London as well. It did more to launch and perpetuate the travesty of the Negro wharf laborer and the Negro worker generally than any single item perhaps.

Imitators of Rice's impersonation soon organized themselves into groups known as minstrels and opera troupes. Hundreds of performances by those companies were given in Pittsburgh, as in most American cities. The Sable Troubadours, Christy's Minstrels, the Empire Minstrels which were later known as Williams' Original Operatic Groups, and the Sable Harmonists all appeared here time after time at Wilkins Hall, Apollo Hall, or the Odeon Theater. The Empire Minstrels at one time ran for five weeks. Several so-called Ethiopian companies are said to have been organized in Pittsburgh, either partly or wholly consisting of Pittsburgh performers. The Ethiopian Warblers and the Ethiopians are said to have been entirely Pittsburghers, and exceedingly popular for "the high quality of the musical performances in Apollo Hall."

Against this background the songs of Stephen C. Foster became famous. Some of his earliest compositions were written for T. D. Rice, E. P. Christy, and members of the Nelson Kness Great Original Sable Harmonists. Foster as a child had gone to church with the family's Negro servant to hear the singing and as a youth listened to the stevedores singing on the Monongahela wharf. Foster, with other boys of the neighborhood, fitted up a theater in the Foster carriage house, where Stephen starred in singing "Coal Black Rose," "Jump Jim Crow," and similar songs. The proceeds of these performances were used for tickets to the pit of the Pittsburgh Theater from where they saw Junius Brutus Booth, and Edwin Forrest, while Negro patrons, the Vashons, the Pecks, and the Delanys "to add to the comfort of the frequenters of this part of the (gallery) house," were restricted to two boxes on the left hand side.

When a patron of the Odeon Theater complained by letter to a Pittsburgh paper of the discomfort of walking up three flight of stairs to hear Christy's Minstrels, he also suggested that Mr. Andrews equip his Eagle Ice Cream Saloon for such performances. Mr. Andrews did. He sold Ice Cream tickets at 12½¢ a piece, a cover charge, to hear performances and hired Nelson Kneass as manger of the shows. Kneass organized The Original Kneass Opera Troupe, consisting of a former Sable Harmonist, and several Pittsburgh singers. For those shows Stephen C. Foster wrote "Oh! Susanna," which became the marching song of the forty-niners on their way to the gold mines and the farm lands of the west. For

Kneass he also wrote "What Can a Fairy's Dream Be" and "Way Down Souf," with its illegitimate dialect, as well as "Old Uncle Ned," and "There's a Good Time Coming."

Foster said of his first songs: "I had the intention of omitting my name from my Ethiopian songs, owing to the prejudice against them by some, which might injure my reputation as the writer of another style of music."

But Foster's nostalgia for romanticized Negro cabin life in the South caught on, and his songs were sung all over the world. Then Foster said, "By my efforts I have done a great deal to build up a taste for the Ethiopian songs among refined people." The Fosters were Democratic and strong anti-abolitionists.

Foster has been credited with displacing the minstrel interpretation of the Negro as a loud and flashy individual with the "kindly and devoted darky" typified by "Old Black Joe." His songs are said to be broad enough to represent the Negro, the South, and the longing for home of human beings everywhere. He is said to have "sung for the Negroes" and to have influenced their music, also to represent the race. One of Foster's earliest lines is, "white folks I'll Sing for You." Foster and minstrelsy did not grow out of actual Negro life in Pittsburgh or in the points east, west or south. Foster has not been generally accepted by the Negro people, nor have the minstrel songs. Foster and minstrelsy reflect the mid-nineteenth century white man's attitude toward Negro life. Nevertheless Foster's songs, though they made the resignation and the spuriously traditional faithfulness of the slave lyrically charming, did nevertheless help change the popular conception of the slave as a chattel to that of a human being.

Of the work of Joseph Miller and the "famous Choir of Old Wylie Street Church," nothing is known except this slight reference, but the choir must have been famous in the 1840's and 1850's. Their singing followed the choral type instituted by Bishop Payne perhaps more than it adhered also to evangelical hymns.

The age of the sorrow songs or spirituals was represented by Fred Louden and Benny Thomas, members of the original Fisk Jubilee Singers. Louden had been trained by Samuel Neale, who taught in the Pittsburgh schools and privately promoted musical activities by "getting up" concerts at Lafayette Hall. At these concerts his pupils sang choral works interpreted with solos, duets, quartets, instrumental music and readings. Mrs. Mary Liz Hill was a well-known soprano at Neale's concerts.

In the later age of minstrelsy, when the Buck and Wing, the Coon Song, and the folk blues were featured, Callender's Georgia Minstrels frequently appeared in Pittsburgh. In the company Willie Lysle, a Pittsburgher, sang as a female impersonator with a fine soprano voice. Lysle, too, had studied with Samuel Neale and wrote music for orchestra and chorus.

In the age of ragtime, vaudeville, and musical comedy, when "The Octoroons" played, a Pittsburgh woman named Kate Dimey sang in the company. The "Creole Show" with its chorus of Negro girls, W. C. Handy with "Mahaly's Minstrels," demonstrated in Pittsburgh the re-appearance of true Negro rhythms and harmonies and true Negro technique of singing and playing. Black Patti's "Troubadours" brought Sisseretta Jones with her operatic repertory and one of the first fine Negro choruses. Bob Coles' "Trip to Coontown," Will Marion Cook's "Clorindy and Cole" and Johnson's "Shoofly Regiment" all gave Pittsburgh opportunities to enjoy this aspect of American Negro music.

The popular songs of those days were as popular in Pittsburgh as anywhere else. "Go Way Back and Sit Down," "Ta-ra-ra-Boom-de-ay," "Smokey Moke" and "I don't Care If You Never Come Back," were whistled on street corners and sung to the rhythm of slapping shoeshine cloths. "There'll Be a Hot Time in the Old Town Tonight" came with the Spanish War. A number of Pittsburgh Negroes carried on to the vaudeville stage the barber shop quartet, the clog, the Pigeon Wing, and the minstrel ballad with the stale, "Pseudo-Negro" misrepresentation which corrupted the taste of the time. Cakewalks were popular with fraternal orders.

The rapid growth of churches after the Civil War resulted towards the end of the century in a number of excellent choirs and smaller groups of singers. Teaching of music in the schools, and growing number of Negro teachers of voice and of instrumental music produced a greater number of trained singers and skilled readers.

The last decade of the nineteenth century and the first of the twentieth were a kind of golden age of church music in Pittsburgh. The choir of John Wesley Church on Arthur Street was at the time the oldest in the city and was for twenty years directed by D. M. Washington, the first professional choir master in the city, who also conducted the Varrick Sextet organized in the same church in 1898. Members of John Wesley Choir from time to time became leading singers in other choirs. There was the Trinity A.M.E. choir, directed by James Brown and later by Robert A. Lewis. For this choir Miss Iona Smallwood of Allegheny arranged religious and secular songs. There was also the Warren A.M.E. Church choir and in the same church a male quartet, the Osceola female quartet, and the Warren Patriotic Quartet. Ebenezer Baptist Church choir was directed by H. S. Brooks. There were also trained choirs at Rodman Street Baptist Church, Carron Street Baptist Church and St. James Church on Euclid Avenue.

A contemporary writer on musical affairs says of the Euclid Avenue Choir:

> The members are all naturally musical, but almost all studied music and are rapid sight readers. They have been so coached by Mr. Kelly that they

now almost unconsciously produce the effective crescendos and diminuen-dos, singing as one person, and with an astonishing power of unison and chorus that is worth going far to hear. The very best kind of church music is sung, some masses and voluntaries that high-priced white choirs do not find easy to accomplishment.

Zachariah Coleman had been for many years a singer of spirituals. Coleman had been "discovered" by a white Methodist minister in Allegheny twenty years before. While the choir of Rev. Charles Avery Holmes's church was rehearsing a Mozart mass in their church on Arch Street, in old Allegheny, some time in the late 1870s, a Negro wandered in and sat by himself in a rear pew. As the choir re-hearsed he hummed the airs. Rev. Holmes, hearing the voice, came forward and invited the man to join the rehearsal. Choir, organist, choir master and minister were amazed at "the glorious voice." The singer was Zachariah Coleman. He was given training and traveled extensively in concert. The reviewer who wrote of the Euclid choir says of Coleman:

> While Mr. Coleman is a trained musician and a graduate of the Boston conservatory of music, he is a staunch advocate of the pure, primitive African form of singing. He sees beauties in this form of music that are attainable in no other style of singing and believes and has received good proof that his views are wisely taken, that the best musicians of the country agree with him in this stand. He was a musical director for a number of seasons of the origi-nal Tennessee Plantation Jubilee singers, an organization which was formed in 1873 under the auspices of the Central Tennessee College, Nashville, Tenn., and traveled extensively with them. Later he joined forces with the Fisk Jubilee singers, and toured in Europe with them, creating a most favor-able impression wherever they sang.
>
> He took his singers to Chautauqua when it opened in 1875, and had the privilege of sitting within a few feet of the late General U.S. Grant on the oc-casion of the President visiting the grounds. His course of study in Boston was most thorough, receiving vocal instruction under Toerge and the late Doctor Sherwin. Since coming to Pittsburgh he was associated with the Rodman Street Baptist Church as a chorister, but left that organization some-time ago. Prof. Coleman is now holding under consideration a proposition made by Dr. Kincaid, of the New Castle Industrial School, to form another company of jubilee singers, and tour the country.

Many members of church choirs formed secular quartets, quintets, and sex-tets that sang at general public affairs, and a number of which traveled to give concerts. The Acme, the Ladies Four-in-Hand, the Climax, the Black Swan, the

Lindsay and the Lone Star Quartets were famous in their day. The earliest and by many considered the best of these was the Lone Star Quartet organized in 1885, when few or no others existed.

The Lindsay Quartet illustrates the kind of patronage which in large part made such groups possible. Before it took the name of the Lindsay Quartet it had become known as the Wisteria Quartet. A reviewer says,

> At that time the quartet had been making as high as five or six engagements a month for Mr. Lindsay, of the Carnegie Steel Company, on which occasion he always insisted on giving them twice as much as asked for their services. One day Mr. McCloud was struck with the idea that it would be a great help to the quartet if it could be named after some prominent man like Col. Lindsay, and after thinking over the matter for several weeks he went out to see Col. Lindsay and obtained an audience. He explained his errand and Mr. Lindsay at once declared the idea a good one. McCloud then said that as Mr. Lindsay had done so much for them they felt like calling their quartet after him if he would permit them. This was agreed to on condition that the quartet would allow Mr. Lindsay to purchase their uniforms and instruments. He also gave them some excellent advice and has since done everything in his power to stimulate the quartet and assist the members in gaining a prominent place in the city's musical affairs.
>
> The quartet's first appearance in public before prominent men was on the occasion of a dinner given in honor of Charles M. Schwab a few days after his election to the presidency of the U.S. Steel Co., when all the big officials of the concern were present. The next year they appeared before Andrew Carnegie at a banquet given by the Carnegie officials. In July 1904, the quartet sang and played before Gov. Samuel Pennypacker and his staff at Gettysburg, and in July 1905, they entertained Gov. Stokes, of New Jersey, and his staff at Sea Girt, New Jersey.

A curious discussion took place in the *Pittsburgh Press* at this time which, inept as it may be sociologically, indicates the importance of music in the community. The writer says:

> There have been, quite as many suggested solutions of the Negro problem as there are phases of the problem itself. Seldom does a noted educator fail to air his pet theory on the social evolution of the colored race. Every conceivable and possible method, beginning with lower education up to the universities, industrial plans by which the colored man shall bring about his own evolution: agriculture, calculated to give him that independence without which it is sometimes contended he can never be anything but a menial;

teach him the rudiments of sciences so that he can be made to feel that he is capable of something better than mere labor, and the greater and perhaps better plan advocated by men of hard common sense that the Negro be left alone to work out his own solution, which he may eventually do by the constant and growing intercourse with the white race.

Recently one of the best known of the Negro race, a man of intelligence, set up the plea that music is likely to be the avenue along which the colored man is most likely to attain that degree of efficiency which will place him beyond the barrier of prejudice. . . .

It is his theory that there is and can be no prejudice in art. That the Negroes may arouse from present condition by applying themselves to the art of music. He is a fine basso and his knowledge of music is wide, valuable and varied.

He takes the position that the restrictions placed upon the Negro slaves brought out the heart and soul of the race in song. That is why the colored man is recognized in the art of music more than he could ever hope to be in any other way. That is the only avenue to which the Negro can turn to raise himself from present conditions.

"Higher positions will be accorded to the Negro in the musical world," said Mr. Payne.

"Here prejudice has no place. It has no place or standing what so ever in art. By this, I do not mean there are places for them in grand opera. No one but a Negro can get that quaint melody of their songs proper. We are against songs such as we hear today. The melody may be there but the literature should be offensive to every person. What the race needs more than anything else is a writer of lyrics. His day is not here yet, though we have several famed song writers of our color. When they come, the day for the uplifting of the Negro throughout the avenue of music is reached. What use is education to the Negro if there is no opportunity for him? He might as well be ignorant and back in the shackles.

"Jubilee singing is distinctly a product of the colored race. During the darkest days of the colored race the Negro slaves at work in southern fields were not allowed to go to church during the day or during the night," says Mr. Payne. "It was this restriction placed upon them more than anything else that caused Jubilee singing to become more popular among the colored people.   ·

"When a meeting was arranged, darkies would pass through fields singing, 'Steal Away, Steal Away.' The words notified the colored people that there was to be a meeting that night. Among the most popular of Jubilee songs are: 'Steal Away,' 'Good News,' 'The Chariot is Coming,' and 'Swing Low.'"

A reply to Mr. Payne follows. The reviewer says:

The pioneering colored lawyer in Pittsburgh is W. H. Holmes. Mr. Holmes is a highly respected member of the Allegheny County bar, and probably as good an authority on the subject of the Negro problem, as can be found on this side. There is little of the sentimentalist or philanthropist in his views, regarding the advancement of the colored man. He has little faith in the paying theory of music and does not hesitate to say that the uplifting of the colored race can only be brought about in the same manner, and by the same methods that have been applied to all races.

"That is an unjust and unreasonable view for an educated colored man to take," said Mr. Holmes. "Music is all very well for those who have an aptitude for it, but how many of us have this aptitude? So far as the old Negro folk songs go, they serve to display the emotional side of the Negro character at a time when he felt the release of pent-up emotion, which becomes unrestrained with his freedom from slavery. But times have changed for the Negro, as they have for everybody, and those songs are of no more use or good to the colored people of today than the old ballads are to you. Besides it is just as well to forget them. It is more to the purpose to apply himself to industrious pursuits, that will bring him or give him a chance to acquire a competency, rather than to dreaming and fooling his time away with a vague notion of the higher ideals and aesthetic notions of some over-sentimental chap who has more melody than muscle.

"It is an injustice to the Negro, especially on the part of the member of the race, to be preaching such lofty notions of art in music and other ideals in aesthetic character. Men who advocate this everlasting concern over the welfare and the future of the Negro are not so much his friend as many people imagine.

"The Negro will do a great deal to evolve himself from his present lowly condition, and set about to cultivate his own ideals, if he is given a fair opportunity to earn equal wages as the white man, according to his capacity. Where this opportunity has presented itself, the Negro has made good on the greater majority of areas than is generally supposed. Where the Negro has shown unusual capacity he has generally received courteous treatment from the white man in the station to which he aspired. There is one thing, however, that is imperative in the Negro whose ambition leads him into the higher professions. He must show an almost greater degree of proficiency than most of his white competitors to gain the recognition he deserves. That is where the prejudice against his color comes in. It imposes upon him a task infinitely harder than is really necessary for the white man. While the bench and bar have always accorded the most courteous consideration to the colored law-yer, just think of the unreasonable antagonism in an ignorant jury. Conse-quently it calls for extraordinary display, not only of forensic talent, but a convincing demonstration of his knowledge of both law and practice to en-able him to bring a jury of white men to accept his view.

"There are many successful colored men in the higher branches of whom the world knows nothing. It is largely because the white race refused to learn about them. They never understand the better element of the colored people. There is no fraternity by which they can learn of his accomplishments, either mental, commercial, or otherwise. They see him only at a distance and judge him by the standard of those men of the Negro race with what they came in contact in a servile capacity.

"The idea of solving the Negro problem by making them musicians and singers is utterly absurd. Give a Negro a full opportunity to become a skilled artisan and he will find his way into the arts of his own accord."

The visits of Samuel Coleridge-Taylor to America spurred the development of Negro American music. His appearance at Carnegie Music Hall, November 28, 1906, with H. T. Burleigh, Melville Charlton, Clarence White and Mme. Skeeve-Mitchell gave an impetus to choral singing, especially of Negro composi-tions. A group of seventy-five singers, accompanied by an orchestra of twenty pieces, this year sang for the first time in Pittsburgh Coleridge-Taylor's "Hiawatha's Wedding Feast" at North Side Carnegie Music Hall.

A few years later, Mr. Rogers Walker developed the North Side Choral Group. Mr. Walker taught for years in the Night High School of the city, then left Pittsburgh for several years to teach and study in New York. Meantime the H. T. Burleigh Choral Group was organized, one of hundreds that developed through-out the country in the resurgent interest in Negro music in which Burleigh played so great a part. This group also sang "Hiawatha's Wedding Feast," "The Holy City" and many a cappella numbers. The Burleigh Choral group was in existence from 1916 to 1919. The North Side Choral and the Burleigh Choral group merged under Rogers Walters in 1922 as the Clef Choir and for years was the leading Negro Choral Group in western Pennsylvania. Mr. Walker wrote choral arrange-ments of spirituals maintaining the Negroid qualities of the music, and performed works of Coleridge-Taylor, and composed original choral works for women and mixed voices.

The Timeson-Hardy singers devoted much of their program to spirituals. Mr. Lawrence Peeler, and James Miller are music graduates of the Carnegie Insti-tute of Technology. Lawrence Peeler, the first full-time Negro teacher employed by the Board of Education in the Public School system, organized the Watt Evening School Chorus. James Miller also teaches music in the schools, is master at Bethesda Presbyterian Church and recently turned to composing.

The Mary Cardwell Dawson Singers, organized in 1925, devote themselves chiefly to Negro music—H. T. Burleigh, Coleridge-Taylor, W. C. Handy, Jean Stor, C. C. White, Nathaniel Dett and others. The Dawson singers have given performances of music by Pittsburgh composers, Mr. Harvey Gaul's, "I Hear America Singing," and Miss Marianne Genet's "Hymn to the Night." They have featured the songs of Stephen C. Foster. The Dawson concert production had brought to Pittsburgh audiences William Allen, pianist; Hazel Harrison, a pupil; and Orrin southern, organist. The Dawson singers were guests at the Mountain Lake Festival in 1936 and in the Forbes Field singing Festivals, winning trophies for several successive years. The director organized and trained a Negro chorus of three hundred voices for the visit of Rosamond Johnson, W. C. Hardy and Jean Stor in 1937.

In September, 1919 the War Camp Community Service sponsored a Song Festival at Forbes Field at which over a thousand Negro singers, including church choirs, choral clubs, soldiers and sailors and individuals appeared. The stated purpose of the festival was to awaken interest in Negro folk music, especially the spirituals.

When Rubi Blakey[3] in 1932 asked that a group of eighty boys and girls between the ages of ten and eighteen be sent twice a week from Herron Hill Junior High School to the Coleman home for boys to sing Negro spirituals, folk songs and choral works by Negro composers, these young people came to know the richness and variety of Negro music for the first time. At Somers Trade School Mr. Blakey directed a boy's glee club. It began about the same time to sing choral works of Arthur Sullivan, H. C. Burleigh, Dett, Gedman, besides spirituals and work songs. Blakey then went further afield and gathered together the Blakey Jubilee Singers to sing Negro music, emphasizing spirituals and work songs. Then as part of the WPA Federal Music Project with Dr. Will Earhert's encouragement, Blakey assembled a group of unemployed musicians, singers, and teachers around a core of people from the Jubilee singers with the purpose of establishing a higher regard for good choral music in general and Negro choral music in particular. Mr. Blakey says,

> I think we proved to our own satisfaction that we ourselves, when we have something of our own, don't very often give it much attention. It's just another something. I had always noticed, in regard to Negro singing groups, that there was a strong tendency to sing some well-known "Gloria" or concertized, operatized versions of the spirituals that sounded like anything any

3. Blakey is sometimes spelled Blakely. Frank Bolden, interview with author, July 26, 2002.

group could sing. For my own part I had come to realize that from my experience in Pittsburgh concert halls that I knew much more about good, standard music and what is called classical music than I did about the spirituals and contemporary Negro music.

One night, while I was still a student, I heard the Fisk Jubilee singers. I heard something in that music that I had never heard in all this music I had listened to before. I determined to go somewhere and find out all about it. Shortly afterwards, I heard a group of forty or fifty youngsters—I think they came from Russia, and from them I got a similar feeling. I was determined to go to Fisk and study. There I was filled with a love of the Classics. I studied voice. Negro music was still for a time secondary with me. But at the persistent persuasion of Mrs. John W. Work, I began to sing with the Negro groups. I began to get a real background for a study of Negro music, as we researched out in the back woods churches and listened to the simple rich improvisations of these singers, I knew I had found a very real thing for which I had been searching. These songs were not just got up to make some money for tomorrow. That was the way the people felt about things and that was why such songs were born. The deep sincerity of them made me want to stick with the simplicity of spirituals, not concertize them.

The Blakey Jubilee Singers, as a WPA choral group, were given an appropriation for ten weeks. At their concerts they talked to the audience about Negro music. Within a month they were giving two to four concerts daily, and continued until 1936 as part of WPA to take choral music, especially, Negro music, to thousands of people who had never heard it before. The Blakey singers were the only Pennsylvania Negro choral group in Pennsylvania.

After their WPA career the group remained intact, giving concerts, broadcasting over WCAE[4] on a sustaining program, doing commercials over KQV, singing at colleges and universities in Pittsburgh, in Youngstown, and Columbus, Ohio, and in Philadelphia. They included in their programs works of Bach, Palestrina, and Russian Gregorian church music.

Rubi Blakey also directs the Blakey Glee men, a group of sixteen men at the Center Avenue (Negro) Branch of the Y.M.C.A. "Every group I have ever had," he says, "has been recruited from the lower incomes of my people. There are some unemployed teachers and singers, but there are common laborers and maintenance workers, among whom so many of my people are found." A group of Negro and white singers, the white singers from Dr. Harvey Gaul's choral group at the Y.M.C.A., sang with Paul Robeson in "Ballad for Americans" at Carnegie

4. WCAE went on the air in May 1922 and would later become WTAE.

Music Hall in February 1941. "It is my hope," Mr. Blakey says, "to get people of every nationality to sing together in such groups."

"The standard musical organization of the fifties," says Alain Locke, "was not the orchestra but the band." And the band remained the standard musical organization in Pittsburgh until the first quarter of the twentieth century was completed, that is, among instrumentalists.

When at a mass meeting in the Market House in September 1850, which met to protest the fugitive slave law, William Lloyd Garrison, one of the speakers, wrote to his wife that a fine band had played. The Duquesne band seems to have been the only one of its kind until the end of the century. But in the last ten years of the century, the era of the "cake-walk," and the "Buck and wing," not less than five such organizations were in existence. By 1891 the Twin City, the Lincoln Cornet Band, the Pittsburgh Military Band, Lloyd's Orchestra, Kelly's Orchestra, and the Avery College Orchestra, dispensed music publicly and privately for parades, dances, picnics, and concerts. Churches and fraternal orders developed bands and orchestras.

The Great Northern Band was composed of youth between the ages of twelve and eighteen led by Frederick Jones. The Williams Orchestra was also composed of young Pittsburghers. St. Benedicts was advertised as giving "a grand musical and literary concert in the church hall" in the winter of 1898.

Early in the present century a newspaper man wrote that "Pittsburgh's colored population has made a marked advance in music as well as along almost all the other profession or business lines." He spoke of the natural musical endowment of the African. He said it had produced a few notable musicians among the Negroes but that within the last ten or fifteen years the Negro's knowledge of music had been primitive. He knew a "pretty tune" when he heard it, and was able to sing whether alone or in a chorus correctly but merely by instinct. Knowledge and training played little part. That was why Negro chorals possessed "a peculiarity, a weird, half-barbaric sweetness. found in no other race." The music of the Pittsburgh Negro was, at this writing, he said, a vastly different thing. A surprisingly large percentage of the members of church choirs were trained musicians with a solid grounding in principles and theory. Many had by now studied under prominent and expert teachers and were earning a comfortable living through music as a profession.

When Harvey B. Gaul, pupil of Guillemant, Widor, D'Indy and others, composer, conductor, and critic, came to Pittsburgh as organist at Calvary Episcopal Church, he began, as he had been advised by Coleridge-Taylor in London, to investigate Negro music in the city. He frequented the churches, walked the streets of the Hill District listening to street calls and songs of bean-sellers, coal-vendors, pie-men and other peddlers. Themes he gathered from these people he used in his choral compositions. David B. Peeler, Rogers Walker, Ethel Ramos Harris, and Rubi Blakey have all studied composition with Dr. Gaul.

About 1920 Father Bishop Brown wanted a boys choir at Holy Cross Negro Episcopal Church. Under Dr. Gaul's direction and training the first Negro boy's choir west of the Allegheny Mountains was formed of forty boys.

At the time of Dr. Gaul's arrival in Pittsburgh, and for more than a decade afterward, the choir at the Seventh Day Adventist Church on Wylie Avenue was still improvising spirituals in the traditional manner. A member of the congregation would throw out a line of song, another would be added, the song developed, and improvisation would continue to the music of a piano, tambourine and, traditional for establishing rhythm at the creation of spirituals, the beating of sticks upon the floor. To dancing and ecstatic clapping of hands, the song would run its course, then the singers would sit down until some one else was "inspired" and another spiritual was born.

Among professional musicians who influenced musical development in Pittsburgh was William A. Kelly, who had been a coal miner, studied for a term at Oberlin, returned to the mines, and then completed his work at Oberlin. He opened the first musical studios for Negroes in Pittsburgh and organized the first Negro orchestra, the Kelly Orchestra of eleven pieces, a purely professional organization. His studio contained a piano and an organ, violins, cellos, horns "a number of mysteriously shaped instrument canes," and stands. Mr. Kelly kept a supply of instruments because many of his pupils could not buy them.

Contemporary with W. A. Kelly, and continuing much later in service was Henry Waters, an excellent musician who organized and conducted a number of bands in fraternal societies and whose musicianship and energy developed taste, appreciation and activity in Pittsburgh. Mr. Waters worked among musical circles in Pittsburgh until about 1920, when he went to New York.

In 1909 Dr. C. A. Taylor, a dentist who had come to Pittsburgh from Toronto and who had studied music at the Toronto College of Music and the Toronto Orchestral School and had played first violin with the Toronto Civic Orchestra, organized the first Negro concert orchestra in Pittsburgh. The orchestra numbered twenty-five members and gave a yearly concert, the receipts from which paid for scores and rehearsal space. After several years the orchestra was discontinued but was shortly revived under the direction of Frederick Hawkins, a native of Baltimore. Mr. Hawkins was a chemical engineer at Crucible Steel Company and a partially trained musician who had organized a professional dance orchestra in great demand for social affairs. He had become the president of the Pittsburgh Local 471 of the musicians union and at the time was the best known Negro musician in Pittsburgh. Frederick Hawkins worked with the Pittsburgh

Symphony Orchestra—as he called his concert orchestra—[and] was a sound pioneer in music among Negro Pittsburghers. He carried over his work as leader of [a] dance orchestra from the earlier years of ragtime into the later development of jazz. He also conducted the Peeler Symphony Orchestra and Concert Company.

The Peeler Symphony Orchestra played church and concert music between 1915 and 1927 under the leadership of David L. Peeler, a Negro contractor and builder.

Finally, in 1937, Dr. A. R. Taylor drew together the members of various groups into a symphony orchestra of forty-five members who rehearsed and gave concerts at the Center Avenue (Negro) Branch of the Y.M.C.A. The following year Dr. Taylor had an orchestra of advanced players with all sections of a symphony orchestra represented. Negro musicians from every part of Allegheny County and as far west as Washington, Pennsylvania, whose opportunities for playing had been restricted to dance orchestras of varying quality of musicianship now had an opportunity to play with a competent concert orchestra whose repertoire would include standard orchestral symphonies and concert compositions. Rehearsals have been limited because of practical difficulties of commuting from distant points. The present "Y" symphony orchestra is the culmination of years of work on the part of Negro musicians to establish themselves in the musical activities of a northern American city. The present orchestra pays no fees, and plays no professional engagements. Its members look upon it as a civic project on a large scale, not a Negro orchestra, but just one more orchestra in the musical world. It does not intend to devote itself to American Negro compositions such as those of Clarence White, William Dawson, Florence B. Price, and other Negro composers, but to music as a whole.

Aubrey Pankey was born and raised in the Hill District. His recital at Carnegie Music Hall, sponsored by the Administrative Committee of Grace Memorial Church in 1940 showed his people that he was one of the outstanding Negro baritones of the country.

Mr. Pankey began his singing career when he was very young as a boy soprano in Holy Cross Church Choir. At the death of his parents, he left home for Hampton Institute to became a mechanical engineer. There his baritone voice was discovered, and after warm encouragement from such musicians as R. Nathaniel Dett and Roland Hayes he abandoned his engineering for concert singing. He studied at Oberlin Conservatory of Music, the Hubbard Studios and Boston University's College of Music. In Europe Aubrey Pankey studied in Vienna under Dr. Lierhammer, and in Das Neue Wiener Konservatorium, and in Paris with Cesar Daniel and Charles Panzera. He has made more than two hundred appearances in recital, with symphony orchestra, and in radio performances, in sixty cities, twenty-four countries, including Egypt, Palestine, and Syria. Pankey covers the full concert field of lieder, opera, and other forms.

Ralph Banks died too young to achieve his splendid promise. Banks as a Peabody High School boy, began a pre-med course at the University of Pittsburgh, took a B.S. at Howard, and studied medicine at Northwestern. He had begun voice study in Pittsburgh, continued for two years in New York and finished in Rome, Berlin, and Paris. His appearance at Steinway Hall, New York City, in 1929, established him as a fine interpreter of Italian and French classics, and of moderns like De Falla and Nin. Ralph Banks sang to audiences in his own city and was struck down by the most fatal of Pittsburgh diseases, pneumonia.

Out of the jazz age have come Fate Marable, Earl Hines, Mary Lou Williams, Louise Mann and others. In the ten years following the world war Pittsburgh shared the nationwide interest in jazz, and in the Hill a number of small night clubs sprang up where good jazz could be heard. The three most popular "hot spots" were Collins Inn, the Humming Bird, and the Leader House, located upstairs over the C. & G. Coffee Shop. But there were also Derby Dad's, Fullerton Inn, and Paradise Inn. Besides there were Marie's and Lola's, here in small, stuffy rooms reached by many steps and along narrow hallways, and where the air was thick with cheap incense and dim with red or green lights, juke boxes played until during the latest hours of the night or the earliest of dawn, musicians came up from the river boats, or in from dances they had played. Visiting musicians with name bands sought out their places. Here they would sit out the night, drink, play, and improvise in jam sessions. At these spots might be heard Earl Hines, Casey Harris, Fletcher Henderson, Honey Boy Jones, Louise Mann, and from time to time other musicians who have enlivened night life and jazz history in Pittsburgh. A trumpet, a saxophone, a piano, and a double bass would "jam" together, and improvised figures seized upon and carried away by memory to be used later in playing and recording. Fate Marable carried jazz up the Mississippi and Ohio to every town along the banks. He himself played it. He picked up one man after another, trained him soundly in musical technique, and watched him leave the river to carry the gospel into cities inland, on lake shore, prairie, mountainside from coast to coast.

Pittsburgh was the northern pole, New Orleans the southern, of the river axis around which jazz evolved, and along which were scattered the star towns of Natchez, Memphis, Paducah, St. Louis, Cincinnati. Fate's home has been the river, and not for very long at a time any single town between New Orleans and Pittsburgh. He drifts in the winter between St. Louis, Kentucky, and Pittsburgh. The Bailey Hotel and the night clubs of the Hill have known him as much as the towns along the one thousand miles of river across the night waters of which his music has sounded for more than thirty years. St. Louis is his favorite town because of the fine Negro orchestra to be heard there. But there are weeks at a time when the C. & G. (Crawford) Grill at the head of Wylie Avenue is his favorite haunt. Here he sits, drinks, and talks with musicians. His favorite drink is gin, not shots, but water glasses of gin, washed with whiskey or beer. He hardly ever goes to bed, just dozes in chairs.

Fate is a small, slender man, light coffee-with-cream colored. He wears well-made, expensive suits, is slightly bald, has nice eyes, long arms and long hands, and always smokes a cigar. He has a strange manner of speech—runs his words quickly and obscurely together, but breaks into long pauses. He is notoriously reserved on all subjects but music, slightly touched by arrogance, used to telling people what to do.

Before Fate had plied the river many years as a member of another man's band, he took over Charlie Creath's band.

Fate had not achieved the heights of some other players, but he is revered in every night spot between New Orleans and Pittsburgh, a fine musician and a noble drill master. If any man in his band were not following right, Fate would stop him then and there. If any musician were known to have come from Fate Marable, he was known to be O.K. He could read; he could play. Fate plays a little Beethoven, some Bach. But jazz is his field. He is a sound musician, a little pedantic. He plays, not with flash, but freely, easily. He is of course an excellent reader.

One record of legend of Fate's first job is that as a kid of sixteen he was standing one day by the river bank, a piece of hot sweet potato pie in his hand. How the band leader on the J.S. knew young Fate's talent is not told, but he is said to have asked, "Want a job playin' piano?" "Sure," was the monosyllable answer, "Come on." And the transition seems to have been complete. But the real story of Fate Marable's entrance into the world of river music, the musician himself has left in an autobiographic fragment, written for Miss Wilma Dobie. In the third person singular. Fate writes a brief, unfinished chapter of musical history in an unliterary style no writer could well duplicate:

FATE MARABLE

It was the year 1907 in the month of September in Paducah, Ky., that a colored youth riding on his delivery wagon with a friend of his who worked for the (then) Dry Goods Store of L .B. Ogolbie, was hailed by a passerby, and abruptly his driver friend pulled the reins of the horse (as automobiles were not so common in that year) so to make it as brief as possible. Fate was asked of how he wanted a job playing on the Steamer J.S., an excursion steamer then in port at Paducah.

She was 175 feet in length and had a capacity of 2,000 people. The steamer J.S. the previous Sunday had run an excursion from Paducah to

Cairo, Ill., and Fate at that time was working in a barber shop on Broadway between 4th and 5th and while shining shoes kept hearing about a 2 piece band on the J.S. (where violin player—Colored piano player) and the wonderful playing of the two and their names were Chas Mills and Emil Flindt. Emil Flindt (violinist) is the *absolute composer* of Wayne King's theme song, the "Waltz You Saved For Me," but at these early days it was called the "Dance of the Poppies"; to make a long story short about Chas. Mills the pianist on the J.S. was anxious to leave the boat to go to music school. And any piano player was alright, that is for him to get away so Fate was eventually rushed into the job and naturally following a great pianist as Chas. Mills it seemed impossible to make the grade and on top of playing the piano he had to double on calliope and that was his hardest job to master the calliope.

The J.S. laid over in Paducah from Monday morning to Friday a.m. and left for Evansville, Ind., for two excursions to Queensboro, Ky., (a distance of 50 miles) and while there Fate mastered on (Everybody's in Slumberland But You and I), number on the steam Calliope and downstairs on the dance floor, Fate a musician and born leader from birth had the crowd screaming and yelling over his playing of the "Grand Old Flag," written by Geo. M. Cohen and very popular in those days.

On the piano, Fate was an immediate success, but upstairs on the calliope, he was still a "rookie" and so green that if he got too much steam it would blow up.

He would go on the bandstand and keep the people enthused but upstairs on the calliope he still "soared."

Now this year of 1907 of October was an epoch in American History. Theodore Roosevelt, then president of the U.S., and father of the 9 ft. channel idea from Pittsburgh to Cairo, Ill. So on our arrival in Cairo there was a steamboat parade with the steamers, Alton, Spread Eagle, Mississippi (Cov. Boat), St. Paul, Quincy, Dubuque, David Swain and many others and the President's abode was on the Str. Mississippi.

During the parade the J.S. passed all the boats and pulled up along side the Mississippi and Fate getting better on the calliope started playing the old rural number "Turkey in the Straw," and to everyone's amazement with the calliope playing, the President of the United States came out and danced a jig atop the Mississippi and continued until the master of the Mississippi, who was also the boss of the river parade, yelled over and told the Capt. of the Str. J.S. to turn around as she was not supposed to be in the parade, so she turned around and went back to Cairo.

Charles Mills left the boat at Cairo and left Fate and Emil Flindt to take her to New Orleans and the two boys handled the musical job all the way

down the river until they got to Bayou Sara, La. was there that the Capt. told
Fate he was not satisfied with his calliope playing and insisted that he play
the calliope until he got back from uptown, so Fate kept playing and playing
and old man Capt. John Streckfus, who told Fate to continue playing was still
up in the city hearing the calliope and told his eldest son Capt. Joe Streckfus
"That fellow is still playing." From that day on, Fate has asked no quarter
from any calliope player living today and still is tops among calliope players.

The trip continued South to New Orleans and that was where Fate got his
idea of the New Orleans swing. (Jazz in those days.)

Arriving in New Orleans with a two piece band (violin and piano with
Emil Flindt the violin player doubling on banjo, trumpet, and piano) and
breaking the house down each note with rhythm and the crowd kept getting
larger so that Capt. John decided to put another instrument in the band, so
he had Tony Catalono (now he has a band in Rock Island, Ill.) a very good
cornet player, to join, as he already knew Tony as he had previous service
with the company before Fate became an employee of the company and so
the two piece combination became a rousing 5 piece band and with business
continuing to pick up, a drummer was added to the combination and with
the coming of the drums, Flindt and Fate considered that they had a Big
Band (4 pieces), so that was long before 10 to 16 piece bands were heard of,
so the summer of 1908 was spent in St. Paul, Minn., also 1909 on the Steamer
J.S. and the crowds from New Orleans to St. Paul went wild over the Super
Band and their successes continued through 1909 Fall and Winter.

Fate Marable's bands were always good, solid. Nothing showy, nothing fancy,
but good jazz bands. He has changed with the times, and consequently had
played each phase of popular music as it has passed from the early barrel-house
blues, into jazz, "sweet music," and swing. With Fate have played Louis
Armstrong, Jimmie Blanton, Ernie Nappolo, Fletcher Henderson, Chuck Webb,
and others. When Fate's boat puts in at Paducah, Irvin Cobb used to come and
sit and talk with Fate and listen to him play. And the great Bix Beiderbecke too
came to listen and talk. Bix once introduced Fate to some friends as the boat's
cook. But Fate got sore at that idea of a joke.

Musicians tease Louis Armstrong about being fired from Fate's band, because he couldn't read music. But Louis has said that is not only admirable, but
almost affectionate. He had much to say about Fate Marable in his "Swing That
Music." Armstrong met Fate Marable in the autumn of 1919 when Armstrong had
been with Kid Ory's band at the Peter Lalas Cabaret in New Orleans for a year
and a half. Armstrong had just finished a street concert with another band when
a man walked up to him and said he wanted to talk with the young trumpeter, said

he had heard him blow and wanted him for his band. It was Fate Marable, the hot pianist and leader of the band on the Dixie Belle. The two made a deal, although Armstrong at the time could hardly read music, but could already play with much promise of his later . . .

Fate was planning that summer to take the first Negro jazz band to go north on the river. The old "Dixieland" band and Freddy Keppard's band; each had but five pieces. "King Oliver's "Magnolia Band" and Kid Ory's band had only seven. But Fate had got together a twelve-piece band of crackshot musicians. Fate was already a fine swing pianist. "Boy" says Armstrong, "could he make those keys sing!"

Once the Dixiebelle, during a storm ran on to a sand bar. With the bow fast on the bar and her stern free in deep water, the Dixiebelle swung and heaved that people were thrown to the floor. The chairs and instrument racks of the band were tossed about like corn stalks in a wind. And a wind blew open the doors, rushing into the cabins with such force that the boats' mates had to force them shut, two men at a door with their shoulders. Fate shouted to his men to play. And while men and women put on life belts and the life boats were got ready Fate's band played up to distract their attention until they were sure they would not have to swim for the shore, which was "only half a mile away." But the storm abated, coffee and sandwiches were served, and Fate and his men played for dancing the rest of the evening.

Fate Marable is one of the finest calliope players in the country. And as the "Senator" leaves the Monongahela wharf in Pittsburgh on summer evenings for its excursions down the Ohio, its decks and pilot house garlanded with brilliant lights that shatter their reflections on the water, its paddle wheels clinking and kicking up a foamy cascade that settles into a misty wake, Fate may be seen on the deck sitting at the calliope in a swirl of steam, his ears stuffed with cotton, his fingers releasing the keys for the steam to thrill through the pipes in the notes of "Beautiful Ohio."

Fate Marable doesn't even have to say that he will ever leave his river music on the John Streckfus line of river boats. Everyone who knows him knows that.

Earl Hines was born and grew up among the steel mills of Duquesne. The usual tales are told of his being called from ball games after school by his mother's, "Earl, come and practice." The cigar-smoking, arrogant Earl that led a band so properly, rose to fame with his six-year stay at the Grand Terrace, Chicago. Hines is probably the best Negro musician aside from Cab Calloway. He is tall, broad-shouldered, built to wear clothes and known to wear pastel suits. He was unquestionably the greatest jazz pianist living in his hey-day. When every other pianist, like Jelly Roll Morton played a rocky rolling piano, Hines played a trumpet piano, the type that picks out clean hot figures with the right hand.

Hines was the original hot piano player, the "Daddy of hot jazz." Formal training does not show on Hines piano. Hines hits terrific heights, over and above the conventional playing. He reaches almost mysterious step. He carries away the listener. One does not think of technique while Hines plays. Hines seems to have a fantastic twist to his brain which comes out of his music. The result of jamming all one foggy night in Chicago with Bix Beiderbecke was the song "In a Mist."

Hines played his first band job at the old Leader House, now the Crawford Grill on Wylie Avenue. He played with Lois E. Deppe, in the early twenties. In one of the early jam sessions Earl ran across Mary Lou Williams and the result was some fine dust playing.

Mary Lou Williams was born in the East End of Pittsburgh. No one seems to know authentically of her early training. She is said to have been somewhat of a child prodigy and to have played the organ in church. She is another person whose real career as a jazz musician began in the steel town of Homestead in the late 1920s when she played in dingy, little cabarets. She too played around Duquesne and has played a lot with Earl Hines off the stand. She made her name, however, as the key figure in Andy Kirk's band. She has played as guest artist with Benny Goodman, but as player and arranger has stuck close with Andy Kirk. Her arrangement of "I Can Do Most Anything For You" put her on the map. Musicians say she is one of the greatest pianists in the country. Her playing is on the Ellington side, not bassy, although she plays "a lot of piano." Her work is musicianly jazz, in good taste, formal training showing through everything she does. She has made many recordings, in a number of which she does excellent solo work. Among them are "Night Life," "Drag 'Em," "Wednesday Night Hop," and for Benny Goodman, "Roll 'Em." There is a distinct quality about her arrangements for Andy Kirk, especially where she accompanies a slow tune by a lot of chords for full band, and where the arrangement seems to swell with restrained power, her arrangements are never too involved, and intelligent rhythmically.

Louise Mann was one of the best regarded musicians ever to play in and around Pittsburgh, a rich personality, a pianist who could play anything from boogie-woogie to Chopin. Louise Mann had an excellent musical background, was a fine technician. At the Benjamin Harrison Club and the Pittsburgh Playhouse, out of town musicians would hang over her piano rapt with attention. As a singer, Louise was the definite blues type, husky, powerful; she didn't need a microphone to fill a room. She never used a score. Louise Mann loved the classics and hated doing the off-color things for which she was so often called upon. She did not actually compose, but her revisions were characterized by real musicianship. While singing at the Old Benjamin Harrison Literary Club, she used her voice so hard she was compelled to look for someone to relieve her. It was then that she brought in a young woman from Homestead, Maxine Sullivan.

When Maxine Sullivan went to New York, Louise Mann went with her for a while, but returned to do two years work at the Pittsburgh Playhouse grill. In 1937 as Connie Compton, she broadcast over station WCAE as part of the Night Club of the Air. In the autumn of 1939, Louise Mann died of cancer in a Philadelphia Hospital.

When Maxine Sullivan came to the Benjamin Harrison Club to work with Louise Mann, she had been doing honky-tonk work around Homestead at little clubs where steel workers spent their evenings and their money. Her grandfather was a miner, her father a barber. Her brother became a mill worker, a pit man. Her uncles were steel workers. Maxine Sullivan had been singing and dancing all her life, but dancing was her chief interest; singing was secondary. In Homestead there was no recreation center. Maxine Sullivan, with other worker's children, danced and sang in the streets creating what pleasure they could among themselves. She was a precocious child. In school she made a complete "A" record for her first year. But at the death of her father she left high school in her last year to work as a domestic until her brother was old enough to get a job. She had already done some youthful sculpture, and had won first and second place in a scholastic poster contest. One of her hobbies was oil and water color painting. "She should have been a painter," says a friend. She had sung a lot at house and church affairs, and sang for six months in Akron, Ohio with Harry William's six-piece band, all of whom were steel workers, and brothers and cousins of Maxine. She also sang over station WWSW. But in 1926–27, she had won several Charleston Contests in Braddock and Rankin and had given up singing. While she was singing with Louise Mann at the Benjamin Harrison Club, however, a girl in Ina Ray Hutton's band, then playing at the Stanley, heard her and got her a New York contract.

It was her singing at the Onyx Club in New York, where she had gone with Jenny Dilliard as her accompanist that won Maxine Sullivan her name as a unique singer of ballads with a definite swing in her voice, not powerful, but good for microphone singing. After her Onyx Club nights, Maxine Sullivan worked in Baltimore and Detroit, and in Hollywood at night club work, she was Titania in "Swing The Dream," the swing version of Shakespeare's "Mid-Summer Night's Dream." For the past year she had been studying dramatics.

Roy Eldridge, of the wild high trumpet, is of the North Side born. In high school Eldridge played the violin. But he didn't like it. He bought a nickel-plated second hand saxophone but didn't like that either. His brother Joe, a real musician, decided to use it. Roy Eldridge laid down his saxophone. He got a second-hand trumpet. That he found was the instrument he liked. He started playing by ear, knowing few of the fundamentals of music. He has been a self-taught musician except for what training his brother gave him. Roy Eldridge played for a time

at Hendel's Roosevelt Theater. When Eddy Marshall organized his Cotton Pickers, he chose men who could play whether by note or by ear. He built his orchestra around a few who could read music. Not unlike other orchestras, the Cotton
Pickers had their way of learning dance numbers They would play, for instance,
a Fletcher Henderson record such as the "Watcha Call 'em Blues," an extremely
popular piece. The fact that Benny Carter was sax man in the recording perhaps
explains the choice. Such recordings the Cotton Pickers reproduced, spelling
them out slowly note by note until they had a repertoire that "put them on the
map" in the tri-state area—Ohio, West Virginia, western Pennsylvania, and Kentucky. The men in such bands taught each other. Roy Eldridge and his brother
Joe played with the Cotton Pickers as long as the band was in existence, about
five or six years. Here they got their foundation for later work. Roy Eldridge and
Horace Henderson drifted from one spot to another until they joined Fletcher
Henderson in Chicago. Here Eldridge went in for serious work with the trumpet
and developed a style of his own. He entered jam sessions sponsored by "Down-
beat" and various organizations. He got good notices from judges, and from then
on "Went to Town." He can play any instrument in the band and also arranges
dance tunes. Although Eldridge's trumpeting is rather wild, it is popular. He was
once considered a trumpeter of great promise. Apparently Eldridge has or had
great ideas which he couldn't quite express.

Other Pittsburghers made interesting music, either with bands around the
city or with large bands in other. Honey Boy Jones created a sensation for a while
as drummer. Those who listen to Honey Boy Jones differ in their appraisals.
Some say he is a flash, that his amazing tossing and juggling of his sticks in tempo
does not make him a legitimate drummer. But Gene Krupa is reported as having
gone up to the Hill once while he was playing at The Stanley Theater, and hearing Honey Boy, to have said, "He's the best I've ever heard." Others say this gum-
chewing drummer, if a flash, is a natural flash, that he can reach a drummer's
heights, and that if his reason for being is to stimulate a band, then Honey Boy
does that. Honey Boy is one of those people who got started in the steel town of
Homestead. Honey Boy came into notice there at the Club Mirador.

Don Redman is a native of Harpers Ferry, West Virginia, where he played in
the town band when he was so small that, they say, he sat on his father's arm to
toot his horn. His first real job was with Lois Deppe's band at Burke's Hall on
Fullerton Street, which later became the Java Jungle, upstairs from the Ritz Cafe.
Redman's alto sax is heard on some of Louis Armstrong's best old recordings, as
Earl Hine's piano. Redman stayed in New York with Fletcher Henderson, then
went to Detroit where he organized and directed McKinney's Cotton Pickers.
Since then he had various other bands. He is a hard working musician, an accom-
plished pianist and is most noted as an arranger. From his arrangement of

"Stormy Weather," Tommy Dorsey is said to have got his idea for his famous "Marie" record.

Lois Deppe had the first Negro band in Pittsburgh and the best. Before he appeared at the Paramount Inn with his swing orchestra from 1919–21 to 1925–26, Deppe had a brief and successful career as a concert baritone with Mme. Florence Talbert. But, like many Negro musicians, Deppe found swing music a more secure and profitable profession than occasional concerts during the intervals of which he worked as a porter. With Deppe at the Paramount Earl Hines played for sometime. Deppe's band made successful recordings during their stay at the Paramount, and gave Pittsburgh swing fans their first protracted opportunity to hear good swing music.

Jimmy Blanton played on the river boats with Fate Marable for several summers, and Fate said of him, "That boy can play bass with anyone in the country. When the boat puts in at the wharf Blanton, like many other good musicians, would spend his time on the Hill playing at the C. and G. coffee shop. Sonny Woods, vocalist with Louis Armstrong, is another musician who comes from the steel center of Homestead. Chuck Jefferson, who was with McKinney's Cotton Pickers, was a "bassy" pianist with unusual cording and rhythm. Leroy Brown has been playing a beautiful tenor sax at the Benjamin Harrison Literary Society and the Southern Hunting and Fishing Club. Casey Harris also entertained the clientele of these places with a fine boogie-woogie style of piano playing, though some connoisseurs say his fine rolling left hand is marred by "too much piano," too many keys played, and by an exaggerated rhythm.

One highly significant painter was born in the Pittsburgh community. Henry Ossawa Tanner (1859–1937), the son of Benjamin Tucker Tanner, African Methodist Episcopal Church Bishop, and Sarah Miller, a graduate of Avery School and a noted Pittsburgh teacher was born on Fulton Street, now Fullerton, near Wylie Avenue. While he was still a child, the family moved east. In the children's division of the Continental Exposition of 1876, one of Tanner's drawings won a prize. At the Philadelphia Academy of Fine Arts he was an outstanding student under Eakins and Chase, but did not receive any of the foreign scholarships his work merited. Embittered, he went south to Atlanta where for four years he taught and sold his drawings. His first exhibit in Cincinnati was a financial failure, and family opposition to his art career was strong, but with the aid of friends he was able to study in Paris where he worked under Benjamin Constant, and for five years at the Julian Academy. Tanner may truly be said to have placed the Negro artist before the world's judgment on a purely aesthetic basis, without regard to race. His early work suggested that he founded a school of American Negro art. But even though he was awarded the Lippincott prize in 1900, and medals at the Paris, Buffalo, St. Louis, and San Francisco expositions and finally the

French Legion of Honor, Tanner was more and more embittered by emphasis on his race, became a recluse, and shunned America. Through Rodman Wanamaker, he made the journey to Palestine which resulted in the series of religious painting upon which his fame chiefly rests.

In the late 1890's, two men, father and son, opened a studio on Collwell Street for the crayon portraits so popular at the time. But few Negroes could afford, or were interested in, such portraits, and the men closed up shop and moved away. A year or two later a Mr. C. L. France opened a studio at No. 45 Roberts Street. A note in the *Press* said on one occasion that Mr. France "has just completed a life-like oil portrait of one of the leading men of the race which he intends to send to a Negro exhibit in Jamestown, Virginia.

One other notice of Negro painters has come to light. A Mr. Leguen, who was also a musician, had a studio for a time but gave up the painting he did and moved to New York to study music. None of the art schools of Pittsburgh have graduated any Negro painters or sculptors. Two Negro men—Mr. John Gore and Mr. Emmett Hill—are employed on the WPA Easel Project. A dozen or so amateur painters have once or twice attempted to form a club for the encouragement of painters but nothing has come of the venture.

CHAPTER 14

The People Speak

Typist: E. Saunier / Rewriteman: J. Ernest Wright /
November 7, 1940 / Final

In this chapter the Pittsburgh Negro speaks for himself. Here is what he has to say about living in Pittsburgh, about his problems, his achievements. Here are a dozen different attitudes toward his community, toward his fellow Pittsburghers, Negro and white. With varying degrees of articulateness, men and women from a dozen walks of life have put together their words and sentences to write this chapter. The housewife of moderate circumstances, the paperhanger and his wife, the trained social worker, the minister, the college student. The unemployed worker with no particular training for a job; the young woman who is a tinter of models on a WPA project, takes typing and shorthand courses in evening classes, and wants to paint and does paint an occasional still life in oil; the woman who lives on relief; the watchman in a downtown bank; the seamstress who has directed a Negro theater group and won critical recognition from Pittsburgh dramatic reviewers; the teacher who cannot find employment in city schools and works as a domestic in wealthy white families—these and others say what it means to be a Negro in Pittsburgh. Some belong to families long established in the city; others are newcomers. Consequently some see one shape of living more sharply outlined than another. Some are indifferent to things that make others resentful or angry. Some speak harshly. Some speak with optimism. But here is what they have to say about work and recreation, about being one of a minority group, of obstacles or progress. Of the church and politics, of strata within the

334

Negro community and the social attitudes prevalent in each, of attitudes imping-
ing on them from the white community.

What these people have to say has been put down as nearly verbatim as possible or, where it has been written down by their own hands, with no editing except for punctuation or an occasional change in spelling to make reading easier.
The value of these pages lies in the fact that here is what people think, as they say
they think about their lives. What one states as true another denies. What one
thinks is a solution another thinks ineffective. Where one praises another criti-
cizes. Whether what they say is true for all is not the important thing. The important thing is that this is what people do think and say. Whether they speak with
approval or disapproval, with hope or resentment, whether they express clarity of
perplexity, frustration or achievement, these are human moods, existent because
of the interplay between men and women and the conditions under which they as
individuals and as members of a particular group live.

In the kitchen of her second floor home in the Hill District, a middle-aged
Negro woman sat facing her sister at a little round table spread with white oil-
cloth. The light from a sixty-watt bulb gleamed over the white enamel of the sink,
the frigidaire, and the kitchen cabinet. If one sat sideways at the large table there
was barely room for the shaggy brown dog to move between one's chair and the
walls, or among chair legs and furniture. The sisters wore freshly laundered
house dresses. The elder was slightly grayer and wore black glasses over her
nearly blind eyes. From time to time a tall, black-skinned youth in his mid-twen-
ties came and stood in the door-way to button his collar or link his cuffs, listening as his mother and his aunt talked, now animated, now quiet-toned and mel-
ancholy, again wistful or eager, or their voices rising with subdued fire. The blind
sister laid her hands on the table before her or raised them to adjust her dark
glasses, or stretched them full length across the table, the dark brown hands
clenched as she agreed in low tones with her sister's talk. And the younger sister
said:

> I was a good sized girl before I realized that complexion made any differ-
> ence. We lived in Lawrenceville; it's one of the most rubbish places now.
> There were a lot of big mills there then. There was Clark's and the Black
> Diamond and several others.
>
> Yes, we Negroes have just about every problem there is. We have people
> that are disreputable just as the whites have. But then their faults are visited
> on most all of us. We don't feel that way towards the whites; no matter what
> opportunity they have every problem to fight against—how to make a liv-
> ing—how to live in decent homes and how to live in a decent neighborhood.
>
> I've often thought since I've become a mother that it's almost impossible

to bring up our children. Our love for our children has nothing to do with the color of our skin. Our love is just as great as a white mother's and it wants our children to grow up with the same opportunities and be just as happy as white children. Nobody can ever know but ourselves our misery and our pain. It costs us more, probably more misery and more pain even than it costs a white mother to bring our children into the world. We love our children just as dearly. We aspire to just as much as white people. There's only one thing in the world would make me want to be white and that's to have a white woman's opportunity. I'm surprised to see so many of them throw away their opportunity. They waste so many opportunities, so much of their time, doing things without any purpose, things that are useless, things that don't benefit them or their children. If we could do the same we'd hold on to them like golden precious hours. For instance, my son tells me he went downtown to file an application to enlist. Ever since he was a boy he's wanted to be an aviator. But he couldn't enlist because he was a black boy. Now does a man's skin have to be white to make him handle an airplane? Just because my son is black can't he learn to pilot a machine?

This equal rights bill, all bills are a farce. They shouldn't be introduced to give us our rights. They shouldn't have to be introduced. Our rights should come to us naturally. People should be tolerant. We're all God's children, there's no difference between us in the sight of God, why shouldn't we all be free among ourselves, free to partake of all the opportunities there are. Opportunity should be free just as the air; it's free; it's free to breathe for all of us.

There shouldn't be any distinction. There's no distinction in our tax dollars. We pay them just like the rest. And our tax dollars come high, higher than the whites; they cost us more because we get less salary and have to pay for it with more labor. Yesterday my sister attempted to give our ice-man a tip. He refused to take it. He said, "You've been buying ice from me for twelve years and you always pay for it. You can't afford to give tips." That's what I call Christianity.

We wouldn't have so much to face with the relief of some economic problems. Among the poorer people is where the rub comes in. They don't want to see a Negro holding down a job they ought to have.

Many a black man who has known nothing but abuse have taken the white man's children to their bosom and there are some white families have brought up our children and have been good and kind to them and loved them like their own. But the black man has done it much more often. Many a time they've taken them to their bosom and they loved them in their hearts.

Some of our people are very timid. Especially since we've had this welfare business they have a fear of the people they come in contact with. They think they're snooping and spying.

You want to know if we're doing all we can do to put an end to this discrimination and segregation. No, they are not doing all they can do. Most of them come to the place that they say, "What's the use." Lots of our people say "There is no use giving this child an education. He can't do anything with it anyhow." Education isn't the whole story; it won't end our problem. But a child has something to look forward to if he has an education. You never can tell when opportunity come. If you're prepared they may give us a chance temporarily, and at least that will give us a chance to make good. Take nursing opportunities, those hospitals downtown won't take colored girls. We can't train to be nurses. They ought to take our girls. They don't have to house them in the same building *if they don't want.* I was in a hospital the other day. It made my blood boil to see how those doctors treat patients. They don't seem to think our people have any feelings. You'd scarcely believe it, but there was one woman lying in a bed and they all stood around her and questioned her so everybody in the ward could hear and they laughed and they pointed at her, and they talked about the color of her skin and whether her hair was straight or kinky and about her features and her feet and everything. All the clubs of colored people do what they can to help the hospitals. They make clothes and they make gowns and they make layettes for babies. They give the hospitals plenty. Our opportunity ought to be to work and get training in those hospitals. The Negro has proven that the Negro is capable of love for this brother.

The Negro is not known to hoard like the white man. We like to live, but it costs us more to live. If we had the opportunities to live like we want, we would spend our money. If we had the opportunity to live we wouldn't hoard. Of course classes exist just as much among Negroes as whites. There are some wealthy Negroes of course and I don't believe every rich man makes his money dishonest, even the whites. Lots of them do by paying cheap labor. But most Negroes if they have any more than it takes them to live—what do they do?—they don't hoard, they invest. They try to put their money into property or land or some business our people will patronize.

There certainly is a Negro problem, but far too many don't think about it. So many are blinded by the type of religion that's handed to us. We're told to look forward to a mansion and starry crown. I'd like a decent home right here on this earth and I can wait for my starry crown. Maybe I'll get one, or what it means but in the meantime I have to live on this earth and make my home

on it. I go to church but I don't believe everything the preacher tells us. I
don't want you to think I have no religious training. My sister and I had good
religious training. It was real and it was sound and we tried to live by it. But
it didn't come just from the church. We got it at home. So many of our people
are told to bear up with this world and to wait to get to heaven for their reward.

Politicians hand out a dollar or two and make them think they're living.
They remember them until Saturday after election day—and election day
comes on Tuesday. Sometimes they remember them just until the polls close,
but I'll give them the benefit of the doubt and say until the Saturday after.
Then they'll be on their own again.

The remedy is to tell people the truth. Tell us the truth. Don't lie to us.
Tell us the truth about everything. Tell us the whole truth. Let the preachers
tell us the truth. Let everybody tell us the truth.

When I go out I try to make sure that I'm in a place where I'm welcome. I
don't intend to pay for insults. I go to movies in my own community. Our
people are too meek, too submissive, too timid.

When I moved into this neighborhood they didn't want us here. We were
colored. But a year after we moved in the woman next door said to me, "Mrs.
J.—I have to tell you the truth. God forgive me I have to tell you the truth.
When you moved here I cried and I worried. I said to my husband, 'I don't
want them for neighbors' and I didn't. God forgive me I didn't. But now I
could love you. You've been so good, you've been so kind. You're clean as
anybody, you keep a good house, you are quiet and respectable, you helped
me. You're the best neighbor I have on this street."

C—— is a social worker. She lives at the edge of the Hill district where the
Negro and white populations mingle in neighboring houses, and in the better
houses of the Hill. She is a graduate of an eastern college and has done graduate
work at the University of Chicago. She buys season subscriptions to concerts and
the Theater Guild performances.

In her large bright living room, its wine colored carpet a plain background for
the tapestried chair and the chaise lounge by the window, she sat at her maple
desk. Her princess housecoat brike[1] its figured hem over silver slippers. Through
the windows that filled the far side of the room you looked out over a sun-porch
that was also a dining-room, through tree tops and into distant space. But below
the tops of the trees lay the city, its grimed roofs, its billboards, and cupolas, its
church spires and the tall bulk of hospitals or office buildings. Below the window

---

1. Spelling is as in original.

sill a long shelf was lined with books. Over the studio couch hung a water color of blue and yellow iris. And on the desk in a blue bowl stood a cluster of calendulas. As she talked she drew her feet up under her on the chair and leaned forward to adjust the orange flowers.

I think of myself as a Negro—first, last and always; I don't think of myself as an American, or an American citizen, but as a Negro woman. That is perhaps because I'm always struggling to make inroads for Negroes, not colored people, but just Negroes. I don't have to worry about my color, and passing, and all that. I think of myself as just that kind of person. I identify myself with the underprivileged groups, I think, with the underprivileged Negro.

You see, the thing is all a matter of development. Arriving at this position is a matter of growth. Every Negro starts out in life as an individual, a very individualistic person, like everyone else. That is why you hear them say "I am before everything else an American." But after the Negro reaches a place where he has achieved this great asset of education, which is such a privilege to the Negro, he is finally faced with the fact that he is still a Negro. The barriers are still just as high as for the lowest Negro. The barriers are as high, but living is so much easier because of one's particular interests and pursuits and adjustments and understanding that one doesn't see them. You just don't see them, you don't feel them.

Take as an example the Negro who owns a car. If he is traveling he doesn't necessarily come up against the barriers. He can travel from the deepest South, say New Orleans, to the farthest point in northern Maine and never feel that he is different from anyone else. But let him get stranded, let him have a breakdown on the way and he is just as much a Negro as the man that works on the plantation. The same thing is true in the North. Of course, there are degrees. The North, however, is not all that it's cracked up to be. The Negro no longer thinks of it as "Nigger Heaven." That's why the smart Negroes in New York and Chicago have banded together, recognized themselves as Negroes, as underprivileged Negroes at that, and have pressed for their rights. That is why they have used legal redress for many of their deprivations. It hasn't been handed to them, you can make sure of that.

Since I have been here I have come to feel that the Pittsburgh Negro's feeling about his problem and how to improve his position is analogous to the geographic position of Pittsburgh. I mean by that, that Pittsburgh finds itself in between, halfway between West Virginia and New York. Pittsburgh Negroes, as Negroes do everywhere, reflect the attitudes and opinions of white people, not of their leaders, who think of themselves as liberal. And so the Pittsburgh-born Negro is conservative, like his white friends. Both groups are opposed to the newer methods of handling their problems, and of handling the Negro's problem in particular. The new point of view is that the progressive Negro asks for voluntary segregation. If they want Negro teachers in the schools, as so many do, they go, if they are progressive, to the Board of Education, and say, "We want Negro teachers in the schools in the Hill District, where most of the pupils are Negro children." The same is true if they want Negro swimming pools, and Negro life guards at swimming pools.

The conservative Negro began to make his demands known by asking for Negro lifeguards at white swimming pools, or for Negro teachers throughout and the public school system. That was the first technique employed, and it was a beginning, but it isn't the way things get done. If they have Negro hospitals they will be segregated in those hospitals. But too many Pittsburgh Negroes will not make it known that they want voluntary segregation.

I've never known just how to cite the problem if people say to me, is there a Negro problem, or what is the Negro problem, or how is the Negro problem to be solved. I suppose there is a Catholic problem, and a Chinese problem. I am never quite sure whether what I am saying is what I believe as a social worker, or what I believe as a Negro social worker, or what I believe just as an underprivileged person, or just how objective my opinion is. I believe that if more people would start from that point of view more would get done. There are a lot of fallacies and myths that people want to keep circulating and these fallacies and myths simply stand in our way, in anyone's way.

I don't grant very readily that there is a middle-class Negro. There isn't a middle-class Negro. I think of the Negro as being a laborer or a non-laborer. I don't think of the doctors as being a kind of head group, the teachers being a middle or intermediate group and the laborer being the lowest group of the three. The white middle-class group is analogous to our group that we think of as the cream of our people. The poor doctor or poor teacher in the white group is the middle-class person—numbers of them make up a middle-class. In Pittsburgh the Negro man who is "tops" got there by luck. Someone died and left him a little money or else he got his start by hitting the numbers, maybe for four or five thousand dollars and then went into some racket temporarily. Let the Negro get two or three thousand dollars on the numbers and usually he will open up a little night club until he loses it or moves from that into something else.

The Negro thinks of living well until he dies, not storing up for posterity. He wants to send his children to school; he wants to have a machine and summer vacation, a good home, and its comforts. He doesn't buy big insurance policies. Heaven has been so alluring to him all these generations he thinks, "If I can just make it until I get there everything will be all right." But the Negro minister doesn't have the hold over Negroes anymore. They aren't any more leaders than are the ministers among the white group. Who listens to Fosdick on Sunday afternoons when the symphony's on?[2] They do give spiritual comfort to thousands, of course, and the church is still one of the greatest forces, if not the most powerful institution and a religious guide. It doesn't dominate, however, in real leadership.

The church is still one of the greatest social factors in the life of the Negro, but I won't agree with the idea that it is the most powerful force for leadership. It is still a great social center because we have nowhere else to go. It still has a good social influence, but I don't agree that it gives the greatest leadership on vital questions. I think it can and may with the new type of minister that is coming through, and of whom we are getting more in Pittsburgh. But our ministers are not actionists enough.

In fact until recently there has been too little drive on the part of the Negro generally. He has been awfully comfortable here. He thinks, "Here I am in the North, I'm not in the South, I don't have to achieve any particular rights or privileges." There have been no pressures such as there have been in the South or in Chicago, where it's so hard to get a living. So here we have sat. Living comes comparatively easy here. Most of the people were servants a generation or two ago. Some wealthy family bought us houses, gave us the winter's coal, gave us some very good left-over clothes. We had it lovely in Pittsburgh. Then came the influx from the South and competition with the new southern Negroes. For the most part we didn't even try to compete. We thought the newcomers weren't worth competing with and the Pittsburgh families have tried to live on the merit of their names, which is of course characteristic of any old settlers. In the "fine old families" there were a lot of old maids. Frequently the daughters didn't marry; they wouldn't mix with the new families. They weren't good enough. I remember my mother telling about her and her sisters peeking out the windows to see the southern people going by to church.

It's too bad, but many of the old families are referred to by the newcomers with derision. They have a name, but they have no money, no training. They don't do things. Oh, they do beautiful needle point, and they have beautiful silver which is a family tradition and was given them by early employers. Such things are almost a cult. They have family reunions of 200 or

2. Harry Emerson Fosdick was a prominent Baptist minister, professor of theology, and author of popular books on religion. His fame was such that in 1925 his picture was featured on the cover of *Time* magazine.

300 people in South Park. They have a culture, a very distinct and thorough culture; but it is a culture of manners, of behavior, of religious affiliation.

But intellectual culture isn't easily attainable for the Negro. We can go to the International Art exhibit and I always see many Negroes in the halls while the International is in progress. And we use the libraries a lot. But when it comes to the symphony or the theater or when your culture has to do with the purchase of tickets the Negro is at a disadvantage. A white friend always buys my tickets with hers. Maybe it is absolutely necessary, but the fact that we continue from one season to another to do that is commentary on the situation enough. The fact is that I don't want to take a chance on being sold something that I prefer not to have, and likely wouldn't have if some white person wanted the same seats, or if I applied in person.

The R——'s one-room home is typical of many of its kind. It's on the third floor, the attic floor of an old house, in a grubby street on the North Side. The halls have no light. You grope your way up uncarpeted stairs, turn and follow a narrow second floor hallway to the front of the house, and turning at the bathroom, open a door that leads to the attic stairs, steep and bare. At the top you find yourself in a large, gabled room. It could be attractive. It serves as kitchen, dinning room, living room, and bedroom. But sixty dollars a month in wages doesn't allow much for paint or even inexpensive bright wallpaper. And the dormers and stair banister give little scope for arrangement of furniture, which, though several pieces are well made and tasteful, must stand where it can, most of it stacked along one wall. An old over-stuffed davenport juts into the room, opposite the large, substantial, neatly made bed. The gas range is an old white range. There is no cupboard space. The corner behind the stair banister and the davenport is stacked with boxes.

R—— is by profession a seamstress, but she finds employment at present as attendant in women's washrooms. She has passed a number of civil service exams but has not been placed. E——, her friend has taught in Negro schools in Maryland but works in Pittsburgh as a domestic. Both women have taken typing and shorthand in evening schools.

R——: I have funny ideas about colored and white. I take a man for what he is, and damn his color. Some white people you have to put in their place. Now, there's a boy out at the club where I work. He was carrying something in the other night and he called, "Open that door there," you know, with that southern brogue, because I was a Negro. Well, I just didn't pay any attention to him. I just thought, you're not speaking to me, and you can just open that door yourself so far as I'm concerned. Well, he knew what was happening, and he said to me when he got up to the door, "Will you open that door for me?" And I said, "Sure, why not." And I haven't heard any southern brogue from him since. But it just amuses me when the girl at work says, "You're the best *one* we've had out here yet." She doesn't say *what*, just "nicest *one*."

E——: Well, I laughed today, and I told the woman I work for how I feel. She's a pretty nice person, and she treats all her help pretty well. She really didn't mean anything by what she said. But it shows how people pick up things and hold on to them, and use them when they don't intend to. She was sitting there on the chair, and there was just one butler and me there. He's colored too. And she was saying, "Why I worked so hard, I worked all day, and on into the evening. I worked like a Nigger." Well, I just looked at Charley, that's the butler, and then I looked at her, and Charley looked at her, and she looked at us, and then she got red and she started to say, "Oh, I didn't mean to say that." But I stopped her dead in her tracks. I said to her "Don't apologize. Don't apologize." And I wouldn't let her apologize. I said, "The minute you apologize, then you insult me. After all, you weren't talking to me." And after all I use the word too. That word's used more among Negroes than among whites. It's a kind of slang.

R——: When we lived on Island Avenue as children there was no difference and we didn't even know there was any difference. But I know now.

E——: Yes, so do I. The minute you step out the door and get on a street car, even while you're waiting for the car you know it. People stare at you. On the car they walk right past you, even if there were fifty seats beside you they'd walk on past and take one somewhere away from you. Consequently, I never sit on a car beside a white person. Now today, I did, and I said to myself, "Why am I? Just why am I sitting here?"

R——: I won't. Now you notice if there are three or four colored people on a car they're bunched in one spot. They'll bunch together every time. After a while they'll fix that spot.

E——: I just don't sit beside a white person.

R——: I don't know why it is. I don't think of it as an honor, and I don't think of it as a dishonor. If I see three or four colored people sitting together, all bunched in one place I'll go and find me another place. If it's beside a white person, they don't usually move. And if they move, they move.

E——: Since they refuse to sit beside me if they can, I don't want them to think I feel it an honor. But that's a feeling of inferiority. And, after today I'm going to think that way. I'm going to get on a car and take whatever seat offers.

Now on 71 I don't have that feeling because there aren't colored and white like there are on an 82. I think of myself as a Negro and I'm proud of it. Then I think of myself after that as an American citizen. But America hasn't given me anything to be so American about.

R——: So far as citizenship goes it rarely crosses my mind. I'm a Negro and I can't get away from it. I don't want to get away from it. That's just what I am and I'm not proud of it or disproud. It's just me, that's all. I don't see that there's anything to be *proud* of, not as if you had done something well for yourself or for some one else. I am just a Negro. There's that color on my arm and I have to take it with me everywhere I go, and if people don't like it, it's just too bad, that's all. Lots of people it doesn't make any difference to. There are white people who think about us Negroes just like I think about them. They take a man for what he is and color doesn't make any difference. I'll grant you they are few and far between, but there are some.

E——: Well, I'm a person that tries to make opportunities, and if I weren't black I could make a lot more. But damn it, I'm proud of being black. I'm honest to God proud of it. I'd certainly like some more opportunities to do a lot of things I can't do, to go places and get jobs, especially to get jobs, but I certainly wouldn't change the color of my skin to do them.

R——: I'm very conscious of being a Negro in most restaurants. A colored man isn't the prettiest sight in the world, but when he's well dressed he isn't so bad at that.

E——: I'm not sorry I'm a Negro and when it's thrown in my way I'm going to raise hell. We're born under a handicap, and because we are that's no reason why I'm sorry.

R——: I have no race pride. Race pride doesn't mean a thing to me.

E——: Well, I'm proud of being a Negro. What the white man wants is for us to be ashamed of being a Negro. I'm not a hybrid. These Negroes that have white blood are proud of having white blood. So what are they proud of? Not their Negro blood. But I am. I'm pure blooded as far as I know.

R——: I'm a hybrid, as you call it, and I can put my finger on my white blood and I'm not proud of my white blood or of my Negro blood. It's just there mixed up together. I don't see anything to be *proud* of over either one of them.

E——: Mixed Negroes' morals isn't as high as others! Mixed blood can't think the way I can. You're a Negro and as a Negro you have certain advantages. But as a Negro you can't use those advantages. I certainly wouldn't rather be white, but since I'm black, I tell you I'm proud of it. After all, life is nothing but seeking happiness. And you're crippled from birth by being black.

R——: I've never said I wish I was white. I've said I wish I could do this or that. You can go as far as the Harlem Casino—Period! You can go to South Park-Period! Our life would be so damned unhappy if we sat around and wished we were white! Lots of people do regret that they're colored. My father, for instance. There are so many more places you can go if you are not colored.

E——: We're used to it and we don't expect so much. We're satisfied to go around in a limited circle. It just burns me up. We certainly are a worry to the white man. Now when I hate a person I let him alone. But when a white man hates a Negro he goes to so much trouble to make it plain. He puts up signs, and tells you to stay out, and he passes laws, and he does all kinds of things. He doesn't hate us for our customs, or our cooking, or our habits. He hates us for our color. Take all those ads for light brown-skinned girls. Dark is associated with filth. I have a hymnal here that says, "Wash me Whiter than Snow." White's supposed to be the cleanest you can get—Wash me Whiter than snow! But the blackest mammies nursed white children. If you can pass you pass. That's all right if they want to. I don't.

R——: Yes, and a Negro can spot a Negro every time. I can. I can spot colored feet and colored hands. I've seen people on the street cars; there's a girl rides the car with me almost everyday. She could be white if you could hide those feet and those hands. And I don't care how much they've had their hair straightened I can tell it.

E——: The Equal Right Bill has helped some. But there are still some places, some theaters especially, and lots of restaurants, but there are still some theaters where they try to say "Upstairs," or "The only seats available are upstairs." But rather than find out if it's effective I don't bother. I'm not going to pay to be insulted. There's going to be a complete revolution in this country sometime. Then things will be different, and they won't be different until then. Take a poor white man, he'll call you a Nigger any time. Take a wealthy one he'll be polite and all that and ask you to come back. He might not think so behind your back, but he'll do it all the same.

R——: I say put the bill into effect.

E——: So do I. Put the bill into effect. Right efforts definitely are being made to enforce it.

R——: I don't know what would help, really I don't. I don't know. I wish I did.

Mrs. —— lives in one room of a small house in the center of the Hill District. The rest of the rooms she rents and lives on what she gets from them. Her room is in the center, on the ground floor and the people who live in the back and in the upstairs rooms must pass through room to reach theirs. Her room is well kept, the linoleum floor scrubbed, the windows brightly polished. A large, old fashioned side-board almost fills one side of the room. A coal stove stands almost in the center of the room in front of the mantle piece. Beneath the window stands the cot on which she sleeps. She sits in her rocker, her head bound in a kerchief and talks steadily and quietly:

I'm a southerner, I'm a real southerner. But I've lived here eighteen years. I came in 1922. I wanted and I wanted to come. I've always been a working woman and had saved much and I came here to make my home.

I'd been in the South all my life and hadn't seen much. I wanted to be among the Yankees and see what was going on. I decided to come here to work and better my condition, out of curiosity, to find something about the North. I liked Pittsburgh and decided to come here. I'd been in New York, on Long Island. And I didn't think there were enough of my people in New York for me to be happy. I hadn't been to Harlem, but I knew there were a lot there. I had acquaintances here but no black kin. A friend of mine, a woman who was my friend come on ahead. She likes it, and I come on ahead. She was a working woman just like I was. She told me the laws were better, my people were rated better, they got better wages, we got more consideration with our jobs and our work.

I'm a nurse and a housemaid. I'm a good nurse. I can recommend myself as a nurse. I really know how to take care of babies and small children.

I was born in Calhoun County, Alabama. My parents were farmers. We had a very small family. There were just three children. Mother put me out to service, and the people trained me. I was very young. I was about 13 or 14 when I began to get paid for my work. I liked it. I had to like it. No need to find fault, I had to work for my living, and that was my job. They were kind to me mostly. I got a good deal of pleasure out of it.

In the winter the Government gave us government funds for January, February, and March and we could go to school then. Just a little, for three months. The rest of the time my parents had to scrape up whatever they could to pay to have us taught. As soon as I got large enough to work that was all over. I had to go to work.

As it happened we lived near the school house. I was sorry when I had to quit. I read a little, but didn't have much to read. When we weren't in school, I burned brush, or I spent time knocking cornstalks. Or I had to help clean up new ground and get ready for planting. That's why I couldn't go to school longer than March. We had to help with the planting. We'd plant corn one year, plant cotton in the next. That's why in between we had to clear the ground.

Father was a good farmer. He was a Kentucky man and liked to raise a little tobacco. He liked to try to put in a little wheat too, and a few vegetables for us to eat in the winter. Father stood well in the community. We all stood well. Father rented on shares. We were sharecroppers, real sharecroppers, that you read so much about. The planters manage in a way that [they] didn't have anything left at the end of the year. Maybe a little corn to feed your hogs on. But the run of sharecroppers never had to sell. You always come out in debt.

I came here from Birmingham. I spent the best part of my life there. I came up by train, 800 and some odd miles. It was exciting. I couldn't bother about reading. I was looking out the window from the time the train pulled out till I got here. I didn't even get to sleep. I'd talked so much about it I felt like I was coming home, to my people.

I liked Pittsburgh, I felt very much at ease. I got a job with a nice family in Mt. Lebanon. I was nicely treated. I did general housework. I got the job through a friend, a kind of social worker. I applied to her. Pittsburgh wasn't strange. It was like Birmingham. They're both mineral towns. There's lots of coal and steel in both of them.

I just naturally felt more freedom. I was working for a newspaper man. He used to have stacks of papers. He had all kinds of papers. Being a newspaper man he got all the papers. They gave me news of Mr. Debs, everything he did. And I searched the papers for everything he said. I got hold of one of Mr. Debs speeches and I just searched the papers for everything he did at that time. And I got hold of one of Mr. Ruthenberg's speeches. I read everything that came out in the papers about Mr. Ruthenberg and Mr. Debs. Every move that Mr. Debs made came out in the Atlanta papers, and the *Kansas City Star*, and the *Detroit Free Press*—all the papers. I looked through those papers and read whatever I could find to read. I knew when Mr. Debs was sent to Atlanta and I watched the papers for everything he did. I knew I was a radical. That is another thing that made me want to come here. I wanted to use my strength too. I read about Mrs. Rankin, the woman suffrage woman. I wanted to get into some of those societies. I wanted to have a hand in it somewhere.

I fell off the step up here at the church one day and broke my hip. When I got well, my one leg was shorter than the other. I been crippled ever since. But I joined the Unemployment Councils. First, I went to the Shipton Street Local, and that went down. Then, I went to the Bloomer Way Local, and that went down. Then, I went to Our Way Local. But they all went down. But then, the Workers Alliance was organized out of a lot of the unemployed organizations. I've been a member ever since they started. I always felt my people ought to go a little further. I was never satisfied. It seems like they're not interested. You can't get them interested somehow. I have a friend who's got four boys, but there isn't one of them belongs to any organization. I feel like my people could do better. I think they should take an interest in the labor movement and work to our advantage.

I've lived ten years in this house on the Hill. I was in Pittsburgh six weeks before I got permanent work. Then I was in Mt. Lebanon for a long time. There's a difference, of course. Mt. Lebanon is a suburbanite district. I knew it was rough here, but I didn't have any trouble from the first time I came to live here. It's a rough neighborhood. It's disorderly, there are fights, and people get drunk and things like that. And a heap of times I've seen the patrol wagon come along and I knew the law was hunting somebody. But anywhere where people got something to drink, they get that rowdy way. It's the same thing exactly as in Birmingham, because there's so many of the same people here.

I don't do much. I just stay around home. I read the papers. Sometimes I go to church. Sometimes I go into the park. Maybe to watch a ball game. But mostly I just read my papers. I've been reading a continued story. I began it in the *Birmingham News* when I was in Alabama. And then when I came here I found it in the *Chronicle-Telegraph*. It was called the *Chronicle-Tele.*, then. That story started in 1916. I kept up with it till 1929. It's still going, but I just stopped reading it. Now it's called *Marriage Meddler*. It's the revelations of a wife. But it's changed its name, that's all. But now I don't like that kind of thing.

I go to church, but not a great deal. I'm not religious. I never was. I desired to be good and all that, but I was disgusted. The preacher was dishonest. I didn't like the management, so I didn't take any thought for it.

It was very difficult in the Unemployment Councils. Our meetings were very business like. Hardly a week we didn't meet at some eviction. And we'd be in demonstrations. Sometimes we'd go down to the Mayor's office. Or we'd picket somebody's home. We picketed Senator Coyne's home and the William Penn Hotel. That was in the early days of the Unemployment Councils. There was always a good crowd, men and women. We were all unemployed anyhow, and so we'd just be there.

I remember my first picket line. It was at the relief station of Fifth Avenue. We went up to the police station, too. I believe it was for getting checks enlarged for our rent, or for getting coal. When I went on my first picket line I was trying to get on relief. I applied in March and got on in June. I was crippled at that time and couldn't work. I was working up on Wylie Avenue and fell off a step-ladder and fractured my hip.[3]

I had heard about these things and read about them in my papers, but I never went into them. My people are some better off here, the law is more equal here. But we're certainly not equal in the eye of the law in Pittsburgh.

Since we have people in the struggles that tell us what to do, I think we should follow our leaders. They know what it's all about. If we follow them, we'll overcome in the struggle. We'll not be left in the dark, not knowing what to do, if we follow their instructions.

Things aren't good on the Hill here. The housing is not so good. The general living conditions are not good. Most houses and sidewalks need repairing. We need better garbage and rubbish service. My people here on the Hill don't fight hard enough. They don't try hard enough. Not enough of us fight. If everybody on this Hill had the same ideas I have, we'd get a lot done. We got to do more than complain.

We got to do it together. Some white men are our enemy, but we got enough white friends that, if we work together, we'll get what we want.

This girl that just came in don't like my organizations. I talk to her a lot. I tell her she ought to join, but she don't like our organizations because they say Negro. A lot of our people object to them on that account. But I tell them to get in and they can have it stopped. I don't like it either. I think it is better to say Black Man. Negro is just a nickname; I like Black Man better. If they're in the black race, that's what they are. The other sounds like what they're used to in Virginia. I don't like it, but I couldn't fall out with these organizations just because of that, because I don't like it. I have really got a nationality. If they say colored people I like it better. But since that's just the way I like it, that seems kind of silly. When all my people get a nationality and get a name, maybe they'll stop saying Negro. I'm not Mary Watkins. That's my father's master's name. I should have an African name. Negro means strength, but it's been a scandalous disgrace so long that we dislike it so. I do. I hate to hear that word.

We're supposed to be Muslims. If we accept no religion, then we go under the Moroccan flag and then we are called Moorish Americans. But that's all right. We'll just pass that up. When I'm introduced to a Mohammedan, I give him my Mohammedan name. He knows I am a free person. That's what counts. That's the reason I don't say anything. There was a Moorish Science

3. It is unclear whether the interviewee injured her hip falling from the church step (as stated a few paragraphs back) or a stepladder.

Temple here, about 1927. In a way they're carrying on yet. There's a big one in Braddock. They've got a Mosque there. In Homestead, they've got a Mosque and quite a lot of people. Once they had 1,800 here. But they don't stick to it. Just like they don't stick to anything. Why don't my people stick with anything?

I remember my father got hold of some union buttons once. He wore them in his cap like he should have done. But then when he went to the meeting a lot of people said, "Oh, you're a radical nigger." But father said he didn't mind that, they said the same thing about Mr. Lincoln and Mr. Grant. And I remember when we children used to be in the cotton field playing, the Republican children would be on the other side of the fence and they'd shout Hooray for Cleveland and Hendricks. But most all of the blacks in that part of the country were Republican on account of what Mr. Lincoln did.

I've seen a lot of the presidents. I saw Mr. Harrison and I saw Mr. Roosevelt, Mr. Teddy Roosevelt. I saw Mr. Harding at a distance. He came to Birmingham once and there was a great crowd. I saw Mr. Roosevelt several times when I went to New York.

My father was radical before me. He'd been a slave and so he took the radical side quite naturally. Quite naturally he sided with them. Everybody who was a slave was grateful to the northern people for what Mr. Lincoln did.

You'd be tickled to death if you knew what I thought about the Yankees when I was a child. I thought every Yankee had to wear blue, just like the northern soldiers wore. And then later I had another idea about the Yankees. When we were children, my father took us to a circus once. And I saw the men and women in tights riding the horses; so then I thought because the circus men and women were Yankees and wore tights, that all Yankee men and women wore tights. I thought for a long time that the Yankees had to dress like that.

And you know, ever since I have been grown, I wanted to see Miss Russell, Miss Lillian Russell. And Billie Burke. They were such beautiful women in their pictures. I knew Miss Russell's home was Pittsburgh, and I thought if I came to Pittsburgh, I'd see her. Then she died just before I came. Just two months before I came here. Oh, I had funny ideas when I was a child. Just think of my thinking every Yankee must be dressed in blue and that I didn't know that was just the uniform of northern soldiers.

Mrs. —— is the wife of a physician, a graduate of West Virginia State Teachers College and, for a time, a teacher in southern schools. She now devotes her time to keeping house and working with young women's community and civic groups. Mrs. —— wrote the following:

I am made conscious that, due to the fact that I am a Negro, I cannot get a job in any of the large stores in the city although I have much more education than many who are working in said stores. Until recently, no Negro teachers held positions in the city schools. In many sections of the city, members of the other races object to Negroes moving near them although the Negro may be buying and they can only afford to rent. Negro pupils must be more than outstanding to be recognized in the universities. They cannot join some of the white fraternities.

I cannot see immediate remedy in many of the above situations. I would advise that the Negro continue to do his best work at all times—continue to try to convince the other races that although the skin is pigmented, the features not too regular in many cases, accepting of all this, there beats a willing, able heart, there also dwells a soul that's as white as his neighbor's and a mind that if given a chance, can function as effectively as his white brother's.

However, our Negro leaders have a great opportunity here to touch this community in interracial get-togethers, not just political, as seemingly is being done chiefly for personal gain, but from a civic standpoint. Interracial clubs and forums could be organized so that the problems and questions of the community can be discussed and a better understanding gained.

I admit much is being accomplished through the above-mentioned organizations, but there is still great room for improvement in the clubs in furthering the program of the Negro race.

In reply to the minister who said, that as much has to be done among Negroes to make them tolerant toward whites as must be done among whites to make them tolerant toward Negroes, that is not true. Take the Negro from a young child—he loves to play with his little white neighbor friend and the little white friend likes to play with him. This is a beautiful thing. Until the white child's social life becomes an issue in his development, the parent or white society makes the white child realize he cannot continue playing and associating with that Negro child and hope to be accepted in the white race. The Negro has remained faithful until the white child breaks the ties of love and friendship. The Negro race dislikes the white race only when the white race has some way discriminated against or in some way injured its pride.

I believe that the Negro is making some contribution to his community through civic clubs. There is a greater civic pride in the Hill District since the city is hiring Negro school workers. The standards of living are slowly but surely improving; there is a greater effort than ever before towards home ownership. Such clubs as Hill City, Y.M.C.A., Y.W.C.A., "K" club and recreational centers show much progress.

I must say, Pittsburgh is a grand city. But it is still in its pioneer stages as far as the opportunities it offers to Negroes is concerned. I wonder if the Negro has not sat back to a large degree and not asked for what he wanted? Other cities are older in their cultural background for Negroes. This is a laborer's city. I feel if the Negro qualifies and then convinces the public he can do the job, there will be great opportunities in Pittsburgh.

I have not been in the city long enough to give an accurate statement or comment on the Equal Rights Act. There are pros and cons on this question. I imagine in some instances the law is avoided, others ignored. I have no statistics on this question, therefore I will not commit myself. However, it should be enforced.

M—— R—— is active in social work among young Negro men in Pittsburgh. He is a university graduate, is interested in interracial relationships and adjustments, in establishing forums for the discussion of social and economic problems, and in promoting cultural activities. He says:

I never walk down the street without discomforting consciousness that I'm a Negro. One reason is that I'm extremely interested in Negro problems and race relations, because my school, college, and vocational experience, and also my social relationships, have impressed upon my mind that there is a definite limitation and separate, circumscribed sphere within which my activities must be confined. If I'm downtown I know there are very few restaurants where I will be welcome. Movie houses accept, but do not generally wish for, the patronage of Negroes. While attending the University, the treatment I received by faculty and student body, while not what might be called unfriendly, was anything but warm. I become more and more aware of being a Negro because of the fact that as a Negro goes about his daily activities, regardless of what they may be, he is aware that he can go so far and no further, and that from only certain people can he receive decent treatment. The Negro learns from the time he leaves grade school, that he can move in a certain, restricted category of people, and can never be wholly accepted in civic or social life. When a Negro goes to get a job he knows it is almost useless to apply for anything in the factories and shops except manual work. We're conscious in the field of religion, too, that we can attend only Negro churches. As far as social relations between Negroes and whites, I think most Negroes have been friendly. But there are definite, precise limitations to that social relationship. The whites have a completely decided, biased opinion, which makes them feel bitter towards the Negro. This is due to the combination of a carry-over from slavery and a prejudice against color. So long as a Negro is a decent individual and behaves himself well, he should be accepted on equal grounds. Whites do not appreciate the potentialities of the Negro either in the past or the present. One day I went to buy a car. The salesman tried to be courteous. He asked me where I lived. I said "In Homewood." Then he asked, "Where do you attend church?" I told him and he replied, "Our maid goes to that church too, and she says they sure do shout and rant and have a good time." I resented that very much.

One day my wife and I went into a store. A number of men who had been working in the street were sitting on the stools at the counter. We sat at the end of the counter and asked to be served. The waiter said, "You'll have to go over in that corner," and he pointed to the rear of the store. I said, "But I want to sit here." He went over to the head waiter and they whispered together for a minute. Our waiter returned to us and said, "We're out of dishes right now, but we can wrap what you want to take out." I walked out of the place and across the street to a policeman. The policeman came back to the store with me, and tried to smooth out the difficulty as well as he could, but we weren't served. My wife and I walked out of the store with the policeman and stood talking with him on the street. He told us to go to a magistrate and swear out information on the incident. I did, but have had no report from the magistrate. This is typical of what we have to face in a city like Pittsburgh. When a Negro gets himself an education and is a highly trained, socially useful individual, there is no reason why he should be treated in this condescending way.

Since the Negro does not have an equal opportunity with the white man it is almost presumptuous for him to go ask for a job.

As to the remedy for this kind of thing, I believe that the people who profess a Christian faith should expound from the pulpit that discrimination and shackles be removed from 12,000,000 people. The Negro himself must in the first place become conscious of what his problem is. A lot of Negroes are fighting the wrong thing. Those who have interests in institutions, clubs, political organizations and all such institutions have a definite picture of what they are seeking. I think the churches represent the largest organized body among Negroes. And consequently through the churches a lot can be done. Club life gives an interchange of ideas. If Negroes are accepted into political and civic life, they would be readily accepted by whites.

Negroes are restricted and segregated into certain districts in Pittsburgh. If I want to rent a house I can rent only in particular districts, not anywhere I might like to live. Here I am, an educated, law-abiding, well behaved man, but I can't choose where I want to live. I have to take the district offered to me as though I were guilty of some misdemeanor. The Negro will not progress so long as this blatant injustice is practiced.

The outlook for the Negro is, of course, much brighter in the North than in the South. Interchange of ideas is greater in a city like Pittsburgh because we do get a chance to mingle with a little more freedom than we do in the South.

The Civil Rights Act is being evaded. Even the least corrupt judge will evade when he does not ignore the law.

Mrs. —— does secretarial work at one of the leading Negro social institutions in Pittsburgh. She and her husband live in the East End of the city, own their own car, and are members of the Negro middle class of the city. Mr. —— is an automobile mechanic. Mrs. —— is active in church work and the work of a new community center opened in the lower Hill District. She was born and grew up in Pittsburgh, and graduated from high school. Here she wrote out her impressions and ideas:

In nearly every instance where there is interracial contact, there is always, more or less, an attitude of condescension, or (sometimes unconscious) exhibit of superiority complex, which always creates a resentment in the heart of the Negro. We come daily in contact with open antagonistic feelings and expressions of dislike, and racial hatred which has the tendency to create the same spirit, and arouse the spirit of retaliation in the breasts of the Negro. This will have to be eliminated, dispelled from the hearts and minds of both the whites and Negroes before interracial peace and harmony can exist. It will take generations to bring about such peace. The Negro is not pleading for social equality, but justice, fair-play in the courts, a chance to make a decent living of which he is denied on every hand.

Yes, I think there is a remedy, but not an immediate one, it will have to be a gradual process. Through interracial adjustments, the white race having closer contact with the more intelligent Negro; and unbiased study of the Negro history, their past, present, and a clearer insight into their future outlook. When the white man shall cease to judge the Negro race as a whole, by the short-comings of the illiterate and criminal element of the race, and accept a Negro as a man with the same propensities, the same proclivities, and the same ideals as the white man, then I think we will be getting one step nearer [to] solving the so called "Negro Problem."

The Negro must prepare himself educationally, he must insist upon his rights as an *American citizen*. Mixed schools for our American youth. The working together of interracial groups, and organizations solving kindred problems together, all which will surely have a tendency to create a mutual respect and understanding, one race for the other.

The Negro *must be educated industrially*; the teaching of Booker T. Washington is not obsolete. One of the greatest needs of today is *training in indus-trialism*, preparedness. This may not be the whole need, but undoubtedly one of the most essential, the training of the *hands*, as well as the *head* and the *heart*.

The named organizations have been a salvation to the Negro race, but they still have not reached the limit of their service to the race. The church is still wielding the strongest influence through its educated ministry, intelligent evangelism, and social service program.

The Negro minister is still the great torch bearer, the greatest influence and leadership among the Negro race. The church must emphasize the great need of *Home Missions*, to help alleviate the suffering of their own people. The Negro church today must stand for the Emancipation from an un-American standard of living; it must stand for, and contend for the highest ideal of manhood, and honest living unhampered by political intrigue or monopoly and graft.

Organizations are seriously hampered by economic conditions, the lack of finance to carry on the much needed work that otherwise might be accom-plished.

The thousands of Negro youth that are annually coming from the schools and colleges are demanding an educated ministry, and the type of sermons that are practical, and can be applied to the everyday life.

I think that the expression of this minister that as much must be done to make Negroes tolerant of whites as to make whites tolerant of Negroes is prevalent thought of the intelligent Negro. There is a surprising amount of prejudice existing among Negroes against whites, and we realize the vice-versa. Among thousands of Negroes, we might say millions, there exists sim-ply a spirit of toleration. I think, however, that the interracial movements, the education of Negro and white youth, combined with religious influence, again plays an important part towards the progress of creating a better under-standing between the two races.

Such organizations as the recent "Hill City" movement to help prevent crime among the youth, will help solve the problem. The Y.M.C.A., and the Y.W.C.A., the Kay Community Club, the Sojourner Truth Neighborhood House, all have character building programs, lofty ideals, fair-play, which excites a desire for a higher standard of living. Our social workers, the Urban League with its extensive civic and industrial program, the Harriet Tubman Guild, Inc., with approximately 200 organized workers, are doing splendid work among the hospitals for Negro convalescents. The Tuberculosis Ser-vice League, with an annual program, and an annual Donation Day, they make and present hundreds of garments and clothing to the patients.

James —— is a night watchman in a downtown bank. His wife does housework to help enlarge the family budget. Mr. —— likes to talk with anyone and everyone about things that are close to his interests. For several hours he sat in the
living room of the family for whom his wife works and talked. He said:

Yes ma'am, I like living in Pittsburgh. I was raised here you might say, and
I'm used to conditions. I was eleven years old when I came here from North
Carolina. Been here 22 years. Came here to visit and stayed. A lot of people I
know came here to visit and just stayed.

Well, now, I'm going to talk candidly with you. Only difference is a little
more freedom than the South. Living conditions are just as bad and intolerance isn't much better. In a way, I guess I'd rather live in the South. From the
color standpoint, it's easier. In the South you *know* you can't go into restaurants and places, and there's no temptation. I'd rather live there; you know
where you stand, and here in Pittsburgh, you can't always tell.

Remember the night of the Conn-Pastor fight? I was standing in front of
a restaurant there in East Liberty with some friends. A couple of men came
out after the fight was over—they'd been listening to the radio, and one of
them, he was a foreigner but he talked pretty good English, he said to the
man he was with, "Well, Conn beat Pastor . . . now he'll be ready to fight that
nigger!" He said it to this man but he looked right at me all the time and I was
mad for a minute and I turned to my friend and I said, "Louis will be ready
to fight that peck." Now that's a fightin' word. It's the same when we use it
like whites using the term "nigger." Maybe he didn't hear me and maybe he
wouldn't know that anyway, but for a minute there I was mad.

Where I'm working at now I asked my employer about buying a car. He
said I couldn't afford a car and he looked at me and said, "You don't need a
car." Now, maybe I can't afford a car but a lot of people who have cars can't
afford them. And what he meant was that I shouldn't have a car because I'm
colored. It was from a racial view point he said that.

After I lived in Pittsburgh for a while, I got a job in Indiana, Pennsylvania.
There was no color question or trouble there at all. There were only about
five Negro families in the community and they were employed in the hotel
and bus stations. Everybody knew everybody else and I wasn't there two
days before the whole town knew there was a new colored boy in town. The
Negroes there went into the white stores and were invited to white parties.
They gave a big dance there and what colored was there danced with whites.
It made me uncomfortable, somehow. I wasn't use to it. A boy I knew there,
Freddy, married a white girl and they were happy. They had children and

they'd all go shopping and around together and everybody accepted it just as if she were colored or he was white.

But take Clarksburg, West Virginia, about 75 miles from here. The attitude there is typically southern. A boy I knew worked there and he came back. I guess Pittsburgh is more like Clarksburg. One day on Wylie Avenue . . . It was a nice sunny afternoon . . . I met two white girls. One of them I knew pretty well and she was married to a colored friend of mine. She was a very nice girl and she lived in Mt. Washington. She introduced me to her friend and we were talking about a new job her husband just got. I said to give him my regards and they walked on down the street. Just then, a radio car pulled up and said, "What are you doing?" I said I knew her, and her husband was a friend of mine. And they asked me her name and where she lived and I said, "Mt. Washington," and I told them I didn't know anything about the other girl and then they drove off. My brother-in-law, he said about Hitler and the Negroes, he said, "The Negroes wouldn't be any worse off under Hitler than they are now." I don't quite agree to that though. That Hitler, he'd have a problem on his hands with all of us, wouldn't he? Ha!

I believe in equality of rights, but not exactly social. I just want the same chance to better myself and have things. I heartily believe in the Equal Rights Law but it's not being enforced. The —— Theater downtown. Colored people are supposed to sit in the last ten rows. And —— Restaurant. A Negro in —— is not wanted anymore, like he used to be. We used to go in there all night and get something to eat, but we're not wanted during the last few years or so. Different managers or different policies or objections from white customers. Mostly lower classes of whites look down on the Negro as inferior. Middle classes just don't think about it. I think the Equal Rights Law should be enforced in all places open to the public. I don't ask [for] equal social rights. There's too much race misunderstanding on both sides. I know of some Negroes who actually hate whites, hate them as a race just as a lot of whites hate the Negroes, and I mean hate.

They had a forum here, a Catholic, a Jew, a Negro, and a Japanese. I don't know how it came out. Forums might find the cause and the answer. I don't know. It is good for people of all kinds to set up and discuss problems together and talk things over without any trouble. Education in both races is the only thing to look forward to. The Parent Teachers Association does a lot of good. Out at Garfield school, the P.T.A. secretary is a Negro. I don't think children have such race consciousness at first. Some white children come along every morning and pick up Bessie, my niece, and they all walk to school together.

But here's one thing in our school systems here. They're harder on you than they are on the whites. When I came I was put into 4A and I had been through all that but they put me there and I stayed there the rest of the semester and I didn't feel like studying too hard because I knew all that. I learned the hard way. And Bessie, just the other day, was talking about a little girl who got a better mark than she did, but Bessie was just as bright. You've got to be better than the next person if they're white, even in athletics.

Living conditions here are pretty poor, I think, even in better places. When the whites move out, rents are raised for colored people and landlords refuse to fix up places. It's not much better than in the South. Wages are higher here but then so is the cost of living. I'd venture to say that housing and living conditions in the South are improving more rapidly than here in Pittsburgh. Of course the housing projects here elevate some, but there's an awful lot left.

From what I've seen in Philadelphia, conditions are worse than they are here. Houses are all crowded together. In New York, most Negroes get by as easily as possible. They're largely contented because of economic betterment. They have representation in pretty much everything and now they're not concerned much with bettering themselves. In Cleveland, sometime ago, there was picketing. They picketed white business houses there because they wouldn't employ Negroes. It was violent, perhaps, but they gained their objective and now they have a Negro judge and police captains. We're about fifty years behind times here. Negroes don't have much successful business here except the *Pittsburgh Courier*. We don't even have a colored police magistrate. Take our third and fifth wards . . . we have some business men . . . the theaters there employ Negroes but are not owned by them. In the last five years I know they've been working in chain stores. . . . Until we awaken to the fact that the Negro of the third and fifth wards can gain our objectives by writing and voting, we'll never get anywhere. Power of the polls is our only weapon.

The majority of colored boys with specific training get work easily enough in laboring classifications. But there's not much for the educated ones. A lot of them go South where there are Negro schools for them to teach in and Negro businesses. There are no opportunities for them here. The *Courier* got one teacher here in music in the public schools. We're too contented to let things go as they are.

There was the Negro Cooperative. It worked pretty well for a while, but it died completely out just from the lack of interest. Now, on Frankstown Avenue, there are seven beer gardens, one of which is owned by a Negro. But the other six are better patronized by colored people because they are not so badly managed. He just didn't bother to keep good order. When he first opened up he had a pretty good class of trade, but when fights and rumpuses started, the trade fell off. "Bucket of Blood," I called it, and we don't go there because it's so tough.

In getting somewhere you've got to get somewhere yourself. Even with bad heredity and bad environment, you still do only what you *want* to do. My parents lived around that old rubble, but I got out. Things like this . . . people say that prostitution among Negroes is due to necessity, that they're forced into it. I think it's just because it's easy to get by that way. They'd rather do that than work. A lot of us would starve to death before we'd do anything like that. Yes, you do what you want to and to get somewhere, well, like I said, you've got to get somewhere yourself.

Howard MacKinney has done wonderful work with that "Hill City" idea of his. He relieved petty crime 60%. Homer Brown is our great salvation, I think. He's in contact with all classes of his race most of the time. He knows us, believes in us, and tries to help us all. Some other prominent Negroes are not reliable. They stick to their own economic and social class. And color snobbery is pretty bad, too. Some social clubs send invitations to only light-skinned Negroes, and it's understood if you receive one you shouldn't take a very dark-skinned person as your guest. Larger churches don't do much good either because of class distinction and snobbery. People can't work together that way for race betterment.

Racial prejudices through ignorance have to be broken down and they will be some day, but it will take a long time. If white people who don't know of us would stop judging all by the actions of the few, the criminals who make headlines with murder, rape, and theft, we'd have a better chance. We'll have to promote more understanding, a lot more on both sides, before prejudice can be broken down.

MEMORIAL OF PITTSBURGH'S FREE CITIZENS OF COLOR

Memorial of The Free Citizens of Color in Pittsburgh and its Vicinity.
Relative to the Right of Suffrage
Read in Convention—July 8, 1837
Harrisburgh
Printed by Thompson & Clark, 1837
Historical Society
*Call #V.S.*2*

Lewis Woodson
Reference:
Proctor Hair Shop
616 5th Avenue
Pittsburgh, Penna.

Mrs. Carolyn Stevenson
Great Grand-Daughter of
Lewis Woodson.

MEMORIAL

To the Honorable Convention assembled for the purpose of proposing to the people of Pennsylvania, amendments to the existing Constitution of Pennsylvania.

The Memorial of the undersigned free citizens of color, residing in Pittsburgh and its vicinity, respectfully represents:

That they have heard, with surprise and alarm, of an intention seriously expressed by some of the members of your honorable body, so to amend the Constitution as to make the right of suffrage depend not on the fact of being a freeman and a tax-payer, but on the complexion, whether dark or fair, which it may have pleased God to confer on the good people of the Commonwealth.

That such an attempt should be meditated by a single individual in the year eighteen hundred and thirty seven, may well be regarded as a matter of astonishment.

It has been deemed both at home and abroad, a matter of just sarcasm, that, whilst the Declaration of Independence boasts of the universal equality of men, in many of the States one half of the community is the absolute property of the other subject to the despotic will, nay to the passion, caprice, and cruelty of a master. In Pennsylvania, while sentiment has triumphed over this glaring inconsistency, the brave spirits who achieved the Revolution laid the foundation of a system by which slavery has been extinguished. The preamble of the noble act of the first of March, 1790, breathes a spirit which surely cannot have departed from the land. We beg leave to recall its imperishable language:

> When we contemplate our abhorrence of that condition to which the arms and tyranny of Great Britain were exerted to reduce us, when we look back on the variety of dangers to which we have been exposed, and how miraculously our wants in many instances have been supplied, and our deliverance wrought, when even hope and human fortitude had become unequal to the conflict we are unavoidably led to a serious and grateful sense of the manifold blessings which we have deservedly received from the hand of that Being, from whom every good and perfect gift cometh. Impressed with these ideas, we conceive that it is our duty, and we rejoice that is in our power, to extend a portion of that freedom to others, which hath been extended to us, and release from that state of thraldom to which we ourselves were doomed and from which we have now every prospect of being delivered. It is not for us to inquire why, in the creation of mankind, the inhabitants of the several parts of the earth were distinguished by a difference in feature and complexion. It is sufficient to know that all are the work of an Almighty hand. We find in the distribution of the human species, that the most fertile as well as the most barren parts of the earth are inhabited by men of complexions different from ours and from each other, from whence we may reasonably, as well as religiously infer, that He who placed them in their various situations, hath extended equally His care and protection to all, and that it becometh not us to counteract His mercies. We esteem it a peculiar blessing granted to us, that we are enabled this day to add one more step to universal civilization, by removing as much as possible, the sorrows of those who have lived in undeserved bondage, and from which, by the assumed authority of the Kings of Great Britain, no effectual legal relief could be obtained. Weaned by a long course of experience from those narrow prejudices and partialities we had imbibed, we find our hearts enlarged with kindness and benevolence towards men of all conditions and nations; and we conceive ourselves at this particular period extraordinarily called upon, by the blessings which we have received, to manifest the sincerity of our profession, and give a substantial proof of our gratitude.

Such were the sentiments promulgated fifty-seven years ago, by the fathers of the Commonwealth: The undersigned cannot but believe that to discard these now and to fall back upon barbarous prejudices, would be not less impolite than unjust and cruel.

The danger under which some of our sister states is now trembling is, that they hold within their bosom a population cut off from social rights, and looking with sullen discontent or eager hostility on all around them. In Pennsylvania, the colored man, under her liberal and enlightened policy, has been taught to feel that he has an interest in common with the white man in sustaining her free institutions. He has felt that he shared in the blessing of her condition; and it has been his pride to show by his conduct as a citizen, that he is not unworthy of having been restored to the rights of humanity.

Believing that information would be interesting, we beg leave to submit to your honorable body, certain statements which accompany this memorial, (marked respectively A, B and F.) They show our present condition, the stand that has been taken in the useful pursuits of life, in the requisition of property, and the efforts made to ameliorate the condition of our race.

And your memorialist will ever pray, etc., Pittsburgh, Penn. June 26th 1837.

John B. Vashon,

A. D. Lewis,

O. R. Lewis,

R. L. Hopkins,

Otho Mathews,

James McKnight *(His Mark)*,

Daniel Smith *(His Mark)*,

Othelo Darsey *(His Mark)*,

Samuel Berry,

George Parker,

B. J. Colder,

Samuel Sanders,

Va. Johnston,

Matthew Jones,

Samuel Bruce *(His Mark)*,

Owen Barrett *(His Mark)*,

John Cook *(His Mark)*,

James Gillard *(His Mark)*,

B. W. Wilkins,

A. Ball,

E. Sears,

Steaven McGill *(His Mark)*,

A. Bedfort *(His Mark)*,

Samuel Johnston,

John M. Mitchell,

Chambers Peters,

George Powell *(His Mark)*,

H. Vashon,

C. Jones,

Robert Bailey,

J. W. Brown *(His Mark)*,

Zelicher Newman,

Henry Anderson,

Samuel Collins *(His Mark)*,

Charles Cook *(His Mark)*,

O. S. Williamson, Jr.,

Thomas Norris,

Peter Ennis *(His Mark)*,

George Woods *(His Mark)*,

S. Norris *(His Mark)*,

John Graham *(His Mark)*,

Henry Woods *(His Mark)*,

Solomon Phillips *(His Mark)*,

Charles Weddly *(His Mark)*,

James Parker *(His Mark)*,

Peter Starks *(His Mark)*,

Edward R. Parker,

Issac Sheldon *(His Mark)*,

Hugh Tanner,

Henry Collins *(His Mark)*,

Samuel Ranyolds,

Benjamin Jones,

Charles Clark,

James F. Douglass,

Richard Bryans,

Lewis Davis,

George W. Boler,

Thomas Knox *(His Mark)*,

George Spearse,

Lewis Woodson,

George Carney,

Geo. Wheeler *(His Mark)*,

Robert Henderson *(His Mark)*,

Reuben Farmer *(His Mark)*,

Nathaniel Dixon *(His Mark)*,

John Peck

William O. Krow,

Henry Myers *(His Mark)*,

Joseph Manks,

Abraham Strawdeo,

Edward Talbert,

Henry Seaton,

Robert Brown,

Jube Newton *(His Mark)*,

Benjamin Russel *(His Mark)*,

David Body *(His Mark)*,

Joseph Mahonney,

James Coleman,

Ebenezer Findley,

The committee appointed by the free colored citizens of the city of Pittsburgh, at their public meeting on the thirteenth of June 1837, to make certain inquiries concerning the moral, social, and political condition of the colored population of Pittsburgh, and its vicinity, have performed the duty assigned them and beg leave to submit the following report:

The number of colored population of the city of Pittsburgh, and villages immediately adjacent, is supposed to be about two thousand five hundred. Their manner of living is generally the same as that of those among whom they are located. The sacred obligations and duties of the family relation are respected and practiced among them, as it is among all Christian people. They are believers in the doctrines of the Bible and the worshipers of that God whose attributes and character it more fully unfolds. They are the decided friends of good order, and the supremacy of the laws under which they live; and feel a warm interest in the peace, safety, honor and prosperity of the Commonwealth.

The colored population of the city of Pittsburgh have under their exclusive government, one African Methodist Episcopal Church of two hundred and five members. The house in which they worship belongs to them, and is a substantial brick building, newly enlarged and repaired, and furnished with comfortable pews, carpets, Venetian window blinds and opaque lamps, and is valued at ten thousand dollars. The congregation is large, orderly and well attended. Their doors are always open to all well behaved people; and no person has been excluded from the best of their seats, on account of the complexion which it may have pleased the Almighty to give him. Besides these, there are a number of colored persons assigned to the Presbyterian, Episcopalian, Baptist, and Catholic congregations of the city.

They have a very flourishing Sunday School of ninety-seven scholars and fifteen teachers; furnished with a Library, selected chiefly from the publications of the American Sunday School Union. This school is exerting a most happy influence on the moral character of the rising youth.

They have a common day school, taught by a young colored man, a graduate of the Ohio University. The number of scholars now in regular attendance is eighty-five, many of whom are making rapid progress in their studies, and are preparing for future usefulness and respectability in society. The house in which it is taught and the lot on which it stands, both belong to the colored people, and is valued at two thousand dollars; and the school is supported entirely by the colored people.

They have a Temperance Society of about one hundred and seventy members. This society is now in active operation; and no institution ever exerted a more happy influence on the moral character of any people than this has done on the moral character of the colored people in Pittsburgh. They have purchased with their own funds, and distributed gratuitously, three hundred copies of the Temperance Almanac; besides a considerable number of Temperance tracts. And they are now regularly taking eighty copies of the Pennsylvania Temperance Recorder.

They have a moral reform and literary society, whose object is the improvement of the morals, the promotion of the mechanic arts, and the diffusion of useful knowledge among all classes of the colored people.

They have among them four benevolent society, male and female; the oldest of which has in its treasury, a fund of two hundred and twenty dollars. And the treasuries of the others are solvent and well supported. The object of these societies is to relieve the wants of their members and friends; when in sickness or distress; thereby preventing the disgrace of their become chargeable to the State as paupers, or going to the common poor-house.

The amount of property and poll tax paid by the colored citizens of Pittsburgh, amounts to about four hundred and twenty-two dollars, according to the report of the City collector, which accompanies this report and is marked F. The amount of water tax paid by them is about four hundred dollars. The amount of house rent paid by them is about ten thousand dollars. And the amount of real estate owned by them is valued at ——[1] thousand dollars.

In the city of Pittsburgh there are colored mechanics embracing the following trades viz.: carpenters, blacksmiths, bricklayers, stone masons, boot and shoemakers, plasterers, painters, tanners and curriers, copper-smiths, and shipwrights; and in the vicinity of the City there are several farmers. All these are constantly, and some of them very successfully employed in their several avocations. It has been frequently remarked by impartial observers, that there is less idleness and drunkenness among the colored people who actually live in the City than among any other class of her population. The amount of pauperism among them is extremely small and, accord-

1. Number is missing in the original manuscript.

ing to the report of the overseers of the poor, which accompanies this report, and is marked B, does not average more than three in a year (his own language was "perhaps only a little over two; and the annual expense of these is about $75 each.")

In the village of Arthursville, immediately adjacent to the City on the east side, about seventy-one colored families reside. Thirty-six of these are the owners of real estate; the very lowest estimate of which is thirty-six thousand dollars. For some of the lots as much as two thousand five hundred dollars has been offered. The remaining thirty-five families are tenants, at from three to four dollars a month rent; amounting in the aggregate to about fourteen hundred and twenty-eight dollars. The people of this village have erected for themselves a small church, in which divine service is celebrated every Sabbath day. They have a Sunday School from eighty to eighty-five scholars; and also a very full common school. The people of this village have done much to acquire the property they possess—to improve and make their dwellings comfortable—to educate their children, and to prepare them for future usefulness and respectability.

In the borough of Allegheny town, lying immediately west of the City, twenty-seven colored families reside. Seven of these are the owners of real estate, some of which is highly valuable, lying near the centre of the business part of the borough. Eight are the owners of valuable leases and twelve are tenants, whose aggregate rent is four hundred and fifty-eight dollars. The property tax of some of them is ten dollars and forty cents, whilst some is as low as three dollars seventy cents. All the others pay the usual poll tax.

The Committee have not had time to pursue their investigations further. They believe, however, that enough has been exhibited, to satisfy any unprejudiced mind that the colored population appreciate their present privileges; and are endeavoring to sustain themselves honorably, and respectably in the community in which they live. Whatever of ignorance or degradation there is among us, owes its existence chiefly to our former condition in life. Slavery, that unrighteous, and unnatural state in which many of us were raised, deprived us of every means of moral cultivation, and caught its own sordid interest in shutting out every ray of intellectual light. The fathers of this Commonwealth abolished this wicked system; and the wisdom of their deed is evinced in the fact that as we further recede from the fetters of the slave, we are better prepared to sustain the honors and high responsibilities of freemen.

In conclusion, the committee would say, let it be the chief pride of our existence to render ourselves worthy the land of William Penn.

> John B. Vashon, - of Pittsburgh
> Joseph Mahonney, - of Alleghenytown
> Samuel Ranyolds, - of Pittsburgh
> Thomas Knox, - of Arthursville
> Lewis Woodson, - of Pittsburgh
> Committee
> Pittsburgh, June 19, 1837.

The foregoing report was read, and unanimously adopted in public meeting of the free colored citizens of Pittsburgh, and ordered to accompany their memorial to the Convention for proposing amendments to the existing constitution of Pennsylvania, now met at Harrisburg.

Lewis Woodson, Secty.

Pittsburgh, June 28, 1837

- B -

Pittsburgh, July 3d, 1837.

The colored population of the City average three persons chargeable, or something like $75.00 per year for each person.

Chas. Craig,

Overseer

- F -

J. B. Vashon	pays	130.00
Ch. Richards		46.00
Geo. Gardner		24.00
Frone Logan		22.00
A. Lewis		30.00
J. Mitchell		20.00
T. Morris		18.00
Mrs. Lewis		7.00
Total		$297.00

The above named persons pay the amount of city and poor tax, and there are at least one hundred men who pay a poll tax of $1.25 each.
Thos. Dickson, City Collector.

BIRTHDAY MEMORANDUM OF LEWIS WOODSON

Written by Lewis Woodson on His 50th Birthday
Pittsburgh, January 22, 1856.

This is my birthday. Today I am fifty years of age. On the 22nd of January, 1846, when I was forty years old, I felt very solemn, and had an unusually clear and distinct recollection of all the principal events of my past life, and was very deeply impressed with the thought that I had lived out full half of my days on earth. And deeming it as a turning point in the duration of my natural life, I thought it a proper time to begin my life anew, and devote it more strictly to the will of God; and lest I should forget the promise and covenant which I then made, I wrote it down in the form of an item, or memorandum which I have now before me. On reading it over I see nothing objectionable in it, but on the contrary I approve of it all, and do hereby solemnly and deliberately renew it. And as I have not willfully violated it in any particular heretofore, I pray God to help me to keep it hereafter with unfailing fidelity.

When I was just forty years of age, and wrote the memorandum before alluded to, I thought that when I should be Fifty, I would feel the effect of age quite sensibly; but today, I find myself most happily disappointed, for I feel quite vigorous in body, and more clear, strong and vigorous in mind than I ever felt in all my life. In fact my taste for learning, and for mental improvement of every kind, is still improving. And although there I have no assignable reason to assign for it, my spirit is still buoyant, and my hope of the future is bright. One thing I think is very remarkable in my past ten years experience, and that is its sameness or uniformity. All my feelings, habits or pursuits have been almost daily the same throughout the whole time. Sameness of employment, locality, and association may have contributed to the sameness of feeling for such a considerable length of time.

Only one thing seems to cast any shadow upon the prospect of the future, my poor wife who has been the sharer of my varied fortune for the last thirty-two years, has apparently lost her health, and to all human appearance, unless she soon recovers it again, must be soon taken away from me. My hope was that, as we had been so long together, God would permit us to continue together until the end of our earthly pilgrimage. But nevertheless I bow in submission to His blessed will. And to the most holy Trinity be everlasting praise, AMEN.

TWO POEMS BY GEORGE B. VASHON

Typist: E. Saunier / Rewriteman: J. Ernest Wright /
September, 1940 / Final

Vincent Ogé (1854)

There is, at times, an evening sky—
The twilight's gift—of sombre hue,
   All checkered wild and gorgeously
With streaks of crimson, gold and blue;—
   A sky that strikes the soul with awe,
And, though not brilliant as the sheen,
   Which in the east at morn we saw,
Is far more glorious, I ween;—
    So glorious that, when night hath come
    And shrouded it in deepest gloom,
    We turn aside with inward pain
    And pray to see that sky again.
    Such sight is like the struggle made
    When freedom bids unbare the blade,
    And calls from every mountain-glen—
From every hill—from every plain,
   Her chosen ones to stand like men,
And cleanse their souls from every stain
   Which wretches, steeped in crime and blood,
   Have cast upon the form of God.
   Though peace like morning's golden hue,
With blooming groves and waving fields,
   Is mildly pleasing to the view,
And all the blessings that it yields
   Are fondly welcomed by the breast
Which finds delight in passion's rest,

That breast with joy foregoes them all,
While listening to Freedom's call.
Though red the carnage,—though the strife
Be filled with groans of parting life,—
Though battle's dark, ensanguined skies
Give echo but to agonies—
To shrieks of wild despairing,—
We willingly repress a sigh—
Nay, gaze with rapture in our eye,
Whilst *"Freedom!"* is the rally-cry
That calls to deeds of daring.

The waves dash brightly on thy shore,
Fair island of the southern seas!
As bright in joy as when of yore
They gladly hailed the Genoese,—
That daring soul who gave to Spain
A world—last trophy of her reign!
Basking in beauty, thou dost seem
A vision in a poet's dream!
Thou look'st as though thou claim'st not birth
With sea and sky and other earth,
That smile around thee but to show
Thy beauty in a brighter glow,—
That are unto thee as the foil
Artistic hands have featly set
Around Golconda's radiant spoil,
To grace some lofty coronet,—
A foil which serves to make the gem
The glory of that diadem!

If Eden claimed a favored haunt,
Most hallowed of that blessed ground,
Where tempting fiend with guileful taunt
A resting-place would ne'er have found,—
As shadowing it well might seek
The loveliest home in that fair isle,
Which in its radiance seemed to speak
As to the charmed doth Beauty's smile,
That whispers of a thousand things

For which words find no picturings.
Like to the gifted Greek who strove
To paint a crowning work of art,
And form his ideal Queen of Love,
By choosing from each grace a part,
Blending them in one beauteous whole,
To charm the eye, transfix the soul,
And hold it in enraptured fires,
Such as a dream of heaven inspires,—
So seem the glad waves to have sought
From every place its richest treasure,
And borne it to that lovely spot,
To found thereon a home of pleasure;—
A home where balmy airs might float
Through spicy bower and orange grove;
Where bright-winged birds might turn the note
Which tells of pure and constant love;
Where earthquake stay its demon force,
And hurricane its wrathful course;
Where nymph and fairy find a home,
And foot of spoiler never come.

And Ogé stands mid this array
Of matchless beauty, but his brow
Is brightened not by pleasure's play;
He stands unmoved—nay, saddened now,
As doth the lorn and mateless bird
That constant mourns, whilst all unheard,
The breezes freighted with the strains
Of other songsters sweep the plain,—
That ne'er breathes forth a joyous note,
Though odors on the zephyrs float—
The tribute of a thousand bowers,
Rich in their store of fragrant flowers.
Yet Ogé's was a mind that joyed
With nature in her every mood,
Whether in sunshine unalloyed
With darkness, or in tempest rude
And, by the dashing waterfall,
Or by the gently flowing river,

Or listening to the thunder's call,
He'd joy away his life forever.
    But ah! life is a changeful thing,
And pleasures swiftly pass away,
    And we may turn, with shuddering,
From what we sighed for yesterday.
        The guest, at banquet-table spread
        With choicest viands, shakes with dread,
        Nor heeds the goblet bright and fair,
        Nor tastes the dainties rich and rare,
        Nor bids his eye with pleasure trace
        The wreathed flowers that deck the place,
        If he but knows there is a draught
        Among the cordials, that, if quaffed,
        Will send swift poison through his veins.
So Ogé seems; nor does his eye
    With pleasure view the flowery plains,
The bounding sea, the spangled sky,
    As, in the short and soft twilight,
The stars peep brightly forth in heaven,
    And hasten to the realms of night,
As handmaids of the Even.

        The loud shouts from the distant town,
        Joined in with nature's gladsome lay;
        The lights went glancing up and down,
Riv'ling the stars—nay, seemed as they
Could stoop to claim, in their high home,
        A sympathy with things of earth,
And had from their bright mansions come,
        To join them in their festal mirth.
        For the land of the Gaul had arose in its might,
        And swept by as the wind of a wild, wintry night;
        And the dreamings of greatness—the phantoms of
        power,
        Had passed in its breath like the things of an hour.
        Like the violet vapors that brilliantly play
        Round the glass of the chemist, then vanish away,
        The visions of grandeur which dazzlingly shone,
        Had gleamed for a time, and all suddenly gone.

And the fabric of ages—the glory of kings,
Accounted most sacred mid sanctified things,
Reared up by the hero, preserved by the sage,
And drawn out in rich hues on the chronicler's page,
Had sunk in the blast, and in ruins lay spread,
While the altar of freedom was reared in its stead.
And a spark from that shrine in the free-roving breeze,
Had crossed from fair France to that isle of these
And a flame was there kindled which fitfully shone
Mid the shout of the free, and the dark captive's groan;
As, mid contrary breezes, a torch-light will play,
Now streaming up brightly—now dying away.

The reptile slumbers in the stone,
Nor dream we of his pent abode;
The heart conceals the anguished groan,
With all the poignant griefs that goad
The brain to madness;
Within the hushed volcano's breast,
The molten fires of ruin lie;—
Thus human passions seem at rest,
And on the brow serene and high,
Appears no sadness.
But still the fires are raging there,
Of vengeance, hatred, and despair;
And when they burst, they wildly pour
Their lava flood of woe and fear,
And in one short—one little hour,
Avenge the wrongs of many a year.

And Ogé standeth in his hall;
But now he standeth not alone;—
A brother's there, and friends; and all
Are kindred spirits with his own;
For mind will join with kindred mind,
As matter's with its like combined.
They speak of wrongs they had received—
Of freemen, of their rights bereaved;
And as they pondered o'er the thought
Which in their minds so madly wrought,

Their eyes gleamed as the lightning's flash,
Their words seemed as the torrent's dash
That falleth, with a low, deep sound,
Into some dark abyss profound,—
A sullen sound that threatens more
Than other torrents' louder roar.
Ah! they had borne well as they might,
Such wrongs as freemen ill can bear;
And they had urged both day and night,
In fitting words, a freeman's prayer;
And when the heart is filled with grief,
For wrongs of all true souls accurst,
In action it must seek relief,
Or else, o'ercharged, it can but burst.
Why blame we them, if they oft spake
Words that were fitted to awake
The soul's high hopes—its noblest parts—
The slumbering passions of brave hearts,
And send them as the simoom's breath,
Upon a work of woe and death?
And woman's voice is heard amid
The accents of that warrior train;
And when has woman's voice e'er bid,
And man could from its hest refrain?
Hers is the power o'er his soul
That's never wielded by another,
And she doth claim this soft control
As sister, mistress, wife, or mother.
So sweetly doth her soft voice float
O'er hearts by guilt or anguish riven,
It seemeth as a magic note
Struck from earth's harps by hands of heaven.
And there's the mother of Ogé,
Who with firm voice, and steady heart,
And look unaltered, well can play
The Spartan mother's hardy part;
And send her sons to battle-fields,
And bid them come in triumph home,
Or stretched upon their bloody shields,
Rather than bear the bondman's doom.

"Go forth," she said, "to victory;
Or else, go bravely forth to die!
Go forth to fields where glory floats
In every trumpet's cheering notes!
Go forth, to where a freeman's death
Glares in each cannon's fiery breath!
Go forth and triumph o'er the foe;
Or failing that, with pleasure go
To molder on the battle-plain,
Freed ever from the tyrant's chain!
But if your hearts should craven prove,
Forgetful of your zeal—your love
For rights and franchises of men,
My heart will break; but even then,
Whilst bidding life and earth adieu,
This be the prayer I'll breathe for you:
'Passing from guilt to misery,
May this for aye your portion be,—
A life, dragged out beneath the rod—
An end, abhorred of man and God—
As monument, the chains you nurse—
As epitaph, your mother's curse!'"

A thousand hearts are breathing high,
And voices shouting "Victory!"
Which soon will hush in death;
The trumpet clang of joy that speaks,
Will soon be drowned in the shrieks
Of the wounded's stifling breath,
The tyrant's plume in dust lies low—
Th' oppressed has triumphed o'er his foe.
But ah! the lull in the furious blast
May whisper not of ruin past;
It may tell of the tempest hurrying on,
To complete the work the blast begun.
In the voice of a Syren, it may whisp'ringly tell
Of a moment of hope in the deluge of rain;
As the shout of the free heart may rapt'rously swell,
While the tyrant is gath'ring his power again.
Though the balm of the leech may soften the smart,

It never can turn the swift barb from its aim;
　　And thus the resolve of the true freeman's heart
May not keep back his fall, though it free it from shame.
　　Though the hearts of those heroes all well could
　　accord
　　With freedom's most noble and loftiest word;
　　Their virtuous strength availeth them nought
　　With the power and skill that the tyrant brought.
　　Gray veterans trained in many a field
　　Where the fate of nations with blood was sealed,
　　In Italia's vales—on the shores of the Rhine—
　　Where the plains of fair France give birth to the vine—
　　Where the Tagus, the Ebro, go dancing along,
　　Made glad in their course by the Muleteer's song—
　　All these were poured down in the pride of their
　　might,
　　On the land of Ogé, in that terrible fight.
　　Ah! dire was the conflict, and many the slain,
　　Who slept the last sleep on that red battle-plain!
　　The flash of the cannon o'er valley and height
　　Danced like the swift fires of a northern night,
　　Or the quivering glare which leaps forth as a token
　　That the King of the Storm from his cloud-throne has
　　spoken.
　　And oh! to those heroes how welcome the fate
　　Of Sparta's brave sons in Thermopylae's strait;
　　With what ardor of soul they then would have given
　　Their last look at earth for a long glance at heaven!
　　Their lives to their country—their backs to the sod—
　　Their heart's blood to the sword, and their souls to
　　their God!
　　But alas! although many lie silent and slain,
　　More blest are they far than those clanking the chain,
　　In the hold of the tyrant, debarred from the day;—
　　And among these sad captives is Vincent Ogé!

　　Another day's bright sun has risen,
　　And shines upon the insurgent's prison;
　　Another night has slowly passed,
　　And Ogé smiles, for 'tis the last

He'll droop beneath the tyrant's power—
The galling chains! Another hour,
And answering to the jailor's call,
He stands within the Judgment Hall.
They've gathered there;—they who have pressed
Their fangs into the soul distressed,
To pain its passage to the tomb
With mock'ry of a legal doom.
They've gathered there;—they who have stood
Firmly and fast in hour of blood,—
Who've seen the lights of hope all die,
As stars fade from a morning sky,—
They've gathered there, in that dark hour—
The latest of the tyrant's power,—
An hour that speaketh of the day
Which never more shall pass away,—
The glorious day beyond the grave,
Which knows no master—owns no slave.
And there, too, are the rack—the wheel—
The torturing screw—the piercing steel,—
Grim powers of death all crusted o'er
With other victims' clotted gore.
Frowning they stand, and in their cold,
Silent solemnity, unfold
The strong one's triumph o'er the weak—
The awful groan—the anguished shriek—
The unconscious mutt'rings of despair—
The strained eyeball's idiot stare—
The hopeless clench—the quiv'ring frame—
The martyr's death—the despot's shame.
The rack—the tyrant—victim,—all
Are gathered in that Judgment Hall.
Draw we the veil, for 'tis a sight
But friends can gaze on with delight.
The sunbeams on the rack that play,
For sudden terror flit away
From this dread work of war and death,
As angels do with quickened breath,
From some dark deed of deepest sin,
Ere they have drunk its spirit in.

No mighty host with banners flying,
Seems fiercer to a conquered foe,
    Than did those gallant heroes dying,
To those who gloated o'er their woe;—
    Grim tigers, who have seized their prey,
    Then turn and shrink abashed away;
    And, coming back and crouching nigh,
    Quail 'neath the flashing of the eye,
    Which tells that though the life has started,
    The will to strike has not departed.

    Sad was your fate, heroic band!
    Yet mourn we not, for yours' the stand
    Which will secure to you a fame,
    That never dieth, and a name
    That will, in coming ages, be
    A signal word for Liberty.
    Upon the slave's o'erclouded sky,
Your gallant actions traced the bow,
    Which whispered of deliv'rance nigh—
The meed of one decisive blow.
    Thy coming fame, Ogé! is sure;
    Thy name with that of L'Ouverture,
    And all the noble souls that stood
    With both of you, in times of blood,
    Will live to be the tyrant's fear—
    Will live, the sinking soul to cheer!

                    Vashon, George Boyer, 1824–1878
                    Syracuse, N.Y., August 31st, 1853.

A Life Day (1866)

MORNING.

The breeze awakes with morn's first ray,
Like childhood roused from sleep to play;
The sunshine, like a fairy sprite,
Comes to undo the wrong of night;
And earth is jocund with the glee
That swells from hill and vale and tree.
It echoes music fitly set
For mocking-bird and paroquet;
And, joyous as a ransomed soul,
It hears the notes of the oriole.
The murmur of the wide-swept cane
Hymneth the rapture of the plain,
And mingles with the brooklet's song,—
A mirthful brook with fitful gleam,
Hasting to Mississippi's stream,
And glad'ning both its banks along,
Surely, to be mid scenes like this
Doth render like a dream of bliss—
A treasure-store without alloy;—
Here Joy's alive, and Life is joy.
Oh! what a joy it is to him
Who for this scene has left the room
Where sickness, hollow-eyed and grim,
Hath held, for years, its court of gloom,—
Whose shrunken limbs too clearly own
That there the monster had his throne!
They tell not all his tale of woe,—
How friends and brothers from him fled,
And left him to the fever's glow,
The ulcered frame, the throbbing head,
With no defense against the grave
Save this—the care of one poor slave.
That faithful one is by his side;—
What more of bliss can now betide?
What matter that the earth is fair?
What matter that the glad bird's sing?

His pleasure, is that she doth share
The balmy breeze's welcoming.
    Her sweet smile is the sunshine bright
    That floods the landscape wide with light;
    Her gladsome youth the genial morn
    That doth his happy day adorn,
    And her soft voice the music sweet
    With which no warbler can compete.
    And now that Life and Hope again
    Open to him paths long closed by pain,—
    Now, while her tawny cheek, her eye,
    Are bright with modest ecstasy,
    The hushed shades of the orange grove
    Smilingly hear his tale of love.

NOON.

How swiftly glide our mortal years,
When Love doth wing each blissful hour,—
    When all our hopes, and all our fears,
Are minions of his magic power!
    Twelve years! Twelve moments in her life,
    Since she became a happy wife!
    All chains are riven save the tie
    Which links her to his destiny.
    What cares he for the glance of scorn
That mock him in his daily walk?
    What, that each coming night and morn
Echoes his neighbors' gibing talk?
    She, once his slave and now his bride,
    Out-values all the earth beside.
    And 'neath the orange trees he strays
    With her, as in their younger days;
    But not with her alone; for now
    His hand doth press a maiden's brow
    Whose flaxen curls and eyes of blue,
    From her fond sires have caught their hue.
    Beside them stands a dark-eyed boy,
    Whose laugh rings out his infant joy,
    As, now and then, comes flashing by,
    The many-colored butterfly.

Oh! with such pledges of fond love
As thou dost mark in either boon,
Say, mother, hath not He above
Granted thy morn a fitting noon?

NIGHT.

Alas! that noon should yield to night
Its treasured joys of life and light!
Alas! that sun-bright happiness
Should be o'erclouded by distress!
The noble soul who gladly gave
A wife's name to his faithful slave,
Hath passed away, and those who fled
In horror from his stricken bed,
Have come, like vultures to the dead,—
Have come to batten on the store
He left to those he held so dear—
To claim them in their anguish sore,
As born thralls to a bondage drear.
And one whose guilty deeds hurl shame
On white-robed Justice's sainted name,
Holding no sacred thing in awe,
Dared to proclaim the marriage tie
Shielding them with its purity,
A fraud upon the slaver's law.

A wailing comes upon the breeze,
That sighs amid the orange trees;
And she is there, and all alone.
Oh, linger, night! for with the day
Her children will be far away—
Her children! Ah! no more her own!
O, mother! mourning by the spot
Hallowed by sweetest memory,
And bidding fancy shape the lot
Each little one is doomed to see.
Alas! thy poor heart knows too well,
What to itself it dares not tell!
Hundreds of boys as gently born
As he who was thy joy and pride,

Have by the cruel lash been torn,
And 'neath its bloody scourgings died.
  Hundreds of maidens full as fair
As she whose little life you gave,
  Know what a dowry of despair,
Is beauty in a female slave.
    And thou, lorn mother!—thy sole part
    Is weeping, till it breaks thy heart.

    Shades of the heroes, long since gone!
Was this your glory's end and aim?
  Was it for this, O, Washington!
That welcoming the rebel's name,
  Halter and battle you defied?
  For this, O, Warren! that you died?

Vashon, George Boyer, 1824–1878

TRANSCRIPTIONS OF SELECTED NEWSPAPER ITEMS

Weekly Advocate and Emporium—April 30, 1841, p. 4

PITTSBURGH AND ENVIRONS

Were a Pittsburgher who left this city in 1820 to return now, he would be fairly puzzled to identify the "old landmarks" of the town. Indeed, he would fancy he had come to a place which he had never before seen, if he considered the artificial appearance of Pittsburgh alone, without reference to the physical features of the city. In illustration of this supposition, we will point out a few—and they will be but few of the more prominent locations which were peculiar 20 years and less since, to mark that "old things have passed away and all have become new," with almost Aladdin-like enchantment.

Twenty years ago, our Monongahela front did not present its present improved appearance. At that time, the houses on Water street, for the most part, were small frames, with here and there a two story brick. A steep and ragged bluff froze up from the river and frowned down upon the turning water instead of the paved slope now so gently rising from the wharves, there were two banks which lead down the bank, at Wood and Fairy Streets. There were then no wharves, and a steamboat was something of a curiosity! Rafts, canoes, flat boats, and keels might be found, but the later craft might be deemed ne-plus-ultra of water architecture! Everywhere along the river where persons are now forbidden to throw rubbish, under a "penalty of fine," all the filth and garbage of the city were thrown—coal ashes, clippings of tin from the tinners, pieces of woven wire from the wire-workers and fender makers, the sweepings of shoe makers' and saddlers' shops, shavings from the carpenters, the cleanings of stables and other nuisances—were thrown down the high precipitous bank, to be swept away by the floods in the Monongahela! Watermen in those days went down in

The appendix contained numerous transcribed newspaper articles, totaling over two hundred pages. Most of these dealt with the general history of Pittsburgh, the region's labor movement, and the general history of the United States. A moderate number of articles related directly to the history of blacks in Pittsburgh. Those that seemed most illuminating have been included here.

the river with their carts and having filled their hogs-head returned into the city and vended the water at a fip or ten-cents the hogshead—"the water-works" had not been "dreamt of in our philosophy." We were truly a set of "uncivilized barbarians" in comparison with our present light and knowledge. Bible and Tract Societies were scarcely thought of, although we were not without philanthropists who went about doing good." The Rev. patriot "Father Patterson," as he was affectionately termed, was our "home missionary," and many a tract and bible did he distribute among the boatman and others, while he gave them counsel and his blessing.

The ranges of the warehouses and stately stores, toward the foot of Wood Street were not in existence, but small tenements of frames straggled along the streets, as they were ashamed to be seen in too close proximity! Where the fine block of brick buildings on the northern side of Wood Street from Diamond Alley to Fifth Street, now stands, there was a tavern and wagon-yard, well known as the best and most capacious in town. Here, the traveling showman occasionally pitched his tent, and exhibited his elephants and painted horses while the clown cracked his whip and jokes at the same time! How we have degenerated!

Further up Wood Street, in the triangle spot now known as "Baird's Row," facing on Wood, Liberty and Sixth streets, a few years ago stood the old "round church," which was torn down on the erection of the present Episcopal church on Sixth Street—the ground on which this edifice was erected being then, at the present, a burial place.

Nearly opposite "Baird's Row" on the Allegheny side of Liberty Street, below Fifth Street, but the other day might be seen a very handsome cottage house of Jas. Adams, Esq. almost hidden from view by the trees and shrubbery of his ample garden, and considered as a suburban retreat. The cottage and garden were converted into a tavern and wagon yard which, in turn, gave way to the present pile of brick and mortar.

There were twenty years ago, comparatively few houses, and these country residences below St. Clair Street and northwardly of Liberty Street from the Point upward. Many of the present squares in this district were at that period "vegetable gardens" where our citizens got their salad and onions! The ranges of dwelling and stores on either side of St. Clair Street and Liberty Street to the bridge were not in existence. "Patterson's Row" was thrown up about 15 years since, and the bricks made on the spot from the clay of the cellar. The location where the exchange and other large building may now be found, about the same period, was filled with wooden tenements of the meanest kind. A fire, however, one bitter cold night, swept away the "baseless fabrics," and left not a "wreck." How has the scene changed! In those old fashioned days, fire-buckets were used instead of engine and hose, and the devouring elements was extinguished by men, women and children, forming long lines, and passing the buckets from hand to hand from the pumps and rivers to the dwelling under flames.

The sight of the present beautiful structure of the Third Presbyterian Church, scarcely fifteen years ago, was the scene of the most fearful riot, originating in a circus, under the direction of an Italian named Pepin. We refrain from mentioning the cause of the riot. The walls of the surface, however, were speedily demolished; missiles of stone of bricks torn up from the pavements, flew in every direction, and fire-arms discharged their leaden messengers till a victim was stretched in death! The awful recollection! We rejoice that our city has not since been disgraced by such scenes, and from the characters of our people, we need not anticipate them for the future.

Ten years ago we had but one bridge over the Allegheny River! Now there are three noble avenues of our neighboring city, besides the Aqueduct, bringing the canal into the heart of Pittsburgh! The vicinity of the canal basin was not then built up, where is now so much life and bustle. Upon the ground where the forwarding warehouses are now located, a very few years ago, might be seen lumber yards or unclose lots. Bayardstown was a village "far away," and the Old Catholic Church was out of town! The "city on the hill" above Seventh Street, was an orchard, where the urchins would steal the apples in spite of dogs and farmers. Where the splendid New Court House now stands was, the other day, the country residence of James Ross, Esq. and the large town over Grant's Hill and along Sukes' Run, easterly, between Prospect Boyd Hills, were orchards and meadows and groves. Who does remember the beautiful grove on Boyd's Hill, where the "young fellows'" came away out from the city to play at Cricket! How merrily they knock the ball in those days! The wood has been cut down, and the place is a brick-yard! Oh tempera! But improvement has disdained to rest here. Further on, she has found it a colony of the gentry of our city; and beautiful and princely are the abodes of wealth and luxury. If Pittsburgh continues to advance at this rate for another fifty years, the Youghiogany River will form another side of our "Western Emporium," and "Braddock's Fields" will be formed into streets miles long! What a contemplation? Yet who will say!

On the Allegheny side turn we, and what do we behold! Why twenty years ago, "Allegheny City" did not dare presume to celebrate a dignity! The town was not even a burgh! We remember the first Burgess well—and why not we—since the thing happened only a few days ago! Allegheny City, in our boyhood and we are not old yet by any means—was in considerable village; indeed, hardly that,—for "few and far between" were the cottages! Now what a city! The road on the other side of the lower bridge of Allegheny leading up toward the hill, was a perfect quagmire fifteen years ago! "Robinson's Row" was not even dreamt of—that spot was an orchard! The many factories now seen, were not contemplated; the "Theological Seminary," on Hog's Back had not appeared. The town of Manchester was woods where our citizens spent Fourth of July "without distinction of party!" Men could then differ in Politics, and eat a dinner together on our National holiday! Oh! the good old days! On the very spot, where the splendid residences are now found, on the lower of Hog's Back towards the Ohio river, used to be a "great place," in Juvenile Parlance together blackberries. The elegant seats of Opulence, on the north of the city of Allegheny, did not present their fronts and look down with disdain from their lofty heights, upon the scarce cultivated planes below. Twenty years ago the Penitentiary did not present its towers and massy walls. There were no churches in Allegheny then, if we except the frame house occupied as an academy, where the good and luminated Mr. Stockton occasionally preached. How many are there now? We will go and count!

But why attempt to note all the improvements! Indeed we cannot, and will here stop to take breath. The fact is old Pittsburgh has almost entirely rebuilt. Wood Street, may be said to be altogether new; and every block in this city is witnessed of some change for the better, to say nothing of the extension of the city in every direction. Verily, we are an utilitarian people, and it is pleasing to witness that we have built no palaces in the skies, but have constructed our fabrics imperishably as the everlasting hills by which we are environ?[1]

Pgh. Daily Commercial—Oct. 23, 1865, p. 2
Worker—M. Hoyleman / Received—Dec. 30, 1940 /
Typed—Dec. 21, 1940 / Typist—A. Pummer

NEGROES AS WITNESSES

The emancipation measure has commenced its raid upon the slave code, as we sometime since predicted it would. The question of admitting Negroes as witnesses in courts is discussed in So. papers, and is finding its way into So. politics. And, we may add, it is getting along unexpectedly well. Some object to their admission in cases involving the interests of white parties, on the ground that they do not understand the nature and obligations of an oath. This is well answered by others, who say that the objection implies that, in cases involving only the interests of Negroes, it is of no consequence whether the black witness understands the oath and tells the truth or not. It is, however, a foregone conclusion evidentially, in the reconstruction policy, that colored witnesses shall be admitted, and have the protection and privileges of courts, like the rest of the people. The old slave code will have to give way on the point.

Pgh. Daily Commercial—Sept. 23, 1865
Worker—Hoyleman / Received—Dec. 31, 1940
Typed—Jan 2, 1941 / Typist—W. Funkhouser

FREEDOM IMPROVING

We never expected miraculous advancement in the Negroes, by their emancipation. We never anticipated that, the moment they were made free from their hereditary bondage and disseminate, they would rise to gigantic proportions of intellectual manhood, and become models of industry, enterprise and thriftiness. Human nature

1. Sentence is as in original.

is usually slow in its social ascents, and it never had a lower standing point than that of slave who had been for generations left of his manhood and classed among chattels. It is occasion of surprise or disappointment to us that he does feel perplexed by the novel possession of freedom, that the necessity for forethought and calculation finds him unprepared for it, or that amid the confusion consequent on the great change of condition, both in himself and all around him, his poor, uncultivated wits are bewildered.

But we should be glad to see as promising indications of an upward turn in tendencies of the white populations of the South as there are among the blacks, as prompt recurrence to the paths of honest industry, as good evidences of attachment to and confidence in the Government as patient awaiting for its movements of favor towards them, as cheerful as readiness to acquiesce in the stoppage of the Government rations. In these respects, the blacks, lately made men have honorably distinguished themselves, where they have had the opportunity, on the plantation and in the military service of the country. Give them a fair chance, and the freed men will become free men indeed.

Pgh. Daily Commercial—Nov. 4, 1865
Worker—Hoyleman / Received—Jan. 2, 1941
Typed—Jan. 3, 1941 / Typist—Saunier

PITTSBURGH PACKET LINES

Some fifteen years ago the trade of Pittsburgh, westward and southward, was dependent wholly on navigation, and in those times the vessels which composed our packet lines were regarded as floating places. The business was large, competition great, and elegant and substantial boats composed a very extensive fleet. But the introduction of railroads seriously impaired the river trade, and in a brief time our magnificent steamers forsook our port for the lower Mississippi and western waters, where railroads were not yet known. Although river traffic was depressed for sometime owing to the introduction of railroads, the expensiveness of shipments of heavy goods by the latter and their inability to transact all the business offering, necessitated a return to first principles, and now we have three first-class lines of packets, plying between the city and Zanesville, and Brownsville and Parkersburg, points of inestimable value to the wealth and business of Pittsburgh.

The Muskingum river packets often to the merchants and manufactures of Pittsburgh a wealthy agricultural region, whose prosperity in a mercantile point of view, as well as increasing richness in agriculture, is in a great measure dependent on this city. The products of the valley, being among the choicest of their kind, find a ready market here, and the producer, on the other hand, supplies all his wants before leaving the city, at less prices than would be demanded of him at home. The steamers composing the line between this city and Zanesville are the "Julia No. 2," Captain

Coulson, and clerk J. C. McVey and "Emma Graham," Captain Stull—the former arriving here every Thursday evening and leaving Saturday, at 4 p.m. and the latter arriving every Sunday night, and leaving Tuesday at 4 p.m. These boats are commodious, and are elegantly furnished for passenger travel, besides being in command of officers of experience, well-known for their courtesy and integrity. These packets touch at every important point between this city and Marietta on the Ohio, and between the latter place and Zanesville on the Muskingum. Between the hours of their arrival and departure passengers have ample time to convert their produce into cash or trade for such articles as they may want, and return in charge of their freight. The convenience of this packet line, however, is too well known and appreciated by the inhabitants of the Muskingum Valley to require further education. Among the points not reached by railroad, at which these boats make regular landings are the following: On the Ohio river—Moundsville, Powhattan, Sunfish, Bearsville, New Martinsville, Sardis, Sisterville, Cochransville, Matamoras, Grandview, St. Marys, Newport, Bull Creek, Mariette and Harmar; on the Muskingum—Union Landing, Lowell, Coal Run, Beverly, Waterford, Centre Bend, Roxbury, Windsor, McConnellsville, Malta, Eaglesport, Gaysport, Taylorsville, and Duncan's Fall.

Next in importance to the Muskingum, is the Monongahela Steam Packet Company, whose splendid steamers leave and arrive at the wharf twice daily, landed every trip with products of Fayette and Greene counties, of this State, and of Monongahela or other counties of W. Va., and the Dunkard gold and oil region. The steamers comprising this line are—"Fayette," Captain S. C. Speers; "Telegraph," Captain D. Bugher, "Franklin," Captain Z. W. Carmac, and "Gallatin," Captain A. S. Carlisle. The boats are all first-class side-wheel Packets, elegantly equipped, and in command of gentlemen and officers of the right stamp judging from the number of passengers carried over the Monongahela Slackwater by boat, it would seem that railroad travel has passed away. The development of the South, Pennsylvanian and W. Va. oil regions will in a brief time multiply the trade and travel by river, and even now the boats are frequently scarcely equal in capacity to the demand made upon them.

The Marietta and Parkersburg Packet line was but recently organized, and for the period it has been in existence has built up an extensive and rapidly growing trade between this city and the prosperous town of Parkerburg. At present the traffic is confined mainly to the oil region of Burning Spring and Horseneck, W. Va., and it also accommodates a large passenger travel. The packets comprising this line are "Forest City," Captain Gordon, and "Bayard," Captain G. D. Moore, Daniel Moore, clerk—the former leaving every Wednesday and Saturday at noon, and the latter every Monday and Thursday at 11 a.m. Both boats are first class and commanded by capable officers.

The three packet lines above referred to contribute in no small degree to the prosperity of our mercantile and manufacturing interest, and the merchants and manufacturers, it is pleasant to know, appreciate the fact by giving liberal encouragement of the business of the boats, which, in turn, enhances the value of their own interests.

Commercial—Dec. 7, 1865
Worker—Hoyleman / Received—Dec. 27, 1940
Typed—Jan. 2, 1941 / Typist—Saunier

ENLARGEMENT OF CIVIL LIBERTY

In observing the day designated by the chief magistrate of the nation for returning thanks to Almighty God, we are called upon to thank Him for the "great enlargement of civil liberty."[2] This is no unmeaning expression merely thrown in to fill the measure of a neatly formed sentence. It has form, substance and spirit which give to it a living, earnest and solemn power. It embraces the grand central principle irrevocably established by the war, and from which it is not in our power to escape. It may be that at times we will allow it to be temporarily forgotten, but soon it will recur to us again to remind us that the sacrifice of a million lives and of untold treasure, and the unparallel sufferings of our gallant soldiers in southern prison pens, have not been in vain.

The president does not direct attention to it as a separate cause for Thanksgiving, but he makes it the companion of each specific blessing we now enjoy. He does not regard it, nor indeed is it, a boon that could have been granted us independent of our blessings. Therefore, while we have immunity from civil war, it is with great enlargement of civil liberty; while we enjoy peace, it is with the same fractious blessing; while unity again exists, it is with the like favor; and while harmony abounds among us, it is with the same "great enlargement of civil liberty."

While the president may have had reference to the deliverance of the whole people from the perils and dangers which but lately beset them, there can be no doubt that the mind was more especially fixed upon the fact that the shackles of slavery have through God's Providence fallen in broken fragments from four million of his creatures; and it is to this point that we wish to address ourselves at present.

The same profound statesman in his message which had just been given to this country says: "It is one of the greatest acts on record to have brought four million of people into freedom." It will be a greater act to take charge of the host just brought into freedom, and, by the exercise of a generous philanthropy, provide the means to cultivate their minds and hearts, and to teach them how they may become useful and industrious citizens, and be entitled to the full protection of our laws and the hearty respect of their fellow men. We must remember that the charge that the freed men are ignorant, gross and degraded is no reproach to them. Whatever they are is attributable to the system which oppressed them, and in a great measure to the people of the

2. Thanksgiving had no fixed date until Abraham Lincoln set it as the last Thursday in November. Before that, Thanksgiving was set by presidential proclamation; in 1865, it was celebrated on December 7. After Lincoln's death, Thanksgiving remained an unofficial holiday, and on two occasions, 1865 and 1869, its date was shifted. Finally, in 1941, President Roosevelt declared the fourth Thursday in November an official national holiday for the celebration of Thanksgiving.

North, who for generations lent a passive approval to the iniquitous system. But to-day we thank God that the wicked system is destroyed and civil liberty has received a great enlargement. But yet the condition of freeman, mentally and morally, remains the same. It is not enough that we have given him freedom—we must see him fit to enjoy his new political status. It will not do to say that his former master, who enjoyed the fruits of his whole life's labor, should provide for this duty. We must remember that the South is well exhausted, while we in the North have enjoyed unexampled prosperity. We have wherewith to give and to give with liberality, while they have not. While theirs was the sin of enslaving their fellow men, it would be pharisaical in us to avow ourselves blameless.

It will not be much less than a mockery of God if we lift up our hearts to give thanks to him for the great enlargement of civil liberty if we fail to contribute the means to make freedom a reality to those who have just been brought out of bondage. In this matter we believe that faith can have no existence. Let us make this a day not only of Thanksgiving but of thanks-offering. Let hand go with heart and purse with prayer. In this way only can we do our duty to the freedman—this way only can our Thanksgiving be acceptable to "God."

Much would be needed for this noble mission, and we indulge the hope that the contributions this day received will go towards making up a sufficiency. The Freed-man's Aid Association has made an appeal to the Christian churches, and we trust it will meet with a liberal response. From all we can learn the contributions in our churches will be unusually large. We hear of benevolent citizens offering to contribute large sums toward making up much larger sums in their respective churches, and we are persuaded that such offers will induce more liberal contributions from others. Each man, woman and child should go to church this morning prepared to contribute to this great work and to contribute with unusual liberality. Aside from all that, we have already suggested it should be appreciated that for American missions there is not such a field upon earth as the southern States. To spread the gospel among, and to raise up from their degradations, four million of accountable beings, is a grand mission work which will lay up for us "treasures in heaven" more abundant than if we rest content with having merely freed them from the form of slavery. This work is a legacy of the war, and is as binding in morals upon us as the national debt is in law, and while the Secretary of Treasury has not control of the figures, the account is reg-istered above, and will have to be answered there. Let the debt be paid with thankful hearts and unsparing hands.

FREE SPEECH WITH A VENGEANCE—A COLORED MAN ATTEMPTS TO SPEAK FOR GREELEY AND GETS "SNUFFED OUT."

The Post—July 27, 1872

Last evening another large and enthusiastic meeting of colored radicals was held at the Franklin Street school house. The meeting organized by calling John F. Butler to the chair and appointing Bros. Woodson and Hammon secretaries. A "man and a brother" named Wilson addressed the assembled to go for Gomely and that pure and unimpeached patriot, Hartranft, who like Washington, is "first in war, first in peace, and first with his hands in the treasury of Pa." After a little gymnastics proper to the occasion, while this was going on the meeting began singing "John Brown's body," etc., while this was going on some disloyal "pusson" began chirping.

> How Hartranfts hopes are drooping
> The ring can't put him through;
> From hillside, heath and valley;
> Comes the cry—For Buckalew!

Mr. Linden a Second Ward "cullud" man who carried dis guberment from Frotress Monroe to do so. California on his shoulder, told what he "knowd about farming." At this juncture, Capt. Ward stated there was a colored gentleman who desired to present the claims of Horace Greeley. A scene of wildest confusion ensued, and many of the sable brethren rising to their feet and shouting "put him out," "chuck dat nigger out de window." While the air was rent with yells a portion of the audience began singing "Rally round the flag boys," which seemed to have a soothing effect on the temper of the audience. The Greeley man seeing that there was no show for a plea for the earliest and best friend of the colored race, departed disgusted with "dem hill niggers." Brother Woodson concluded after a few remarks from Brother Wilson, the curtain dropped and the meeting adjourned.

Pittsburgh Leader—February 6, 1874
Worker—Hoyleman / Received—December 23, 1940
Typed—December 30, 1940 / Typist—Saunier

Colored Troops Getting in Line

Pursuant to a call made by the committee, the colored people held a mass meeting at the Franklin St. Schoolhouse last night for the purpose of considering who they should support in the coming election. The meeting was not very large, but those present appeared to be representative men. At 8 o'clock there was about 40 colored men present, and about ½ dozen white folks, most prominent amongst whom was Mr. Boothe, scribe to common council. He was the mightiest man in the assembly until Mr. Smith came puffing and wheezing. Mr. Boothe gave up the chair and left the meeting. It was nearly 9 o'clock before the meeting was organized by calling Mr. Louden to the chair. He stated the object of the meeting was to determine who they should support at the coming primary elections. He believed the time had come for them, as a class, to take a commanding position, and suggested that there be a general expression of opinion in regard to candidates.

Mr. Jackson favored trotting the candidates for Mayor out and trying them on the course before election day. He wanted to have the records brought up for inspection.

Mr. Louden came down from the chair to offer the following resolution: *Resolved*, That we, the colored voters of the city Pittsburgh, in mass-meeting assembled, do hereby express the opinion that the Republican party of this city and county, in whose support we have been unwavering, has totally ignored our claims upon the distribution of the offices and positions in its gift, at which we feel aggrieved; and be it further—

Resolved, That we believe our interests will be best subserved in the nomination and election of William C. McCarthy, of the 11th Ward.

Resolved, That we hereby pledge ourselves to work as a unit for his nomination and election.

Mr. Bailey took the floor for McCarthy. He thought he was the best man on the track, and he had a good record, and he was sure that he would not forget the colored folks, as some others had (Cheers). He always was our friend, stood by us when it meant something to be a friend of the colored man.

Mr. Louden followed in a stirring speech, in which he eulogized McCarthy highly. He regarded Gross as a man who had joined the dominant party for the purpose of being on the winning side, to keep on the tidal-wave, and for the purpose of being popular. He didn't have as much faith in this kind of man as in those who had always been on the right side. He was opposed to supporting those who were always promising to do something until after the election, and then forget their promises, and urged the colored voters to stand their ground, and he believed they held the balance of power, and whichever side they supported would win. This being the case they could turn the election, and it was their duty to put their votes where they would do the most good.

Mr. Harris, one of the prominent young politicians on the Hill, moved as a amendment to the foregoing resolutions that McCarthy be stricken out and Dr. Gross inserted instead thereof, (Cries of "never, no, no; cheese it"; besides hisses and confusion). He said that McCarthy had never done anything for the race, and did not possess dignity necessary for the chief magistrate, while Dr. Gross had done as much—

The chairman—That ain't so. He hasn't.

Harris—He has been.

Chairman—He never did anything. He was a democrat and—

Harris—You'd better call a fellar a liar.

Chairman—I did call you.

Harris—You have no right to interrupt me in that way.

Chairman—That's so, I beg your pardon sir; hope there's no offense, I was a little excited.

The crowd laughed heartily at this little tilt, and seemed disappointed at its sudden termination.

Mr. Gibson—I have known McCarthy as long as any of you; and like him very much, but don't propose to be sold out to him or Mr. Gross, or to any party or sect. I don't know anything about McCarthy ever being a conductor on the underground railroad. There were lots of things whispered against him while in office before, but I don't know that they were true. He is a good man, but I don't mean to sell out to no man nor party, but will support the Republican nominee. I am personally opposed to McCarthy, but will support him if nominated.

These remarks, coolly and dispassionately made were well received, and, as far as they related to supporting the nominee of the party, seemed to fairly represent the sentiment of the meeting.

Mr. Louden—Until after Lincoln's first election, Dr. Gross was a democrat of the old school, and you all know in what estimation we were held by that party. He was smart enough to see that he must change his coat in order to be in the ascendancy. I am going to stand by the man who stood by me when I needed a friend. We are under no obligations to support any party, but rather to support the men who have been true to us. McCarthy was a true Republican, even more, an abolitionist, when Gross was a democrat.

Mr. Harris took the floor for Gross, and said: "When McCarthy was in office before the 'dew drops' and 'mudlarks' had their own way, and it wasn't safe for a colored man to go on the sts. after night. Grant and Logan, and Butler were not always Republican, but now are the most reliable. Who knows but Gross will be another Grant? Give him a trial." (Cries of "No, we won't.")

Mr. J. C. Brown said he know all about the "dewdrops," and he knew that Mr. McCarthy did all that a man could do to suppress them. He advised as to arm ourselves for self-protection, and he would tend to any of them that were caught, and he did.

Mr. Morton arose and said: I is not a sect man, and has all de time stuck by de 'ole party. I is goin' for to support de best man. If Mr. Butler takes de field, I is Mr. Butler; if Mr. McCarthy takes de field, I is Mr. McCarthy, or I is Mr. Gross if he be de man. Mr. Butler was always a good man ever since he was a lispin' take in his mother's arms (Immense laughter). The Republican party is de sure foundation stone for us to stand upon. Jerry Brush is my man too. He made dem "dewdrops" mighty scarce when he was runnin' Municipal hall. If dey knocked my long silk hat off, I just knowed war to go fo justice.

Here Mr. Morton was called to order, but refused to give up his eulogy on his friend Jerry until the chair compelled him to do so. He then declared for the support of the nominee and against the resolutions.

Mr. Louden—You came to me about twenty times and wanted to cut in the Republican party. I think you are in the ring.

Morton—I in de' ring? Dat's the greatest consumption I ever heard of. How could I get in de ring? Dat's a mistake.

Paul J. Carson opposed the resolution arguing that it was unfair to compel their supporting candidates. He was not in favor of supporting Gross, personally, but would support the nominee. That Gross was once a democrat was no argument against him, for St. Paul was once a Jew, Grant was a democrat, and so was Butler such a bad one that he voted for Jeff Davis. If we leave the republican party, where shall we go? (A voice—To the devil. Great laughter). When the dewdrops found us we never could find an officer. There is where the trouble was. It wasn't the mayor's fault. They melted before Jerry Brush; as the dew before the morning sun. We want a man of firmness and dignity. If we stay away from the election the democrats will be successful, and from them we cannot expect anything. No one can make any promises, nor it is unconstitutional. We want a Republican, whether or not he saw the great light like Paul, and turned from the error of his ways when the war for freedom commenced.

Mr. Louden saw that his resolution was not meeting with much favor, and he took the floor again, and made the loudest speech of the evening except Morton's. He appealed to their manhood, and said the Republicans had never done what they should. He would support the party that held out the greatest inducements, by way of elevating and supporting him, and would not stick to any party that wanted his vote and then kick him out the next day.

Mr. Harris moved to indefinitely postpone the resolution. Here the storm raged furiously, after a division of the house the chairman announced the motion had carried. (Applause)

Mr. Brown said the Republicans had not a majority without their vote, and offered the following resolution:

"That we select a candidate upon whom to center our votes and support him." Lost.

Mr. Harns offered a resolution in favor of Mr. Gross.

Mr. Loome thought this was worse than Mr. Louden's—said: I will never vote to put Mr. Gross ahead of always our friend. Gross came into the Republican party because he saw it was going to win. McCarthy stuck to the old abolition party when its day star was almost entirely hidden, when it cost something to be a friend to the black man. It would be ungenerous for us now to go and support a life-long democrat in preference to our best friend.

A voice—Wasn't Gross in the army?

Loome's—Yes, but what for?

Several voices—For the money. He was after the lucre. He was not fighting for us, and never will. We want to stick to our friends, and not be tied to any particular man or party. Butler and Grant are good men, but I would rather trust Summer or Phillips in the long run.

A call for the vote on the resolution was made which resulted in one vote for Gross and the remainder of the house against him. A motion was made to adjourn, but was lost. Notwithstanding the result of the vote the majority left for their homes, satisfied that nothing would come of the meeting, and that every man would vote as he pleased anyway. It was generally supposed that Mr. Louden's object was to get the voters pledged to McCarthy, and then favor running him independently if Gross was nominated. The indications are that the colored troops will fight the Republican trenches.

Gazette—Feb. 14, 1874
Worker—*M. Hoyleman / Received*—*Dec. 23, 1940*
Typed—*Dec. 30, 1940 / Typist*—*A. Pummer*

COLORED VOTERS IN COUNCIL

Last evening, a "delegate" meeting of colored voters, was held in the Franklin Street school house, pursuant to public call to take some action in reference to an union of their forces for political purposes.

The meeting was organized by calling Mr. Grandison to the Chair.

The gentleman in assuming this position said the object of the gathering was to effect an organization for the purpose of advancing the political interests of the colored voters of the Co.

Mr. Hall was named Sec'y. But at his own request was relieved and Mr. John H. Jones was chosen for the position.

Mr. Louden said that there seemed to be some misunderstanding in reference to the meeting or that sufficient publication had but then given to the matter. Hence there was not a full attendance from all the election districts. He therefore moved that a committee of five be appointed to prepare resolutions, to be reported to another meeting, at which action could be taken.

Mr. Brown did not favor an adjournment, because it would throw the action of the colored voters too late to have any influence on the coming election. He thought the districts not represented could be filled by appointment of the chair, and the meeting could take action without delay.

Mr. Louden thought the design of the Comm. was not so much to effect the coming election as it was to concentrate the influence of the colored voters, so as to protect their future political interests.

So far as the coming election was concerned, he thought there was no necessity for formal action, for the colored voters so far as he knew were all going to vote the one way to cast their ballots for Mr. McCarthy. He thought therefore they would be standing in their own light by attempting at such a late day, to interfere with the elections next Tuesday.

Mr. Lovett thought they should go ahead with business, and not adjourn.

Mr. Coleman thought "a bird in the hand was worth two in the bush." He thought there had been a lack of energy upon the part of the committee in charge of spreading of the call. He believed in going to business at once, with little talk but plenty of action. There was an old adage that "nothing would hurt a mouse but its mouth," and so he thought they injured themselves by talking too much, (laughter) and not acting with energy.

The vote was then taken on Mr. Brown's motion to fill the representation for unrepresented districts, and it was carried.

The delegates then handed in their credentials.

The chair then appointed the following persons as representatives from the city not represented: R. A. Hall, F. J. Louden, Scott Taper, D. W. Thomas, Geo. Lovett, Jas. H. Loomis, Mr. Morton, J. C. Brown, John H. Jones, Emanuel Jackson, Robert Jackson, Grandison Singleton, William Simpson, John Bell, Mr. Boss, Mr. Barkley, John Russell, M. H. Johnston.

Mr. Paul J. Coperton and Mr. Richman appointed for Allgh. Mr. Louden moved that a committee of five be appointed on that committee by the chair.

While the committee was out deliberating, Mr. Zacariah Coleman was called upon for an address and responded fittingly.

The committee then returned and reported as follows:

Pres.   F. J. Louden
V. Pres.   E. Jackson, J. Grandison
Sec'y   J. H. Jones
Treas.   M. Dietcher

The list was approved and Mr. Louden upon taking the chair made an address in which he beheld that the colored voters should vote as they fought and stand in solid rank at the polls.

The Convention then endorsed the following resolution which had been passed at a meeting of colored voters held in the 8th Ward.

WHEREAS we the colored voters believe the time has now come when if we desire our political strength to be felt in this Commonwealth, we must concentrate our scattered forces by compact organization as a means to reach certain attainable ends; therefore be it

Resolved, That we have abiding faith to the ability, honesty and integrity of James H. Johnston, and we the colored voters of the 8th ward, do hereby pledge ourselves to use all honorable means to secure his election to a seat in the Common Council of the City of Pittsburgh.

The Convention then adjourned to meet at the same place Feb. 27.

Pittsburgh Leader—February 4, 1874
Worker—Hoyleman / Received—Dec. 23, 1940
Typed—Dec. 30, 1940 / Typist—Saunier

OUR COLORED CITIZENS

THEY WANT SOME "PROBING" DONE—A BIG MEETING MON. NIGHT.

The Franklin St. Schoolhouse was the scene of an interesting gathering of our colored voters. The object of the gathering was twofold, namely, to get a good "ready" on for the coming elections, and also to do a little "investigating." The meeting was organized by calling James H. Loomis, to the chair, and appointing John H. Jones to the position of secretary.

THE TROUBLE

The main "rub" is about as follows. In May 1873, the present incumbent in the prothonotary's office wrote a letter to colored voters over his own "sig" and signed by witnesses, to the effect that if elected to the office he pledged himself to appoint a colored man to a clerkship in the prothonotary's office. This letter was read by the secretary at their meeting, and called forth the inquire "why hasn't the writer fulfilled his promise?"

Mr. Kennedy, who was present, said our informant made a brief speech, admitted that out of all the applications for a position which he had received that if Mr. Jones, the secretary, possessed the most favorable claims to notice. As an excuse for not fulfilling his pledge however, the prothonotary is said to have referred to the clause in the new constitution punishing the candidate who shall use any promise of any kind to his supporters, as an inducement for support. But as Mr. Kennedy was elected long before that revised document went in force, it does not seem clear how this reason can have weight in the matter in hand.

Mr. Haymaker, who was also present, made some remarks on the situation, but the substance of Mr. Haymaker's statements did not transpire. After considerable discussion, the matter was tabled for action at the next meeting. It was also agreed to appoint a committee of one voter from each ward in the two cities, who should be authorized to call a mass meeting this week.

BIBLIOGRAPHY

Typist: A. Turner / Rewriteman: J. Ernest Wright /
May 28, 1941 / Final

MANUSCRIPT COLLECTIONS, PRIVATE PAPERS, ETC.

The Henry Bouquet Papers, 1758–1761, in the possession of the Historical Society of Western Pennsylvania; the Holmes-Wallace Family Journals and Letters, 1813–1938, in possession of Miss Rachel Holmes and Miss Carolyn Wallace, Grantsville, Md.; clippings file on Negro Activities, in the Pennsylvania Room of the Carnegie Library of Pittsburgh.

NEWSPAPERS, PERIODICALS, AND ALMANACS

Allegheny Daily Enterprise. Pittsburgh, 1850–1851.

Beacon, The. Published Weekly by the Beacon Publishing Co., Pittsburgh, 1939–1940.

Bulletin Index. Pittsburgh: Bulletin Index Publishing Co., 1925–1939.

Commercial Journal.

Competitor, The. Robert Lee Vann, ed. Pittsburgh, 1920–1922.

Crisis, The. A Record of the Darker Races. NAACP. 1935–1940.

Daily Morning Post. Pittsburgh, 1851–1855.

Informer, The. Grace S. Lowndes, ed. Pittsburgh: The Urban League of Pittsburgh, 1928–1939.

Mercury, The. Pittsburgh, 1811–1832.

Opportunity. Journal of Negro Life. N.Y.: National Urban League.

Pittsburgh American. Pittsburgh, 1919–1920.

Pittsburgh Courier. 1939.

Pittsburgh Daily Advocate and Advertiser. 1834–1840.

Pittsburgh Dispatch. 1860–1903.

Pittsburgh Gazette. 1787–1939.

Pittsburgh Leader. 1880–1903.

Pittsburgh Press. 1897–1939.

Pittsburgh Leader Almanac. Pittsburgh: Leader Publishing Co. 1875.

Pittsburgh Press Almanac. Pittsburgh Press Publishing Co. 1895–1901.

Pittsburgh Saturday Chronicle. 1859–1861.

Pittsburgh Saturday Visitor. (weekly) 1848–1854. (incomplete file)

Pittsburgh True Press. 1852–1861.

Pittsburgh Weekly Mercury & Manufacturer. 1842–1845.

Saturday Evening Visitor. Pittsburgh, 1836–1839; 1841–1842.

Spirit of Liberty. Pittsburgh, 1846.

Tree of Liberty. Pittsburgh, 1800–1804.

Western Pennsylvania Historical Magazine. Pittsburgh Historical Society of
    Western Pennsylvania, 1918–1939.

DIRECTORIES

The Pittsburgh Directory for 1815. Pittsburgh: Joseph M. Riddle, editor and
    publisher, 1815.

The Pittsburgh City Directory for 1819. Pittsburgh: Joseph M. Riddle and M. M.
    Murray, comp.

Pittsburgh in 1826. Pittsburgh: Samuel M. Jones, comp. 1826.

Harris' Pittsburgh Business Directory for 1837-1838-1839-1841-1842-1847.

Directory of Pittsburgh and Vicinity for 1856–57; 1857–58; 1858–59. Pittsburgh:
    George H. Thurston, Pub., 1856–59.

THESES[1]

Allen, Gerald Edgar. "The Coal Miner in the Pittsburgh District." 1927.

Anderson, J. V. "Unemployment in Pittsburgh with Reference to the Negro." 1932.

Bell, William Y. "Commercial Recreation Facilities among Negroes in the Hill
    District of Pittsburgh." 1938.

Berkeley, C. Clifford. "Analysis and Classification of Negro Items in Pittsburgh
    Newspapers" 1917–1937. 1937.

Bikle, Horace Waters. "A Study of the Intelligence of a Group of Negro Trade
    School Boys." 1930.

Bond, J. Max. "The Rosenwald Y.M.C.A. Development for Negroes." 1931.

Brice, Maryann. "Vocational Adjustment of 101 Negro High School Graduates in
    Allegheny County." 1932.

Clarke, Elsie Rosalia. "A Study of Juvenile Delinquency in a Restricted Area of
    Pittsburgh." 1932.

Covington, Floyd C. "Occupational Choices in Relation to Economic Opportuni-
    ties of Negro Youth in Pittsburgh." 1928.

Daniels, U. R. McD. "Attitudes Affecting Occupational Affiliation of Negroes."
    Ed.D. 1938

Gould, Howard David. "Survey of the Occupational Opportunities for Negroes in
    Allegheny County." 1934.

---

1. Masters' theses from University of Pittsburgh, unless otherwise indicated.

Hall, Wiley Albanus. "Negro Housing and Rents in the Hill District of Pittsburgh, Pennsylvania." 1929.

Harris, A. L. "New Negro Worker in Pittsburgh." 1924.

Lowman, Ruth M. "Negro Delinquency in Pittsburgh." M.A. thesis, Carnegie Institute of Technology, 1923.

Moron, Alonzo G. "Distribution of the Negro Population in Pittsburgh, 1910–1930." 1930.

Morrison, Anna Canady. "Study of One Hundred Forty-One Dependent Negro Children Placed in Boarding Homes by the Juvenile Court of Allegheny County." 1938.

Pittler, Alexander Z. "The Hill District in Pittsburgh: A Study in Succession." 1930.

Rathmell, J. N. "Status of Pittsburgh Negroes in Regard to Origin, Length of Residence, and Economic Aspects of their Life." 1935.

Redmond, Pauline. "Race Relations on the South Side of Pittsburgh as Seen through Brashear Settlement." 1936.

Reid, Ira De Austine. "The Negro in the Major Industries and Building Trades of Pittsburgh." 1925.

Richey, Donald J. "The Legal Status of Education for Colored People as Determined by Court Decisions." 1932.

Seawright, Delmar Clarence. "Effect of City Growth on the Homewood-Brushton District of Pittsburgh." 1932.

Smith, Fred C. "Neglected Factor in the Determination of the Price of Pig Iron." 1928.

Stevenson, Ruth Lucretia. "The Pittsburgh Urban League." 1936.

Walls, Jean Hamilton. "Negro Graduates of the University of Pittsburgh for the Decade 1926–1936." Ph.D., 1938.

Westmoreland, A. H. "Study of Requests for Specialized Services Directed to the Urban League of Pittsburgh." 1938.

Yarbrough, Dean Scruggs. "Educational Status of Negro Public School Children as Reflecting Economic and Social Problems." 1926.

Yarbrough, Dean Scruggs. "Racial Adjustment in Small Communities." 1934.

BOOKS

"Appeal of Forty Thousand Citizens Threatened with Disfranchisement, to the People of Pennsylvania." 1838.

Baker, Paul Ernest. *Negro White Adjustment*. New York: Association Press, 1934.

Baldwin, Leland. *Pittsburgh, The Story of a City*. Pittsburgh: University of Pittsburgh Press. 1938.

Barnes, Gilbert H. and Dwight L. Dumond, *Letters of Theodore Dwight Weld, Angelina Grimke Weld and Sarah Grimke*. New York: D. Appleton-Century Company, Weld Co., 1934.

Beatty, John David. *Our Changing Occupations: A Statistical Survey Comparing the United States, Pennsylvania, and Pittsburgh*, by John D. Beatty and Herbert Grau. Pittsburgh: Pittsburgh Personnel Association.

Boucher, John Newton. *A Century and a Half of Pittsburgh and Her People*. New York: Lewis Pub. Co., 1908.

Boucher, John Newton. *Old and New Westmoreland*. New York: American Historical Society, 1918.

Boyd, Rev. R. Earl. *The Strip*. Pittsburgh: Christian Social Service Union, 1915.

Brawley, Benjamin G. *A Short History of the American Negro*. New York: MacMillan Co., 1931

Brawley, Benjamin G. *Your Negro Neighbor*. New York: MacMillan Co., 1918.

Brawley, Benjamin G. *Negro Builders and Heroes*. Chapel Hill: University of North Carolina, 1918.

Brawley, Benjamin G. *Early American Negro Writers*. Chapel Hill: University of North Carolina, 1935.

Brawley, Benjamin G. *The Negro in Literature and Art in the U.S.* New York: Duffield & Co., 1929.

Brissot de Warville, J. P. *Memoire sur les Noires de l'Amerique Septentrionale, fait en 1789*. Paris: 1789

Brookes, George S. *Friend Anthony Benezet*. Philadelphia: University of Pennsylvania Press, 1937.

Brown, Hallie Q. *Homespun Heroines*. Xenia, Ohio: Aldine Publishing Co., 1926.

Brown, Hallie Q. *Tales My Father Told*. Wilberforce, Ohio: Eckerle Printing Co., 1925.

Brown, Ina Corinne. *The Story of the American Negro*. New York: Friendship Press, 1936.

Brown, Trevor, and Ira DeA. Reid. *Divine White Right*. New York: Harper & Bros., 1934.

Buck, Solon and E. H. *The Planting of Civilization in Western Pennsylvania*. Pittsburgh: University of Pittsburgh Press, 1939.

Bunche, Ralph J. *A World View of Race*. Washington, D.C., 1936.

Carnegie, Andrew. *The Negro in America*. 1907.

Cayton, Horace R. and George S. Mitchell. *Black Workers and the New Unions*. Chapel Hill: University of North Carolina Press, 1939.

Church Survey of Allegheny County, Pennsylvania. The County Commission, Pittsburgh: Council of the Churches of Christ, 1934.

Dahlinger, Charles. *Pittsburgh: A Sketch of Its Early Social Life*. New York and London: G. P. Putnam's Sons, 1916.

Davies, H. B. *Labor and Steel*. New York: International Publishers, 1933.

Deland, Margaret. *If This Be I*. New York, London: Appleton Century, 1935

Delany, Martin R. *The Condition, Elevation, Emigration and Destiny of the Colored People of the United States, Politically Considered*. Philadelphia: 1852.

Detweiler, Frederick German. *The Negro Press in the United States*. Chicago: University of Chicago Press, 1922.

Douglas, Mrs. Dorothy, Sybil Wolff and Katherine DuPre Lumpkin. *Child Workers in America*. New York: R. M. McBride, 1937

Douglass, Frederick. *Life and Times of Frederick Douglass*. Hartford, Conn.: Park Publ., 1881.

Douglass, Frederick. *My Bondage and My Freedom*. New York, 1855.

Dreiser, Theodore. *A Book About Myself*. London: Constable & Co., Ltd., 1929.

DuBois, W. E. B. *Black Reconstruction*. New York: Harcourt, Brace & Co., 1935.

Dumond, Dwight Lowell. *Antislavery Origins of the Civil War in the U.S.* Commonwealth Foundation Lectures. University College, London. Ann Arbor: University of Michigan Press, 1939.

Dutcher, Dean. *The Negro in Modern Industrial Society: An Analysis of Changes in the Occupations of Negro Workers, 1910–1920*. Lancaster, Pa: Science Press, 1930.

Federation of Social Agencies of Pittsburgh and Allegheny County, Child Welfare Division. *Services for Negro Unmarried Mothers in Allegheny County*, 1938.

Foster, William Z. *The Great Steel Strike and Its Lessons*. B. W. Huebasch, Inc., 1920.

Commission to Locate the Sites of the Frontier Forts of Pennsylvania, *Report of the Commission to Locate the Site of the Frontier Forts of Pennsylvania*. Harrisburg: C. M. Busch Pub., 1896.

Fuller, Thomas Oscar. *Pictorial History of the American Negro*. Memphis: Pictorial History, Inc., 1933.

Ferguson, Russell J. *Early Western Pennsylvania Politics*. Pittsburgh: University of Pittsburgh Press, 1938.

Garrison, Wendell Phillips and Francis Jackson. *Life of William L. Garrison*. New York: The Century Co., 1885.

Gibson, John William. *Progress of the Race*. Naperville: J. L. Nichols & Co., 1929.

Gosnell, Harold F. *Negro Politicians*. Chicago: University of Chicago Press, 1935.

Hanne, C. A. *The Wilderness Trail*. New York, London: G. P. Putnam's, 1911.

Harmon, John Henry, Jr., Arnett Lindsay and C. G. Woodson. *The Negro as a Business Man*. Washington, D.C.: Associated Publishers, 1929.

Hadden, James. *Washington's Expeditions and Braddock's Expedition*. Uniontown, Pa., 1910.

Harris, Abram L. *The Negro as a Capitalist*. Philadelphia: American Academy of Political and Social Science, 1936.

Hare, Mrs. Maud Guney. *Negro Musicians and Their Music*. Washington, D.C.: Associated Publishers, Inc., 1936.

Hill, T. Arnold. *The Negro and Economic Reconstruction*. Washington, D.C.: Associates in Negro Folk Education, 1936

Holland, Frederick May. *Frederick Douglass*. Rev. Ed. New York: Funk & Wagnalls Co., 1891.

Holmes, S. J. *The Negro's Struggle for Survival*. Berkeley: University of California Press, 1937.

Housing in Pittsburgh, 1934–1937. Pittsburgh Housing Association.

Irving, Washington. *Life of George Washington*. New York: Putnam & Co., 1855–1859.

Johnson, Charles Spurgeon. *The Negro in American Civilization: A Study of Life and Race; Relations in the Light of Social Research*. New York: Holt & Co., 1930.

Johnson, James W. *Negro Americans. What Now?* New York: Viking Press, 1934.

Johnson, Julia. *Negro Problems*. New York, 1921.

Kellogg, Paul Underwood, ed. *The Pittsburgh Survey*. New York: Russell Sage Foundation, 1909.

Killikelly, Sarah E. *History of Pittsburgh: Its Rise and Progress*. Pittsburgh: B. C. Gordon Montgomery & Co., 1906.

Kirkland, Edward C. *History of American Industrial Life*. F. S. Crofts & Co, 1932.

Klein, Philip et al. *A Social Study of Pittsburgh*. New York: Columbia University Press, 1938.

Labor Research Association. *Labor Fact Book*. New York: International Publishers, 1931.

Larsen, Arthur J. *Crusader and Feminist*. St. Paul, Minn.: Historical Society, 1934.

Locke, Alain LeRoy. *Negro Art, Past & Present*. Washington, D.C.: Association in Negro Folk Education, 1936.

Locke, Alain LeRoy. *The Negro and His Music*. Washington, D.C.: Association in Negro Folk Education, 1936

Locke, Alain LeRoy. *The New Negro: An Interpretation*. New York: Albert & Charles Boni, 1925.

Locke, Alain LeRoy. *The Negro in America*. Chicago: American Library Association, 1933.

Loggins, Vernon. *The Negro Author*. New York: Columbia University Press, 1931.

Mangum, Chas. S., Jr. *The Legal Status of the Negro*. Chapel Hill: University of North Carolina Press, 1940.

Mays, Benjamin and William E. Cigale. *The Negro's Church*. New York: Institute of Social and Religious Research, 1933.

McKnight, William James. *A Pioneer History of Jefferson County*. *Philadelphia*: J. B. Lippincott & Co., 1898.

Miller, Annie Clark. *Chronicles of Families, Houses, and Estates of Pittsburgh and Its Environs*. Pittsburgh, 1927.

Minton, Bruce and John Stuart. *Men Who Lead Labor*. New York: Modern Age Books, 1937.

Mulhauser, Roland August. *Library Service to Negroes*, 1939.

National Association for the Advancement of Colored People. *Annual Report, 1917–1919*.

National Association for the Advancement of Colored People. *Can the States Stop Lynching?* 1937.

National Association for the Advancement of Colored People. *Racial Inequalities in Education.* 1938.

National League on Urban Conditions Among Negroes. *Bulletin* V. 2, No. 3, 5; V. 3, No. 2–3, 6–8; V. 4, No. 2; V. 5, No. 1, 1913–1915.

National Tuberculosis Association, Committee on. *Tuberculosis Among Negroes.* 1937.

National Urban League. *A Quarter Century of Progress in the Field of Race Relations.* 1935.

National Urban League. Research Department. *Negro Membership in American Labor Unions.* New York: Alexander Press, 1930.

Nell, William C. *The Colored Patriots of the American Revolution.* Boston: Robert A. Wallcut, 1855.

Parke, John E. *Recollections of Seventy Years and Historical Gleanings of Allegheny, Pennsylvania.* Boston: Rand, Avery & Co., 1886

Payne, Daniel Alexander. *Recollections of Seventy Years.* Nashville: A.M.E. Sunday School Union, 1888.

Payne, Daniel Alexander. *Semi-Centenary and the Retrospection of the African Methodist Episcopal Church.* Baltimore, 1866.

Penn, Irvine Garland. *The Afro-American Press and Its Editors.* Springfield, Mass.: Wiley & Co., 1891.

Pennsylvania Archives. First, Second, Third, Fourth Series. Philadelphia and Harrisburg, 1852–1902.

Pennsylvania Department of Public Welfare. *Negro Survey of Pennsylvania.* Harrisburg, 1926, 1928.

Pennsylvania Colonial Records. Harrisburg, 1851–1853.

Pickens, William. *The New Negro, His Political, Civil and Mental Status.* New York: Neale Pub. Co., 1916.

Pittsburgh Survey. Edited by Paul Kellogg. Russell Sage Foundation. "One Hundred Negro Steel Workers" by R. R. Wright. New York: Survey Associates, 1914.

Proceedings and Debates of the Convention of the Commonwealth of Pennsylvania to Propose Amendments to the Constitution. Harrisburg, 1837–1839.

Reid, Ira De A. *Social Conditions of the Negro in the Hill District of Pittsburgh.* Pittsburgh: National Urban League, 1930.

Reid, Ira De A. *The Negro Membership in Labor Unions.* New York: National Urban League, Alexander Press, 1930.

Roberts, Thomas P. *Memoirs of John Bannister Gibson.* Pittsburgh: Jos. Eichbaum, 1890.

Robinson, Jesse S. *The Amalgamated Association of Iron, Steel and Tin Workers.* Baltimore: Johns Hopkins Press, 1920.

Rollin, Frank A. *Life and Public Services of Martin R. Delany*. 1868.

Schenkel, E. N. *The Negro in Allegheny County, Pennsylvania, 1789–1813*. Bellevue, 1931.

Scott, Emmett Jay. *Negro Migration During the War*. Oxford University Press, 1920.

Siebert, Wilbur H. *The Underground Railroad*. New York: MacMillan Co., 1899.

Sipe, C. Hale. *The Indian Wars of Pennsylvania*. Harrisburg: Telegraph Press, 1929.

Smedley, R. C. *History of the Underground Railroad*. Lancaster, Pa.: 1888

Smeltzer, Wallace Guy. *Homestead Methodism*. Pittsburgh: D. K. Murdoch Co., 1933.

Smith, Chas. Spencer. *The Life of Daniel Alexander Payne*. DD. LLd.

Spero, Sterling and Abram Harris. *The Black Worker*. New York: Columbia University Press, 1931.

Styles, Fitzhugh Lee. *Negroes and the Law*. Boston: Christopher Pub. House, 1937.

Swisshelm, Jane Grey. *Half a Century*. Chicago: Jansen, McClurg & Co., 1886.

Turner, Edward Raymond. *The Negro in Pennsylvania: Slavery, Servitude, Freedom, 1639–1861*. American Historical Assoc., 1911.

United States Bureau of the Census. *Negro Population, 1900–1915*. Washington, D.C., 1917.

United States Bureau of the Census. *Negroes in the United States, 1920–1932*. Washington, D.C.: U.S.G.P.O., 1935

United States Department of Labor. Negro Economic Division. *Negro Migration, 1916–1917*.

Veech, James. *The Monongahela of Old*. Pittsburgh, 1852–1892.

Wesley, Charles H. *Negro Labor in the United States, 1850–1925*. New York: Vanguard Press, 1927.

Wilson, Eramus, ed. *Standard History of Pittsburgh, Pennsylvania*. Chicago: H. R. Cornell, 1898.

Wilson, F. Alden. *Occupational Status of the Negro in the Iron and Steel Industry of Pittsburgh and Environs*. Pittsburgh: Bureau of Business Research, University of Pittsburgh, 1934.

Witchen, Elsie. *Tuberculosis and the Negro in Pittsburgh*. Pittsburgh: Tuberculosis League of Pittsburgh, 1934.

Woodson, Carter Goodwin. *The History of the Negro Church*. Washington, D.C.: Associated Publishers, 1921.

Woodson, Carter Goodwin. *The Negro Professional Man*. Washington, D.C.: Association for the Study of Negro Life and History, 1918.

Woodson, Carter Goodwin. *A Century of Negro Migration* Washington, D.C.: Associated Publishers, 1918.

Woodson, Carter Goodwin. *The Journal of Negro History*. Washington, D.C.: Association for the Study of Negro Life and History, 1916–.

Woofter, Thomas Jackson. *Negro Problems in Cities*. Garden City: Doubleday,
    Doran & Co., 1928.
Work, M. N. *Negro Year Book: An Annual Encyclopedia of the Negro*. Tuskegee:
    Negro Year Book Publishing Co., 1912. Issues used: 1912, 1913, 1914, 1915, 1937–
    38.
Wright, Richard R. *The Negro in Pennsylvania*. Philadelphia: A.M.E. Book
    Concern, 1912.

LIST OF MICROFILMED MATERIALS

Ch. no.	Chapter sequence on film	Stage	Notes
—	Table of Contents	Final	Included names of authors for each chapter
—	Table of Contents	Final	Outline format with subheads; chapter titles and order are similar to the first version
—	Table of Contents	Final	Outline format; different chapter titles and order than the other two versions
II	The Negro on the Frontier	Final	
III	The Early Community, 1804–1860	Final	Chapter appears twice in microfilm (see below) in somewhat different forms; the two are blended for this published edition
IV	Abolition Years	Final	Chapter appears twice in microfilm (see below) in somewhat different forms; the two are blended for this published edition
V	Civil Rights	Final	
XII	Folkways	Final	Chapter appears twice in microfilm (see below) in somewhat different forms; the two are blended for this published edition
XIII	Arts and Culture	Final	
XIV	The People Speak	Final	
—	George B. Vashon poem "Vincent Ogé"	Final	
—	George B. Vashon poem "A Life Day"	Final	

Ch. no.	Chapter sequence on film	Stage	Notes
—	Bibliography	Final	
I	The Shadow of the Plantation	Pre-final	
III	The Early Community	Pre-final	
IV	Abolition Years	Pre-final	
VI	The Negro Wage Worker	Pre-final	
VII	Church, School and Press	Pre-final	Appears as one chapter in the microfilm, despite what the original table of contents implies
VIII	The Later Community	Pre-final	
IX	Folkways	Pre-final	
—	Appendices		

- Lewis Woodson's "Birthday Memorandum" of 1856
- Clyde Davis Funeral Home advertising flyer and interview by Coleman, 2/27/41
- Presidential election returns for Pittsburgh, 1892
- "Memorial of Free Citizens of Color of Pittsburgh," 1837
- Notes on the size and union membership of blacks, their housing and health conditions
- Essay: "Our Gay Village—The South Side"
- Newspaper articles relating to the history of labor in Pittsburgh
- Excerpts from *The Pittsburgh Survey: Wage-Earning Pittsburgh*
- Articles on the history of the South Side and on steamboating in nineteenth-century Pittsburgh
- Brief descriptions of local social agencies
- Research notes for a history of blacks in North and South America and the Caribbean
- Excerpts from several published histories of blacks in labor
- Excerpts from *Homespun Heroines* by Hallie Q. Brown
- Excerpts from several masters theses and Urban League studies of blacks in Pittsburgh
- Note on plans to include twenty to thirty photographs by Luke Swank and Rosalie Gwathmey
- Newspaper articles relating to the history of blacks in Pittsburgh

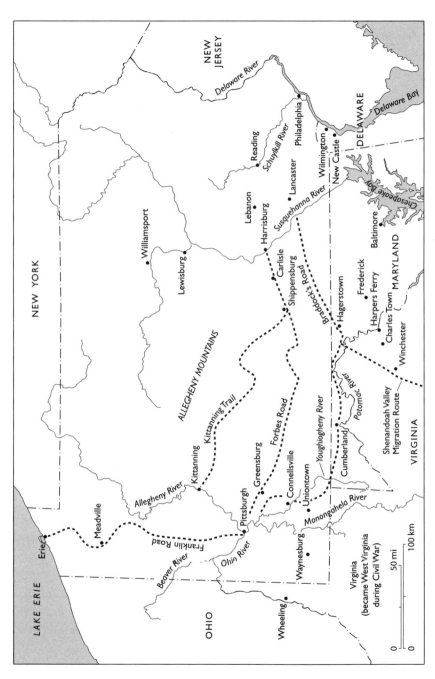

African American Migration Routes to Pittsburgh, 1760–1860

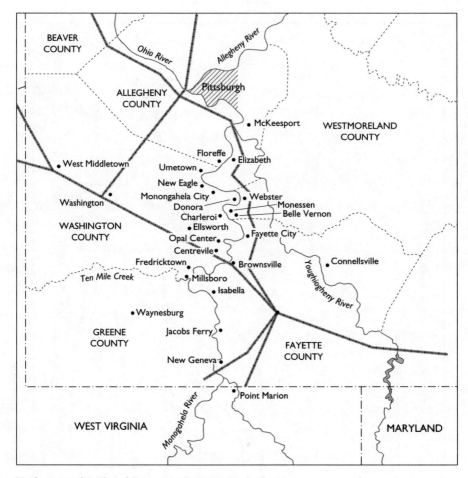

Underground Railroad Routes in Western Pennsylvania

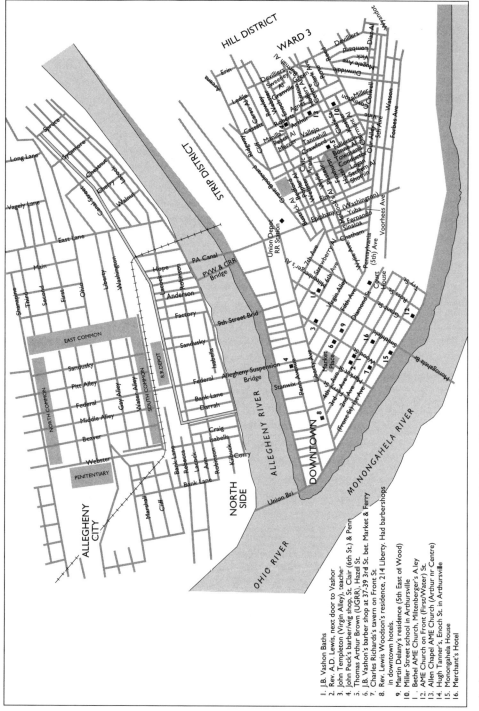

Pittsburgh Downtown, Hill District, and Allegheny City (North Side), ca. 1850

1. J.B. Vashon Baths
2. Rev. A.D. Lewis, next door to Vashor
3. John Templeton (Virgin Alley), teacher
4. John Peck's barber/wig shop, St. Clair (6th St.) & Penn
5. Thomas Arthur Brown (UGRR), Hazel St.
6. J.B. Vashon's barber shop at 37-39 3rd St. bet. Market & Ferry
7. Charles Richards's tavern on Front St
8. Rev. Lewis Woodson's residence, 214 Liberty. Had barbershops in downtown hotels.
9. Martin Delany's residence (5th East of Wood)
10. Miller Street school in Arthursville
11. Bethel AME Church, Miltenberger's Aley
12. AME Church on Front (First/Water) St.
13. Allen Chapel AME Church (Arthur nr Centre)
14. Hugh Tanner's, Enoch St. in Arthursville
15. Monongahela House
16. Merchant's Hotel

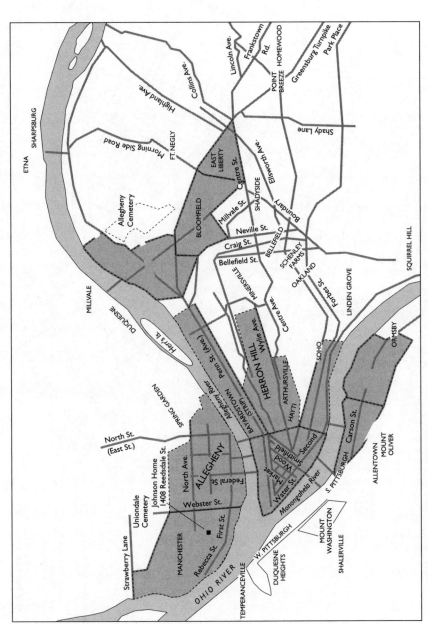

Pittsburgh Neighborhoods and Settlements, 1865

INDEX

Abolition Act of 1780, 42–43, 53, 169

abolition movement, 116, 162; colonization movement *vs.*, 102–5, 125; conventions of, 87–88, 105, 251; and fugitive slaves, 108–12, 114; leaders of, 56–59, 62–64, 150–51, 157–59; newspapers of, 88, 105, 155, 157, 159–62, 245–47; participation in, 63, 75–77; popular opinion of, 119, 133, 153–54, 157–58, 164; relation to democracy, 118–19; support for, 75, 104; violence against, 87, 131–32. *See also* Abolition Act of 1780; abolition societies; antislavery movement; *Mystery*

abolition societies, 102, 175

Africa, 89, 103, 121. *See also* colonization movement

African Education Society, 59, 80, 175, 240–41

African Public School, 56

"Afro-American Notes." *See Pittsburgh Press*

Albatross (abolition newspaper), 160, 247

Albriton, James M., 9

Allegheny area, 27, 267, 366, 385–86

Allegheny County, 47–48, 53

Alsberg, Henry, 3–4, 7

AME Church, 13, 96, 364; early churches, 231–33; number of, 233–34. *See also* churches; religion

American and Foreign Antislavery Society, 134

American Colonization Society, 121–22, 127–29

American Federation of Labor, 220, 225. *See also* trade unions

American Guide Series, 3

American Negro Labor Congress, 211

American Revolution: and Fort Pitt, 40–41; not extending rights to slaves, 43–45; Pittsburgh's support for, 117–18; reasons for, 66–67

anti-lynching activity, 104

antislavery movement, 118, 133, 160; colonization supporters switching to, 128–29; leaders of, 130–32, 142–44; lectures sponsored by, 140–41; newspapers of, 130, 245–46; in Pittsburgh, 102, 116; political involvement in, 134–35; publications of, 132–33; rejecting gradual emancipation, 130, 151; relation to abolition, 162; splits in, 133–34; support for, 143–45, 164, 197; tactics used by, 130, 140, 157; violence against, 131, 245

antislavery societies, 13, 59, 104–5, 175; activity of, 136–37, 184–85; membership of, 142–43; and other organizations, 131; records of lost, 135–37; and state convention, 136–38; Western Pennsylvania Antislavery Society, 133, 136–40, 157

"Appeal of Forty Thousand Citizens—Threatened with Disenfranchisement," 179

art, 332–33

Arthursville, 55, 66n14, 234, 366. *See also* Hill District, the

assembly. *See* legislature, Pennsylvania

assimilation, 227, 254

Avery, Rev. Charles, 128–29, 171, 232–33, 243

Avery College, 27, 243

Ayres, Rev. Robert, 48–49